CHALLENGE TO POWER

CHALLENGE TO POWER

Trade Unions and Industrial Relations in Capitalist Countries

Klaus von Beyme
University of Heidelberg

English translation by Eileen Martin

SAGE Publications · London and Beverly Hills

For information address

SAGE Publications Ltd
28 Banner Street
London EC1Y 8QE

SAGE Publications Inc
275 South Beverly Drive
Beverly Hills, California 90212

British Library Cataloguing in Publication Data

Beyme, Klaus von
Challenge to power.
1. Trade unions
I. Title
331.88 HD6483 79-41782

ISBN 0-8039-9840-6
ISBN 0-8039-9841-4 Pbk

First Printing in English

For Maximilian and Katharina —
our happily syndicalizing family sub-system

Contents

Tables

Introduction

There is no lack of literature on trade unions. But most studies consider trade unions only in a national context and are inclined to premature typologies and generalizations which will not stand up to comparative analysis. In view of the different origins, organizational forms, conflict habits and integration mechanisms of the various political systems even the terminology, which is usually transferred unhesitatingly from one country to another, is not always appropriate. The French union specialist, Jean-Daniel Reynaud, summed up an international symposium recently with these resigned words: 'From what we have heard it is literally true that a ''strike'' is not a ''grève'' nor is it a ''sciopero''; a ''Gewerkschaft'' is not a ''syndicat'' nor a ''union'' and a ''Tarifvertrag'' is neither a ''collective agreement'' nor a ''convention collective''.[1]

The social sciences, particularly sociology and political science, have so far considered many aspects of unions, but the extent to which union organizations are embedded in the complicated network of norms, ideologies, expectations and conflict patterns of the labour relations of individual societies has hardly been systematically studied. Research so far has mainly focussed on[2]:

— historical analysis of union 'organization' in connection with 'industrialization';

— sociological analysis of 'class formation' in the context of the emergence of different forms of organization in the labour movement; here the Marxist studies are mainly descriptive and narrative and the non-Marxist studies rarely go beyond general typologies;

— economic analysis of 'employment structures' in relation to changes in the conditions of union organization and action. This offered relatively the best possibilities for quantitative work;

— organization theory analysis on the basis of theories of bureaucracy, devoted mainly to the internal organization structure and deficits in union democracy, but only in isolated cases do these studies indicate a connection with the degree of democracy in other sub-systems in society.

Work on strikes (cf. Chapter 3) is best systematized and quantified, and some schools of economic thought emphasize the political aspect, but the political scientists have shown astonishingly little interest in this. It is only with the growing interest in 'non-conventional political behaviour' since the development of new patterns of conflict in the protest movement at the end of the sixties that they have turned to the study of collective behaviour in strikes. But a prejudice in favour of union militancy has blurred recognition of the real value of strikes and led to exaggeration of their 'mystical' power to create class consciousness and group cohesion in opposition fringe groups. The more fashionable the subject of the unions became among left-wing conflict theoreticians, the more damage was done to the academic reputation of that branch of sociology which was concerned with the unions and labour relations.[3]

Scarcely any other branch of scholarship has been so strongly affected by the polarization of the meta-theoretical and theoretical positions; as a result consensus cannot even be reached on the concepts. While a certain agreement is possible on what can be called a 'union' despite the great differences in terminology and meaning, ranging from the conservative *Patronat* to the radical literature on changes in the system, consensus hardly seems possible on the expression *Arbeitsbeziehungen* or 'industrial relations'. *Industrielle Beziehungen* is a not very successful translation of 'industrial relations' and in German it has further implications. Firstly, in an economy in which the services sector is growing in importance, *Arbeitsbeziehungen* are no longer mainly industrial. Secondly, the transfer of the conflict pattern of *industrielle Beziehungen*, as the working class developed it, to the growing public sector, invalidates the old term. Finally, the term has the disadvantage of an inherent reference to the employers' standpoint. *Arbeitsbeziehungen* does more justice to the fact that the human factor 'labour' cannot really be equated with the substance 'capital'. *Arbeitsbeziehungen* is, therefore, the better term if not only job relations but the wider context of society as a whole and the political sphere is meant.

In Great Britain, too, the tendency is increasingly to move away from the older 'industrial relations' to 'labour relations'. The employers' standpoint is felt to be too prominent in the older term. Linguistically, therefore, it is not a coincidence that the Conservative Industrial Relations Act of 1971 was replaced by the Labour

Trade Union and Labour Relations Act of 1974. Nevertheless, the terminology in Great Britain appears to be so established that authors like Flanders, who argued that certain concepts were untenable (he would have liked to replace 'collective bargaining' with 'joint regulations') have resignedly continued with the old usage.[4]

In Germany the development is still wide open and diverging. Unwieldy composites such as *Arbeitgeber-Arbeitnehmer-Beziehungen* are still being used (in government publications) and we have *Austauschbeziehungen zwischen Kapital und Arbeit*, the phrase preferred by the project group Gewerkschaftsforschung (Union Research) in the Institut für Sozialforschung in Frankfurt.[5] Time will show whether these phrases will remain in use.

Labour relations depend on the concept of a system of relations between the main protagonists, capital and labour. They imply an ideology over and above the partners in conflict or at least an awareness of certain rules of behaviour in the representation of interests.[6] For the groups concerned, the unions, employers' associations and state agencies, they include both internal constitutions and institutionalized formulae such as collective contracts, agreements, arbitration arrangements and norms for company constitutions, as *integrative items,* and the habits and rules of the labour conflict as *dissociative elements* in the relations between the parties on the labour market. The concept of the system, on which the idea of the interdependence of 'industrial relations' is based, has the advantage of marking this sub-system off from the economic sub-system. It also presupposes the interaction of the state or the public sector right from the start, and does not include this on the side of capital on all too abstract a level through some sort of 'state induction'.

Even some of the Marxist theoreticians have regarded the concept of the system as indispensable for an analysis of labour relations. They rightly, however, reject the concepts of balance of the functionalist school. Neo-Marxists and neo-pluralists are today largely in agreement that the term 'the parties in the bargaining process' hides real imbalance of power and that the status quo of labour relations may be stubbornly defended by parity ideologies but is increasingly untenable in view of the rising expectations of the rank and file with regard to the distribution of income and participation chances on the job.

Like Richard Hyman I see labour relations as a power struggle. It is unlikely that any state of balance could be long maintained in industrial relations. But in contrast to the Marxist position which Hyman takes, I do not regard the 'elimination of industrial relations' by the class war as very likely.[7] Labour relations as a whole are only clearly polarized in times of open revolutionary conflict and usually they do not remain so for long, because new rules become accepted and a new distribution of power furthers the stabilization of industrial peace. However revolutionary the victorious powers may have been before the open conflict, all revolutions so far have shown that new 'industrial relations' are almost always imposed from above by revolutionary regimes, and that they do not always further the original aims of the spontaneous groups of workers in the conflict. As long as there are authority relations in working life a theory of labour relations will not be superfluous. Many non-Marxist scholars also hope that these authority relations can be minimized.

The adoption of the concepts 'industrial relations' or 'labour relations' from the writings of American systems theoreticians and the Oxford school of industrial relations in Great Britain (Clegg, Flanders, Fox and many members of the Donovon Commission) is an acknowledgement that there are common ideological elements and rules in these relations. The facts in Chapter 4 of this book especially prove this; even if they do not fit into the Manichean view held by a group of authors who can only conceive of the unions as in a class war between two normatively and clearly separated hostile units, 'capital' and 'labour'. On the other hand the use of these terms does not mean accepting all the harmonist concepts of the relations between the parties in the bargaining process which the 'human relations school' and other integrationist American writers put forward for their country. They have been especially uncritical in their introduction of these concepts to comparative literature on labour relations in Europe, which are much more conflict-ridden and at times have been and are caught up in a class war. In the European context neither the evolutionary stage theories of the growth of the unions to increasing 'maturity', i.e. peaceful behaviour, nor a view of certain stages as absolute levels — the relatively peaceful labour relations in the reconstruction and fine-weather phase of post-war capitalism, for example, — is really an adequate basis for the assessment of union movements.

A comparative study should consider the historical individualities of the various countries and groups of countries, but at the same time consider the astonishing continuity in organization and conflict behaviour, without losing sight of the systematic aspect. Despite this dual aim the result will still be fragmentary. There are only a few hypotheses which can be plausibly applied to all systems of labour relations. By far the best and most of the studies on labour relations are from Great Britain and the USA. The former are usually descriptive and the latter incline to theory or the use of the methods of empirical social research; only rarely, as with Lipset and some others, is an attempt made to integrate theory and empiricism.

These differences in research approach cannot be explained by the fact that the research on unions in the USA has had more funds at its disposal.[8] The stronger historical and organizational approach in Great Britain is certainly in line with the general trend of British sociological literature. Most of the British studies produced so far — even the Marxist ones are less dogmatic and more inclined to detail than many on the continent — are reserved in their use of general theories and at the same time more critical towards the qualities of their own system.[9]

Both trends are well worth following. A complex study like this, which aims to represent all the essential aspects of labour relations and identify the causal relations between individual factors in the macro-system instead of concentrating on one problem in detail, cannot offer a general theory of labour relations. Many of the results of the research will have to be seen as relative to certain types of organization and behaviour. The typological method is certainly an obstacle to the formation of a general theory. The step to quantification, which could be facilitated by the formation of less abstract types, is only possible in a few areas and, as will be apparent in many cases, by no means in the most relevant.

The author's grateful thanks are due to all the European head union associations — with the exception of the Italian, to whose lack of cooperation I owe a second visit to Rome — for their readiness to make material available. The main sources, as one would expect with this subject, were from the sixties and seventies. Where it seemed necessary the development of certain features which are still influential today has been traced back to their origin, mainly the debates of the 2nd International. But a systematic comparative analysis cannot present all the historical details and reference is made to the comprehensive literature on the genetic aspects in the various countries.

The complexity of the material need not necessarily involve a conceptual loss. The main thesis of the book is that the current interpretation of the behaviour of unions through organizational details (loss of members, bureaucratization, 'the shift to the middle class' through the integration of white collar workers, etc.) is an inadequate as is the confrontation of unions with their programmes and ideology to deduce either that they are making exaggerated power claims (conservative criticism) or 'betraying the workers' (neo-Marxist criticism). Union behaviour is only explicable in the context of labour relations as a whole and the political system. In many areas the unions have remained a sub-culture despite their growing strength. In any case they have only rarely and always only for a time been a dominant formative factor in the system. Their behaviour has always been in some part an answer to measures by other groups — their main opponents, the employers and respresentatives of state power.

But simple schemes of stimulus response, as we sometimes find in American union literature, according to which the unions only 'react' to pressure from without, are not adequate either. Institutional factors in their own organizations, such as the degree to which they are embedded in the system of labour relations and bound by their own ideological aims and ideas, are independent factors which must be examined. Hence one part of the book is devoted to each of the concepts in the title. Part 1 is concerned with the main factors which have been an essential part of the concept of a large organization since Max Weber: organization (Chapter 1) and ideology (Chapter 2). Part II is devoted to a closer examination of the external relations of the unions in the system of labour relations: firstly the conflict response (Chapter 3) to decisions, most of which are taken outside the unions, and the integration mechanisms (Chapter 4), which aim to reduce the conflict potential in the system and bring the unions to accept complex co-responsibility in the political system.

I

The Internal Structure of the Unions

1

Organization

1. A GENERAL UNION OR A PLURALISM OF UNIONS ON AN IDEOLOGY BASE?

In the union theories of the various neo-Marxist schools, the dichotomous concept of society, according to which the dominant conflict of a capitalist society is the opposition between capital and labour, produces a strong normative prejudice in favour of union unity: 'Strictly speaking unity is essential to the trade union movement: it has proved to be a practical necessity in every hostile action and largely determines the success or failure of these'.[10] The Catholic social theorists who work on trade union questions have been equally dogmatic on the inevitability of pluralism on the grounds that plurality of values is inevitable in a democracy.[11] Neither of these 'fundamentals' of the labour movement has actually been generally decisive in the real world of union organization.

Paradoxically, precisely in those countries where unions are most strongly oriented to ideology the essential unity of the labour movement is not apparent. In fact, the more dogmatically certain groups insisted on the uniform nature of the movement the more did plurality develop in reality.

There has never actually been consensus on the organizational form for a general union. We can identify three different concepts:

(1) A general union *for the entire workforce*, including clerical staff and civil servants. This was the aim of Hans Böckler and the union leaders in the western zones of Germany after 1945. The

specialist groups were only to be sub-sections of the head organization and not independent industrial unions. However, this idea was opposed not only by the Occupying Powers but also by the chairmen of the largest individual organizations.[12] If one seriously regards this concept of a general union as desirable and measures the result of efforts to achieve unity against such an ideal (and, as I have said, it was certainly held in Germany after 1945, and not only by the Communists in the Free Federation of German Trade Unions [FDGB] in the Soviet occupied zone) then there is, no doubt, justification for the harsh verdict that the general union 'failed' in Germany because there were still splinter groups such as the Christian unions and clerical organizations.[13] Certainly, if this tight form of organization is the only one which deserves the name 'general union' (its opponents call it a 'hotch-potch'), then it has not been realized in any capitalist democracy where unions are not subject to state control.

(2) *A head association with industrial unions as members*. The Swedish and West German systems come closest to this.

(3) *A grouping of unions on an ideology base*, as we find in Italy, France, the Netherlands and Luxembourg. These are known as 'general unions' but the re-integration process, which has been only partly successful in Finland and the Netherlands, usually, as experience has shown, leaves such strong independent wings that the term is not really applicable. Political difficulties also prevent the principle of the industrial union from being strictly practised here.

One can identify five reasons why the ideal of the general union, in the less rigid interpretation of the second and third types, has not really been established so far:

(1) Difficulties arose where a workers' party did not achieve primacy and syndicalist traditions of *direct action* by unions remained strong, competing actively with the workers' parties (Belgium, France, Italy).

(2) The same applies to systems in which party primacy was impossible because several parties of numerical significance were competing for the workers' votes (in the latin countries and Finland). Israel would appear to be an exception to this. In view of the important role played by the parties in the Histradut the elections to its central bodies have occasionally taken on the character of pre-parliamentary elections. So far the Histradut has survived the now intense conflict between the parties without splitting, first-

ly because the external threat has proved a strong incentive to unity (despite the embittered conflict over the question of the role of Arab workers in the Histradut),[14] and secondly because for a long time the Mapai formed a hegemony in the union and accounted for up to 85% of its members. Party decisions often pre-determined union decisions.[15]

We find another set of particular problems in Ireland. For a long time efforts towards unity encountered difficulties as after 1924 organizations like the Workers Union of Ireland (WUI), based in the Irish Free State, were competing with the ITGWU. There are still a large number of unions operating in Ireland and some are represented only in Northern Ireland and some in Great Britain as well.[16] In 1970 twenty-four of the ninety-five Irish unions had their head offices in Britain. They accounted for about 14% of the organized workers in Ireland.

(3) In countries with *a highly fragmented political culture* organizational unity has rarely been achieved in the labour movement (Belgium, Luxembourg, the Netherlands, Switzerland). But not all the consociational democracies have developed as fragmented a pattern as the Netherlands. In Austria, for instance, the influence of the German concept of party primacy was sufficiently great to prevent fragmentation on religious grounds. But fragmentation is not always due to the confrontation between inflexible ideological blocks. In the USA it has been the result of power struggles between different groups and interest coalitions, which have simply used ideology as legitimation for the bitterness of the conflict. 'The boss mentality' and corruption have often also fragmented the movement further.[17]

(4) *A failure to realize the industry principle* has also tended to increase fragmentation on ideological grounds. Often when a general union split, status consciousness was strengthened in some of its organizations. In France, for instance, after the split of the Confédération Générale du Travail (CGT), the teachers did not join another head association but made themselves independent in the Fédération de l'Education Nationale (FEN).[18]

Ideological fragmentation is now largely cemented in *the international trade union movement*. This also began with the idea of unity when, on 3 October 1945 the World Federation of Trade Unions (WFTU) was founded, which most of the major unions, with the exception of some Christian unions and the American Federation of Labour (AFL) (in contrast to the Congress of Industrial Organisations [CIO]) joined. During the Cold War the World Federation split over questions relating to the Marshall Plan and the policy towards the Third World. At a special conference under the chairmanship of the British Trades Union Congress (TUC) and the American unions in London at the end of November/beginning of December 1949 the International Confederation of Free Trade Unions (ICFTU) was founded. Its main focus was in Europe. However, the big Western European unions, such as the CGT and CGIL, remained in the World Federation. In addition, a Christian confederation has existed since 1920, the International Confederation of Christian Trade Unions. In 1968 it changed its name to the World Council of Labour.[19]

We can point to three main areas of conflict which have been responsible for splits in the union movement:

(1) conflict between a Communist minority striving for disproportionate influence and Socialists, Social Democrats and other groups;

(2) conflict between a Christian section of the workers and a dominantly Socialist sub-culture;

(3) conflict between the 'economically peaceful' and nationalist groups, known as the 'yellow' groups, and class-conscious worker unions.

Other groups, such as the liberal unions, have been of less significance. In Germany, as the Hirsch-Dunkersche Gewerkvereine, they have always played only a marginal role. In Belgium, too, the liberal unions (Centrale Générale des Syndicats Libéraux de Belgique [CGSLB]) occupy only third place and are concentrated in certain public services (trams and buses).[20]

(1) In some countries such as France, Italy, Finland and Luxembourg, conflicts with Communists caused the collapse of a general union which had been formed only after great difficulty. In Germany, too, a central union body did not emerge as a matter of course, it was built on memories of the catastrophe of the union collapse in 1933 and experiences of the fight against National Socialism. It has been called 'the foundling of organizational history'.[21] But many critics regard the price paid for unity in Germany as too high: 'The Social Democratic majority among the officials has largely succeeded in realizing its claim to power within the organization and in changing the industry-oriented general

union into one oriented to the Social Democrats'.[22] It is particularly regretted that the change could only be brought about with 'the sacrifice of the traditions of class war'. These harsh judgements usually overlook the other side to the question: the tone adopted by those groups in the Federal Republic today who would like to continue or revive the 'traditions of class war' does not suggest that in view of the growing differentiation of the variants of 'pure' doctrines of class war a general union could be maintained. Unfortunately, general unions based on traditions of class war are only conceivable under a Leninist party dictatorship. In a free society, as experience has shown, Marxist and Socialist sects are usually torn apart. Where a large organization has been successfully built up it has had to make compromises with the Social Democrats. This applies to the large organizations in the pluralist structures of the Latin countries (CGT, CGIL) as well.

A more problematic feature of the German central body is its strong anti-Communism; this spread with the division of Germany and became one of the main binding forces in the general organization, even if it did not feature so markedly in the programme as in the 1961 Constitution of the American head organization, the AFL-CIO, where 'protection against Communist subversion' was added to the main aims of the organization under Point 10 of the Principles of the Federation and during the Cold War eleven unions were excluded for 'Communist activities'.[23]

The inconsistency of the Left in proclaiming union unity on the one hand and on the other holding rigid views on the degree of 'infection with opportunism' in the organization, was apparent even before the creation of the Federal Republic. All the Socialist groups in the labour movement in Germany have always paid lip service to organizational unity. But even the General Federation of German Trade Unions (ADGB) during the Weimar Republic usually subordinated unity to its own tactics in practice. This was also characteristic of the Revolutionary Union Opposition (RGO), whose mystification of unity in the proletarian class war actually achieved the opposite of what it claimed to be working for.

The strength of anti-Communism, which is not restricted to this side of the Iron Curtain, has always made union unity vulnerable in Germany. Even the emergence of merely left-wing Socialist groups, like the union wing around Viktor Agartz, which could not be accused of subservience to Moscow, aroused a disproportionate reaction from the opposition and threatened to split the unions. This threat is renewed even when there are signs of too close ties between the DGB and the present Social Democrat Party (SPD). In 1953, for instance, representatives of the Catholic Workers Movement and the social committees of the two conservative governing parties, the CDU (Christian Democrats) and the CSU (Christian Social Democrats) more or less presented the DGB Federal Board with an ultimatum to enforce ideological neutrality and balance as a condition for the preservation of unity. A threat by Christian Democrat union members to form a party group is a sanction which usually precedes the threat of a split.[24] In 1955 a CDU union was eventually formed with the participation of two members of Parliament, Winkelheide and Even; its membership was estimated at about 20,000 but it has not won much support either from the Party Executive Committee or the Board of the Confederation of German Industry (BDI). The threat of a split in the union movement even played a part in the 1976 federal election campaign.

All the Communist groups in West Germany have learned from the mistakes of the old RGO policy and they are careful not to be driven into complete isolation. A publication from East Germany emphasizes that the Communists do not see themselves as 'opposition within the union', nor are they aiming to unite the forces which are dissatisfied with the opportunist course of certain union leaders, in separate 'pure' organizations.[25] The Maoist groups also reject the idea of separate organizations or union opposition, but propound more deliberately than the unionists close to the Moscow-oriented DKP (the former Communist Party of Germany, KPD) the function of the unions as transmission belts. The new (Maoist) Communist Party of Germany (KPD) announced that 'for us there can be no list of demands for the construction of a revolutionary union opposition which differ from the Party's programme',[26] while the West German Communist Federation (KBW) wants party groups within the unions: 'The party groups are not independent organizational units, they are levers to enable the members of the KBW to act on a common plan in their work in union meetings and on union bodies'.[27] Both groups say they have learnt from the experience of the RGO in the Weimar Republic, which was too rigorous in its refusal to cooperate with the 'reformist' unions, and both of them support the central body in order not to be cut off from the 'mass of the workers'. But from a certain strength their tactics amount to the same as the old RGO policy, because the majority of the unions will not admit these minorities; if necessary they can be excluded from entire Land associations since in April 1973 the first DGB unions, the Metal Workers (IG Metall) and the Chemical, Paper and Ceramic Workers Union (IG Druck, Papier, Keramik) passed delimitation resolutions.[28] There is little prospect of legal protection against this exclusion. Complaints have been rejected so far on the grounds that the unions are organized under private law and are not registered associations under civil law. The autonomy of the association, on which the Left usually puts so much emphasis, can thus become a boomerang in times of conflict. The chairman of the German Trade Union Federation said in an interview in 1975: 'I have always said that the unions can take the individual Communist, but we will not tolerate organized Communism in the unions in any form whatever'.[29]

The polemics of the Maoist groups make it easier, even in the Federal Republic, where anti-Communism can assume strange forms, to tolerate Moscow-oriented Communists, at least on union level. In contrast to the Maoist groups, the DKP is not usually named in the exclusion resolutions. However, the relation between the DKP and the union leaders is anything but relaxed. The loyal cooperation of many DKP members in the unions is not actually denied by the union leaders, but their 'acknowledgement of union discipline' is still largely viewed with suspicion and regarded as 'conformity for opportunist reasons'.[30] The DKP's support for unity (*Statements by the DKP Düsseldorf Party Congress*, Statement 30) goes hand in hand with a rejection of the attempt to bring the unions into line with the principles of the three parties now in the Federal Parliament.[31] At the same time it is emphasized that the party's aims are more far-reaching than those of the unions. At present the DKP is not propounding the transmission belt function of the unions but in contrast to the Maoist groups it does not simply impute to the unions the arrogance of its own party principles. We must wait and see how far this is a sign of a permanent change of attitude.

Groups which support the principles of Leninism traditionally find it difficult to forget Lenin's verdict that without leadership by the party the unions develop 'just a trade unionist mentality'. Even Communist leaders who developed independent ideas in Western Europe have passed on these prejudices, like Antonio Gramsci, who ultimately saw in the unions only another manifestation of capitalist society and not the potential to change it; in his view the unions tended to follow a 'bread-and-butter policy' and had proved organically incapable of establishing 'the dictatorship of the proletariat'.[32] However, widely as Gramsci is still acknowledged as the theoretician of Italian Socialism both in the CGIL and the Italian Communist Party, neither organization would publicly express such a harsh verdict today. But these views are held by groups to the left of the Communist Party and, in contrast to other Western European countries, Italy had many of these even before the 1968/69 demonstrations. The Lotta continua and Potere operaio groups and the group around the paper *Quaderni Rossi* had been agitating since 1962/63. They were joined in 1968/69 by Il Manifesto (a wing of the Communist Party) and Avanguardia operaia. All preferred spontaneous structures like those which emerged in the rank and file (CUB) but they entertained only brief ideas of a completely new workers' organization. Their aim was to form wings and *correntocrazia* in the union movement.[33] But they were never a serious threat to the unity of the CGIL.

After the Second World War an attempt was made in Italy, as in West Germany, to create a general union on the basis of the cooperation of the opposition groups in the resistance movement against Fascism. The Communists, Socialists, and Christian Democrats were equally represented in the leadership of the CGIL and a minority representation was accorded to two other anti-Fascist groups, the PRI (Republicans) and the Partito d'Azione (a left-wing middle-class party which collapsed between 1946 and 1948). But shifts of power, particularly in favour of the Communists, made it impossible to hold this balance. At the CGIL Congress in Florence in June 1947 the voting was as follows:[34]

PCI	57.8%
PSI	22.6%
DC	13.4%
PSLI (Social Democrats)	2.2%
PRI	2.0%

With support from the Vatican and Catholic organizations on the one hand and financial and ideological support from the USA and American unions on the other, the split in the CGIL was driven further on the grounds that the Communist domination must be broken. On 1 May 1950 the Confederazione italiana sindicati lavoratori (CSIL) was founded in Rome, a Christian Democrat union under Giulio Pastore as Secretary-General. Its membership quickly reached 600,000. In March 1950 the Socialist unions of the Romita group had been excluded from the CGIL because they had left the PSI. They founded the Unione italiana del lavoro (UIL) under Italo Viglianesi as Secretary-General, which was close to the Republicans and the later Social Democrats. Again in 1950 a small Fascist pseudo-union was founded, the 'Confederazione italiana sindacati nazionali dei lavoratori' (CISNAL), which emerged from the neo-Fascist MSI.[35]

De Gaspari and the DC élite had from the outset a much more corporatist conception of the trade union; this was to include, according to Catholic conceptions, even the farmers and artisans.[36] After the split the CISL understood its organization as concentrated on the factory, not trying to organize political activities outside the enterprises, and as representing its members but not the whole of the working class as the CGIL conceived of its role.[37]

In France the split began after conflicts with the Communists in 1921. However, the CGT was twice reunited for brief periods as a Popular Front movement: from 1936 to 1939 and 1943 to 1947.[38] On both occasions the reunification was made possible by rapprochement between the parties behind the groups. In 1946 the Anarchists split off. In May 1947, when Ramadier removed the Communist ministers from the Government after conflicts over the Marshall Plan and finance policy, union unity was impossible to hold. After bitter strikes at the end of 1947 Jouhaux and his friends, mostly old *confédérés* from the first phase of disunity, resigned. In April 1948 the 'CGT-Force Ouvrière' was founded, taking its name from the periodical round which the group had gathered. But the CGT was not a purely Communist union. Some non-Communist leaders such as Léap and Le Brun remained and many moderate unions like the Fédération de Livre also remained in the head association. But the Fédération de l'Éducation Nationale, after some hesitation, decided to make itself independent.

In Belgium, too, the general union, which had been agreed in principle in 1945, split when the Fédération Générale du Travail de Belgique (FGTB) expelled the CBSU delegates after the Prague coup d'état in February 1948. The last Communists in the Central Committee thereupon resigned on 27 April 1948. The balance of power in the FGTB was as follows:[39]

	Membership	**Secretariat posts**
CGTB	248,259	3
CBSU	165,968	2
MSU	59,535	1
SGSP	51,789	1

In contrast to the situation in France and Italy, the Communists were only the second strongest group and the initiative came largely from conservative forces which did not split off but 'purged' their organization.

Although Finland had the third largest Communist party in Europe, the Social Democrats kept the upper hand in the Finnish head union association (Suomen Ammatiyhdistysten Keskusliitto [SAK]), which they had founded in 1930 after the old organization had come under Communist control after the civil war. In 1948 the Social Democrats controlled twenty-five and the Communists fourteen unions. The progress made by the Communists in the union movement caused the Social Democrats to fight them with their own weapons. In 1945 a 'Committee for Union Affairs' was founded in the party — the Communists already had one — to defend the Social Democrat position in the unions. This was stabilized with a deliberate and effective policy. In 1955 the Chairman, his deputy and the Secretary-General of the SAK were elected on to the Executive Committee of the Social Democratic Party.[40]

However, the conflict was not solved without repression. In the Spring of 1947 the Social Democratic Party launched the slogan 'That's enough' in a campaign against Communist tactics. In 1948 seven unions were expelled from the association because their Communist leaders were pursuing an independent policy against the SAK. Five were later readmitted after they had undertaken to keep the SAK rules in future. Against embittered opposition from the Communist minority which remained in the SAK the association left the World Federation of Trade Unions which is dominated by the Socialist states.

In 1960 the movement split further. By 1969 there were three blocs:

	Unions	Membership
SAK	24	298,000
SAJ	16	90,000
Independents	5	128,000

In the same year there were negotiations on reunification but this was not achieved because the SAJ did not support the agreement. A new central organization of the SAK was formed with twenty-four former SAK unions, five independents and six SAJ unions.[41]

As the Communists increased in strength and became coalition partners in the Government, the ideological conflict in the Finnish unions flared up again. In some (Construction and Groceries) the Communists now have control and the Social Democrats have gradually lost the leadership they once had in the largest union (Metalworkers). But the conflict does not always follow party lines. As during the period of the bitterest conflict the Social Democrats were not always consistent in their union policy — during the general strike of 1956, for instance — considerable divergencies emerged among the Communists in 1976 over the question of a prices and incomes policy. While the moderate majority of the Communists, together with the Social Democrats, supported Kekkonen's 'overall solution of an incomes policy', the left wing made every attempt to undermine a peaceful solution, making appeals 'to the people' and causing unofficial strikes.

(2) But in all these countries the unity of the union movement was threatened repeatedly not only by conflicts with the Communists but also by disputes with a strong *Christian Democrat* movement. In Italy the union of the five parties was destroyed by the Cold War, as was the *tripartisme* in France. The Christian Democrats usually had a reservoir of lay organizations in the background to fill out organizational gaps in the labour movement.

In Belgium the ideological fragmentation was furthered by the nationality issue. The Christian union movement had always been largely Flemish in orientation. While the Walloons account for over 40% of the members of the FGTB, they make up only 18% of the Christian CSC union.[42]

In the Netherlands, on the other hand, the ideological split was reinforced by conflict between the religions. Catholics and Protestants also split, as on the party level where the Protestants formed two separate organizations, the Anti-Revolutionary Party (ARP) and the Christian-Historical Union (CHU), until a Christian Democratic federation of parties was formed.

The labour movement in the Netherlands is now in three blocs:

	Membership	
	1978	**1966**
Nederlands Verbond van Vakverenigingen (NVV)	724,996	550,000
Nederlands Katholiek Vakverbond (NKV)	341,804	432,000
Christelijk Nationaal Vakverbond (CNV)	231,800(1974)	237,000

Source: EEC: *Gewerkschaftsinformationen. Die Gewerkschaftsbewegung*, loc. cit., Part 2, p. 10 for the CNV and 1966; 1978: *Trade Unions affiliated to the FNV-partners,* Amsterdam, 1978, pp. 3ff.

The strongest shifts in the last decade have been between the Catholics and the Socialists. But the Protestants in the CNV have also suffered losses, although of the three organizations they put most emphasis on ideological purity and are most fierce in their resistance to any attempts at unification.[43]

But the efforts towards unity continue in the Netherlands. The unions have actually been more successful here than the parties in their attempt to form one Christian Democratic party. Underground movement discussions in 1943 led to a loose federation of the unions, the Raad van Vakcentralen. The experiment came to grief in 1954 because the NKV withdrew when an episcopal edict forbad Catholic workers to join non-Catholic organizations. The Protestant CNV, however, emphasized its readiness to cooperate with every organization, even those which did not accept 'the gospel as a guideline for human behaviour'.[44] In 1959 a loose Raad van Overleg was formed. But when the NVV insisted on federation plans to lead to complete unity, the Protestants too insisted on an independent organization of their own. Finally, in December 1975 the NVV and the Catholic union NKV formed the

Federation of the Dutch Union Movement (FNV) which began work on 1 January 1976. In January 1974 the CNV had withdrawn from the preparatory work for this federation. But the individual unions in the two other head associations were strong motivating forces for unity. Three NVV and NKV unions (Transport, Construction and Agricultural and Food Workers) actually merged.[45] There were no specialized and concentrated metalworkers' unions, which in other countries have been the main advocates of unity, in these two head associations. The ideological union was only able to produce vague compromise formulae such as 'The equality of all people, freedom, justice and solidarity' and it entailed concessions to the Christian part of the new federation: 'The FNV recognizes the importance of faith and religion as a source of inspiration for union activities'.[46] A further step on the path to unity is the joint platform of the three unions, which agreed on a political programme for 1976/77 with an appeal to the Government and Parliament to use the remaining legislative period for reforms to benefit the workers.[47]

In Luxembourg, too, the main stumbling block to unity is not so much the Communists, who are organized in the FLA, as the Christian unions, which still cling to their concept of pluralism and fear, with some justification, that they will otherwise be driven ideologically into a hopeless minority position.[48] (3) Genetically speaking, the earliest conflict which threatened the unity of the labour movement was that between the largely Socialist unions and those desiring 'economic peace' and supporting the *national idea.* These groups have become known as the 'yellow' groups, after members of economically peaceful works associations in Le Creusot and Monceau-les-Mines stopped using the colour red after 1901 to mark themselves off from the Socialist unions, and instead of red wild roses wore yellow gorse as a badge, and used yellow paper and placards. In 1904 a head association was founded in France for the economically peaceful national works associations, called Fédération Nationale des Jaunes de France. So what was originally a term of derision for strike breakers became a proper name. When the term was adopted in Germany it was sometimes also used for the Christian unions and Hirsch-Dunker associations. Franz Mehring regarded these as 'deformities' unworthy of the name of union.[49] In Marxist criticism the Social Democrat unions were then duly castigated by Lenin and others for their treatment of groups ideologically out of line with too liberal a use of the term 'yellow'. Later the term was generally used for the national groups. The MAN works association in Augsburg wanted to use the term in its name but the national works and workers' associations protested (although without much success).

Similar groups emerged under quite different conditions in the English-speaking countries, in Great Britain in conjunction with the old liberal unionism which was aiming for a partnership between employers and workers, and in the USA under the influence of the propaganda for 'human relations', a form of works association ideology with academic trimmings.[50] The 'yellow-dog contracts' which American employers often insisted on their workers and clerical staff signing on appointment, promising not to join a union, also recall the hostile meaning of the term 'yellow'. It was not until the Norris-La Guardia Act of 1932 that these contracts became non-actionable in the national courts.

In Germany two types of 'yellow' groups emerged: firstly the nationalist and monarchist workers' associations, some of which did not reject strikes altogether for the achievement of economic aims, and secondly the economically peaceful associations, which did reject any form of strike on principle and had usually been formed on the initiative of the employers or conservative or nationalist liberal members of the middle class. The opposition from the Socialist unions — which the 'yellow' groups denounced as terror — often actually achieved the opposite of what it was aiming for and rather served to bind together the dissentient groups. So it is not a coincidence that the economically peaceful national workers' movement collapsed at the beginning of the Weimar Republic when this pressure eased. The agreement between the unions and the employers' associations of 15 November 1918 was a milestone because the employers, in return for concessions to the unions for their labour market policy and the reintegration of returning soldiers in the reconstruction of the post-war economy, had to give up their open financial support for the 'yellow' groups.[51]

The conflict between the general union movement and the 'yellow' groups only became obsolete with the mutual recognition of the partners in collective wage negotiations and the strengthening of the legal framework for labour relations, or at least with the establishment of rules for arbitration on a voluntary basis as in Sweden in 1938. During the period of full employment after the Second World War the employers found big concessions in wage policy and fringe benefits in the plant to be a more effective means of hindering strikes than support for the 'yellow' strike break organizations.

Only in political systems where democracy and free trade unionism were reintroduced very late, as in Spain, did the fight against the 'yellow' organizations still play a part in the seventies. The attempts to maintain a kind of government-dependent organization after the collapse of the state syndicalism of the *movimiento* or to create organizations sponsored by the employers was fought by the Comisiones obreras and the UGT under the label of 'yellow trade unions'.[52] But even in Spain the position of the Comisiones obreras, which was organized semi-legally in the last years of the Franco regime, was strong enough to give the yellow organizations little chance.

Of the three main lines of conflict over which the unity of the labour movement came to grief only the third can be regarded as no longer relevant in most of the highly capitalized countries. Efforts to eliminate the two other conflict areas have been only partially successful. Attempts like those in the Raad van Vakcentralen in the Netherlands up to 1954 and in the Mouvement syndical uni et démocratique in France of June 1957 to achieve an institutionalized federation process have not proved effective, any more than federation processes on a state level. Efforts towards unity have now become multi-frontal and are progressing in small stages. Although at first sight it would appear that there are many failures the outlook for unity in the eighties is actually better. There are several reasons for this:

(1) *The removal of class distinctions* through the levelling process of modern labour policy and the gradual establishment of the *industry principle* in union organization are furthering unity. Groups with a high degree of organization where the industry principle is largely realized, like the metal workers, have become the pacemakers of unity. In Italy, for instance, while the central associations of the unions called their three *consigli generali* together for 'informal talks' in Florence at the end of October 1970, the metal workers' unions decided in March 1971 to take definite steps towards unity during the year with joint actions and publications.[53] It was not until July 1972 that a loose Federazione CGIL-CISL-UIL was founded. Despite some resistance from the

political wings in the organizations, the confederative character was stressed with equal representation in the Secretariat. If the class conscious groups had profited most from the splits in the past, we now find members of the clerical staff and civil service unions calling for mergers (this is the case in Germany, France and Sweden).

(2) A further factor which is encouraging unity is *cooperation between competing workers' parties*, particularly Communist and Socialist parties. The increasing orientation of 'Euro-Communism' to a pluralist democratic system of Socialism is removing the conflicts which emerged during the Cold War, when the Italian Social Democrats in the UIL, for instance, and the moderate Socialists in France in the CGT-FO were not prepared to cooperate with the Communists on any account. So it is becoming less and less possible to identify the parties behind the partly Communist-oriented unions with all the negative acts by their 'brother parties' in the Eastern bloc, as large sections of the electorate and the press have done in the past. The non-Communist members of the French union movement, for instance, were deeply impressed when Georges Séguy and Henri Krasucki (CGT) stood up for union freedom in the Eastern bloc countries during the riots in the Polish harbours in 1970,[54] although Krasucki's tribute to the unions under Socialism was a little overdone. The Communists in the unions have also increasingly moved away from the concept of the transmission belt. The programmatic document of the three Italian trade unions which decided to build up a confederation in 1971 already contained not only a verbal declaration on the complete independence of the unions from the parties (which we find in many documents) but reaffirmed strict incompatibility rules between leading functions in the parties and the unions as had already been realized in some of the autonomous organizations since 1969.[55]

In Spain the independence of the trade unions from the parties was the equivalent of the postulate put forward by the Eurocommunists that the unions should be completely independent of the state — which they had not been in Spain since 1937.[56] In some documents the Spanish Comisiones obreras went further than any other organization dominated by Communists in admitting that there is no coincidence between the objectives of 'the party' and those of the working class.[57]

The CGT in France has come to be much less ruthless in the pursuit of its own interests in regard for efforts to achieve unity. The polemical war has become a conflict in which there are limits; there are joint actions, particularly with the CFDT. After the Congress in Nîmes in 1972 the CGT offered to draw up a list of the problems on which agreement had been reached but at the same time not to hide the differences of opinion and to continue to discuss these openly. Tactical cooperation had developed well in many fields for the CFDT as well, although the organization still feels 'patronized' by the CGT in the ideological sphere, where the CGT presents a more united front and can lay claim to the philosophical basis of dialectical materialism. This causes all the more bitterness in the CFDT as it can justly claim to be more responsive ideologically, giving serious discussion to a wider range of different concepts and really striving for the transformation strategies while the CGT in the views of its competitors is still inclined to leave the strategic work to the party.[58]

But the CGT's responses in this dialogue have lost their former sharpness and have an almost resigned tone. Georges Séguy, the CGT Secretary-General, admitted in 1975: 'The road to unity is very long. Progress is held up by those who speculate on natural divergencies of opinion to keep the splits open'.[59] The attitude has even changed towards the FO although this has always been anti-Communist, very much in contrast to the CFDT which, although it was much more open over its disagreement with the CGT on 'democratic Socialism', was never, after its reorganization in 1964, anti-Communist on principle. While there used to be frequent attempts to play the rank and file off against the FO leaders, recent efforts towards unity have not completely excluded the FO. This process is also loosening the bonds between the parties and the unions. The *incompatibility regulations* which were brought into force in Italy in 1969 and in Belgium and have been repeatedly discussed in France with varying degrees of intensity[60] are the external expression of 'détente' by the parties in order to facilitate an 'entente' among the unions.

(3) A further factor which will strengthen union unity is the *secularization of the Christian union movement*. This has been encouraged in France through a new nationalist conservatism within the Gaullist movement. The decline of the old left-wing Catholic movement, MRP, which had been one of the main pillars of the régime in the Fourth Republic, accelerated the process. The old CFTC expressly supported the principle of union pluralism. It was

not until 1953 that a minority under Bouladoux as Secretary-General made a declaration in favour of the idea of unity. At a Special Congress on 6/7 November 1964 the CFTC then decided to change its name to Confédération Française Démocratique du Travail (CFDT). To stress the move away from the Christian orientation Article 1 and the preamble to the statutes were revised to cut out the reference to 'Christian humanism' and the acknowledgement of humanism was given a lay meaning. The decision was supported by about 70% of members. The out-voted minority largely remained loyal to the organization, with the exception of a small intransigent opposition around Joseph Sauty and Jacques Tessier, which decided to continue the old CFTC tradition. But the group remained marginal in the union spectrum. The CFDT suffered its largest losses in the Fédération des Mineurs, most of whose members stood behind Sauty.

The left wings of the Christian union movement fought for autonomy from Christian Democratic parties and the accumulation of offices at an early date. In Italy these were mainly the metal workers in the CISL.[61] In Belgium the 1953 Congress of the Christian CSC union stressed its independence of the Christian Socialist Party (PSC) and expressly forbad the accumulation of offices.[62] De facto, however, the process was a long and wearisome one, as it was in the other countries, particularly in the CSC-dominated Flemish regions.

The Christian unions in France and Italy increasingly moved to Socialism in the sixties. Some members of what had been the Christian unions moved to the left of those which had always been Socialist in tendency. This has been apparent in the CFDT since 1968 and spectacularly recently in the battles for the LIP watch factory in Besançon. The CGT, which is still largely regarded as Communist-oriented, has been reproached with not having a clear strategy in the battle for Socialism, of concentrating too narrowly on wage demands and not pursuing long-term Socialist aims with enough determination despite its verbal assurances.[63]

The conflict between Christian unions and their related parties also broke out, although in a weaker form, in countries with relatively conservative social and political structures, like Switzerland, where not even the SGB, a union close to Social Democracy, is pursuing Socialist aims so that the Christian unionists do not come under pressure to accept Socialism. Nevertheless, in January 1976, for instance, the CNG and CVP found themselves opposing their parties, the Christian People's Party and the Protestant People's Party, because the unions were supporting the SGB over co-determination and the majority of the Christian party members rejected this or were at best unenthusiastic.[64]

The reorientation of many leaders and members of the Italian Christian workers' organization (ACLI) to Socialism also led to a noticeable cooling of the relationship to the Church. The Vatican stressed on several occasions that the ACLI could no longer be regarded as a Catholic organization. Nevertheless, it would be premature to say that the Christian tradition in the organization is no longer of primary importance. The CISL in Italy, for instance, although it is in favour of further integration within the *confederazione*, does not exclude new splits under certain circumstances.[65]

In Italy, and even more so in France, the former Christian unions are concentrated in areas where Catholicism is still a powerful political force, in the west and in the east. But it has not made much headway in the traditionally 'heretical' south or in the *balcon rouge* of the Midi and around Paris. In most countries the Christian unions have been won over to the idea of unity, but they are more cautious than the traditionally Socialist unions. The leaders of the French CFDT have declared that they are prepared to help realize unity. But unlike the 'enthusiasts' they want this to 'be built on a rock' and they maintain that this is a more serious attitude than the mere ideological postulate of unity.[66] Much as the Moscow-oriented Communists welcome the move to Socialism in some Christian unions, they still strongly reproach the international Christian movement for its pluralist ideology, which is splitting class unity, and its negative influence on the re-integration process within the national workers' movement.[67]

(4) *The international union movement*, too, is aiming for unity for the national organizations, with a reorganization on a European level, although it remains split into three world associations. The European Trade Union Confederation (ETUC) was established in Brussels in 1973 as successor to the European Confederation of Free Trade Unions, which was more strongly anti-Communist. The ICFTU unions still dominate this (see Table 6). But most of the European unions in the Christian world association WCL have, one after the other, joined the European Confederation and with the acceptance of the largely Communist-oriented Italian CGIL by

the Executive Committee on 9 July 1974, the first step was taken to close the gap between the organization and the Communist-oriented Western European unions in the World Federation. The French CGT, which until 1974 had a joint office with the Italian CGIL in Brussels, has revised its basic attitude to the EEC and is considering joining the European Confederation. As condition of its entry it is demanding, among other things, continued membership of the World Federation and the right to remain independent — which is justifiable in view of the fact that other unions were not required to change their membership of a world organization on joining the European association.[68] In the meantime the Italian CGIL has cooled down its relations with the World Federation in Prague in order to facilitate the federalization process of the three unions in Italy, and in 1978 even the CGT criticized the Socialist countries and their unions at a congress in Prague; Séguy withdrew from the membership of the General Secretariat of the World Federation.[69]

The growing integration of unions of different views in the battle against the multinational corporations will be a further incentive to unity on the national level. It is not by chance that the metal workers are again the most active supporters of international cooperation, as they are the strongest advocates of national unity for the trade unions. Solidarity against the multinational corporations has led many unions to more politically-oriented strategies; we find this even among those who were formerly reluctant to organize solidarity strikes and political manifestations, as in some Christian unions or in the Social Democratic unions in Northern Europe.[70]

It is not possible to generalize yet on the success of efforts toward unity or the factors which will favour them. Conditions vary too much in the different countries. In Belgium and the Netherlands the fragmentation on an ideology base is combined with a high degree of organization and a comparatively highly developed readiness by the leaders to reach minimal consensus on the lines of a consociational democracy even without federal unity. In the Netherlands especially it is emphasized that there was never a fierce struggle for 'exclusive representation' as there was in other countries. The traditions of consociational democracy occasionally had a healthy effect on the union movement. The unity of the Austrian union movement would hardly be conceivable without the possibility of political factions in the Socialist union party (FSG) which accounts for about 70% of the members, the Christian union party (FGC) and the Communist union party which has operated for some years under the characteristic name of Union Unity (Gewerkschaftliche Einheit — GE). But unity amid variety is not possible without the traditions of a consociational democracy, and this demands a certain restraint by the Social Democrat majority. On the occasion of the thirty years' anniversary of the Republic of Austria the President of the Austrian Union Federation (ÖGB), Anton Benya, declared: 'Unanimity is often reached because the majority group in the organization is concerned to be able to achieve what it wants not only with majority decisions'.[71]

In those Latin countries with a high degree of fragmentation but without the traditions of consociational democracy unity is much harder to achieve. The first Latin country to try to take advantage of a new beginning for the unions on a legal base and achieve unity is Spain. In the Spring of 1976 the Workers' Commissions (Comisiones obreras) which are dominated by members of the Communist Party, established the first contacts with those unions working throughout Spain, the USO, the UGT and the CNT. The Anarchist CNT, legalized in 1977, which was a considerable force in the Second Republic but remained astonishingly weak in the seventies, excluded itself from further negotiations. In the elections for the representatives of the trade unions in the plants the comisiones proved to be the strongest group (with nearly 40%), the UGT was second with about 30% of the votes.

The pluralism of unions in Spain was not simply a repetition of experience in other Latin countries after the Second World War. There is no Christian or right-wing union. Rumours that one was to be founded with the help of the German Adenauer Foundation were immediately denied by the Government. The moderate head organizations, Comisiones obreras and UGT, have conquered a hegemonial position against the radical organizations such as the CSUT, SU and CNT and many regional groups. Instead of working for further unity these organizations have to consolidate their positions and defend themselves against the radical groups on the one hand and on the other attempt to build up 'yellow groups' as a substitute for the old 'vertical unionism' of the *movimiento*. The smaller organizations have accused the CCOO and the UGT of abusing their hegemonial position in the plants.[72] The repercussions of the 'decreed unity' of syndicalism under Franco are still too strong for a general union in the Northern European sense to be possible, although the Euro-Communists in Spain have made more concessions to internal pluralism than have the Communists who dominate some other organizations in the Latin countries.[73]

Efforts to reach unity have progressed further in Italy than in France. French union leaders who have been closely following the reintegration process in Italy see two factors as responsible for this: firstly the decision to restrict efforts to integration to an industry base and to the rank and file, and secondly the fact that ideological differences are rather of secondary importance because the CGIL, CISL and UIL do not have 'Socialist aims'.[74] But this is rather a simplified view. Certainly the union movement in Italy is more centralized and the work of the activists is less localized or fragmented than in France. Thus initiatives on unity from the rank and file can be better coordinated in the central offices. And it is true that the Italian Communist Party is less dogmatic than the French, so it is certainly easier for other groups to join the CGIL. The gap between the FO and the CGT in France is still very much wider than that between the three Italian unions. But it is an over-simplification to say that the Italian unions are not motivated towards Socialism. The CGIL still maintains that a *sindicato di classe* must be realized and however much independence there may be of the parties the aim is still for the unions to function as a political power as well.[75] Only recently 'agnosticism' before political power was advocated by some leading CGIL ideologists.[76]

The French attitude might suggest that united efforts for Socialism make unity easier to achieve. But the conflict between the Communists and the Socialists is rather greater in Italy through the policy of 'historic compromise' with the Christian Democrats than it was at least for a time between the two French parties when they had agreed on Mitterand as a candidate and a common programme. And the attempt to induce all union members to agree on a political programme for Socialism has not been successful. In those countries where the unions are highly political and avant-garde in their ideas the degree of organization has always been lowest. A former German historian said succinctly: 'The party is dependent on an idea, unions on success. A party can take political setbacks for years and still grow; a union sees every setback reflected immediately in its membership figures'.[77]

As the expectations of the Socialist parties become less comprehensive the idea no longer plays so great a role as the cohesive centre, even for the Socialist parties of Western Europe, as it did in times of out and out class war ideology. The statement still holds for the unions. But as the Socialist parties cease to become the prophets of ideas and take on practical responsibility in govenment the comparison becomes increasingly difficult. It soon becomes apparent that the parties, too, are dependent, if not on the numbers of their members then on the number of voters, as we saw in the power struggle between the French Communist Party and the Socialist Party under Mitterand. Parties are no less dependent on success than the unions, and their voters fluctuate much more than the unions' membership does.

2. INDUSTRIAL UNIONISM OR CRAFT UNIONS?

Scarcely any of the first unions corresponded to the Marxist concept of the organization of the working class *in itself* and *for itself* with an acknowledgement of the unity of the proletariat. The 'Trade Union Associations', the early organizations in Germany, had relics of status symbols in their official designations and traces of these have remained to the present day, even where support was avowed for the industry principle right from the start. Highly qualified groups such as the book printers, who always remained aware of their special position and the progressive role they sometimes played, although they regarded themselves as members of the working class, were often the object of suspicion and polemics. Kautsky coined an early form of the phrase 'the aristocracy of the working class' in criticism of the printers, accusing them of a 'guild spirit' and lack of solidarity with the working class as a whole: 'Sometimes the organized members of certain crafts draw a distinction between themselves, the aristocrats, and the mass, on whose shoulders they would like to climb higher'.[78] The industry principle was seen as a means of countering the guild spirit and was repeatedly demanded by the international labour movement, most insistently wherever the parties had a certain leadership in the movement. In the debates of the 2nd International on the relationship between the parties and the unions the victory, despite the compromise formula on equal rights, really went to those who tacitly assumed party primacy and dissociated themselves sharply from the syndicalist ideas of the French Socialists and the primacy of union-organized general strikes. At the Socialist Congress in Stuttgart in 1907, however, the supporters of both the majority and the minority resolution agreed that too close a cooperation between parties and unions in countries with a fragmented Socialist movement could also have negative repercussions on the unity of union organization. The majority resolution contained a warning against enforcing 'occupational organizations' and the minority resolution by Kautsky, Legien and others demanded first 'a united organization of the workers in industrial associations' as 'the core of the Republic of Labour'.[79] This was in itself an indication that a general union and the industry principle were in theory intended to be inter-related if not identical. That is not quite so in fact, even if, in theory, general unions permit a better realization of the industry principle. The development in both Great Britain and America shows that the two concepts are not identical. Although there is a relatively comprehensive head association in both countries this has had little influence on the realization of the industry principle. The Danish Landsorganisation is an even clearer example of the same point.

The historical development of the labour movement reveals specific circumstances which were unfavourable to the realization of industrial unionism.

(1) When the union movement did not, in the main, *adopt Socialist aims* (as in the USA, Great Britain and Ireland); even in the organizational debate in Germany during the Weimar Republic the Revisionists did not, as it happened, derive their main support from the occupational associations while the dogmatic Centrists dominated the industrial associations.[80]

(2) When, as in some countries with a British tradition, obligatory registration strengthened the tendency to a 'Balkanization' of the union movement, as registration did not, of course, facilitate the process of mergers.

(3) When the union movement, and usually the Socialist parties as well, remained fragmented and ideological conflict prevented organizational unity (the Latin countries).

(4) The industry principle was realized best in countries where there was close *cooperation between a big Social Democrat party* and *a relatively centralized union movement*. Whether there was a

direct organization link between the party and the unions (Denmark, Norway and Sweden) or only an informal relation (Germany and Austria) was only of secondary importance.

On the factors which favoured the realization of the industry principle union research has several explanations to offer. It has been suggested that this correlates with:

(1) The degree of concentration of one branch of industry or monopolization in the capitalist system in any country. However, an international comparison shows that in the most highly capitalized countries such as Great Britain and the USA the industry principle has hardly been realized and the unions are largely organized on craft lines. In those English-speaking countries in which there is not an old craft tradition — mainly the USA, Australia and New Zealand, however, the term 'craft union' does not seem very appropriate. Membership of the unions here is not so much dependent on certain skills as on work in certain occupations. The term 'occupational union' would therefore, one might suggest, be more accurate.

In the USA the industry principle and the craft or occupational principle had been rivals since 1935, when the Congress of Industrial Organizations (CIO) was created as a counter movement to the craft-organized AFL. The fusion of the two head associations to the AFL-CIO in 1955, however, blurred the former conflicts over this issue. But other problems (accusations of corruption among the Teamsters) and the arbitrary policy of the automobile workers under Reuther led to another breach. Some big industrial organizations, which had become outsiders, had no objections to joining up with smaller craft-oriented unions in the Alliance for Labor Action (ALA).[81]

Although the USA has remained free of the guild traditions of the early European labour movement a functional equivalent of status factors has remained and hinders the further realization of the industry principle: discrimination against unskilled workers, especially in many of the AFL unions, and the protection of old-established workers against repeated waves of immigrants who came on to the market as cheap labour.[82] The industry principle seemed all the more desirable in the United States as the union movement was confronted with the problem of corruption to an extent inconceivable in Europe. Industrial unions were less prone to this and the CIO was more sensitive to accusations of corruption than the

AFL before Meany.[83]

In Great Britain, the mother of highly developed capitalism, the industry principle has not been realized either, although TUC publications have always proclaimed its advantages. But in view of the fierce fighting in the wings of the TUC there would appear to be little point in carrying this conflict between the two principals in the loose federal organization on to the front line as well. The TUC has therefore limited itself to a cautious encouragement of the process of concentration. As it has few means of exercising direct pressure on its members it tries to encourage concentration when considering new applications. In 1974, for example, it rejected the application from the National Association of Licensed House Managers on the grounds that the organization should merge with other unions which were already affiliated. In 1975 the union again applied for membership and explained that the other unions were not prepared to merge. But the General Council of the TUC remained obdurate and did not accept the organization.[84] Between 1958 and 1970 the total number of British unions dropped through mergers from 673 to 534 and the number of TUC unions had gone down to 115 by 1977. 'Text-book unions' like the Jewish bakers union with twenty-four members, which find their way into most studies, have died out.[85] But there are still ten different unions representing the workers in mechanical engineering in Britain, the smallest being the Society of Shuttlemakers with 128 members.[86]

A concentration process is taking place in most countries where there are a large number of unions, both among the unified general unions (in Denmark the Landsorganization Congress decided in 1967 to create nine large industry unions but there were still fifty organizations in 1973, and forty in 1977),[87] and among the ideology unions, where the desire for unity is encouraging concentration (cf. Chapter 1, 1). The greatest progress has been made in the Netherlands and Finland. But although the Netherlands are among the most highly concentrated countries (cf. Table 1) with fifteen (NVV) and nine (NKV) unions in one head association, even the federal association created in 1976 from the NVV and NKV, the Federatie Nederlandse Vakbeweging, still contains such curiosities as the Football Trainers Union with 2,267 and the Professional Footballers Association with 757 members (in the NVV) or the Kappersbond (Hairdressers) in the NKV with 1,389 members.[88] It is perhaps less surprising that a small country like Denmark should

TABLE 1
The number of unions in the various head federations (about 1978)

Luxembourg	*CGT*	*5*
	LCGB	*9*
Belgium	*FGTB*	*12*
	CSC	*17*
Netherlands	*NVV*	*15*
	NKV	*9*
	CNV	*13*
Federal Republic of Germany	*DGB*	*17*
Austria	*ÖGB*	*16*
Switzerland	*SGB*	*16*
	CNG	*13*
Sweden	*LO*	*25*
	TCO	*24*
Italy	*CGIL*	*28*
Finland	*SAK*	*28*
Norway	*LO*	*40*
Denmark	*LO*	*40*
Ireland	*ITUC*	*90*
Great Britain	*TUC*	*115*
New Zealand	*FOL*	*117 (346 altogether, 1971)*
Australia	*ACTU*	*124 (305 altogether, 276 registered, 1973)*
USA	*AFL-CIO*	*105 national unions*
		51 state federations
		741 local central labor councils

Sources: *The Labour Movement of the European Community*. Brussels, 1975, 2 parts.

B: *Connaître la CSC*. Brussels, September 1977, p. 18.

CH: SGB: *Tätigkeitsbericht 1972, 1973, 1974*. Berne, 1975, pp. 173ff; *Die wichtigsten Arbeitnehmerorganisationen ausserhalb des Gewerkschaftsbundes*, NZZ, 14 October 1976, p. 11.

DK:	LO: *Kampens gang*. Copenhagen, 1973, p. 518 still listed 50 members. In January 1977 there were only 40 mentioned, in August 1977, 41 member unions.
	LO Beretning 1976. Copenhagen, 1977, pp. 85-87.
	The Danish Trade Union Movement. Copenhagen, LO, 1977, p. 1.
GB:	*TUC Report 1977*. London, 1978.
I:	'Il finanziamento del sindacato', *Rassegna sindacale*, No. 50, 1970, p. 60.
Irl:	ICTU: *List of Affiliated Organisations*. Dublin, 1975.
N:	*Labour Relations in Norway*, Oslo, 1975, p. 50.
NL:	*Trade Unions Affiliated to the FNV-Partners*. Amsterdam, 1978.
NZ:	M. H. Howells, et al. (eds.): *Labour and Industrial Relations in New Zealand*. Carlton, Pitman House, 1974, pp. 18, 318.
S:	*LO: Verksamhetsberättelse, 1977*. Stockholm, 1978, p. 3.
SF:	*Statistisk arsbok for Finland*. Helsinki, 1977, p. 282.
USA:	Information from the AFL-CIO to the author in February 1979.

---

have among its forty unions the Engine Drivers Union (private railways) with 130 members and a Union of Railwaymen (private railways) with 273 members.[89]

In Finland when the SAK was founded it was decided that the individual organizations of what used to be the SAJ should be dissolved by 1972 and their sub-organizations should join the parallel unions of the SAK. The process lasted until 1974.[90] But the policy of mergers did not enable the principle of industrial unions to be realized in every country. In Great Britain, for example, it did little to blunt the rivalry between the various unions. The TUC has increasingly had to act as arbitrator in 'demarcation' disputes.[91] Nor have the structures become any sounder. On the contrary, the monopoly position of the big 'amalgamated unions' reduces mobility in the reorganization question, as a meaningful reorganization would not be possible without their splitting, and they are now the largest unions.[92]

(2) *Ideological unity* and *class consciousness*. External factors such as monopolization and the development of concentration in industry do not necessarily produce the appropriate Socialist mentality. Even where class consciousness would appear to be an inherent element, as in the case of unions based on a strong Socialist ideology, the industry principle has not proved realizable, largely owing to the jealous rivalry of other unions. In France the CGT has

upheld the industry principle since the Charter of Amiens in 1906 but strong corporate and professional elements have stubbornly survived. The CGT still has three independent unions of merchant navy officers (captains, bridge officers and doctors; ships engineers; electrical engineering officers). Even within the large industry federations there are numerous 'craft' groupings: dockers, typographers, etc.

(3) *Close cooperation* between a Social Democrat party and an ideologically united union movement has proved to be comparatively the most favourable factor for the realization of the industry principle, as the 2nd International insisted in its debates on the relation between the party and the unions in 1907 and even earlier (Denmark is an exception). Conversely, the preponderance of the craft unions, especially in the USA, went hand in hand with mistrust of the specifically political organization of the working class in the party.[93]

In Sweden the adoption of the industry principle was decided as early as 1912 in the Landsorganisation. But certain minorities consistently opposed the realization of the decision and at several union congresses heated controversy broke out over the issue.[94] Rivalry from white collar workers' associations, which were more status conscious and were sometimes fighting for the same groups of members, also forced a slower pace in the implementation of the decision. But the fact that many smaller groups came to join the LO shows how successful this cautious policy was.[95] By the sixties industrial unionism had been 80% implemented in Sweden and this is far above the international average. The industry principle was also adopted in Norway, in 1923, but its implementation has not progressed as far as in Sweden.[96]

In Germany the realization of the industry principle was certainly helped by the reorganization of the union movement after the Second World War. But it would be an over-simplification to argue, as is occasionally done, that a necessity for fundamental reorganization is the decisive factor. Italy had the same chance after 1945 and did not use it in the same way, and Finland reorganized the SAK in 1930 on Social Democrat lines after the collapse of the old union movement when the Social Democrats withdrew on account of Communist domination. The industry principle was adopted at the founding congress and reaffirmed at numerous other congresses. But the realities of the situation favoured the continuance of craft organizations. The considerable differential in membership fees was a further factor which broke industrial unionism, as many workers chose the cheapest union rather than the most appropriate one.[97]

(4) Finally, *the legal framework for industrial relations* also influenced the means of realizing the industry principle (cf. Chapter 4, 1). That applies to the right to coalition as well as legislation on relations between the wage partners. Where the unions came under the normal legislation on associations, especially in the English-speaking countries, the fragmentation into craft unions was favoured. In Ireland after the Act of 1941 seven persons could register as a union with the Registrar of Friendly Societies and obtain a licence to negotiate on payment of a fee to the High Court.[98] In other countries, such as Luxembourg, legislation on wage agreements laid down that only one agreement could be concluded for the blue or white collar workers in any plant or branch of industry, clearly working against craft unions.[99] Many continental countries used legislation on wage agreements in an attempt to level out occupational differentials. But few of them attempted to touch the status differentials between blue and white collar workers, if only in consideration for the jealously-guarded rights of the employees in the public sector.

3. THE ORGANIZATION OF THE WHITE COLLAR WORKERS

As the theory of trade unionism — and not only in its Marxist variants — was largely based on the concept of the essential unity of the workers, the social differences between workers and the problems these cause in union organization have not been a main focus of attention in the literature. One differentiation theory, which aimed to sub-divide the working class further, is still regarded in Soviet literature as a 'bourgeois ideology to split the working class, drive manual and clerical workers apart and nourish reformist illusions'.[100] But this kind of dogmatism will not stand up to empirical research into union structures.

British union researchers[101] have made empirical tests of the degree of union awareness among white collar workers and have coined the phrase 'unionateness' to describe the degree of engagement of various groups for the principles of the union movement. Some of their criteria, such as whether an organization declares itself a union, its attitude to collective negotiations and hostilities (e.g. strikes) can be used for all Western countries. Others, such as the readiness to join head associations, cannot be applied to systems with a pluralism of ideology unions (France, Italy, cf. Chapter 1, 1); and the decision to join the workers' party collectively as union members its typical of a Northern European form of cooperation between party and unions which does not occur in Central Europe or the Latin countries (cf. Chapter 1, 2).

The readiness of an organization to declare itself a union cannot simply be deduced from its name. Many organizations of white collar workers or civil servants which are still called 'association', 'federation' or the like may well have moved beyond the middle-class mentality if their style of negotiation and readiness to strike is any indication of their acceptance of syndicalist patterns of behaviour. But the attitude of other organizations to them is also important. Some organizations, judged objectively, are certainly unions (the German white collar workers' association, the DAG, for instance) but their opponents always try to deny this. Willingness to join a central union body is certainly an important test of 'unionism'. But great difficulties arise where the head association is relatively strictly organized on the industry principle (cf. Chapter 1, 2).

The more independent the work processes of certain occupational groups were and the longer their special status awareness lasted the greater was their tendency not to accept industrial unionism and organize themselves in associations outside the central union body. This development was not always, however, dependent on a sense of status. The prejudice of workers' associations against white collar workers and intellectuals often intensified the desire for independence. An ideological proletarian cult, which no longer adequately reflects the variety of modern jobs, can thus help to create an attitude which works against the understandable desire for the realization of the industry principle and the centralization of large unions with a class mentality. This is particularly the case in countries such as France, where the largest union, the CGT, in which Communist influence is very strong, still retains a good measure of the traditional cult of the proletariat despite its verbal assurances that it is open to all groups and ideologies. This has driven other groups, as long as they were not actively Socialist, into the arms of other unions. The FO, which split off from the CGT, profited from this for a long time and the CFDT is still increasingly profiting from it today. The CFDT does not take up a dogmatic avant-garde position in the class war but remains eclectic and cautious, without animosity towards the changing theses of the leading role to be played in the development of class consciousness by the proletariat, the *nouvelle classe ouvrière*, or the marginal groups. The CFDT is equally open-minded with regard to hostilities. It does not recognize a canon of classical rules of behaviour and alliance. The variety of its forms reflects, in its views, the range of possible participants and this has given the union a more creative policy on hostilities in the eyes of many intellectuals, even those who are strongly politically engaged.[102]

The dogmatic preoccupation with the working class (*ouvrièrisme*, *operaismo*) is declining in most of the predominantly Communist-oriented unions. In Spain the struggle for the rights of the unions is meeting with resistance especially in the state apparatus with its latent authoritarianism conserved from Franco's days. In Italy the Communists with the beginning of Euro-Communism have paid increasing attention to this problem and are far more open to middle-class professionals than the French CGT has been so far. The working-class bias of the CGIL gave its Christian rival CISL an advantage in organizing those employed in public administration and the services sector (see Table 2). But if we compare not only the absolute figures but the relative development of proportions within the respective Italian organizations we can see that the opening of the CGIL to non-manual workers has borne fruit in recent years. From 1968 to 1975 the CGIL increased its membership in the public administration by 222%, the CISL by only 148%.[103]

(a) White Collar Workers and Civil Servants

White collar workers are today the largest group in the workforce still partly outside the industrial unions, and they are often the greatest obstacle to the realization of the industry principle. The fact that white collar workers are less highly organized than blue collar workers has often led to the conclusion that they are less

TABLE 2
Representation of the two largest Italian unions in different sectors (in thousands)

	1968		1972		1975	
Sectors	**CISL**	**CGIL**	**CISL**	**CGIL**	**CISL**	**CGIL**
Industry	555	950	851	1497	926	1746
Agriculture	169	588	296	520	441	634
Public administration	457	253	618	393	678	564
Services	195	252	255	349	285	449
Retired and others	144	416	163	454	261	686

Source: Centro Studi Nazionale della CISL: *Strumenti di cultura sindicale.* Bologna, Il Mulino, 1977, p. 43.

'union-minded' although there is no direct correlation between the degree of organization and the syndicalist emphasis in their associations.

The degree of organization of white collar workers is not an independent variable: it is even more dependent on the occupational structure than that of the workers. The following factors are important:

(a) the proportion of white collar workers among the workforce;
(b) the distribution among sectors of the economy and the size of the services sector;
(c) the importance of the state sector in the economy as a whole, because white collar workers in the public sector are usually more willing to organize than those in the private sector;
(d) the degree of organization of the workers, which has a certain spill-over effect.

Table 3 shows that in countries with a large public sector, such as Italy, the white collar workers are not well organized, whereas in countries with a small state sector like Sweden they are highly

TABLE 3
Union membership density among white collar workers and non-manual workers (percentages)

Sweden	70
Denmark	55-60
Austria	60
Norway	50
Great Britain	39.4
Belgium	35-38
Australia	30
Federal Republic of Germany	c. 24
Netherlands	c. 20
France	15
USA	c. 13
Italy (CGIL)	10.4 (public sector)

Sources: Casten von Otter: 'Entwicklungstendenzen bei den Gewerkschaften in Schweden', *GMH*, 1974, No. 8, p. 474; 'Il finanziamento', loc. cit., p. 59; Kassalow, loc. cit., 1969, p. 196f; G. S. Bain: 'Management and White Collar Unionism', in: S. Kessler and B. Weekes (eds.): *Conflict at Work*. London BBC, 1971, p. 15. Reinhard Lund: 'Die dänische Gewerkschaftsbewegung von 1945 bis 1975', *GMH*, 1976, H. 9 (542-556), p. 543; L. Forsebäck: *Sozialpartner und Arbeitsmarkt in Schweden*. Stockholm, Schwedisches Institut, 1977, p. 27.
Figures for some countries in 1972/73 which are too low in most cases now: Hugh Clegg: *Trade Unionism under Collective Bargaining, A Theory Based on Comparisons of Six Countries*. Oxford, Blackwell, 1976, p. 12; C. Crouch and A. Pizzorno (eds.): *The Resurgence of Class Conflict in Western Europe since 1968*. London, Macmillan, 1978, Vol. 1, p. 316.

organized. This is partly because the general level of organization is high and develops certain spill-over effects. In Austria, which has both a large public sector and a generally high level of organization we see the trend confirmed and the degree of white collar organization is high. In the Federal Republic of Germany about 39% out of a workforce of 32 million are organized. The public sector employees have the highest degree of organization (76%) and white collar workers in the private sector the lowest (24%). 45% of workers are organized. Exact figures are difficult to obtain for other countries, and those available are not fully comparable. Firstly, the definition of white collar workers and clerical staff varies from one country to another. In Germany the tendency is to identify legal status signs with the reality of life at work. But the definition of a union also varies. One study on Great Britain gives about the same degree of organization of 'white' and 'blue' collar workers (approximately 50%) but this only holds if 'staff' and 'professional' associations are also included.[104] In countries where the industry principle dominates this would hardly be possible because the definition of a union is very much narrower. The German Beamtenbund (Civil Service Association) is often not regarded as a union and even the White Collar Workers Association (DAG) sometimes has difficulty in being accepted as one. In the English-speaking countries where the civil servants have not inherited so exalted an image as in some continental countries where there is a strong hierarchical concept of public service the public sector employees have had no hesitation in regarding their organizations as unions. But here too organization is a relatively recent phenomenon. It is possible to identify waves of unionization in the USA: the twenties are regarded as the decade of 'craft unionism', the thirties and forties as the decades of industry unions, the fifties as the golden age of the organization of the white collar workers and the seventies would appear to have brought a wave of organization of employees in the public sector.[105]

In the late seventies even the police and the military staff in most Western countries showed a tendency to unionize. In 1977 the American Federation of Government Employees voted 79% to 21% not to recruit military membership. The Senate in September 1977 voted seventy-two to three to prohibit unions in the military services. Military unions — so reluctantly accepted in the United States — certainly do not cause more problems than the existing unions of police in Europe. Even Communist-oriented trade unions in Europe admit that certain groups such as soldiers and policemen cannot 'mechanically' be integrated into the existing unions for governmental employees.[106] Such an integration would only be possible when the rights and the bargaining patterns of the military service and the rest of the public employees were completely equalized, which in most countries is most unlikely to happen. In Germany even the progressive representatives in the 'Commission on the Reform of the Public Service' who advocated a uniform law for the public service were prepared to admit exceptions for the spheres of government activities where state sovereignty is immediately implied, notably the court system, police and military service. But unlike the American Federation of Government Employees its German equivalent, the ÖTV, has tried to integrate the police and used its veto against the admission of the Trade Union of Policemen (Gewerkschaft der Polizei, founded in 1950), as the seventeenth member of the DGB, since it could claim that there were already policemen in its rank and file. Only in spring 1978 was the Trade Union of Policemen after long negotiations admitted with its 141,000 members as the seventeenth member of the DGB, a step which strengthened the idea of unity in the German trade union movement, but which probably does not facilitate the fight of the ÖTV for a unified law of all the officials in the civil service.[107]

A relative loss of status and the removal of privileges due to a more progressive union policy for the workers have played a part in the large-scale organization of white collar workers in the private sector. The employees in the public sector, however, have not suffered this loss of status. On the contrary, attention is increasingly drawn to the risk that the current development may bring them a dual accumulation of advantages: they may retain their old privileges from the time of state patrimony in return for unconditional service and, now that strikes in the public sector — whether legal or illegal — have in many countries become an accepted mode of conflict (cf. Chapter 2, 3) may become as militant as any other modern union. Both popular right- and left-wing literature often paints a picture of the 'civil servants' state' with a growing army of civil servants in control of the levers of power, constantly improving their own position at the expense of the rest of the community; conservatives often see this as an outcome of the progress of Socialism. In fact in some countries the public sector has definitely taken the lead, both in militancy and in wage rises, while it used only to follow the developments in the private sector.[108]

Left-wing literature is as ambivalent towards the question of the white collar workers as those unions which would like to see the proletarian characteristics of the unions preserved. On the one hand it would appear that the argument that the social position of the blue and white collar workers should be equalized as far as possible is firmly opposed, but on the other hand the greater ease with which white collar workers can now be mobilized for strikes is welcomed as a hopeful sign of a growing proximity of ideas.[109]

In itself the high degree of organization of white collar workers is nowhere regarded as a sign of a high degree of class consciousness. The conservatism of the civil service staff associations would otherwise be hard to explain. Pro-union theoreticians regard the willingness of white collar workers to support industrial unions in a central union body as more important. The greatest degree of organization is now in countries like Sweden, where white collar workers in the public and the private sector have formed two organizations independent of the LO (TCO and SACO). The LO formerly often regarded the TCO as a 'bourgeois organization' and not as a union, while the TCO firmly dissociated itself from the LO's ties with the Social Democrat Party (cf. Chapter 4, 2). There have also been demarcation conflicts. Cooperation has recently improved but a joint organization is not at present regarded as a realistic alternative to the existing dualism. Today, even by TCO functionaries, the similarities in organization and bargaining patterns between LO and TCO are emphasized.[110] The LO gave up its hostile attitude towards the white collar unions but is probably not very interested in linking up as it is clear that its 'solidarity in wage policy' would be very much harder to maintain if the white collar workers in the private and the public sector also had to be integrated.

The growth in white collar organizations in Great Britain has been explained as the result of Government policy, which created a favourable climate for such unions. The state could hardly recommend participation possibilities for private industry on the basis of the Whitley Report and deny these to its own employees.[111] But on an international comparison this needs modifying. The situation is different in Sweden, despite the rapid growth in the public sector and increasing Government control. The state has done little to encourage white collar organizations either in the public or the private sector. Nor have these organizations become as radical as in the English-speaking countries. They have not been very militant, do not see themselves as syndicalist but have achieved as much through skilful tactics and behaviour, and with fewer conflicts, as their more militant counterparts in other countries.[112]

In some countries the 'semi-professionals', such as teachers and nurses, have been the most militant white collar organizations. This has been seen as due to the fact that they have little mobility in comparison with the classical professions, doctors and lawyers, since the expansion of the education and health services made theirs mass occupations. The militancy of organizations is certainly due not only to ideological influence but very much more to the development of chances of promotion and mobility in the various occupations,[113] and to political intervention by the state in the occupational spheres of growing numbers of civil servants and other public sector employees.[114] In most countries — independent of the degree of union pluralism or the concept of union unity — the white collar workers do not show a united front. Some are members of independent staff organizations, some belong to industrial unions or sub-organizations of head associations which at least programmatically support industrial unionism.

The less the industry principle is realized in a head association and the greater the fragmentation in occupational organizations the easier it is for white collar workers' organizations to join a central union body. This has been very clear in recent years in Great Britain where white collar organizations have increasingly been pressing for affiliation to the TUC as they wish to benefit from its services. The trend was interrupted for a time by the 1971 Industrial Relations Act, because the TUC expelled all the unions which registered under the Act. The fourteen unions expelled in 1972 and the twenty expelled at the TUC Congress in 1973 were mainly organizations with a craft or white collar mentality.[115] But most of them have since been re-accepted.[116] The repeal of the Act removed one source of friction between the TUC and the white collar organizations which had been more inclined to accept the Act than the large workers' unions. Very few even of the management mourned the repeal of the Act in 1974 and only the staff associations, which had been willing to register, seem to have benefited as the Act encouraged their growth.[117]

As more and more of the white collar organizations join the TUC the balance of power shifts between pillars of the labour movement. As in Sweden very few of the British white collar workers are prepared to support the Labour Party when joining a union. Three of the most important British unions which do not have manual workers among their members (NALGO, NUT and CPSA) are the largest organizations which do not support the party, with a total membership of over one and half million. More than one million of their members are not even prepared to join the party as individual members.[118] The growth in white collar organizations is, in the sense of a close organizational link between party and union, one of the most important reasons for the decline in the proportion of collective union party membership (cf. Chapter 4, 2).

In highly fragmented union movements the increasing organization of the white collar workers does not in any case automatically lead to a lessening of conflict. This arises not only from the different political loyalties of the white and blue collar workers (cf. Chapter 4, 2b) but also from organizational rivalry. In the English-speaking countries where a large number of individual organizations are affiliated to the head association new areas of friction are constantly emerging between the organizations of blue and white collar workers from demarcation disputes. Both in the USA and Great Britain comparative organizational analyses have revealed a certain trend for white collar workers to integrate into blue collar unions.[119] In the Federal Republic at the height of the protest movement and the move by many intellectuals to Socialist ideas, university staff members, for instance, tended to look towards the big Public Service and Transport Workers Union (ÖTV) and avoid the purely white collar Education and Science Union (GEW), until they realized that the ÖTV was, on the whole, no more left wing than the GEW.

Where industrial unionism is as strong as it is in Germany the white collar unions are increasingly forced on to the defensive and white collar workers tend to join the industry unions. The Metal Workers Union (IG Metall) has the highest number among its members although their percentage of the total is lower than in other unions. The ÖTV, IG Metall and the Commerce, Banking and Insurance Union (HBV) represent numerically the largest number of white collar workers. The Artists and Musicians Union (Gewerkschaft 'Kunst') has only white collar members and they also form the majority of the Commercial Union (Gewerkschaft Handel).

All the unions which are members of the head association in Germany (the DGB) are gaining ground among the white collar workers. The strongest competitor of the DAG, the Commerce, Banking and Insurance Union, had an increase of 25,000 in 1974 while the DAG gained only 8,000 members. The DAG is losing ground particularly among the younger generation (up to age twenty-four) and it did not do well in the social elections either. The trend would appear to reflect permanent changes in attitude. A study by the Institute for Applied Sociology (INFAS) in Bonn showed that 58% of salaried workers would prefer to be represented by a union which has both white and blue collar workers among its members.[120] An empirical study of white collar workers published in 1970 also revealed an astonishingly high degree of organization — about 60% — among those questioned. DGB members are often more political in orientation and less status-conscious than DAG members.[121]

The organizational weakness of the DAG means that

— in general it cannot pursue an independent wage policy as its members are too widely distributed;
— it largely has to accept the results negotiated by DGB unions and sell these as its own achievement;
— its diminishing strength will make entry conditions to the DGB tougher (DGB officials: 'It would be better if the DAG gradually dissolved');
— it is leaning towards the CDU (Conservative Party) in compensation; Helmut Schmidt, the German Chancellor, also tried to woo the DAG. Its chairman, Hermann Brandt, is a member of Schmidt's party, but was increasingly under pressure from *fronde* in his own ranks.

Beside such determinants of the readiness to join a union as social background and the attitude of the parents, there is another factor which is changing rapidly — the sphere of work. While the majority of those who wish to join the DGB are in work preparation areas, in book-keeping and material administration (despatch and stores), the group the DAG is aiming for is largely in commercial accounting, i.e. somewhat removed from the production area and inclined to emphasize its clerical status. There is little inclination to join either organization among employees who are close to the management or work directly for the management.[122] There was for a long time a correlation between political engagement and the readiness to join a union: DAG members were more opposed to political activity by the unions than DGB members. Union studies have shown that the inclination of employees to join unions grows as political engagement grows and also with the increasing size of the plant, and that the employees then prefer DGB unions to status-conscious and a-political organizations like the DAG.[123]

Other plant surveys have shown that white collar workers and civil servants do not differ from workers on some questions as strongly as might be supposed (the distribution of surplus wealth, for instance, or the question of fair wages).[124] Considerable attention was therefore aroused by surveys carried out in the second half of 1974 which indicated that white collar workers and public sector employees were increasingly opposed to excessive and de-stabilizing wage demands, but an analysis has yet to be made of whether the crucial threshold of 10% which formed the basis of the study by the Allensbach Institute is justified.[125] But in other matters, too, the views of the 'officials' in the Deutscher Beamtenbund, for instance, differed. However the recent changes in attitude among white collar workers and public sector employees may be explained when more material is available, it is certain that there has been some functional change in the militancy of these groups. The right to strike in the public sector, for instance, is no longer regarded as only theoretically compatible with public service,[126] it is occasionally practised, as the vote by Berlin teachers for a one-day warning strike in September 1974 showed.[127]

More important than such controversial increases in militancy are the attempts to catch up on advantages won for white collar workers and workers in the private sector through the unions while preserving other privileges (Christmas and holiday bonuses and special pension rights). There is a tendency to profit from the workers' wage battles with the attitude 'Don't strike, let others strike for you'.[128] These tactics have brought the public sector employees to the top of the wage scale in some areas in recent years. Conservative labour law experts see this as a particularly ominous trend in some local authority areas where leading figures on the employers' side are also leading union officials. It is feared that autonomy in wage bargaining may gradually be destroyed as one group gains advantage at the expense of the taxpayer.[129] The Beamtenbund, of course, sees this differently. It draws comparisons not only with other income groups, which it maintains are in a better position — although usually the comparison covers only nominal wages and ignores the special benefits in the public sector[130] — but also historically. The price index of 1913 is used to support the argument that the basic wages of some of the higher income grades had still not been fully adjusted to the price index by 1968. Since 1913 nominal wages for the lower grades in Germany have risen by 380%, for the middle grades by 292%, for the upper middle grades by 202% and for the top grades by 191%. So there has been a certain redistribution in favour of the lower grades, which is very justifiable and cannot be taken as proof of the general wage lag in the public sector.[131] Conflicts can always be expected among the public sector employees in times of crisis when their special privileges and benefits are at risk. When the Minister for Home Affairs, Maihofer, was considering freezing the ministerial supplement the DGB supported him, arguing that if the workers' unemployment benefit contributions were to be increased the civil service could take a cut in earnings as well. But the Beamtenbund bitterly opposed the measure and will have had the majority of the civil service on its side.[132]

Although the unions are devoting more attention to white collar workers in their membership campaigns their successes are often the cause of problems, both for the radical supporters of a hostile union policy and the reformists who want to use a step by step alignment of wage policy to achieve further equality, even in areas where the basic opposition between capital and labour is still a determinant factor. Their worries are increased by the fact that the number of white collar workers is growing — in some sectors of the American economy they now make up over 50% of the workforce, and in Great Britain they will reach the same proportion by about 1985.[133]

The more militant unionists complain that the white collar workers and civil servants in their ranks are not active enough. In the Federal Republic the white collar workers remained neutral in many disputes and surveys have revealed a basically sceptical attitude to strikes.[134] Solidarity grew temporarily in the spontaneous strikes of 1969 and 1973. But generalizations on the attitude of white collar workers to strikes are usually one-sided. Solidarity does not grow out of nothing, it is a product of communication. So there is usually less solidarity where there is little direct contact between white collar workers and the workers (in the German mining industry, for instance, where the white collar workers are in tower blocks in Düsseldorf and have little contact with the problems of the miners in the Ruhr). But in the printing industry, where printers and draughtsmen work in the same building in the large plants, there is a strong sense of unity and a long tradition of joint and active wage policy.

Again, it is difficult to generalize on the militancy of white collar workers in the public sector because the causes of conflict themselves are shifting in the nationalized industries. In countries with large nationalized industries, like France, comparative studies on strikes in the public sector have not only disproved the assumptions of the early strike theoreticians that the frequency of strikes would drop as nationalization increased[135] but also shown that the motives for strikes have changed. In contrast to the private sector the main cause of conflict is not wages but working conditions and the classification of wage and salary groups.[136]

Many groups who can certainly be regarded as privileged strike because they feel that the benefit that will accrue to them from changes in wage and salary thresholds is less than that of other less highly qualified groups. So the conflict pattern is rather one of 'status policy' than 'class policy' despite the degree of syndicalist organization.

In comparative union research it has proved difficult to generalize on the attitude and will to strike of white collar workers. Just as the blue collar workers do not always see themselves as a proletariat, the white collar workers are not all conservative and anxious not to lose status. Even the extent to which the industry principle is accepted by the white collar workers is not an indication of their militancy. White collar workers are not very militant in Germany although most of them are in industrial unions. In countries where certain intellectual groups (the SACO in Sweden) are very jealous of their independent status over the general union, they have not hesitated to use methods which are more militant — they organized a teachers' strike (which would be most unusual in Germany) — and in 1966 the civil servants were mobilized to a three-day sympathy strike. In order to maintain the advantages of credentialled personnel, SACO maximized its union role, but then felt compelled to maximize militancy to uphold its reputation as a union.[137] Again the argument, which is plausible for the English-speaking countries, that white collar workers have rather a strong sense of their occupational status — they see themselves as bank employees, insurance clerks or civil servants — is only true in countries where these groups are highly organized in special unions. The bank employees, often known as the 'aristocracy of clerks', were increasingly militant in some countries even before syndicalist patterns of conflict spread generally at the end of the sixties.[138] But even in a highly specialized group, white collar workers such as the technicians became militant since they proved more and more to be generally dissatisfied as individuals, in terms of their career opportunities and as a group, with their present status and treatment as an occupational category within the firm,[139] even in those countries where generalizations on the *nouvelle classe ouvrière* with its exaggerated hopes in the revolutionary capacities of the technicians proved to be premature.

In some countries the white collar workers have proved very loyal in disputes — especially the teachers — and in some areas they have been extremely militant both with and without a status ideology.[140] With the rapid change in earnings patterns and the attitudes of many groups, generalizations which formerly held good on the behaviour of blue and white collar workers have become more problematical. However, one can venture to say that the increasing syndicalization of white collar groups and their adoption of conflict patterns which the workers evolved is creating new and hitherto unknown problems for the union movement in many countries. Not all the unions have grounds for unsullied pleasure at their success with these groups. While workers usually become more militant as their qualifications increase[141] this is not generally true of white collar workers. Even the advocates of a joint wage policy oriented to reform have some fears regarding the growing proportion of white collar workers and civil servants in the unions. While the class war theoreticians are in favour of a plant wage policy and want to see every possible means of negotiation with the employers exploited, the reformists rather fear that the craft unions will use this policy stubbornly to oppose the industry principle. Well organized craft and specialist unions can most easily force wages up above the general average in their sector and the benefit goes to those groups which are least concerned to change the system, and to the real 'aristocracy of the workers'. In the Federal Republic when the ÖTV took the first small steps towards a joint wage policy by demanding a uniform rate for all public employees the DAG opposed the measure as 'the annihilation of everything we have worked for and achieved over the last few years'.[142] In this dispute the ÖTV dropped its joint wage negotiations in June 1976.

But even DGB officials regarded it as too risky to pursue a policy of direct attack on the DAG, fearing that a number of white collar workers would take an increasingly independent line, as the air traffic control staff had done, and might even be supported in this by the employers in the public sector.[143] The DAG in turn after the summer of 1976 joined forces with the Marburger Bund and the Federation of Unions and Associations in the Public Sector (GGVÖD).[144]

Theoretically the fewest difficulties should arise with white collar workers in countries like Great Britain, where the head association is in any case composed of strongly fragmented craft unions. However, the demarcation problems in such a system in fact create a multitude of problems which do not arise when unions are largely organized on an industry base, as in Sweden and the Federal Republic. The conflicts within the TUC can be seen by the number of disputes it is asked to settle. Most of them derive from conflicts between white collar unions and industry unions competing for clerical staff in their particular sector.[145] The TUC asks the craft unions to carry the flag as far as possible in the sectors in which the workers predominate,[146] at the price of a stronger trend to a disunited wage policy, as the specialists and white collar workers become more united.

The expansion of the education and training system, better opportunities for further training and the corresponding policy in the plants are constantly creating new intermediary positions and groups of employees and opening up new chances of promotion which do not increase solidarity among the employees.[147] State education policy is creating new problems for the unions; their own means are frequently insufficient to solve these and the reorganization of what are often old structures is becoming much more difficult. But simply centralized wage negotiations as have been developed in Sweden are not in themselves enough for a constant adjustment of the different levels of claims which arise. Indeed, it is possible that the integration of large sections of the white collar workers into the industrial unions hinders a united policy on wage re-distribution because it creates fear of loss of status among the more highly qualified groups and higher wage earners, bringing further internal conflicts for the workers organizations. Perhaps — although this is contrary to the value usually attached to a consistent industry principle throughout the labour movement in every country — it is actually temporarily an advantage when the industry principle is only established among the blue collar workers and, as is the case in Sweden, the organizations of the civil servants (TCO) and the academics (SACO) remain outside the head association. Too great a strain is not put on the necessity for pecuniary solidarity between these groups and the workers to maintain solidarity in wage policy.

A basic reorganization of union structures would be impossible today in any country without state intervention. In every country the process of reorganization is proceeding over the longer term and is encountering enormous opposition. The first step towards furthering the industry principle and rationalizing divisions which have become obsolete through economic development is the admission of sanctions if individual members do not enter the appropriate union but — for instance when they change jobs and move to another industry — want to stay in their old union or choose the one where the membership fees are lowest (cf. the Swedish statutes of 1941).

(b) Managerial Staff

This is a new group whose emergence must be seen in relation to the problem of the white collar workers. It is gaining in importance as the entrepreneur ceases to be the all-round director of his plant. Moreover, the senior staff are acquiring a special function through the new participation legislation and this is not quite in keeping with Mallet's prognosis of the development of a new attitude among the technocrats.

In the Federal Republic the Association of Senior Staff (ULA) has gained ground in recent years in the social elections and its position will of course be strengthened by the co-determination legislation. The ULA claims to have a membership of 38,000, which unionists doubt, although this would give it a membership share of only about 10%. The DAG is also making increasing efforts to woo the senior staff.[148] The readiness of this group to join unions varies from one industry to another and is strongest among chemists and in the iron and steel industry.[149]

In France the concept 'cadre' covers not only senior staff; technicians, master craftsmen and commercial travellers are members of the Confédération Générale des Cadres (CGC) together with managers. In France too, the growing quantitative importance of the cadres can be seen in the elections to the works councils (see Table 4), although by no means all the senior staff vote for this union. On the contrary, according to statistics from the French Ministry of Labour only 37.4% voted for the CGC candidates, 13.4% voted for the CFDT and 9.8% for the CGF.[150] So the ideological conflict goes through the ranks of white collar workers and senior staff as well. But the break with the industry principle, which results from such special organizations, is not only the product of the attitude of the white collar workers themselves. In France especially, many unionists greatly mistrust intellectuals and senior staff. The demand for *ouvriérisation* of the unions flares up at recurrent intervals.[151] On the other hand even the CGT is not prepared to condemn the senior staff out of hand and identify them with the employers' interests. They particularly caution against exaggerated hostilities such as detaining plant management, as occurred at LIP.[152]

There is distrust on both sides even in the Federal Republic. The officials of the status organization ULA and the DAG are often attacked as 'an early warning system' for the capitalist side.[153] The emphasis put on the special position of the cadre by the CGC and ULA and its readiness to cooperate, together with the special rights accorded under the co-determination legislation, afford justification for this mistrust. Very few organizations are really attempting to bridge the gap between the management and the workers, as is the French CFDT, which has its own cadre organization. This does not always meet with a sympathetic attitude on the part of the senior staff themselves. The Secretary-General of the CFDT cadre organization, Roger Faist, said at one congress that the cadres must be prepared 'to have their own 4 August one day'. It was a reference to the relinquishing of feudal privileges by the ruling classes in France during the revolution.[154]

But in most countries it is too early for such prognoses. The employers have been skilful in their tactics and have kept bringing new groups of employees into positions of power. In Germany there have already been lawsuits over the recognition of the position of the senior staff — there was one at Lufthansa in 1976.[155] There is much to indicate that in future the cadres will strengthen their position on the employers' side.

(c) The Intellectuals

In every country the intellectuals were relatively most strongly affected by the wave of syndicalization following the world-wide protest movement. But it became apparent that too strong a political engagement of the intellectuals' associations hindered rather than helped efforts to integrate them into unions. In many instances the lesson of the French teachers' union which, faced with the ideological conflicts which led to the split in the CGT in 1947/48 decided to make itself independent, was quickly forgotten. Most willing to adopt union patterns of organization were in general those engaged in cultural work and the media, least willing the university teachers. In countries where the ideological confrontation was not as embittered as it was in Europe, however, the university staff also showed a strong tendency towards syndicalism. The change in the education and training system, the freeing of university entrance and the concern to create equality of opportunity for marginal groups had a particularly strong effect on the attitude of university teachers in the USA. As in the media and the entertainment industry a tendency to star quality or individuality did not prove totally incompatible with loyal union support.[156]

But in countries where the ideological confrontation was more bitter, syndicalist tendencies among intellectuals did not make this new potential group of union members more united. In the Federal Republic we can identify some contradictory developments among the intellectuals and their professional organizations and among the promotional groups:

(1) Members of the academic world made greater efforts than before to conceal material interests or put greater emphasis on ideal interests. Welcome as an academic approach to the realization of organizational interest may be, it is not very praiseworthy to point out that the possible effects of a certain measure or product (this happens frequently in pharmaceutical advertising) have not been thoroughly tested and then grant it a period of grace before prohibition by state intervention although the negative effects are already evident enough without further research.

(2) Polarization is increasing within certain potential groups (for example in academic life through the academic professional associations) and party groups of union-oriented members have been formed within the organizations for the intellectuals and the

self-employed. In some cases attempts were made to syndicalize entire groups. But the penalty was the loss of strong minorities. One example is the attempt by the Association of German Writers (Verband Deutscher Schriftsteller) at the beginning of 1973 to take the writers as a group into the Printing Union (IG Druck und Papier), which cost it one-third of its members before it dissolved itself in the autumn of 1974,[157] or the merger of the Association of University Assistants (Bundesassistenenkonferenz) into the Education and Science Union. Only these recent trends among the intellectuals can prevent us from falling back to a kind of 'nothing-new-under-the-sun approach' which prevailed for a time in the research on parties. Parallel to the Lipset-Rokkan hypothesis: 'the party systems of the 1960s reflect, with few but significant exceptions, the cleavage structures of the 1920s',[158] one could formulate: 'The structure of many unions reflects the state of technology and industrial organization at the time of their birth and growth'.[159] The continuity hypothesis for trade unions is far more correct than for the party systems since the old issues of 'industrial unionism' versus 'pluralist structures' where employees and intellectuals can integrate in a head organization without losing their independent status within the organization are still the most important variables which decide whether independent white collar associations prevail (Denmark and Sweden) or whether they become members of the head organization (ACTU, TUC, AFL-CIO). The German DGB — because of its completely new beginning after 1945 — is the only example of a head organization based on industrial unionism which was capable of integrating most of the employees in private and public employment.

4. CENTRALIZATION AND DECENTRALIZATION

Union head associations are rarely so strongly centralized or unified in their competencies as the central offices of the parties they are alllied to. However, the degree of centralization varies according to the structure of the organization and the political culture of the country concerned:

(1) There is least centralization in countries where *the labour movement is ideologically fragmented*. Paradoxically, the excessive centralization in the French state apparatus is not matched by a

corresponding degree of centralization on the side of the interest groups. In the three big unions the local and departmental units are the decisive ones. Even where more central steering bodies have been created, like the strike fund at the CFDT, it is emphasized that freedom of decision rests with the local and branch organizations.[160] Efforts to create a greater degree of centralization after the reunion of the Socialist CGT and the Communist CGTU in 1936 show why the French unions accepted the obligatory arbitration at the time of the Popular Front movement which had been rejected up to then in the syndicalist tradition in France.[161] Tendencies to centralization usually proved more successful under a left-wing government, which is why there was no linear continuation of this trend in France after the Second World War. In Italy, on the other hand, collective negotiations were relatively centralized and it was not until after the 'hot autumn' of 1969 that the practice of negotiations in or close to the plant became more common again, encouraged by the new forms of participation (cf. Chapter 4, 5).

Theorists of union evolution have sometimes regarded an increase in the influence of the central federations as a sign that the unions had become more mature and outgrown their beginnings in the class war. With the merger of the AFL and the CIO in 1955 the USA also seemed to have entered this 'mature' phase. Unfortunately for the evolutionists, however, the new head association did not develop a centralized influence comparable, for instance, to the Swedish Landsorganisation. It did exert its influence very decisively for the six rules of 'ethical practice' to combat corruption in many organizations. But even sanctioning expulsion was not sufficient to solve the problems, it merely created new ones by strengthening powerful outsiders,[162] as those who knew the situation had predicted, as ideological, radical and nationalist animosities could never be entirely excluded from the US labour movement. Even in Great Britain collective negotiations are more centralized than in the USA.[163] It is true that there has recently been a growing trend to large-scale negotiations in the USA too but these are not so successful as in Europe, and the employers are not encouraging the development, unlike their counterparts in many European countries.[164] European employers, especially in Germany and Sweden, have often deliberately used lock-outs against strikes to gain greater solidarity among employers and achieve large-scale collective agreements to restrict the profit squeeze against prosperous plants.

Ideological conflicts in unions can also encourage centralization. In Finland the conflict between the Social Democrat majority and the Communist minority after the Second World War strengthened the central control of the SAK. Although central negotiations did not assume the same importance as in the neighbouring Scandinavian countries the SAK did form a negotiating committee and strengthened the tendency to centralization by cooperating in the establishment of a state wage policy. In its 1971 programme the SAK decided on a compromise formulation between 'sufficient authority for the central organization' to conduct negotiations and autonomy for the member unions to negotiate.[165] The Communists, too, who were always in favour of centralization wherever they were able to gain the majority in ideologically-oriented unions, largely supported decentralization (as they did in France) as long as this appeared to strengthen their position.[166]

The degree of centralization of collective negotiations can vary from industry to industry in countries where the union movement is ideologically fragmented. In Belgium most of the bargaining in the chemical industry is done at plant level while in the engineering industry both the unions and the employers want national agreements.[167] The extension of those areas which are regarded as appropriate for collective agreements also strengthened the trend towards centralization. In France the usual decentralization of the negotiating method was quite considerably undermined by the tendency of the state to conclude general agreements with certain unions on social and political matters ranging from job security to vocational training.

In Italy and Great Britain the trend has been rather the reverse. Where the unions did not progress quickly enough due to the obstacles and restrictions of the expansion of central control by the state, regulations were obtained in decentralized negotiations with companies such as Fiat, Montedison or Olivetti concerning such matters as investment and development policy which had until recently been regarded as the preserve for decisions by the management.[168] In the Netherlands at the beginning of the seventies a strong tendency to negotiations on plant level also developed.[169] But this can also be seen as a reaction to the failure of attempts at a central incomes policy which had not been undertaken to anything like the same extent in any other country in Europe (cf. Chapter 4, 3).

On an international comparison the central negotiation of *global agreements* in many industries is often seen as a successful balance between the French pattern of centralization and Dutch decentralization (after the collapse of the incomes policy).[170] The durability of the trend to decentralization under the pressure of spontaneous movements after 1969 has been over-estimated in almost every country. This can always last only as long as the union actions are concentrated in the plant or where workers themselves take the initiative in unofficial strikes. There has never been a linear development of this trend (cf. Chapter 4, 5).

Where participation on the job is most encouraged by the state, as in Scandinavia, efforts to achieve an 'equalizing' wage policy fortunately hinder a continuance of the decentralization trend, as this of course needs a good deal of central coordination. A major disadvantage of the progress of decentralized 'control by the workers' is the risk to the competitiveness of individual plants as control by the workers cannot immediately reduce international links and dependence on foreign trade.

(2) In the English-speaking countries, too, where there is a large head association, although not all the unions belong to it, decentralization is still very strong and the individual unions have retained considerable autonomy and decision-making powers. The TUC in Great Britain keeps strengthening this with 'rules' and 'standing orders'[171] and its reports state openly that the number of conflicts between its member organizations has not decreased in recent years, despite the tendency to concentration.[172] In many areas the TUC's function in regard to its affiliated unions is limited to training and education, legal aid and arbitration.[173]

This high degree of autonomy also affects the political attitude which can be taken by the head association towards Parliament, the Government and the political parties. In the USA the tendency of some unions to pursue an independent line is stronger even than in Great Britain. The automobile workers under Reuther took this to the point of a breach with the AFL-CIO and it was not until nearly a decade later that an attempt was made under Reuther's successor, Leonard Woodcock, to work towards reunion.

In its policy the TUC is also largely dependent on its affiliated unions. But in many cases, after long internal battles, it can adopt a much more uniform line in representing the workers' interests than the American head association can. This is partly due to its close cooperation with the Labour Party. Moreover, in Great Britain there is not the centrifugal tendency of American federalism, which makes the representation of interests a much more functionalized 'business'. In recent years the TUC has increasingly attempted to exert its influence, if necessary with the use of sanctions. At the 1973 Congress, as already mentioned, twenty unions were expelled (accounting for about 4% of membership) because they had not followed the TUC policy of boycotting obligatory registration following the Conservative Industrial Relations Act.

(3) Centralization is strongest in countries where a *general union* dominates (cf. Chapter 1, 1). However, a general union is not identical with centralism. In the German labour movement Revisionists, Centrists and later Communists were all in their own way 'centralists in waiting', but they made good use of decentralized organizational elements to gain advantages for their groups.[174] Again centralization at individual union level through the gradual realization of the industry principle is not necessarily identical with centralism in the head association. On the contrary, concentration in favour of a few large industrial unions can weaken the head association. The founders of the DGB, Böckler, Tarnow, Reuter, Richter and others, intended it to have much greater centralized powers than were ultimately created in the Munich charter.[175]

Centralization is still suspect to many syndicalists, especially in the Latin countries, as the precursor of bureaucracy. On the other hand it is complained that a decentralized union organization means that the egalitarian aims of the union programme cannot be realized. Solidarity in wage policy can only be achieved with a greater degree of centralization than even the DGB has managed to create. In Sweden there have been attempts since 1956 to negotiate norms for wage increases for industries and plants. The agreements concluded between the central union organization, the LO, and the employers' association, SAF, are not actually legally binding for the sub-organizations but the central organizations have sufficient authority to be able to realize most of their aims.[176] As on state level, in the union movement, too, where the head association can hardly force unity on its members from above, there are tendencies to self-coordination as a few powerful organizations take the lead. In many industrial states it is the metal workers who are regarded as 'the locomotive of wage rises' and their agreements have often proved to be models for other unions.[177]

Again on an international comparison the extent of centralization cannot simply be deduced from certain factors such as the size of the areas covered by wage agreements or the realization of the industry principle. There are several variables:

(1) The degree of realization of *industrial unionism* (Sweden, Federal Republic). Where there is still a relatively high degree of occupational fragmentation, as in Denmark and Norway (cf. Table 1), centralization has not developed to the extent that it has in Sweden. The tendency to centralize was rather in state intervention in labour disputes in attempts to extend compulsory arbitration (cf. Chapter 3, 4d).

(2) *Ideological unity in the head association* (Social Democrat or Labour dominated head associations in Northern and Central Europe).

(3) *Concentration and production specialization* in the economy. This can (in Scandinavia) but need not necessarily (Canada and Switzerland) lead to a strong centralization in the organizational structure and consequently to centralization of wage negotiations.

(4) *The number of unions which have joined one head association* also affects the degree to which collective negotiations can be centralized. Union organization is becoming increasingly concentrated in all the capitalist countries, nevertheless vital differences remain in the degree of fragmentation below the head association (cf. Table 1, Chapter 1, 2).

(5) *The financial strength and strike fund of the head association*. Head associations which are poor (in the Latin countries) or kept short of funds (the TUC) have less centralizing power than those with a fixed revenue and their own capital assets. According to §4 of its Articles of Association the DGB receives from its member unions 12% of their revenue from membership fees. This fixed ratio guarantees that the head association will grow with its member unions, unlike the TUC, which even in the 1978 Rules agreed to accept a fixed sum per member (20p per member, Rule 3).[178]

The financial strength of the head association also affects the influence it can exert in distributing strike aid; this is not the case for the unions in the Latin countries (with the exception of the CFDT) or the TUC. Even if most unions are not prepared to let the head association have a say in their strike decisions its influence is all the stronger in the preliminary discussions the more financial aid it can offer. An important factor for both the DGB and the Swedish LO is the trust administration of the solidarity fund. DM 0.60 per year and member are paid into this fund at the DGB. Between 1950 and 1970 about DM 79.1 million was collected in this way. But the fund is no longer mainly used for strike pay. Federal strike aid is an exception. As one finance expert from the DGB put it: 'The unions have never been so well equipped for strikes as they are today, but most of them have never had to pay out so little in strike pay as in the last twenty years'.[179]

(6) *Company constitution*. The shop steward system was originally intended to strengthen the influence of the unions. But in many industries the shop stewards have acquired considerable autonomy and are by no means an extended arm of the unions. In the Federal Republic, on the other hand, the union representatives in the plant (*Vertrauensleute*) who were also created to bridge the gap between the plant and the union and extend union influence, have in many cases been strongly integrated into the participation system in the dualist company constitution (cf. Chapter 1, 5), because in practice they function largely as preparatory ground for future works councils, most of which are composed of union members.

(7) *The development of co-determination outside the plant and wage policy aims*. State wage policy has a centralizing effect, either through the creation of bodies to clarify preliminary issues and channel opinion (the Federal Republic, Holland, Austria) or without intervention by the state through self-coordination by the associations concerned (Sweden, cf. Chapter 4, 3). The extent of state intervention is not the only decisive factor, wage policy can have a centralizing effect in the form of collective bargaining if it is nationally arranged and conducted according to fixed formal or informal rules. In every country there is a growing tendency to conduct wage negotiations on as wide a scale as possible. However, this is at the same time provoking local union units to aim for a wage policy which is more oriented to the situation in their plant.

(8) *The position of the unions in the economic process*. Where one union functions on a large scale as owner of production means there is a high degree of centralization. This is most obvious in

Israel, where the Histradut employed 22.7% of the workforce in 1971 and 18.2% of net production was in companies owned by the union.[180]

(9) *The centralization of the political system.* A federal system like that in the United States can easily weaken the centralization tendencies in organizations and in the unions. About half of all registered unions in Australia (about 140) are not organized on a national scale. Another particular feature of Australia is that the labour councils are independent of the individual unions. For many smaller unions membership of a metropolitan council does not mean that they are members of the head association, ACTU. But in some federalized countries, Germany, for example, federalism has not had a decentralizing effect, due to older centralist tendencies in the labour movement which did not take the sometimes arbitrary borders of the Federal 'Länder' as a guideline for their own organization. Centralization is not an independent factor. In the Latin countries where there is a high degree of centralization of the administration there has not been a corresponding degree of centralization among the unions. On the contrary, the union movement has retained a rank and file federalism in the tradition of Proudhon and Mazzini which actually emerged as a reaction to state centralization. In countries with more than one language, like Belgium, the Socialist union had to bow to regional characteristics and the percentage of speakers of each language, which again did not greatly further efforts at centralization.

(10) *The political influence of the unions.* Centralization has usually increased as the influence of the unions in politics has grown. A particularly striking instance is the alliance of the CIO with the Democratic Party in the New Deal.[181] But political influence, which usually entails a close link with a party, has not always had these results. In Great Britain the enormous influence of the TUC in certain phases of the Labour Government's policy was not accompanied by corresponding increases in centralization. The old 'guild Socialism' stubbornly resisted many of the efforts by the head association to re-organize and centralize. A relatively high degree of centralization has proved easiest to achieve in fairly small countries such as Denmark, Norway, or Israel. In Norway the LO actually increasingly took the lead in concluding national agreements on an industry basis after the Second World War and strikes were made dependent on approval of the Secretariat.[182] But

this degree of centralization was rare even in this third type of organization.

Regional, religious and social homogeneity also strengthened the power of the head association in larger countries such as Sweden. Until the revision of the statutes it was doubtful whether the LO had formal rights in wage negotiations. It usually intervened only at the request of the individual member unions.[183] Since the revision the LO has much greater possibility of vetoing strikes.

The trend to centralization has never been unilinear, there have always been counteracting tendencies. Unofficial strikes, wages drift, radicalization in some under-privileged regions and tendencies to bureaucratization with growing union membership have all produced efforts at decentralization. The union leaders themselves, facing accusations from their opponents on the growing threat of a 'state of unions' have had to point out that there is a strong tendency to decentralization.[184]

However, the longer-term effects of the decentralization trend should not be over-estimated. The new tendency to plant wage agreements after the end of the sixties brought temporary further decentralization. But this was not encouraged by the state, which was aiming to obtain 'social contracts' through incomes policy agreements, nor by the employers' associations, which were interested in achieving agreements on as large a scale as possible. Here Sweden went further than most other countries when employers' associations threatened some companies with exclusion sanctions if they concluded agreements with unions without prior agreement with the head office of the association. This was put into practice in some cases. At present it looks as if centralization in general agreements and the exploitation of profit margins through plant agreements in industries which are doing well can easily coexist.

There are astonishing discrepancies in the assessment of the centralization and decentralization tendencies in the literature: decentralization is regarded as welcome in the case of a progressive wage policy which can produce a maximum profit squeeze. But it is suspect from the point of view of an equalizing wage policy. Centralization is regarded as desirable where efficiency is concerned, whereby interest groups such as the unions are not simply machines for the maximization of incomes but have a large range of services to offer their members. Judged by some of their work in the field of education and training, social activities or legal protection,[185] quite apart from the possibilities of participation within the organization, however, it is generally the smaller unions which have most to offer. The fetish of the industrial union in Germany has created bureaucratic machines which are not always very functional. In assessing centralization and decentralization, therefore, it should be remembered that here the individual situation in the various countries and organizations is a particularly strong determinant factor.

5. MONISM OR DUALISM IN COMPANY CONSTITUTION?

Company constitution includes all the formal and informal structures which serve the formation of will on the part of the workers. At times when industry was organized on the principle of patrimony only the will of the employer was decisive. Any rights the workers may have had could at best derive from his rights, and, as in the early period of the constitutional state, be revoked at any time on state level. As the power of the labour movement increased, the participation rights of the workers became an independent source of legislation and they were either channelled by regulations which had been conceded and were fixed in legislation, or granted ad hoc after conflict and negotiation. This led to a certain dualism in most systems of labour relations. A strictly monist company constitution is now only conceivable under an authoritarian regime, where a vertical state syndicate (as in Spain under Franco) organizes all the participation functions in the plant from above. The only other possibility is even rarer: the dominance of councils or committees organized by the workers themselves and leading to the demise or freezing of legal institutions. So far these have only existed at times of the erosion of state power (during the dual rulership in Russia in the Spring of 1917). There is dualism in most systems even if the power relations vary. The British shop steward system comes close to a monism of informal structures organized from below. But here too the formal institutions for the formation of will are growing (cf. Chapter 4, 5).

The opposite pole is a system like the West German, where important powers are vested in works councils. There are frequent conflicts between these and the union organizations in the plant, although normally the two are strongly inter-related. A typology could therefore differentiate between:

(a) Monism of company constitution through the dominance of the shop steward system;

(b) dualism of company constitution through competition between legalized works councils and plant union organizations, which are partly protected by legislation on company constitution.

(a) Monism in Company Constitution through the Dominance of the Shop Steward System

The shop steward system is dominant where there are few legalized works councils or means of participation. The system emerged due to a certain alienation between the union bureaucracy and the rank and file. Although the shop stewards are usually members of powerful unions they were by no means always in accord with the union leaders when assuming their office. Nor, as representatives of union power, do they have any legal protection against the employers, in contrast to the situation in a dualist system, where the second, or union, pillar usually has a legal base as well. The management is not legally obliged to recognize shop stewards who have been elected or negotiate with them. Their power depends on de facto support from the workers and their mobilization ability in times of conflict.

In the more recent militant German union literature, particularly, the shop stewards are often seen in an excessively positive light. British union specialists were quick to see the danger of assuming permanent conflict between the local union officials and the shop stewards, as if all union officials were either 'responsible' or 'reactionary' (according to the standpoint of the writer) and all shop stewards either progressive or extremist.[186] The rise of the shop stewards was certainly not coordinated and planned by the unions, it was the expression of *informal monism* in company constitution. Through their close ties with the party the British union leaders had come to concentrate to such an extent on specific reform policies that they neglected the detailed work in the plant. The shop stewards moved into this vacuum and it was only later that the unions attempted to integrate them in their work, mainly in the membership campaign. There are about 300,000 shop stewards and it is difficult to generalize on their activities, which range from negotiations with the management to arbitration in disputes and cooperation in the distribution of work and the appointment of new workers.[187]

It is only in a few industries and plants that the local union officials are more influential than the shop stewards. In one interview study conducted in 1972 the role of the full-time officials was mainly described as 'marginal'. Shop stewards often also hold other offices in the union, although 90% of them owe their legitimation to elections by groups of workers and only 10% stated in 1972 that there had been no election. In view of the fact that several unions are represented in their plant many shop stewards cannot afford exclusive ties to their own union. 41% of those interviewed said that they occasionally also worked for members of other unions. The distance between the union machinery and the shop stewards seems to have grown since the Donovan Report confirmed this, according to more recent studies. Although instruction of shop stewards has long been a TUC aim, work with them does not appear to be one of the most intensive fields of operation of full-time officials. 'Supervising shop stewards' was given only fourth place in a TUC survey of union officials as a time-consuming occupation (after routine office work, negotiations on the job and the preparation of material for negotiations).[188] Managements are increasingly tending to prefer the shop stewards to the union officials for negotiations and often leave it to them to settle details of working conditions on the spot. In a survey carried out in 1972 74% of managers stated that they preferred the shop stewards to local union representatives as negotiating partners for binding agreements on job conditions.[189]

But the absolute figures which have resulted from interviews are not enough for conclusions to be drawn on the determinants of the influence of job organization and consequently British industrial relations researchers have formulated more differentiated questions. A team from Warwick University classified the influence of the spokesman on the job as either dependent or independent of full-time officials. A middle type of relation was classified as 'cooperative'. A study of a number of plants showed that the degree of independence of job organization depends on the structure of the unions concerned and the number of available officials (cf. Chapter 1, 9). But those determinants which were outside the influence of union organization proved to be almost more important: the size of the company (union officials have more influence in small companies than in the more highly differentiated large companies, which tend to keep conflicts as far as possible at plant level), the form of ownership (public or private, as publicly-owned plants tend to be more centralized) and the degree of centralization of the decision-making structures in the plant. In the cooperative type the union officials exercise their influence in the background. The value attached to the shop stewards and the strengthening of the trend to under-estimate the union officials is not substantiated by empirical research, any more than is the global statement in the Donovan Report that more full-time union officials are needed. In many cases concerted action by the two sides has proved to be the best method of expanding the possibilities for collective negotiations.[190]

The greater the power of the shop stewards grows and the more they aim to organize outside the plant and coordinate their work, the more professional their roles become; a progressive management is encouraging this process when it admits the shop stewards to decision areas which until recently were regarded as the prerogative of the management.[191] So there is a possibility that this development may, over the longer term, take much of the militancy out of the shop steward movement which was once apparent in face-to-face confrontation with the union bureaucracies.

The means available to the unions to exert influence in their own interests also depends on the number of full-time officials. In the Netherlands, too, it is feared that a dualist system between co-determination organs and union representatives may emerge, as in Belgium, and even in Great Britain this possibility is not excluded, as we see from the discussion over joint consultation versus shop stewards. But in the Netherlands there is approximately one union official to about 500 members of each of the three large unions, so that it is rightly argued that the Dutch union movement is geared to 'direct representation of interests (including individual complaints) by full-time union officials'.[192]

But where the new forms of participation are not legally fixed but rest largely, as in Great Britain and Italy, on collective agreements (cf. Chapter 4, 5) the union organizations have not yet been finally outmanoeuvred by the representatives of the rank and file. Over the longer term it has always proved possible to extend union power in all forms of participation even where, as in Italy, *consigli* have formed partly through conflict with the unions. They are the result of success with spontaneous action by the workers, some of whom were disillusioned with the friction between the rival unions and the ideological split. The *consigli* were to demonstrate the unity of the working class, whether organized or not.[193] But a union study showed that in Italy as well syndicalized workers formed an important group in all the major plants after the emergence of the *consigli di fabbrica* about 1969. About 40,000 workers out of a total workforce of about 110,000 in the plants surveyed belonged to them; of these only 2,940 were members of the Communist Party. But in the most important of the big plants, such as Fiat, the number of those politically active among the militant workers was much higher. In other plants, too, the survey revealed that Communist Party members enjoyed astonishingly high prestige among the majority of the workers.[194] In many cases party members and union members gained permanent control of participation posts and organs which had originally been created without union initiative or against union wishes. In the elections to the Commissioni interni the CGIL gained about 50% of the votes, the CISL about 30%, the UIL about 15% and the CISNAL 5%.[195]

(b) Dualism in Company Constitution through Competition between Legalized Works Councils and Plant Union Representatives

The situation in Italy shows that both types, monism and dualism, are becoming increasingly over-schematized and that mixtures of monistic and dualist structures are on the increase, mainly due to the extension of participation within the EEC. Even if the participation bodies were at first rejected by class-conscious union leaders as 'capitalist integration tricks' they have very certainly helped union organization.

In France the beginnings of a dual company constitution with participation granted from above to function beside the organized unions in the plant has helped to gain greater recognition for the union delegates since December 1968. Before the 1968 legislation union sections in the plants existed de facto in France but they were not legalized. In 1969 only about one-third of the plants had these organizations (11,600 out of 33,000). The number has been rising steadily since then.[196] Representation at the elections to the *comités d'entreprises* does not yet adequately reflect this growth in the importance of the union representatives, for the unions were in the majority on the committees, though with different proportions, before 1968 as well. Between 1969 and 1970, however, the number of non-union delegates on the committees dropped drastically.

TABLE 4
Elections to the *Comités d'entreprise* in France

	1974 Workers and employees	Workers	Employees	Maitres, techniciens, cadres (MTC)	1976/77 Workers and employees		
					private sector	public sector	public service
CGT	52.5	55.7	32.3	20.7	65	63	46
CFDT	18.3	19.8	25.5	14.6	23	18	15
CGT-FO	7.2	6.1	14.6	6.9	6	13	25
CFTC	2.0	2.4	5.3	1.7	1	6	4
CGC			2.3	19.4			
Other unions	6.8	2.1	4.5	7.0			
Non-members	13.0	13.7	15.3	29.8			

Sources: For 1974: *Le Monde*, 30 October 1976 and Laurent LAOT: *Les Organisations du Mouvement ouvrier francais aujourd'hui*. Paris, Les Éditions Ouvrières, 1977, p. 44. For 1976/77: 'La CGT'. Supplément au journal *Le Peuple*, No. 1021, 15/31 January 1978, p. 23.

A particular form of dualism in company constitution developed in the Federal Republic, where the dominance of the works councils (*Betriebsräte*) made the position of the union representatives in the plant (*Vertrauensleute*) difficult for a long time. The political mobilization of workers and spontaneous strikes gave some of the union representatives a chance to create a more independent position and establish themselves as far as they could as an organ of control. The close cooperation between the works councils and the managements had discredited many works council members in the eyes of the workers and the union representatives often found willing ears when they attempted to influence the selection of candidates and the order on the lists for the works council elections. However, established works councils were never voted out of office on a large scale, even if only because union members had always dominated in purely quantitative terms although they had never succeeded in radicalizing them.

Too much significance should not be attached to short-term reversals of the expansion of the union share in the works councils in Germany, although this dropped from 83.1% in 1972 to 77.6% in 1975. Even the intensification of the conflict between unionists in the political sphere, between SPD supporters and the CDU social committees, rather had a positive effect on the role of the unions in the plant, for they were united in their approach to non-members. Even where there have been some losses union representation is still over 80% in the major industrial sectors. Figures for the plants in which the Metal Workers Union is dominant also show that more progress was made in 1975, particularly in the elections of the works council chairmen. In 1975 93.4% were members of the Metal Workers Union, as compared with 92.1% in 1972 (cf. Table 5). The 1976 co-determination model will presumably not change this very much, although the unions fear that the new proportional elections will not work so much to the advantage of the DGB unions as the former majority elections did, and that there could be 'unholy alliances' and 'phony majorities' between 'yellow' groups which are loyal to the employers and left-wing radicals.

In the long term the development of a dual structure of company constitution, even if it is *intended* by those who grant it as a means of weakening union influence (as the employers hope and the radical left-wing unionists fear) will *functionally* tend to strengthen them further. But the strength of the unions in the plant again does not only depend on the legal form of participation but on other factors, such as:

— the use which is made of participation rights;
— the possibilities for plant-oriented wage policy in and outside the participation bodies;
— the degree of politicization of the workers;
— the other rights for unions in the plant.

TABLE 5
Works council elections 1957-1975

			Works Council Members			
Year	**Plant**	**Total**	**IGM %**	**DAG %**	**CGB %**	**Non-members %**
1957	7,392	46,215	81.6	—	—	13.5
1959	7,165	45,751	81.6	4.3	0.4	13.7
1961	7,049	47,967	82.2	4.3	0.5	12.9
1963	7,564	52,477	82.1	4.3	0.8	13.1
1965	7,980	54,504	82.6	3.6	0.9	12.9
1968	7,744	52,472	82.6	3.4	0.6	13.4
1972	9,578	65,408	81.4	2.5	0.5	15.7
1975	10,041	66,210	83.9	2.2	0.5	13.3

Source: 'Betriebsratswahlen 1975: Ergebnisse', *GMH*, 1975, No. 10 (607-636), p. 627.

These rights have been extended in the Federal Republic by the new Company-Labour Relations Act of 1972 although this did not fully satisfy the unions. This is understandable, since labour court decisions (when, for instance clauses guaranteeing effective earnings rates are declared invalid) tend to fuel desire for representation of the interests of the workers in a dual system, encouraging efforts to reserve parts of wage negotiation for the works council and take them out of the sphere of union competence.

In future, devices of industrial democracy will strengthen the unions in the plants. From the discussion on the Bullock Report it can already be concluded that British trade unions — and this applies to the unions of the Latin countries as well — will in the long run only accept a system of representation on the boards which is strictly monistic and based on the trade union machinery.

6. UNION DENSITY AND THE REPRESENTATIVENESS OF THE UNIONS

The size of the working class of a country is not a parallel development to union membership — 'class per se' does not automatically produce a 'class for itself' if the membership figures can be taken as any guide at all.

However, the data available vary to an astonishing extent in most countries. The figures given by the head association are not always the most reliable. But even in well organized union movements like that of the Federal Republic undisputed figures are hard to obtain. It is therefore useful to compare figures from various sources. The deviations are enormous and the figures become increasingly unreliable the more fragmented the labour movement of the country is (cf. Table 6).

There are a number of generalizations on membership density and its dependence on certain factors. A collection of data by a German magazine offered the rather one-sided comment: 'The more radical the unions, the fewer members they have'. (The figures are in the last column but one in Table 6.)[197] But the comment is not strictly true of Belgium and Finland. Table 6 is based on data from EEC sources and more recent national information.

The density of union membership cannot be deduced from only one variable (political activity), it depends on several factors:

(1) *Class consciousness*. This shows that current relationships are not valid for all periods of the labour movement. In the early days of the movement class consciousness, expressed in the degree of political radicalism and mobilization and not simply in union data on the organization, was a product of largely objective socio-economic factors such as

— the speed of industrialization;
— the speed of urbanization;
— establishment size;
— the proportion of foreign labour.[198]

There has not been a linear development, although some of these factors, such as urbanization and the size of the plant, still correlate with the degree of organization in unions. But this is now far less an indicator of class consciousness than it was in past phases of the battle for legal recognition.

The traditions have shifted. Countries like Germany, where the class consciousness of the workers and their willingness to join a union were once the admiration of the international labour movement, have dropped very much behind. Other countries with conservative class structures, such as the Benelux countries, can hardly point to the greater self-awareness of their workers as the reason for their higher degree of organization. And in Great Britain, where there is an old working-class culture, where the workers

TABLE 6
Union membership density

International head organizations	**Members in 1000** ICFU	WCL	WFTU	**Figures of the European Federation of Trade Unions** %	***Der Spiegel* 1976** %	**Union density Recent figures published by the organizations** %
Australia	ACTU				50	50
Austria	ÖGB 1527			58	58	60
Belgium	FGTB 1062	CSC 1234		65-70	70	70
Denmark	LO 1100					
	FTF 210 (Empl.)			60	70	70
Finland	SAK 951					
	TVK 280 (Empl.)			65	55	80
France	CGTFO 800	CFDT 900 (former CFTC)	CGT 2500	25	23	23
Germany	DGB 7544*			34-40	39	39
Great Britain	TUC 11515			45-50	43	50,4
Iceland	ASI 35			60		
Ireland	ICTU 564			75		
Israel	Histadrut 1161					56,8 (of the population)
Italy	CISL 2510		CGIL 4317			
	UIL 1116					
Luxembourg	CGT 35	LCGB 15		40	55	55
Malta	GWU 26			50		
New Zealand	FOL 386					55
Netherlands	NVV 724	NKV 343				
		CNV 289		35	40	40
Norway	LO 682			55	50	
Spain	UGT 2017		C C O O (not member of the WFTU)			

Table 6 (continued)

Sweden	LO TCO (Empl.)	2017 821			85	85	
Switzerland	SGB	446	CGB SVEA	98 13	25-30	37	38-40
USA	AFL/CIO (in 1969 it severed its ties with ICFU)			13542			24,5 (non- agricultural workers) 20,2 (including agricultural workers)

**Note:* 7400 + 144 GdP since 1978.

Sources on comparisons of figures:

Liste des organisations membres de la CES (31 December 1975); *Gewerkschaftliche Monatschefte 1975*, No. 8, p. 497 figures of the Congress of European Trade Unions; information from the European Federation of Trade Unions, Brussels (May 1979); M. Stewart: *Trade Unions in Europe,* Epping/Essex, 1974, p.4; W. Kendall: *The Labour Movement in Europe*. London, Allen Lane, 1975, pp. 335ff; C. Crouch and A. Pizzorno (eds.): *The Resurgence of Class Conflict in Western Europe since 1968*. London, Macmillan, 1978, Vol. 1, pp. 316ff; *Der Spiegel*, 1976, No. 29, p. 83.

For special countries:

A: P. U. Lehner: 'Die Österreichische Gewerkschaftsbewegung', *GMH*, 1974, No. 8, p. 489.

B: *Flash sur la Fgtb*, Brussels, 1977, p. 1.

CH: *SGB Tätigkeitsbericht 1975-1976-1977*. Berne, n.d., p. 184.

D: *Statistisches Jahrbuch der BRD. 1977, 1978*, p. 533.

DK:LO: *The Danish Trade Union Movement*. Copenhagen, 1978, pp. 1, 15.

E: J. Prieto: 'Una neuva realidad politica y sindical', *Diario*, 3 June 1978.

F: J.-D. Reynaud: *Les syndicats en France*. Paris, 1975, Vol. 1, p. 142; 'La CGT'. Supplement au journal *Le Peuple*, No. 1021, 15/31 January 1978, p. 22.

GB: *TUC Report 1977*, p. 622.

I: L. Lama: *Relazione e conclusioni al IX Congresso CGIL*. Rome, 1977, p. 55 mentions 4,317,000 members for the CGIL. The competitor of CGIL, CISL mentions for 1975: 4,081,000. Centro Studi nazionale della CISL: *Strumenti di cultura sindacale* Bologna, Il Mulino, 1977, p. 43. A recent comparison for 1975 indicates 3,417,000 members of CGIL whereas the figures for CISL are only slightly less than those offered by the organization. For 1977, 3,620,000 CGIL members have been listed: R. Chiaberge: 'Ma sono rappresentativi?' *Il Mondo*, 18 October 1978 (8-13), p. 9.

IL: *Labor and Society in Israel*. Tel Aviv, 1973, p. 250.

N:LO: *Norwegischer Gewerkschaftsbund*. Oslo, 1978, p. 34.

NL: *Trade Unions Affiliated to the FNV-Partners*. Amsterdam, 1978.

NZ: M. Howells, et al (eds.): *Labour and Industrial Relations in New Zealand*. Carlton, 1974, pp. 17, 318.

S: L. Forseback: *Sozialpartner und Arbeitsmarkt in Schweden*. Stockholm, 1977, p. 23; LO: *Statistik, 1977*. Stockholm, 1978, p. 37.

SF: *Statistisk arsbok for Finland*. Helsinki, 1977, p. 272.

US: *The AFL-CIO Platform Proposals. Presented to the Democratic and Republican National Conventions 1976*. Washington DC, p. 56, Col. 1. *Labour Relations Yearbook*. Washington DC, 1978, p. 248. Information from the AFL-CIO to the author in February 1979. The organization stresses the point that these figures are hardly to be compared with other countries, since they exclude all members on lay-off and sick leave or who are temporarily unemployed for whatever reason.

largely think in terms of social dichotomy and the class conflicts are fought out more bitterly than in many other European countries, studies have repeatedly shown that the workers tend to regard their union as an instrument for the achievement of largely practical ends. Despite the strong inter-relation between the unions and the party (cf. Chapter 4, 2) they differentiate clearly between the two functions.[199] So the relatively high degree of union density is largely a relic of past class consciousness, it is not always a product of political activism on the part of the majority of the workers today.

(2) *The structure of occupations.* Concentration and autonomy in industry are changing the structures of employment and occupations and the education and training system is being adjusted accordingly. The 'scientific and technical revolution' is also having its effect on the willingness of the workers to join a union. It is generally assumed that qualifications are rising and to the dismay of left-wing critics of this theory, which assumes that the further development in science and technology will to a certain extent be automatic (we find this in bourgeois economics as well as in the theory of state monopoly capitalism) the general rise in the level of qualifications tends to make the workers less militant but more ready to join a union.[200] Although even the big Communist-oriented unions like the CGT and the CGIL know that growing membership figures do not prove that the individual member is becoming more class con-

scious, all the unions are very sensitive on the point of the trend in membership figures and support all those socio-political and educational measures by the state which might indirectly have a positive effect on the growth of their organizations.

But in times of full employment some economies would appear to have reached the limits of syndicalist growth. This is also due to the integration of more and more marginal groups into employment. The more women (in 1977 the head organizations in Germany and Sweden were composed of about 20% and 26% women respectively), part-time workers, young people (who account for about 10% of the DGB's members), pensioners and foreign workers are employed, the greater is the deceleration in the growth of the unions. In some countries the foreign workers are the main obstacle to further growth. Those countries which until 1973/74 employed the greatest number of foreign workers (Sweden, the Federal Republic, France) are among those with the lowest degree of union organization. There are, of course, exceptions to this, such as Belgium and Austria, due to the intervention of the variable 'corporatist relics' in the political culture.

TABLE 7
Percentage of foreign workers before the economic crisis of 1973-1974

Switzerland	25.7
Federal Republic	10.8
France	9.7
Austria	8.1
Belgium	7.6
Sweden	5.7
Great Britain	5.1
Netherlands	5.0

Source: Die Zeit, 25 May 1973, No. 22.

In recent years it no longer seems true that foreign labour is not joining the unions. In Britain the unions even managed to recruit a sizeable number of black workers. Nearly 60% of the 600,000 black labour force now belong to a union.[201]

(3) *The economic situation*. The functional change in organizations with economic interests has been much more strongly influenced by the overall economic development than the fluctuation in membership. The employers' associations emerged, historically, generally in times of cyclical upswing to deal with claims from the workers. The German Central Employers Association (Zentralverband der Arbeitgeberverbände) was not formed until 1904, when it was created in response to the nation-wide solidarity of workers for the textile strike in Crimmitschau in Saxony. This press notice is characteristic of its defensive attitude:

> The attempt by the Social Democrats to overrun the Saxon employers has caused large sections of German industry to unite in defence under the leadership of the Central Association of German Industrialists. Appeals have been reaching the Association in recent weeks from many different quarters for an association of German employers which would be a lasting institution and be in a position successfully to withstand the unjustified demands of masses of workers who have been incited by agitators... .[202]

In times of recession, on the other hand, the tendency was rather to create business associations, because the recession encouraged state intervention through customs and fiscal policy and business associations appeared to offer the best means of lobbying.[203]

On a comparison in time, however, none of the generalizations on the effect of a cyclical downswing will now hold. During the world recession between the two World Wars union membership dropped in many countries, and in Great Britain between 1930 and 1934, and in Denmark from 1925 to 1932, the decline was clearly in line with the rising unemployment rate. But recent fluctuations in TUC membership have little to do with cyclical movements. The decline in membership in 1971-72 was partly self-amputation, when the TUC excluded unions which registered under the Industrial Relations Act.[204] The low unemployment benefits may have been an earlier cause of decline, as the unemployed economized on their membership fees. This did not happen to the same extent during the recessions in 1966/67 and 1973/74. It was rather at the end of the prosperous phase, in the late sixties, that the danger of declining membership reared its head. But in most countries there has been a rising trend in union membership despite the economic recessions.

In the Federal Republic membership figures are rising in most industries which are not themselves in decline.

(4) *The continuity, degree of centralization and ideological unity of unions* has an effect on the continuity in growth in membership, as we see in Sweden. In the early years here there were only two breaks in the upward trend: in 1909 and 1920, in each case at the end of a period of conflict.[205] As in the party system the fluctuations in membership seem to be least where political buffers are, so to speak, in-built because the union movement is large and moderate, keeping the influence of political conflict on membership to a minimum. As we see in France and Italy, the fluctuation in membership is greatest where the unions are highly political and their membership is low. In countries where Christian unions still play an important role, their membership decreased in most cases when the politicizing and secularizing protest movement changed the climate in Europe after 1968 (NKV, NCV in Holland, but not in some other countries (CSC in Belgium, which actually became the strongest union in the country, and the CISL in Italy).

When Communist countries or groups have taken political action which could be construed as aggressive, Communist-oriented unions have suffered losses in membership. This was the case in France, for instance, in 1936, on the occasion of the 'Popular Front Scare', in 1956 after the Hungarian uprising and in 1968 after the Soviet occupation of Czechoslovakia. Exact figures are difficult to obtain, especially in France. However, a survey of its militants by the CGT showed that even 26.8% of the most active had left the union at least once, although only a small percentage of them stated that this was because they disagreed with the CGT's policy.[206]

The fluctuations were also very great in Italy. The CGIL had nearly 5 million members in 1949. In 1956-57 this dropped to 3.1 million and after a few ups and downs reached its lowest point in 1966/68 at 2.4 million. The unrest in 1968-69 brought a great increase over the medium term, despite the fact that the protest was occasionally against the unions, and in 1974 the organization had 3.8 million members.[207]

Unions which place great emphasis on ideology have proved to be strongly dependent on the policy of the party with which they work and the Communist unions generally have occasionally been held responsible for unpopular policies of the Soviet Union. The head of the SFIO, Guy Mollet, once put it bluntly: 'They are not left or right — they are in the East'.[208]

But membership losses as a result of Soviet actions never lasted for long, the Communist parties and the unions oriented to them usually recovered quickly. In the Latin countries membership of a Communist union was always an act of intellectual protest as well which needed an organizational vent, although membership of the union did not mean full identification with the party and all its dependent organizations. Data on key years in the Scandinavian labour movement show that the fluctuations in membership are extreme when the claim to political leadership by a certain group — usually the Communists — increases polarization in the union movement and the over-politicization of the organization drives the non-political members out. However, Finland should not be interpreted too strictly. Attacks on Communists, as have been usual there since 1930, can cause a drop in membership as much as the excess of Communist zeal after the re-admission of the party did.

TABLE 8
Membership fluctuation in Scandinavia

	Membership of the union federations (in thousands)			
Year	**Finland**	**Denmark**	**Norway**	**Sweden**
1908	24	97	47	162
1918	157	255	108	222
1928	90	156	107	469
1938	70	470	340	898
1948	306	623	456	1239
1956	289	705	545	1404

Source: Carl Erik Knoellinger: *Labor in Finland*. Cambridge, Mass., Harvard UP, 1960, p. 4.

Fluctuations for political reasons are by no means always induced by party political manoeuvres. Too much pressure on the organization (as in several general strikes, England in 1926, Sweden in 1909 and France in 1956) can have serious repercussions. In

Great Britain, where the union movement never had a Socialist majority in its members there was a considerable break in membership growth in 1921 when political optimism as to fundamental structural change had evaporated, and again in the demoralized atmosphere after the failure of the general strike in 1926. However, political engagement in itself does not necessarily endanger membership. Conservative publicity has sought to draw a relation between political campaigns by the DGB, such as the campaign against atomic warfare or the slogan 'Elect a better Parliament' and a crisis of confidence between the unions and the workers but has not produced any concrete evidence for this beyond isolated and manipulated figures.[209]

(5) *State wage policy*. The argument has occasionally been put forward that increasing intervention by the state in wage policy lessens the attraction of union ties to the workers as all the benefits accrue to non-members as well. But a comparison of the membership figures of individual unions reveals no connection between the two factors. Countries in which state intervention in wage policy is most intensive, such as Austria and the Netherlands, are characterized by great willingness on the part of workers to join unions. There are other forms of state intervention which have a greater effect on union membership: compulsory arbitration, for instance, increased the number of unions and their membership in Australia.

(6) *The legal system of industrial relations*, particularly among white collar workers, best explains the variations in union density. The extent and depth of collective bargaining and the support for union security from the employer, through collective agreements[210] or by the state in some continental countries determines the readiness to organize. But Clegg's hypothesis does not apply to the continental labour movements in the early days of industrialization. Then, on the contrary, it was rather the existence of large working-class groups without rights and little bargaining power which determined union density.

(7) *Close organizational links between the party and the unions* have a clearly beneficial effect on union membership, as can be seen from Scandinavia, Great Britain and some Commonwealth countries (cf. Chapter 4, 2).

Fluctuations in membership are rarely due to only one cause and one should be cautious in interpreting them. A decline is not even always bound up with a crisis of confidence in the unions. Surveys have shown that fluctuations do not always depend on the degree of identification with the unions' general policy. More recent surveys which reveal an increasingly positive relation on average in the general population to union policy do not, however, confirm this trend with marked increases in membership figures.

The degree of union organization should not be identified with:

(1) the standing of the unions and the popularity of their aims with members;

(2) their standing with those to whom their influence is directed.

(1) The standing of unions and the popularity of their claims fluctuate much more than their membership figures. This has been particularly apparent with the DGB and the Swedish LO. The unions themselves admit that 'mass organizations' like the unions are generally only popular within their own contact area. But even here they often meet with reservation and scepticism, partly due to their 'bureaucracy and anonymity'. According to surveys which were evaluated in the periodical *Gewerkschaftsbarometer* the support graph for the German unions showed a steady increase of about 3% among members and 1.3% among non-members between 1963 and 1970. But the increase stopped in 1966 and 1974. The unions lost standing together with the Government, independent of the coalition between the parties. The growth in sympathy among non-members dropped from 1.6% to 1.2%. So we see a certain polarization in the attitude in times of crisis. Among more reserved groups such as the self-employed, professionals, those working in family businesses and pensioners sympathy for the unions dropped drastically but it rose slightly among groups of workers who are close to union activity. Strikes especially during such periods become less popular: the readiness to strike dropped from 57% to 51%; even 16% of union members proved to be opponents of strikes.[211]

(2) The degree of representation of a union can generally be deduced from the membership figures in the case of a general union. The problem is, of course, that even a moderate degree of organization as in the Federal Republic only permits conclusions for about a third of the workforce. So it is important to know whether the majority of the population regards the unions as fulfilling a useful role although they are not formal members. According to a survey by the Institute for Applied Sociology (INFAS) in Bonn

only 11% of the total population and 7% of those employed regarded the unions as dispensable.[212] So the membership figures alone do not fully reflect the degree of representation. As we have seen, this depends on many other volatile factors in the economic situation and the political culture of the country concerned.

There is a particular aspect to the representation question in countries with a fragmented union movement. Where there is a general union the degree of representation presents no problems to the negotiating partner, either the state or the employers. In systems where unions are competing on an ideology base more difficulties arise, especially if the principle of industrial unionism is hardly practised. Belgium is in the middle here, with an ideologically fragmented union movement but with the industrial monism principle largely realized. In 1968 the state attempted to define the degree of representation by the head associations according to various criteria: (1) they must cover a range of occupations; (2) they must be organized on a national level; (3) they must be members of the Central Economic Council; and (4) have at least 50,000 members. The last two criteria of course cannot be applied to other countries. The minimum membership figure is related to the size of the population and other countries do not necessarily have a Central Economic Council or similar institution (cf. Chapter 4, 5).

7. NEGATIVE SANCTIONS AGAINST NON-MEMBERS

As the power of the unions grew and the importance of their functions became increasingly recognized, dissatisfaction also grew over the fact that membership was stagnating or even dropping at times while growing numbers of non-members were benefiting from the advantages won by the unions. Efforts were therefore made in many countries to introduce some form of discrimination against these 'free riders'. Four forms have emerged:

(a) Compulsory membership
(b) The 'Closed Shop' and the 'Union Shop'
(c) Solidarity contributions
(d) Special benefits for members

(a) Compulsory Membership

This has so far proved possible only in a dictatorship where it can be enforced through a corporative system (Italy under the Fascists and Spain under Franco). It is not regarded as an acceptable measure in the Western democracies. In some of the German Länder, Hesse and Bremen, for example, reaction to the obligatory membership enforced by the Nazis was so strong that the right not to join an organization is guaranteed in the constitution. Conservative proposals on the introduction of compulsory membership in the Federal Republic were usually made in the hopes of reducing the powers of the unions.[213] But membership is (de jure though not de facto) not compulsory even in Socialist countries where the unions' functions are strongly dependent and membership is almost total at between 97 and 99%.[214]

(b) The 'Closed Shop' and the 'Union Shop'

The closed shop is a milder form of compulsory membership. It has developed mainly in the English-speaking countries. Ideologically it derives from left-wing corporative ideas of guild Socialism which led G. D. H. Cole to call for a closed shop as early as 1913.[215] Its critics have occasionally suggested that the term 'compulsory trade unionism' should be used instead of 'closed shop',[216] which in the eyes of its defendants is more discriminating. Attempts are sometimes made to deny that the closed shop has an element of compulsion with the argument 'Anyone who doesn't want to join can go and work somewhere else'.[217] But there is a certain cynicism here: the argument presupposes acceptance of some of the rules of the employers' side which the unions are usually fighting against, and factually it is, at most, correct in law. De facto it is hardly possible to change jobs in order to avoid a closed shop if the general economic situation is not favourable or if the closed shop is in the majority in that industry and certain unions are exercising a monopoly.

It would seem more honourable to argue that the element of compulsion is a justified part of the fight by the unions. At the end of the nineteenth century Beatrice and Sydney Webb maintained that the unions would have to exercise compulsion against the employers if they were to achieve working and pay conditions that were acceptable, and that this compulsion against third parties would unfortunately also entail a certain amount of pressure on their own ranks.[218] So the closed shop is still generally regarded as justified, for every strike is compulsion, often against neutral third parties. At best the proposal is to enact legislation to prevent misuse. The form of closed shop which demands union membership as a prerequisite to getting a job (pre-entry) is usually viewed more negatively from the legal point of view than the 'post-entry' type (usually known as the 'union shop') because it can cause unwarranted channelling of access to certain occupations.[219]

Most of the criticism of the closed shop comes from medium-sized companies who see in it an attack on the rights of the individual. However, it can be argued that some professional organizations are also de facto closed shops. Medical associations can make life difficult for young doctors who are not willing to submit to their organizational discipline. In some countries, Australia is one, there has been a trend in the seventies to extend compulsory unionism in the white collar sectors. Labour governments in some countries have even exercised a mild form of pressure on public sector employees to join unions.[220] However, it is hardly justifiable to criticize the closed shop as a 'Socialist' institution. It has only developed in countries where the ideological background is largely non-Socialist and the unions use hard business methods to counter discrimination by the employers.

The closed shop has played a particularly large role in America, where the workers are not class conscious and where until the New Deal the unions were under-privileged in law with chronically low membership. Especially during the Depression the employers attempted to weaken the closed shop movement by requiring new members of staff to sign 'Yellow Dog Contracts' promising not to join a union. It was not until the Norris-la Guardia Act of 1932 that these contracts were combatted by the state and made non-actionable. The Taft-Hartley Act of 1947 forbad closed shops but facilitated the emergence of union shops as these were not prohibited by state legislation (Section 8, a, 3). The American states in which anti-union majorities succeeded in achieving what is known as 'The Right to Work' legislation did not on average really hurt the unions. There are instances from states where this legislation coincided with a low membership, but we have just as many cases of the opposite. A low degree of development of the area seems to be a greater determinant of the degree of unionization than repressive legislation.[221]

It has occasionally been argued in the USA that the closed shop was a necessary protection for the US unions against the undercutting of minimal wages by the 'reserve army' of immigrant labour, while the class conscious European unions did not need this. But if this were so we should find the weakest unions making the greatest use of the closed shop. The opposite is true, it is the strongest organizations which have practised it and they have used their power ruthlessly to extend it. Even in a country like Great Britain, where union membership is traditionally much higher than in the USA, the closed shop has been defended with the argument that the benefits accruing to the 'free riders' must be curtailed and the individual workers should be compensated for the compulsion of the closed shop by the greater negotiation power. In countries where many unions have been competing with each other the closed shop has often been as attractive to the employers as the unions as it made negotiations simpler and more representative. The unions have also often tried to make the closed shop more attractive to employers with the argument that it improves industrial relations. But this cannot be substantiated empirically. In Great Britain the industries in which the closed shop is most prevalent (the motor industry, ship-building, dock work and coal mining) are also those with the greatest number of strikes. There are several arguments against the closed shop:

(1) It is an unnecessary restriction on the freedom of the individual.

(2) It threatens to monopolize skilled labour for certain unions. So it does not serve the egalitarian aims which most unions have in their basic programmes but rather tends to secure a 'working aristocracy'. It also conserves obsolete forms of organization by favouring status organizations. These are still hindering the full realization of the industry principle in union organization.

(3) The closed shop can help to increase union membership, as we see in New Zealand, where a Labour Government used compulsory unionism between 1936 and 1961 as a means of countering declining membership. The number of unions also rose (from 410 registered in 1936 to 499 in 1937) but internally for the unions the measure merely caused apathy and an even lower participation rate

than is to be found in countries without closed shops.[222] The Donovan Report also argued that closed shops should not be made illegal in Great Britain because although they had undesirable side-effects they brought some advantages to industrial relations.[223] The Report also doubted whether a prohibition, as was discussed at the end of the sixties mainly by the Conservatives, would be possible to enforce, firstly because only a minority of the workers would be affected (about one-fifth of the British workforce in the mid-sixties) and secondly because in many cases the employers too were interested in maintaining the closed shop. Nevertheless, the Industrial Relations Act more or less made them illegal.[224] In 1974 the closed shop again became possible when the Wilson Government repealed the Act. Some acknowledgement was made of the argument of constitutional right as workers who on religious grounds could not join a union were exempted. But the TUC strongly opposed even this concession. Since 1974 employers, particularly in the public sector, have written post-entry closed shop clauses into their collective agreements with unions. In the past some unions have been tolerant of individuals who for some personal reason did not wish to join a union. Recent studies see signs that such a liberal attitude is disappearing in Britain.[225]

In its fight against Wilson's legislation the opposition drew attention to the negative effects of the closed shop in certain areas — the press, for example, arguing that here it could actually jeopardize freedom of speech. The minister concerned, Michael Foot, promised to include in the draft legislation a clause to the effect that the problem should be settled by appropriate agreement between the employers and the journalists' union. The agreement was not, however, to be legally binding as the Labour Government was still opposed to any increase in legislation which would bring more industrial disputes into court. The legislation was passed in the House of Commons in its third reading at the beginning of January 1976, by 285 votes to 249.

The closed shop has never been a serious problem on the continent. In countries where there is considerable legislation on industrial relations, like West Germany, the constitutional right to form organizations has as its counterpart the right not to join an organization and, as already mentioned, this has been written into the constitution of some Länder as a result of the compulsion exercised by the Nazis. Verdicts in German labour courts give a large degree of protection to the right not to join organizations. Union propaganda which goes beyond 'well-meaning persuasion' and can be regarded as 'pressurizing workmates' has been declared by a court to be 'socially inacceptable pressure' and an offence against the freedom not to join an organization (Federal Labour Court —BAG — 19, 217, 227).[226] In Sweden there have been efforts to move from the solidarity contribution as the weaker form of sanction against 'free riders' to the closed shop. But here too the closed shop was forbidden at high court level.

In countries where industrial relations do not have such a strong legislative base the closed shop has also played very little part, either because union density was too low for it to be practised or because the ideologically fragmented union movement was not interested (France). In some cases the traditional Socialist elements in the unions rightly regarded it as undemocratic, and partly because of their high membership figures did not need it to strengthen their negotiating powers (Sweden). Again in Sweden the closed shop has only appeared in times of high unemployment (after the First World War) or in a few sectors (the cooperative sector, for example).[227]

(c) The Solidarity Contribution

This has largely been the aim where the 'subsidiary principle' has played a part, as in Switzerland (1956 legislation). It is no coincidence that in Germany the Construction Workers Union, which is influenced by Catholic social theory, attempted at the beginning of the sixties to achieve contractual benefits for its members at least on the basis of wage contracts. In Switzerland wage agreements providing for a solidarity contribution were concluded after the closed shop as the stronger form of sanction against non-members had been made illegal. However, the courts would not allow the full amount of the membership fee but only about half, on the grounds that non-members did not enjoy all the advantages of members.

Left-wing unionists have always regarded the idea of receiving financial support from the apathetic mass as an offence against their avant-garde position and rejected it. But ideology is not the only motivating factor, organizational factors have also played a part. Solidarity contributions seemed most appropriate where big industry unions were aiming for exclusive representation. In the USA and Canada the solidarity contribution, when non-members have to pay fees or make some equivalent contribution to the unions' expenses, is known as the 'agency shop'.

The claim to sole representation need not necessarily come from a general union. On the contrary, it seems to be a feature of a climate of rivalry and competition. It has played a large part between competing unions in the USA but hardly at all in the Latin countries where unions are competing on an ideology base and membership is relatively low. Finally, the strike patterns of the unions, which in turn depend on the form of organization, also play a part. Where wage increases are largely achieved through negotiations by the unions without the necessity for a strike, as in the Federal Republic, solidarity contributions are regarded favourably. But where the strike initiative often does not lie with the big organizations, or where, if the strikes are centrally organized the unions can pay little or no strike money, solidarity is dependent on the powers of conviction and agitatory potential of local groups and attempts are not made to enforce it through a bureaucratic financing policy (France, Italy).

Finally, it is hardly possible to obtain solidarity contributions where union membership is low. The Letzeburger Arbechter-Verband (LAV) decided at its 1970 Congress to follow Swiss and Dutch experiments with a solidarity contribution: 'But only in those industries or plants where the great majority of the workers has joined the negotiating organization'.[228]

In the Federal Republic the Construction Workers Union has been in the lead with demands for a solidarity contribution since 1960. During wage negotiations in January 1961 it suggested a contractual agreement whereby non-members should pay an appropriate fee. It was argued that there was justification both in the attitude of the employers and the unions for this: *the workers* had established in surveys of non-members that 70% of them regarded the policy and agreements obtained by the union as in their interests. It was feared that there would be progressively less incentive to join the union if all the benefits obtained through negotiation automatically accrued to non-members as well. *The employers*, according to the Construction Workers Union, had become accustomed to paying the same wages to non-members as members although the agreement only covered members. The fact that this came from the Construction Workers Union, which was integrationist in its policy, made even relatively conservative observers regard it as justified. They hoped that by supporting the claim they would achieve on the one hand a more moderate union policy with regard to membership and on the other less militancy towards the negotiating partners.[229] Such different constitutional lawyers as Herbert Krüger and Helmut Ridder also regarded the claim as constitutionally correct.[230] But despite the union's structural policy aims the employers finally took a stand against the solidarity contribution, although they could have taken an intermediary position as collectors of the fees. The Federation of German Employers Associations (BDA) mobilized reports from leading lawyers such as Alfred Hueck and Ulrich Scheuner arguing that the solidarity contribution was not legally correct.[231]

The fear of moving too close to the corporative and traditional organizational ideologies of other bodies will presumably in future, too, discourage militant unions from reaching for the ammunition of negative sanctions, which would in any case be irreconcilable with their more positive ideas on the creation of a progressive worker mentality. And reassurances to the contrary from those who support the idea of solidarity contributions have not succeeded in allaying the fears of the progressive unionists that the collection of the fees by the employers in the plants could make the unions more dependent on the capitalist side.

(d) Special Benefits for Union Members

The creation of special institutions is actually only another way out of the dilemma when the solidarity contribution cannot be introduced. In the German construction industry a health and rest scheme has been set up, as has a holiday fund, a supplementary benefits scheme, an earnings equalization fund and other similar benefits for union members only. These are to provide the union with at least some leverage against those who do not want to join. Special holiday bonuses, credit guarantees for loyal members (after five years in the union as a rule), insurance against accidents outside work and for legal aid for the family are further services. Some of them are organized only by the union and some are envisaged in collective agreements obtained with the employers. The latter seem rather suspect from the point of view of a 'class conscious' labour movement as they threaten to further the 'trade' aspect of the union movement.[232]

Many legal objectives raised mainly by conservatives to certain forms of differentiation clauses have largely been dispelled, especially where strict parity in the administration of the arrangements seemed guaranteed.[233] Although the development of differentiation clauses is not over some unions are entertaining growing doubts about them. A study carried out by the union Institute for Social and Economic Research (WSI) for the Public Sector and Transport Union ÖTV) sees them as an offence against the unions' image of themselves as entitled to 'represent all the workers' and fears negotiating consequences for the militancy of the unions if apathetic masses are indirectly forced to join.[234]

One variant of this form of negative sanction is the special contribution (usually an annual bonus) which the unions in Belgium have achieved in many collective agreements.[235] But the idea was flatly rejected in Luxembourg, despite its close economic ties with Belgium: 'Such an arrangement may be profitable in terms of union policy. But it still has a taint of favouritsm or compensation for services rendered, if it is not actually a way of repaying union membership fees'.[236]

8. THE UNIONS' FINANCES

Unions are membership organizations and their finances usually come exclusively from their members. There are no charitable contributions and no regular funds channelled from industry. The only exceptions are *corrupt* unions, of which there are some in the USA and the Third World. Organized crime in the USA did not stop at the unions. Business unions, those which least represented the industry principle and unions with a very autocratic leadership have proved most vulnerable to corrupt practices.

On the expenditure side the original function of the unions was to provide funds for strikes and with this in mind they have been anxious not to let the employers provoke them into spending their money at the wrong moment. But the original function is declining in importance in most countries and the unions are looking for profitable long-term investments for their money. The rich Northern

European unions are not very different from big companies in this. They hardly match this picture of union financial administration:

> It scarcely differed from that of the small pensioner who had made enough as a master craftsman to be able to retire; originally he came from the same group as they. Government bonds and mortgage bonds as a fixed investment, an account with a big bank to have ready money for a strike: that was all. Stocks and shares were not acquired on principle. If occasionally a union did buy a few shares this was to give a member the chance to say a few unpleasant things to an aggressive director at the general meeting: it was an outcome of the union's militancy but not part of its financing policy.[237]

The finance policy of the rich northern unions is now hardly dependent on their militancy, and with the DGB the account with a big bank has become the fourth largest bank in the country (the Bank für Gemeinwirtschaft, the trade union bank). The DGB also has holdings in twenty-one companies, ranging from a life insurance company through a housing association to a book club.

In its own words the Swedish LO 'plays a large part as entrepreneur'. It owns the construction company BPA which employs 15,000, one of the largest printing works in Sweden (Tiden-Barnängen), shares in the travel agency RESO, the insurance company FOLKSAM and the second largest Swedish daily newspaper (*Aftonbladet*).[238] According to its financial statements the LO's capital grows each year:[239] from 217 million kroner in 1972 to 340 million kroner in 1977.

The individual unions in Sweden had on average 978 kroner per member in 1977. The sailors, electricians and construction workers were in the lead with 1,800-1,600 kroner per member. The LO statistics showed almost 2 thousand million kroner as per 31 December 1977. The growth in 1976-77 was 9.5% (cf. Table 10).[240]

The TUC in Great Britain shows income from dividends and bank accounts which amount to only a fraction of membership fees.[241] Here the old tradition of solid but unimaginative investment policy is still dominant. Few unions derive income from the stock market. It is more difficult to estimate the wealth of British trade unions than Swedish. Many are reticent in giving the TUC details of the value of the assets they hold. In 1974 only twenty-four unions supplied information, indicating an amount of c. £20 million. Only holdings of land and buildings have grown appreciably in Great Britain since the Second World War. Even in the

USA, where the majority of the unions have not developed fundamentally anti-capitalist feelings, there is little long-term investment and the preference is for security and easily realizable assets.[242]

The richest head associations are those in Northern Europe (DGB, TUC, LO). They are also the only ones to publish figures occasionally on their assets (cf. Tables 9 to 11). The most detailed figures come from the Swedish LO (Table 10) and the least detailed from the German DGB unions. A financial specialist on trade unions published detailed figures in 1972. The DGB officially admits to the principle of 'open finances', with the proviso that it does not wish to participate in the 'polemics over billions' nor lay its cards on its fighting strength open to its adversaries. The most recent statement on the financial position of the German trade unions indicated that on average they have DM 270 per member[243] — which would be less than that of the Swedish unions.

TABLE 9
The wealth of the DGB unions
(31 December 1970 in 1000 DM)

IG Bau	134,800
IG Bergbau	152,000
Chemie	90,988
Druck*	35,496
GdED	27,201
GEW	11,500
GGLF	1,458
HBV	1,500
Holz	31,000
Kunst	1,000
Leder	17,000
Metall	570,746
NGG	39,600
ÖTV	105,000
DPG	35,000
Textil*	27,000
16 Gewerkschaften	1,281,289
DGB	153,185

Source: K. Hirche: *Die Finanzen der Gewerkschaften*, Düsseldorf, 1972, p. 376.

TABLE 10
The wealth of the LO
(31 December 1977 in Swedish Crowns)

Beklädnadsarbetare	77,229,584
Bleck-o Plåtslagare	6,849,087
Byggnadsarbetare	296,810,268
Elektriker	47,450,629
Fabriksarbetare	98,440,669
Fastighetsanställda	8,982,413
Frisörarbetare	1,842,783
Försäkringsanställda	10,962,458
Grafiska Fack	64,247,839
Gruvindustriarbetare	8,816,587
Handelsanställda	104,134,908
Hotell-o Rest-anst-	14,123,892
Kommunalarbetare	172,762,366
Lantarbetare	7,918,903
Livsmedelsarbetare	42,456,160
Metallindustriarbetare	790,367,848
Musiker	4,373,348
Målare	45,851,303
Pappersindustriarbetare	68,465,583
Sjöfolk	26,612,289
Skogsarbetare	11,839,301
Skorstensfejare	2,564,299
Statsanställda	165,111,726
Trasnportarbetare	18,428,725
Träindustriarbetare	89,504,120
Total:	2,186,147,088

Source: LO Statistik 1977, Stockholm, 1978, p. 44.

TABLE 11
The wealth of TUC's top unions (1975)

	Income (£)	Expenditure (£)	Investments (£)	Assets (£)
Transport and General Workers Union	17,140,000	13,297,000	21,477,270	29,304,780
Amalgamated Union of Engineering Workers (Engineering section)	10,240,000	10,416,000	5,199,000	12,943,005
General and Municipal Workers	10,313,000	8,565,000	3,739,000	14,739,000
National and Local Government Officers Association	4,237,000	3,608,000	1,874,000	7,483,000
National Union of Public Employees	4,166,000	3,811,000	3,175,000	4,864,000
Association of Scientific, Technical and Managerial Staffs	3,010,000	2,984,000	75,000	1,867,000
Union of Construction, Allied Trades and Technicians	3,082,000	2,919,000	1,193,000	2,211,000
Union of Shop, Distributive and Allied Workers	2,861,000	2,634,000	2,153,000	3,330,000
National Union of Mineworkers	6,696,000	2,948,000	11,476,000	15,668,000
National Union of Railwaymen	638,000	2,486,000	11,391,000	12,337,000

Source: R. Taylor: *The Fifth Estate. Britain's Unions in the Seventies.* London, 1978, p. 32.

The financial strength of the unions is not an independent variable, it depends on a number of factors. The decisive ones are:

(1) The number of members and the unity of the organization. The richest unions are the big general organizations like the DGB or the LO in Sweden. Few are as conscientious and open in their financing as the LO, which publishes its receipts, liabilities and capital in its financial statements.[244] The financial situation of the DGB and its member unions is not quite so transparent, indeed the affiliated unions do not always fully reveal their financial situation to the DGB itself. In 1969 the DGB had to issue pamphlets in response to rumours that it and its member unions had assets totalling DM 1.5 billion (thousand million). The figure was not confirmed in so many words but it was not denied either and the brochures were devoted to clarifying what is done with the DGB's not inconsiderable wealth.[245]

The TUC, despite its size, is relatively poor compared with the other two Northern European head associations. It does not have capital assets of the order of the DGB or the Swedish LO. Great Britain is an exception to the thumb rule that financial power increases with the number of enrolled members. British unions are caught in a dilemma: the more members they recruit, the more difficult it is to raise the subscription rates. On the basis of the returns to the TUC for 1974 the average membership contribution amounted to about £7 per member, 'just over 13 pence a week which was less than the cost of half a pint of bitter in the pub'.[246] The set amounts (20p per member since 1978, Rule 3 of the TUC Rules) have failed to keep pace with the rate of inflation. The head federation has thus remained poorer than the DGB with its 12% clause or the Swiss who have an index clause in the statutes of their federation (SGB).

As Table 12 shows, the head associations' share of the revenue of the affiliated unions varies considerably. Financially weakest are the ideology unions in the Latin countries. The CGT usually has only a few thousand francs in hand. Where the local organizations are as dominant as they are in France, or where the individual unions are as autonomous as they are in Great Britain, the financial situation of the head association is not so good.

But exact figures are hard to obtain for the Latin countries especially. Those published by the Italian CGIL show that the

TABLE 12
The head associations' share of the revenue of their affiliated unions (percentages)

Federal Republic	12	
Finland	9	(plus 9% for SAK newspaper)
France	c. 2.5	
Great Britain	1-2	
Netherlands	10	(NVV, NKV) — 20% (CNV)
Norway	c. 15	
Sweden	c. 15	

Source: B. C. Roberts: *Trade Union Government and Administration in Great Britain*. London, Bell, 1956, pp. 381, 450. J. P. Windmuller: *Labor Relations in the Netherlands*. Ithaca, Cornell, 1969, p. 180. T. L. Johnston: *Collective Bargaining in Sweden*. London, Allen & Unwin, 1962, pp. 31, 46. Walter Galenson: *Labor in Norway*. Cambridge, Mass., Harvard UP, 1949, p. 41. Knoellinger, loc. cit. (Table 9), p. 144.

percentage of the average wage given in membership fees is usually lower than 1% (see Table 12). In France the CGT only ventured to estimate in 1975 that it received about 1% of its members' pay. If that is correct then the CFDT in France is even lower down the scale than the CGT, as it received 0.7%.[247]

General unions may also be poor in assets, like the Austrian federation (ÖGB), which maintains that in 1974 members' fees made up 96% of its income; but because the degree of organization is higher (about 60%) than is usual in the Latin countries it could boast the proud sum of S. 882.7 million available funds for that year,[248] although membership fees were on average only 1-1.5% of the workers' gross earnings.

TABLE 13
Fluctuations in union fees in percentages of wages in Italy

Year	Union fees as percentage of wages
1945	0.26
1946	0.44
1947	0.29
1948	0.36
1949	0.34
1950	0.36
1951	0.33
1952	0.43
1953	0.42
1954-5	0.53
1956-7	0.70
1958	0.66
1959	0.64
1960	0.61
1961	0.57
1962	0.83
1963	0.70
1964	0.63
1965	0.58
1966	1.16
1967	1.09
1968	1.05
1969	1.00
1970	0.83
1971	0.73
1972	0.67
1973	0.69
1974	0.81

Source: 'Il finanziamento del sindacato', *Rassegna sindacale*, 1975, No. 50, p. 117.

Like the Dutch head association[249] the DGB decided as early as 1955 that union members should contribute about 2% of their monthly income. But it has never been possible to obtain this amount. A particular feature of Scandinavian financing is the special levy for a union press fund. In Sweden for many years about a third and in Finland about half the contributions which had to be handed over to the head association were used for this purpose.

In Sweden the membership dues are not as high as the considerable amount of capital owned by the unions might suggest: they vary from 0.9% to 1.8% of the gross income of the workers.[250]

(2) The relative degree of organization, on the other hand, does not play a decisive role. Unions are always cautious in raising membership fees, especially when they have to take a stand against constant price increases on the capitalist side. Often they do not even act on their own resolutions to raise fees. We can also see that some of the unions with the highest fees also have the greatest number of members (the printers, for instance). So a high fee is not in itself a disincentive, provided that the union is relatively representative of its industry. Where different unions are competing on an occupational base for the same groups of members, as in the English-speaking countries and Finland, some of them try to keep their fees low in the hope of attracting more members. In Australia, for example, doubts have been expressed that it will be possible to realize the resolution of January 1978 to make membership fees 1% of earnings in all the unions affiliated to the ACTU.[251] In Great Britain, too, the low fees of the big mass unions in comparison with highly specialized professional unions have proved a vehicle for centralization.[252] In many countries unions with a low membership have tended to be cautious about their fees. Highly specialized unions like the printers have been an exception to this, in Germany as well. They have often regarded themselves as avant-garde and could afford to keep raising their fees, because their members were relatively active, had rather higher incomes than workers in other industries and the expansion of the services offered by the union made membership attractive to most of the workers in the industry despite the higher fees.

In a historical perspective the tendency is for membership fees to drop in all industries. In the German printers union fees were 3.6%

of the basic rate for skilled workers at the beginning of the fifties. At the beginning of the sixties they dropped to 2.7% and in 1969 to 2%. That rate brings the IG Druck und Papier into line with the DGB guideline of 1955,[253] but it is the only union to be so. In view of this there is little point in recalling the old times, when the working class was ready to make sacrifices, the question is whether the standard hourly wage rate has not become obsolete as a standard for measuring membership fees. There are two reasons for this:

(a) The shortening of working hours since the aboliton of the 60-hour week accounts for the decline in membership fees. Naturally this has caused a divergent development between wages and membership fees.

(b) The differentiation in incomes for the workers is increasingly reflected in a differentiation of union fees. It is usually the higher income groups which come off best. The guidelines issued by the DGB Federal Committee in 1955 on uniformity in membership fees recognized twenty-one classes, finishing with a monthly contribution of DM 15 for incomes over DM 750. At the beginning of the seventies most of the classes ended between DM 950 and DM 1,300. Only five unions (the Chemical, Metal, Leather, Textile and Food-Processing Workers unions) envisage normal fees for incomes about DM 2,000. So wages have developed beyond the limit which once seemed reasonable for the assessment of fees.[254] In countries with greater regional discrepancies in incomes, such as Italy, there are other disparities. Membership fees vary between about 1% (Emilia) and 0.15% (Palermo).[255] Such a wide range is now no longer justified in many cases, according to the CGIL.

(3) *Payment morale* is determined not only by internal attitudes, and in the Latin countries this, like the morale in paying taxes, is not among the highest in Europe. Two American union researchers once said scathingly: 'In France and Italy, where the anarchistic tradition is still strong, the top federations can get people to walk off the job, although they might not be successful in getting them to pay dues'.[256]

Another factor influencing payment morale is the quality of the machine and the efficiency of the collection system. Many US unions have let the plant management collect the fees. In Europe this was not even regarded as acceptable for the solidarity contribution (cf. Chapter 1, 7, c). Where the unions are very militant towards the management this would, of course, have catastrophic effects on their membership, as many workers still dislike a light being shed on their membership in the plant. In the Federal Republic, the Netherlands and Scandinavia the 'check-off' and handling on EDP equipment has spread widely. However, there is a price in participation to be paid for economic efficiency: the Dutch NVV freely admits that the ties between the members and the regional administration loosened when the system of collection by the union was stopped.[257] The shop stewards in Great Britain also regard the collection of fees as one of the most important means of establishing contact with the members in their working group.

In Germany payment morale is regarded as good. A non-payment ratio of only 9% was established. But even some of these were apparently not members who refused to pay but members who had left, who had only just joined or who had moved house.[258] The degree of loyalty is high, especially when compared with the political parties.

However, not even German union finance experts have been able to establish great idealism over the payment of dues. Very few pay the highest rate, and only 0.1% voluntary supplementary dues. With the growing differentation in the working class union membership has become just membership of one association among others and the union is often regarded simply as a service. But even in the best organized union movement with a high payment morale the quality of the financing system leaves something to be desired. Certainly the German system has also come in for its share of criticism.

There are also deficiencies in the financing system among the rich unions:
— §2 of the DGB's Articles of Associaton has for twenty-five years stated that the unions should form an effective unity and create common institutions of administration. The organization is actually dependent on the apparatus available in each case and real comparisons are virtually impossible;
— cashiers book the various dues (to the organization, for self-aid, for solidarity) differently. What one enters as expenditure under wage fluctuation another books as expenditure on conferences;
— there is no common asset administration.

(4) *International financing*. Some of the international federations have common funds, the European Federation of Free Trade Unions, for instance, since 1973. Its purpose is 'to further certain

measures which serve to strengthen the organization of union federations and individual unions in the countries of the Community'. Financial contributions from the DGB to the CGT-FO went through the Fund but some aid from American unions came without this detour through an international organization. On relations in the Communist World Federation and the Christian World Federation there are only conjectures and no exact figures are available.

9. LEADERSHIP PROBLEMS AND DEMOCRATIZATION MOVEMENTS

(a) The Leaders and Officials

Unions are 'cadre' organizations with full-time officials and activists. The number of full officials is a closely guarded secret. However, it appears to correlate with the degree of centralization and the financial strength of the organization. Moreover, the number of full-time officials also depends on the efforts made by the labour movement to mobilize as many members as possible for leadership functions. Great Britain has so far succeeded best here on an international comparison. The Donovan Report assumed that the ratio of members to full-time officials was twice as high even in the fragmented ideology unions in France and Italy than in Great Britain. In the eighteen most important British unions there was one official to 3,700 members at the beginning of the fifties and the Donovan Report assumed 1:3,800. Even the USA had a higher percentage of officials with 1:1,400.[259]

The Federal Republic is often seen by external commentators as the Eldorado of union officials. In 1969 there was one official to 876 members. But the ratio is not quite fairly calculated. An adjustment for administrative staff and those who do no membership work would give about 1,300 members for each of the approximately 5,600 officials (there were only about 1,600 officials in Great Britain at the beginning of the fifties).[260] The Swedish figure needs the same adjustment. According to information published by the EEC the relation of officials to members has changed further since then. La Palombara once established a thumb rule of five officials to 5,000 members. The number of officials should double as the membership figure doubles.[261]

TABLE 14
Relation of officials to members

Netherlands	1:500
Sweden	1:680
Federal Republic	1:800
Denmark*	1:900
USA	1:1400
Italy	1:1500
France	1:1500
Australia (AMWU)	1:1853
Norway	1:2220
Great Britain	1:3800

* = figures for the beginning of the sixties.

Sweden: Calculated from the figures of *LO-Statistik 1977*. Stockholm 1978, p. 15.

Sources: EEC, Gewerkschaftsinformationen: *Die Gewerkschaftsbewegung in der Europäischen Gemeinschaft*. Brussels, 1975, part 1, p. 7. J. David Edelstein and Malcolm Warner: *Comparative Union Democracy*. London, Allen & Unwin, 1975, p. 12. Stan Poppe: 'Mitbestimmung in den Niederlanden', *Amsterdam, NVV*, January 1975, p. 5. R. M. Martin: *Trade Unions in Australia*. Harmondsworth, Penguin, 1975, p. 62.

But these global figures are confusing for two reasons:

(1) They hide the enormous differences in the number of full-time staff in the various unions, as we see from figures on British unions (Table 15). The relation of members to officials can only be fairly assessed on a break-down into industries and the particular working conditions in different sectors.

Where there is a strong organization on the job and where local non-full-time activists and committees have wide discretionary powers, as in the printing industry, the iron and steel unions and the public sector, the number of full-time officials is lower than in industries where the plants are fragmented and there is a high degree of fluctuation among the workers, as in the building

TABLE 15
Differences between the relation of officials to members in individual British unions

Union	Ratio
Amalgamated Union of Building Trade Workers	1:1,300
National Union of Boot and Shoe Operatives	1:1,600
Amalgamated Society of Woodworkers	1:2,000
Transport and General Workers Union	1:2,100
Union of Shop, Distributive and Allied Workers	1:2,500
National Union of Tailors and Garment Workers	1:3,300
National Union of Agricultural Workers	1:3,600
National Union of General and Municipal Workers	1:3,700
Electrical Trades Union	1:4,200
National Union of Public Employees	1:4,700
Transport Salaried Staffs' Association	1:5,000
British Iron and Steel & Kindred Trades Association	1:5,300
Amalgamated Engineering Union	1:5,400
National Union of Mineworkers	1:6,200
National Union of Printing, Bookbinding and Paper Workers	1:10,300
Civil Service Clerical Association	1:12,200
Union of Post Office Workers	1:16,200
National Union of Railwaymen	1:19,000

Source: B. C. Roberts: *Trade Union Government and Administration in Great Britain*. London, G. Bell & Sons, 1957, p. 289.

industry, for instance. Where working conditions are stable, a lower number of officials is needed. But a low number of full-time officials is not in itself generally held to be a good thing. Plant structures and job organization require different inputs from full-time officials even in countries like Great Britain, where the shop stewards are increasingly achieving a leading role in collective bargaining (cf. Chapter 1, 5, a).

(2) Even if one regards the number of full-time officials as significant in itself, it says little on the *effectiveness of representation* among members. It is at best an indicator of the degree of

bureaucratization of the unions but not of the activity of any individual organization. Great Britain, if it has the lowest number of full-time officials, has a large number of shop stewards (nearly 300,000), while the Federal Republic could include its *Vertrauensleute*, the union representatives in the plant, as well as the union activists in the works councils and yet the comparison would not yield a general key to the degree of activity of the organization. In the Latin countries with their fragmented unions the militants could be described as a functional equivalent of the full-time officials and *Vertrauensleute*. In France only 10% are held to be activists. Their motives for above-average participation lie mainly in their job conditions, as a French study has shown (Table 16).

TABLE 16
Motivation for union activism in France
(percentages)

Experience on the job	89
Experience outside the plant (inequality of opportunity, humiliations)	7
Political reasons	3
Religious or ideological reasons	1

Source: Andrée Andrieux and Jean Lignon: *Le militant syndicalite d'aujourd'hui. Ouvriers, cadres, techniciens, qu'est-ce qui les fait agir?* Paris, Denoël, 1973, p. 59.

In countries where the unions are strongly fragmented many union members see themselves as a kind of political avant-garde. And a strong engagement for Socialism is also a feature even of some former Christian unions (cf. Chapter 1,1). The more decentralized the fields of action are and the more anarchic-syndicalist emphasis is put on the autonomous groups in the rank and file, the greater is the conflict of loyalty with the union machine.[262] Where decision-making becomes centralized and industrial unionism creates large and powerful unions the danger grows that the lower-ranking officials will increasingly see themselves simply as transmission belts for decisions that have been taken centrally and less and less as representatives of the interests of the workers.

Referenda and *ballots* are ways in which the individual member can participate in important decisions even in mass organizations. In countries like Sweden and Germany where this is an old tradition, open conflicts have rarely arisen between majorities and recommendations from the body of officials, and the use of the ballot or referendum has rarely been questioned either from above or below. The situation is different when — as was the case in Great Britain under the Industrial Relations Act in 1971 — the legislature attempts to enforce ballots from outside. The union leaders were bound to see this as inadmissable intervention in the internal affairs of the union and reject it vehemently as an attempt to drive a split between them and their rank and file by legislative means. It was one of the main reasons for the boycott of the law by the unions.[263] Ballots had been used in some unions before the Act was passed although this was not always to demonstrate democracy but sometimes to strengthen the leaders' position against left-wing dissenters in controversial strikes.[264]

Where there is a strong orientation to the rank and file, elected representatives (such as the shop stewards in Great Britain or the *delegati* in Italy) are of greater importance than the regional leaders. The emphasis on shopfloor bargaining is changing the job of the full-time officers. Local trade union officials are now expected to have extra skills to cope with productivity deals, job evaluation, work study and written collective agreements. But the territorial form of organization is going through a crisis even in countries where there is no danger that rank and file-oriented organizational forms will develop independent of union structures. In Holland the NVV regards the loosening of the ties between members and the regional office as due to the change in the collection system for fees.[265] But this is only an admission that in the past, as now, most members were passive rather than active.

There has also been a considerable change in the career patterns and leadership style at the top of the union hierarchies, although here again one cannot generalize on an international scale. The stronger the political influence of the unions is in their country and the more they are directly represented in the state apparatus (cf. Chapter 4, 2), the greater is the tendency of full-time officials to follow the behaviour pattern established by Robert Presthus for 'climbers' in bureaucratic organizations: the typology is characterized by a manipulative, externalized ethic, the use of authority and an exhibition of the 'adjustment to the market'. Where the unions have a strong political influence there are fewer internal conflicts. The possibility of taking an active role in Labour Party policy has taken the sting out of many an internal confict in the British union movement.

One problem for the unions as workers' organizations is the importance of the social background of their leaders. Socialist parties have often been led by members of the bourgeois intelligentsia but the unions have objected to this. They have generally been more insistent that their leaders should be, like themselves, workers. There are only a few studies on the social background of full-time trade union officers. But even in Northern Europe where trade unions tend to be less involved in the rhetorics of proletarian class consciousness, about two-thirds of the officials are of working-class origin (Norway 67%, Germany 62%).[266] In Sweden only 57% of a sample were from a working-class family in the narrower sense, but the majority could claim to come from the 'toiling masses' if we include low-ranking employees and workers outside the LO milieu (10%) and the unusually high proportion of those with an agrarian background (15%).[267]

In the early years of the union movement union leaders were sometimes compared to priests of early cultures, administering a number of mysteries in the ideology and needing various almost irreconcilable qualities, such as skill in negotiation, charisma, oratorical skill, ability to organize and ideological initiative.[268] As the field of activity of the unions grew it became impossible for one person to combine and exercise all these qualities. Where the role is largely one of negotiator who has to observe certain rites so as to force the opposite side to give ground but enable it not to lose too much face in its own ranks, the qualities which are needed are rather along the lines of cautious self-repression than militancy and aggression.[269]

We find criticsm of rising 'bossism' in all the mass organizations — even in Northern Europe where there tends to be little radical political dissent and the culture is extremely homogeneous and Social Democrat in spirit. 59% of LO members interviewed criticized the bossism of the top functionaries.[270]

No other interest group has such strong function problems for its leaders as the unions — the labour movement is itself fruitful soil for a hostile image of authority. The union official is by definition a man with a bad conscience, he is too much a creation of the workers' general desire for participation and sense of responsibility not to suffer from his professionalism, his freedom from manual work and the ensuing difficulties in maintaining contact with the rank and file. A DGB chairman once remarked sarcastically on the unions' disadvantage over other cadre groups:

> Full-time officials of employers' associations and the Chambers of Industry and Commerce are more sensible than union officials on principle. It must be the milieu. By general consent officials of the Church are not officials at all. Farmers' Association officials are only occasionally unreasonable — usually they are just 'going it a bit strong'. So it is only the representatives of the blue and white collar workers and the workers in the public sector who are really intolerable. They are stupid, impudent and irresponsible as a matter of course and at regular intervals they get up and jeopardize the state, the economy and the whole of society.[271]

In fact the conservative press often does characterize union officials as 'stupid, impudent and irresponsible' though in rather milder terms. However, the accusation of stupidity must derive from a class-bound concept of intelligence, even though intellectual brilliance is not likely to be the strongest criterion for the choice of a union leader. One Nestor in British union research actually concluded that intellectual brilliance in any prominent form was largely undesired in union leaders.[272] For the oppositon and the negotiating partners certainly a leadership which does not move too far away from its members in its habits of thought and pattern of living, remains representative of the rank and file and is backed loyally by them, is more calculable and easier to deal with than an intellectual, great as the aesthetic attraction may be. But in any case intellectualism would be hard to reconcile with the pragmatism, sometimes criticized and sometimes praised, which union leaders have and need to have.

There are two tendencies which have rather undermined recruitment from the ranks of the workers. The less ideologically-oriented the unions were and the more they aimed for hard 'business unionism' on the US pattern, the more strongly did efficiency rate before democratization, and the results of negotiations were more important than who had achieved them. But less concentration on ideology does not mean that ideology ceases to be important, as has occasionally been suggested under the hypothesis of 'mature unions'. What has happened is simply that the global social ideology has been replaced by the ideology of functional models,[273] and this often means that the unions have to 'shop' for specialists. The more successful they have been politically the more they have needed to attract the appropriate staff. But in many cases the 'bossism' of the leaders who had risen from the ranks remained strong enough to prevent conflict between the members and the intellectuals. This was essentially the case in the USA. The intellectuals were rather appointed for 'window-dressing',[274] and in any case the unions usually attempted first to appoint them from their own ranks. It was only in the USA that professional experts for top management in companies and for the union leaders were recruited on the same market, although the management positions generally carried almost double the salary of the union posts.[275]

In Great Britain the unions on average — despite the extremely low number of full-time officials per 1,000 members — cannot afford specialists of this category. According to a survey by the TUC in 1972 69% of full-time officials had left school before the age of sixteen. In 1959 the figure was 90%.[276] So in Great Britain too the level of qualification is rising. Since the unions have been playing an increasingly active role in economic policy the specialist staff departments at the disposal of the union leadership have grown, especially in Sweden and Germany. Occasionally these staff intellectuals have proved more innovative than their leaders, as was apparent at the specialist congresses of the Metal Workers' Union in Germany in 1973 and 1976.

In the USA, on the other hand, where the unions are relatively wealthy and there is a strong tradition of specialist consultation on policy, the unions themselves have not developed very large teams of specialists. These are rather assembled ad hoc for specific negotiations. The huge organization of the AFL-CLO with nearly 6 million members has a smaller research staff than the Swedish LO which has only about one-tenth the membership of the US unions.[277]

(b) Internal Democracy

Since the debate on general strikes in the International in the first decade of the twentieth century the unions have from time to time asserted their claim to be more democratic than the political parties. Some US unions were an exception, putting more emphasis on efficiency than democracy and showing no interest in appearing as 'praeceptor Americae' in the matter of internal organization.[278] Even in the Federal Republic, where the unions have played a relatively reserved role in politics, the exemplary degree of their democracy has occasionally been emphasized, e.g. by the sociologist Alfred Weber in 1952, who regarded a political mandate for the unions as justified because in view of their aims and inner democratic structure they were particularly suited to further 'the democratic process'.[279] Left-wing critics of the German union movement regarded this impulse from a Nestor of German sociology as 'honourable' but 'not very fruitful under present political circumstances'.[280]

Left and right-wing criticism of the thesis of the unions' potential for democratization was not new. Robert Michels was the first to combine left and right-wing feelings of anger against the bureaucratic machine in his thesis of the iron law of the oligarchy which was regarded as applying mainly to the parties but to the unions as well.

> In the revolutionary union group the leader has plenty of opportunity to deceive those he is leading. The cashier during a strike, the secretary of a union, even the leaders in a conspiracy or on the barricades can betray their followers much more easily and with much more severe consequences than the Member of Parliament or the SPD local councillor.[281]

Even now, left-wing literature often argues that a union which is revolutionary in tendency is bound to be democratic and the French and Italian syndicalists especially have largely proceeded upon this assumption. But they can be shown to have many democratic practices, secret organizations, for instance, elections by acclamation, and authoritarian decisions as to when *action directe* or a general strike is called for.

Michels' exaggeration of the 'iron law of oligarchy' in all large organizations has repeatedly aroused opposition from empiricists in union research. Despite a certain apathy on the part of members a high degree of democratization has always been imputed to the unions by these scholars.[282]

In its proposals for democratization the older literature was largely oriented to the constitutional concepts on state level: legal protection, elections, autonomy for intermediary institutions, internal organizational basic rights were the focus of attention.[283] The later comparative literature also largely went by Anglo-Saxon standards. Often the norm was simply derived from American ideals. One American researcher attempted to refute Michels over the German unions with the following arguments: German unions are no less democratic than others, the degree of participation is no less than in the USA, it is possible for internal opposition to be voiced and in contrast to some American unions there is, according to this American study, no dominant clique in the DGB which monopolizes power. But if the standard of comparison in the study is not another country but the writer's view of what constitutes union democracy, the German unions do not come off so well, as we see from some recent studies. The need for security and fear of loss of status, the difficulties of further advancement professionally or politically after leaving high union office, the strong degree of centralization of the decison-making system and the watchful communication among the union élite have actually caused the DGB unions to be called an almost 'hierarchical-monocratic model'.[284] Unions must allow themselves to be measured and criticized by their own claim to democracy. But the harshness of the verdict will have to be tempered by comparison. And though most European unions can certainly stand comparison with other associations, it is on a comparison of one union with another that more differentiated judgements must be given. Where there is a dual system of bargaining in the plant and the union officials (as in Great Britain) play a less important role in negotiations, there will be comparatively more democracy and more sub-system autonomy (cf. Chapter 1, 5). On the other hand the British union leaders deserve all the more criticism for uncontrollable 'overlapping memberships' or *Filzokratie* as the relations between the party and the unions are very close, as are those between the union élite and the political élite altogether (cf. Chapter 4, 2).

Similar criticism could be made of the Swedish and German identification of trade union leadership with the Social Democrats (98% in Sweden). Though Sweden has a rather active political culture a recent study classified only about a quarter of the trade union units as 'democratically' guided (26%). The rest was classified as 'passive leadership' (30%), 'impotent leadership' (14%), 'manipulative leadership' (14%) and 'therapeutic leadership' (10%).

In systems where relations between the labour party and the trade unions are too close, criticism of the shortcomings of democracy increases, all the more if, unlike Germany or Denmark, the unions have a large number of members who do not sympathize with the Social Democrats (about 18% in Sweden).[285]

In the fragmented system in the Latin countries, on the other hand, there seems to be comparatively most sub-system autonomy, admittedly at the expense of the efficiency and coordination of union work and any continuous political influence on the centres of power.

Comparisons of the degree of democracy between American and European unions, however, are more problematic, because leadership structures are more differentiated in the USA than in any other country. Is one to take Hoffa's gangster methods or the often praised ultra-democratic printers' union as the standard of comparison? This union has provided correlations between organizational features and the degree of democracy which have influenced all the literature on the subject. The most important are:

— autonomy of its member locals;
— decentralized and unconcentrated ownership;
— security of a union in its relations with the management (the less it is obliged to behave like a military organization, the greater the chances are for internal democracy) a proposition which has caused much protest in leftist literature!
— the homogeneity of interests of the members of a union;
— the low degree of stratification in an occupation;
— the attractivity of the job or the occupation;
— the interests of the members;
— the opportunity to learn political skills;
— the amount of leisure time and money that rank and file members have;
— the variation in ideologically relevant background characteristics, and other variables.

In 'union democracy', democracy was largely identified with pluralism, which in Europe too first meant that internal competition was seen as one of the main ways to remove hierarchic and bureaucratic structures.[286]

The Lipset team specialized mainly on informal structures. More recent analyses have again put more emphasis on institutional and formalized conditions of internal democracy and a genuine competition for office. A comparison with European unions put the British unions, for example, in a rather more favourable light with their open competition than most of the American unions in the survey.[287] But Great Britain, too, has to accept certain deficiencies in democracy due to its fragmented union structure. In systems with a large number of unions in one head federation (as in the USA as well as Great Britain, cf. Table 1), the risk increases that some of the large unions will achieve an excessively dominant position,[288] while in head associations which have a relatively small number of affiliated industry unions, as in the Federal Republic, Austria and Sweden, it is not so apparent that certain unions are exerting undue influence. But even in countries with very different organizational forms the weight of some industries in the economy as a whole has made itself felt, not only in the numerical importance of the membership but ideologically too. The miners used to be an example of this, the metal workers are today. Decentralization, often proposed as a means of increasing democracy,[289] has not proved a cure for all ills, even in small countries like Holland. Functional differentiation has often proved a more effective means of combining strength and efficiency together with improved participation than local fragmentation with the danger it brings of local 'bossism'.

Union leaders have occasionally returned the criticism that they are authoritarian and, giving payment in kind, have pointed out that most of their members are apathetic until something which directly affects them shocks them out of their reserve. The expansion of the cadres of union plant representatives and hence the formation of a sub-system have to a certain extent rightly been regarded as a way out.[290]

Comparative research on union democracy, as Galenson understood it, did not reach a clear conclusion on pluralism either. The American studies concentrate on pluralism in the organization. But how does the pluralism of competing unions work in the 'rival unionism' pattern? Precisely where competition was fiercest between unions authoritarian practices by the leaders have been condoned again and again in America.[291] There is no clear causal relation between democracy and union pluralism: general organizations like the LO or the DGB have not proved more despotic than union centres in a pluralist structure.[292] In the Latin countries union pluralism has not produced as much democracy as we find in Holland or Switzerland and the degree of democracy in individual unions varies widely in pluralist systems. In France, today, for example, the CFDT is very much closer to an open democratic-pluralist type than is the CGT.

As a deeply internalized element in political culture pluralism is much more decisive in its effect on democratic structures than the mere existence of competing unions. For the rest it is hardly possible to generalize on different unions in different countries. Their degree of democracy largely depends on their perception of their function in the system. Moreover, the industrial structure of the countries differs too much for general statements on the degree of democracy to be possible.

The degree of hierarchy and bureaucracy depends on two factors:

(1) The *larger* a union is the greater is the degree of hierarchy and bureaucracy. So fragmented ideology unions do not usually have specialized staff to the extent that pragmatic general unions do, and they leave more room for local and plant initiative.

(2) The more strongly *centralized a branch of industry* is, the greater is the degree of bureaucracy of a union.[293] Concentration and monopolization increase the pressure to unity and bureaucracy. The fragmented syndicalism of the Latin countries is in part still the expression of a lower state of development of productivity.

The new impetus in favour of participation by individuals has been directed since the end of the sixties largely against the steering of participation by leaders. Sometimes the relation between the leaders and the members has been seen as too manipulative and it has been suggested that the interests of members mean little in practice. Sometimes this criticism has been bound up with the myth of a revolutionary working class which has simply been deflected from its path by revisionist union bosses.[294] There is also a conservative variant of this attitude, which interprets any tendency to radicalization as excess on the part of the bosses beyond the demands of members and attempts to mobilize conservative prejudices on the part of the union members against their leaders. The second variant has been nourished not only by conflict-oriented researchers as far as they were concerned with the career problems of unionists and followed the efforts of officials to retain their position, style of living and status even after leaving office.

On the other hand the theses of the total manipulation of members by the union leaders have been refuted even by critical union theorists, who have rather shown sympathy for militant union policy. Even *cooperative* unions can never rely completely on the apathy of their members, they always have to reckon that there may be a strike and hold their precarious balance between active participation and passive obedience, avoiding over-motivation as much as resignation.

2

Ideology and the Programme

1. IDEOLOGY AND PRACTICE

In theories of union development an evolutionist view predominated for a long time, according to which unions begin by being radical and ideological and go through a maturation process, ending by being pragmatic and less ideological. Even the American writers, who from their wide perspective were particularly inclined to these generalizations, sometimes recognized that no such uniform trend can be traced in Europe. But only Great Britain, Sweden or Germany were ever included in the comparison, the Latin countries and the smaller countries were left out. According to this evolutionist theory the unions begin as 'political movements' and with growing industrialization tend to become mere 'pressure groups'.[295]

These generalizations were often based on the assumption that the American development was the norm. The move away from Socialist ideas by Samuel Gompers, who headed the AFL for thirty-seven years, as a result of differences of opinion with Socialist sect leaders from Europe, is often seen as an early sign of maturation. But this particular feature of the American development does not mean that the American unions did not adopt ideological principles. These differ, however, from the ultimate expectations of the Socialists, as was once vividly portrayed in an interchange between the Socialist Hillquit and Samuel Gompers before the US Commission on Industrial Relations in 1912:[296]

GOMPERS The best possible conditions obtainable for the workers is the aim.
HILLQUIT Yes, and when these conditions are obtained —

GOMPERS	Why, then we want better.
HILLQUIT	Now, my question is — Will this effort on the part of organized labour ever stop until it has the full reward for its labour?
GOMPERS	It won't stop at all.
HILLQUIT	That is a question —
GOMPERS	Not when any particular point is reached... The working people will never stop —
HILLQUIT	Exactly —
GOMPERS	in their efforts to obtain a better life for themselves and for their wives and for their children and for humanity...it is the effort to obtain a better life every day.
HILLQUIT	Every day and always?
GOMPERS	Every day. That does not limit it.
HILLQUIT	Until such time? —
GOMPERS	Not until any time.
HILLQUIT	In other words —
GOMPERS	In other words, we go further than you. (*Laughter and applause in the audience.*) You have an end. We have not.

This paradoxical conclusion has always astonished Europeans and the voluntary pragmatism of the 'battle every day' was often seen as a total lack of ideology, which is not what Gompers meant.

American pragmatism was very influential in Europe. Just after the war or in the period of growth optimism it emerged from comparable functional constellations as in the United States. In Northern and Central Europe, too, unions began to accept the role of an interest group in a pluralist system. This appears most clearly in the statutes of the Austrian federation, which refer to typical pressure group activities such as 'petitions to the legislature, official bodies or authorities'. The Swiss and Swedish federations too gave all petitions and statements in their reports. It is only recently that objections have been raised to the use of the term 'interest group' with regard to the unions. Only the programme of the Finnish SAK of 1971 still explicitly states that the union movement is operating as a pressure group (*patryckyingsgrupp*)[297] and the AFL/CIO does so implicitly by accepting the general idea of lobby regulation, but rejecting in a recent platform presented to the National Conventions of the two parties in 1976 'those ill-advised proposals which would require unnecessarily cumbersome record-keeping with endless details on the activities of lobbyists or intrude unnecessarily into the affairs of lobbying organizations without increasing public awareness of lobbying activity'.[298]

In 1975 the TUC in Britain realized a plan for 'national lobbying against Parliamant'. On 20 December 1975, 7,000 representatives of all the unions responded to a summons from the TUC and came to Westminster 'to join the lobby'. Labour members of Parliament joined the discussion and answered questions.[299] No pressure was exercised but the weapon of a gathering on a parliament and mass lobbying can in less well disciplined actions certainly blur the lines of distinction between social movements and pressure groups in the traditional sense. Generally, however, the unions have so far, even if they rejected the role of a pressure group, had to rely largely on the weapons of one, as, except for the British unions, during the early Owenist phase, they were never conceived as self-help organizations like the cooperative movement and most of their programmatic claims were clearly outside the immediate sphere of their own influence.[300] In their main actions, not strikes but 'autonomous self-regulation', 'collective bargaining' and 'political pressure', the unions have been described as very conservative, although it is only perhaps in the English-speaking countries that this would not be an exaggeration.[301]

The refusal to integrate fully into the bourgeois pluralist pattern is based in the theory of the labour movement on two arguments:

(1) Unions do not represent particular interests to the same extent as the employers' associations and other interest groups do, they represent the *general* interest (the Frankfurt School has called this the 'concrete-general interest'), which would otherwise not find expression. But it is objected that union interests can conflict with the general interest from the consumer sphere to environment questions and they are certainly not always identical with it. German union leaders like Ludwig Rosenberg saw the unions as 'part of the whole' and did not presuppose that the labour movement should become the state itself, as the third estate once declared itself 'the nation'. That unions are more than an interest group, namely 'a social organization which shares responsibility for society as a whole' was not, however, interpreted by Rosenberg in a revolutionary sense, as it was by the Left, but expressly 'to preserve the state': 'The unions see themselves as an organization which extends beyond the interests of the workers, preserving the state, forming society and responsible to everyone'.[302]

(2) Unions represent not only interests which are inherent in the system but also those which transcend the system;[303] they are, so to

speak, the torch-bearers of a future Socialist society.

Neither of these arguments has ever been used all the time or in every country in the same way and the second has hardly appeared in the English-speaking countries at all. The first was used less frequently in Europe after the Second World War, when the unions' expectations and actions became rather partial, partly because of the negative effects of Socialism under Stalin. It was only when the recognition spread that a form of society is not necessarily discredited if there are premature and brutal attempts at realizing it that the union movement again began to focus on more far-reaching aims.

Even unions which were largely Socialist in orientation could not afford to insist that their members accept the Socialist ideology. Carl Legien, the leader of the German unions' General Commission, wrote in 1903 on the relation to Social Democracy:

> The neutrality of the unions must not be interpreted as that they would refuse to see any party in the Reichstag represent their political views but only that union members cannot be expected to adopt specific political or religious creeds and that no pressure can be exercised on them to do so.[304]

This freedom not to opt for Socialism was a thorn in the flesh of the radical Communists after their party was formed and they put forward motions declaring that membership of a union was incompatible with active membership of the KPD. But Rosa Luxemburg did not share this view and she delayed discussion of the motions by handing them on to a committee to consider.

Communist parties have never been able to maintain this Puritan attitude to ideology and in every country they have made use of the opportunity to attract members from the union movement. But even the union which is most strongly oriented to Socialism, the CGT in France, has stated that unions are mass organizations which cannot demand a homogeneous ideology from their members. Krasucki, one of the leaders of the CGT, actually stated: '. . . You don't have to support Socialism to join'.[305]

But attitudes like this rarely differentiated the political horizon of Socialist unions to such an extent that they could see themselves as one interest group among many. And the 'de-ideologization' during the 'fine-weather phase' after the Second World War did not produce a less far-reaching list of claims. On the contrary:

despite the pragmatism of their policy, in many areas the unions made concrete demands where before they had at most discussed abstract ideas: from the conception of distribution policy to the planning of the production sphere. But with the positive assessment of ideology in critical literature the concept of what could be called ideology also became more demanding. Sometimes it was precisely the lack of a serious and more than verbal ideology that was taken for the ideology itself — in contrast to the general concept of ideology in organization theory literature.

Simply the anticipation of a better future is often taken to be 'ideology' by conservative opponents of the unions. But a critical approach will be careful not to write off the normative programme for an improvement of industrial relations in particular and society in general as ideologically negative, just as a positive assessment of the status quo cannot be called 'ideological' as some radical neo-Marxists have done at times. What is ideological in the negative sense (because it confuses the issue) is perhaps a programme which conceals the normative attitude as an empirical statement on something which cannot be changed[306] and argues that what is desired by partial interest is 'force of circumstances' which it would be irrational to oppose. But the positive assessment of ideology as a programme for the future should not be overloaded with demands for ideological unity in the counterproposal in social theory and political action. Critics of the programmes of the DGB and the affiliated unions complain that the sum of the individual claims does not make a coherent whole and the Frankfurt team takes a negative view of the concept of ideology which is contained in those interpretations of the situation and programmatic claims which are relevant for the unions' own image of themselves and their external representation but are not put into practice.[307] According to this interpretation ideology is mainly the organization's programmatic utterances which are not matched by action strategies or for which there is only an inadequate strategy. The latter is probably over-stretching the concept as it is hardly likely that agreement will be reached in advance on what an adequate strategy is. Actually the most radical strategy papers claim to be 'directives for action' and 'oriented to practice'. Functionally, judged by what has been successfully realized, there has not always been a balance between theory and practice. The Frankfurt group's concept of ideology is only appropriate if the second criterion is not over-stretched and is limited to items in the programme which cannot be taken literally because they are contradicted by other items. The co-existence of items which conform to the system with those which criticize it, which has often been analyzed, especially in the programmes of the German unions, can well mean that the weakest variant becomes the guideline for action by the majority in the organization.

But if their programmes are compared with those of other union movements the German unions appear in a rather better light. There are several reasons for this:

(1) No union group has a programme which is ideologically watertight and entirely free of contradictions. Often compromise formulae and pleonasms confuse the issue. The Socialist creed of the CGT's Executive Committee defines the aim as 'revolutionary change and fundamental change' so that any wing of the union can interpret this in its own way.[308] In Italy the CGIL at its 1969 Congress in Livorno shifted the emphasis from the battle over wages to a battle for social reforms.[309] This was a revision of the old syndicalist illusions that society can be changed through wage claims but it was not possible to integrate the new attitude into a clear strategy, if only because the unions always had to cope with spontaneous action groups which were pursuing quite different strategies, organizing anti-union feeling among the workers and forcing the CGIL to make concessions to local and plant units.[310]

(2) More far-reaching ideological programmatic claims designed to realize a Socialist society and which have been retained in many of the DGB unions' programmes ultimately have no force for action because almost all the unions reject direct political action on principle or for tactical reasons. Even the CGT was very cautious about its role in a 'collective Left' or 'alliance of left-wing parties' which was to help realize these claims while preserving the autonomy of the unions.

The battle over ideological claims, which ultimately has always to be fought by primarily political groups can only ever be partially designed for action. Most honest is the position taken by the Finnish SAK in its 1971 programme, which gives clear instructions beyond a vague offer of cooperation with the parties and speaks of the exercise of pressure to change the constitution.[311] Despite all their revolutionary phraseology the unions usually only move beyond the state of a pressure group in rare periods of mass action. An admission of this may be condemned as 'reformist' or 'revisionist' but it is certainly more realistic than far-reaching but empty revolutionary phrases.

The relation between the ends and means is usually seen quite differently in the English-speaking countries than on the continent. Even unions which are quite prepared for tough measures rarely have radical programmes. A statement like: 'The expression "militancy" refers to the methods but not the aims' would be unthinkable in Germany or the Latin countries.[312] According to this maxim one could just as well reverse the concept of the Frankfurt team: radicalism can only be assessed according to actual behaviour, programmatic claims hardly count or they count only as numerous ad hoc statements, which the TUC prefers to the programmes of principles of continental unions.

(3) Finally, it must be remembered that no union programme (or any party programme) can give full guidelines for action as the situation is constantly changing. In France and Italy too the unions have not worked out new programmes of principles because the number of conflicts keeps increasing and the political constellation keeps changing; they have only made programmatic ad hoc statements, and these were often only made by the leaders. Again realistic union leaders have always emphasized that the unions with their higher membership density cannot be as élitist as the parties or as unyielding over certain ideological claims.[313] As one of the leaders of the CFDT put it, 'a union that wants the moon plus five percent loses credibility to the rank and file'.[314] On the other hand the CFDT has occasionally said that the unions are ultimately a greater challenge to the capitalist system than the left-wing parties, despite these tactical retreats. Jean Monnier once in a discussion said simply: 'The role of the unions in a capitalist system is to put society into confusion. . . the role of the political parties will always be to create a new balance by realizing structural reforms. . .'.[315]

In Germany attempts have been made on the one hand to supplement the programme of principles with longer-term trend analyses for the longer-term items, and on the other to make the programme more operational with shorter-term instructions for action. The DGB attempts to avoid certain faults of the long-term programme of the SPD and make its claims more quantifiable and operational while embedding them in a strategic concept.[316]

Union members often have very different ideas on the importance and feasibility of items in the programme. Modern large organizations test the reaction of their members to certain points from time to time to see whether the functional change of the unions can be accelerated in one direction or another. The cutback in function in wage claims led to an extension of their function in all the social spheres. But from the historical perspective this is only a re-entry of the unions, tolerated by the state, into those spheres in which when there was insufficient state insurance they operated themselves autonomously for the workers' sub-culture. Without this strong social component the concentration of the German unions on positive material incentives would be hard to understand. Hardly any other federation has been so anxious to test the publicity effect of its claims as the DGB. In 1965 it launched a campaign to popularize its action programme. In the following years attempts were made to obtain information on the attitude of members to main points in the federation's work. The selection made by the DGB itself is very much limited to matters concerning the job and the production sphere and does not pay enough attention to the functional change in the distribution sphere.

Repeated surveys showed interesting differences between the objective nature of the aims and the way members saw them: the degree to which the aims were familiar to members often did not correlate with the importance they attached to them. Wage increases and shorter working hours dominated in the mind of members, longer holidays, co-determination, social security and more holiday pay held a middle position. Job security and full employment, asset formation and better training were not well known. Most popular was social security in the widest sense.

On a perspective in time there was a relatively rapid change in members' priority rating. About 1968 co-determination became more important, which was seen as due to successful publicity work by the federation. As recognition of the bad economic situation became more widespread social security and full employment became the main aims. Higher wages declined in importance. Longer holidays, better accident prevention and shorter working hours dropped to the bottom of the priority scale. Little research has been done so far on the attitude of union members to programmes to change the system. A recent study by the Allensbach Institute, however, showed that the attitude of people generally in the Federal Republic has changed and that there is now more real perception of dependence, alienation and wage dependence. Not only are the workers becoming 'more middle class', the middle class are acquiring some of the features of the lower classes.[317]

In some countries recent surveys revealed the danger that programmatic radicalism may lose touch with the rank and file of the workers. A French survey in 1978 showed that in spite of the Socialist terminology in the unions' programmes the majority of workers was more conservative than the trade union leadership. Concerning the constitution of the plant almost half of the workers seemed to be satisfied with the status quo (44%). Only 26% espoused *autogestion* and state-run industries (the CGT concept) was favoured by only 14%. Workers were more favourable to 'participation' in the management of the plants, had a higher opinion of their capital-owners than class-conflict models would admit and were more sceptical about the possibilities of strikes than the official union statements.[318]

Surveys have often shown that union members have a strong political awareness and are very open to social questions. On the other hand, they ranked lower in affinity to authoritarian ideologies and Fascist propaganda than non-members. But older workers are more strongly affected by union activity than younger ones. There was little difference between the younger members and non-members, and the rather harsh verdict was: 'Membership of a union for the younger workers now, if it is not exactly a routine affair, is often as much a matter of course as sickness benefits and social insurance'.[319] This was seen as due to lack of political mobilization of workers by the unions and the restriction of campaigns to full-time officials.

Finally, the programme has to consider not only the union's own members but the effect of certain claims on the population at large. In systems where there are close ties between the unions and the parties (cf. Chapter 4, 2) as in Great Britain, the organizational symbiosis of the two pillars of the labour movement is an unavoidable component of the ideology. Nevertheless, the unions have been cautious about applying sanctions to the members of Parliament they support because they know that the majority of voters within Labour constituencies rather dislike the relationship of close cooperation.[320]

2. SOCIALIST AIMS

The union movement is often seen as the second pillar of the labour movement beside the workers' party and as such it is expected to have a Socialist ideology. But this concept of Socialism is broader than that of the parties. In many countries there have been more marked ideological variants in the union movement than in the parties, and these have often differed from the more or less strongly Marxist-oriented Socialist ideas of most of the parties in the 2nd International. But there were even doubts that the majority of the workers' party were Marxist-oriented, and in 1905 only about 10% of the SPD in Germany were said to have 'some knowledge of Marxist ideas'.[321] In the English-speaking countries and the Latin countries there have been many parties or party groups who certainly did not see themselves as Marxists. Indeed, it could be argued that they did not even see themselves as Socialists. For the Labour Party in Great Britain and the unions which supported it the year 1918, when a constitution was adopted, is regarded as the key year for the adoption of Socialist aims as well, and it has been argued that the move to Socialism was not, as is often assumed in older literature, the cause but the result of the breach with the Liberals, which had become inevitable for organizational reasons.[322]

But even apart from the English-speaking world, where Socialism has been adopted only half-heartedly or not at all, the unions' programmes are generally more pragmatic than those of the workers' parties. The unions concentrate on demands which could be realized over the medium term and avoid general statements on the transformation of society. But only the Christian unions reject Socialism altogether. The Dutch Christian National Union Federation (CNV) contains a reference to the Bible in Article 2 of its statutes and concludes than neither 'the doctrine of the class war nor that of the total state' are acceptable.[323] The programme of the Luxembourg LAV takes the middle path by avoiding in its preamble elaborate prognoses on social development and moving quickly to concrete demands on policy details while taking the opportunity for far-reaching criticism of certain aspects of the system. But its Secretary-General stated the union's rejection of radical Socialist aims at the 1970 Congress: 'Radical aims, such as a general nationalization of land, industry and finance and an authoritarian re-organization of the distributive and services sectors on a common or cooperative basis are not at present part of our programme'. The main reason for this was Luxembourg's membership of the European Community: 'Desirable and important as many of these measures may be, and inevitable as they may also prove to be over the longer term it would be impossible to put through reforms of that nature in a small country alone when it is part of a larger economic area'.[324]

While some American unions have anti-communism in their programmes and even the AFL-CIO included 'protection against Communist subversion' in its 1961 Constitution, and in 1976 blamed the American Government for having 'ceded the initiative to the Communists'[325] a strong non-Socialist tradition does not necessarily lead to anti-Communism. Although there have been some exclusions anti-Communism has played little part in the British union movement, either in the programme or in the political developments. Anti-Communist groups such as are still active in America today have never acquired any real significance in Great Britain, although left-wing groups of Communist Party-oriented Marxists and Trotskyists have been much more active there than in the USA.[326]

There are clearly differences in the adoption of Socialist ideas in the programmes of the Northern European unions and those in the Latin countries. A comparison of the programmatic statements from Socialist unions in Belgium and Holland will show this particularly clearly. Although the two countries have much in common and their pluralist union structures have many similar features the Belgian FGTB has a much stronger Socialist vocabulary than the Dutch NVV, which in turn may seem inconsistent but is more realistic than the revolutionary programmes of some Italian and French organizations. Unions in Northern Europe make much more frequent reference to support for the democratic system, like the Irish Congress of Trade Unions.[327] The unions in the Latin countries avoid any suggestion that they might be prepared to come to terms with capitalist democracy, speaking at most of fighting for basic democratic rights. The Luxembourg CGT again took the middle road when in 1974 it expressed reserved criticism of the 'isolation of political bodies' and an élitist democracy in its own country.[328]

But there have been changes during the past year, especially in the predominantly Communist CGIL in Italy. In its programmatic document for the building of a confederation in 1971 the CGIL subscribed to 'democratic collaboration' on the basis of 'fundamental liberties defined by the Constitution'.[329] In other sources CGIL functionaries stress that even in 'an economy of the capitalist type' alternative propositions and discussions have to take place, and a certain 'agnosticism towards political power' has still to be developed by the CGIL.

The CGIL has abandoned other elements of the Socialist rhetoric. It refuses to speak of a 'breakdown of capitalism' in future, mentioning only 'permanent instability'. But its verbal compromises are not always free from contradictions: the old class conception is not dropped but cooperation within the system is announced, however, only to the extent that no 'corporatist structures' are created.[330]

A Socialist union programme is most highly developed in France, because the two most important unions are now in agreement on their Socialist aims. But the conflicts over strategy and tactics are all the more bitter. The CGT proclaims its Socialist aims in its statutes, which are otherwise limited to organizational matters (Article 1), and in 1971 its Executive Committee published very detailed statements on Socialism.[331] The CFDT, after it left the Christian tradition in the middle of the sixties, developed the concept of 'democratic Socialism' in a more authentic interpretation than the Social Democrat parties in Northern Europe.

The Belgian union FGTB lies between the clear French statements and Northern European abstinence with its claim to *inspiration socialiste*, but its programme contains inconsistencies — the acceptance of 'growth', for instance.[332] And the old syndicalist maxim of *action directe*, which is 'oriented to a democratic Socialist society' is, strangely enough, seldom practised.[333]

Ideas on the transformation of the system are rather apparent in individual measures which presuppose a Socialist system: planning, nationalization or socialization of the means of production, an economic democracy or control by the workers. But the programmes rarely contain strategic details. The Finnish SAK has produced perhaps the clearest framework for militant political activity: its 1971 programme, while respecting 'the legal framework' declares that the legal status quo is not a sacred cow which cannot be slaughtered. In comparison with the tone of the rest of the programme the passage contains sharp criticism of the constitution which has become 'an obstacle to social change'.[334]

Even in countries like France and Italy, where the unions have become the spokesmen of far-reaching social change, they are not seen as revolutionaries by the workers. In 1970 only 10% of those questioned in a French survey regarded the CGT and only 4% the CFDT as revolutionary.[335] To satisfy the CGT the CFDT does occasionally speak of revolution and class war, but 'revolution according to a plan', especially by a party aiming for a monopoly leadership by the working class, is categorically rejected.[336] With the limited prospects for direct social change through union action, consolation is occasionally sought in rather original ways. French theorists see the daily skirmishes in the plant as a contribution to Socialism in that every improvement in working conditions should accelerate the drop in the profit ratio and so intensify the pressure to socialization.[337] The much criticized determinism of Kautsky's old passive *Attentismus* can still frequently be found in the programmes of Socialist unions today.

Unions like the British, which have never been very interested in flowery pronouncements or global Socialist programmes, have travelled comparatively further on the road to nationalization. The tactics of the unions which are oriented to radical social change are now to address their claims to the Labour Party, which they support, and expect in return for concessions such as voluntary wage restraint Socialist measures like municipalization of rented property, public ownership of land, permanent price controls, and further nationalization.[338]

(a) The Nationalization of the Means of Production

Most unions which are not actually opposed to Socialism have the socialization of the means of production in their programmes. Even where the majority are relatively conservative any attempt to change this item usually calls forth storms of protest, as for instance at the Labour Party Conference in Blackpool in November 1959, when Gaitskell proposed that Article 4, of the party's 1918 Constitution, which demands the nationalization of the means of production, should be changed. Gaitskell believed that the claim was preventing the expansion of the movement in view of the growing numbers of white collar workers and clerks, who in his view would not be won over to integral Socialism.[339] In the Federal Republic, too, the majority of the DGB unions did not follow the example set by the Construction Workers Union when it deleted the claim for socialization from its programme in 1957 with very few opposing votes.

But in contrast to the earlier all-or-nothing demands the Socialist unions and parties put forward more concrete catalogues of aims in nationalization policy after the Second World War. However, the political situation in Western Europe was such that Socialist and Communist parties only succeeded in gaining power in coalition with bourgeois parties. So a comprehensive nationalization programme was never possible, and there were usually only political conflicts over the nationalization of individual companies, especially those which had acquired unpleasant prominence during the periods of Fascist rule. It was only in Great Britain that the victory of the Labour Party in 1945 made it possible to tackle the realization of old claims.

The TUC in its 'Interim Report on Post-War Reconstruction' in 1944 demanded nationalization of the 'commanding heights of the economy'.[340] But there was no concrete plan for doing this. The Minister for Fuel and Power, who as head of a department handling key industries was particularly concerned with this question, complains in his memoirs that he had heard the Labour Party talk about nationalization all his life but that when it came to power the party had no plans for its implementation: 'I had to start on a clear desk'.[341] The minister tried to get the unions to participate through an advisory council. But they were at first too disappointed over the limited scope of the nationalization plans and more interested in the question of the allocation of the new top posts, and in their participation rights in the nationalized enterprises, to be prepared to take any of the responsibility for planning from the politicians. In any case they could hardly be expected to do that, and it is not really justifiable to criticize the behaviour of the British unions after 1945, outside the sphere of their close ties with the party, where they do participate in the formulation of many aims but do not play an adequate part in their realization.

From the degree of detail of the nationalization proposals some conclusions can be drawn on the seriousness of the intent to implement them. The programmes of Scandinavian unions generally refer more to the democratization of the plants and their subjection to state control. Not even the 1971 programme of the Finnish SAK has direct nationalization as an aim, although the Communists then had relatively more influence than in any other Scandinavian country.[342] Since the activation of the debate on participation, workers' control and wealth sharing in Scandinavia, the unionists have been less and less inclined to regard dispropriation as the only way to socialization. Organization theorists see better chances of democratization in nationalized industries in Scandinavia than in private industry but fear that the political violence which such a radical intervention in the social order would bring would not further the democratization movement.[343]

The Swedish LO has criticized the expansion of the public sector in that this was mainly in plants owned by local authorities. It argued that these should be more strongly integrated into the work of a centrally coordinated 'efficient economy'.[344] The workers in the public sector are not noticeably more satisfied in Sweden either: on the contrary, in 1969 Sweden demonstrated that the danger of spontaneous strikes is greatest in the nationalized industries, as the unions tend to hold back here for fear of causing difficulties to the governing social Democrat Party which they are allied to. The great wave of unofficial strikes in 1969 culminated in the state-owned mines of the Loussavaara-Kirunavaare Company (LKAB).[345]

So unions which opted rather for 'workers' control' than 'self-administration' in the ideological battle over participation, like the Belgian FGTB, suddenly discovered in the nationalized plants how enthusiastic they were over total *autonomie de gestion*, to prevent bureaucratization,[346] a precursor, one could say, of a Socialist form of participation in every area of working life.

In Germany there was a dominant preference for keeping the word 'nationalization' free of negative implications which it had acquired in connection with bureaucratic Socialism. The unions, too, supported different forms of non-private ownership which they grouped under the term *Gemeineigentum* (common ownership). In its Düsseldorf Programme of Principles of 1963 the DGB simply demanded 'The preservation and expansion of public ownership in business enterprises and its further development to a meaningful and efficient system of public and publicly-linked companies'. No concrete proposals were made, except for the emphasis on the necessity for state ownership of nuclear fuel in view of the importance of the nuclear industry and the need for a coordinated energy policy.[347] Publications by German union theorists are, in view of the division of Germany, still torn between the need to mark themselves off from the nationalization concepts of the German Democratic Republic on the one hand and on the other to bewail the conservative immobility of the Federal Republic, which makes their concept of a 'free commonwealth economy' appear unattainable at present.[348]

The most detailed comments on nationalization are to be found where a left-wing coalition sees real chances of being able to implement a homogeneous policy for the realization of Socialism. In Italy the Communist Party has to be much more cautious in its statements with regard to its aim of a 'historical compromise' with the Democrazia Christiana and it restricts itself to emphasizing that the sector which is already nationalized should be more strictly controlled by the state and parliament. In Great Britain, too, there are constant complaints of the lack of efficiency of state or parliamentary control of the nationalized companies.[349]

The 'Joint Programme' of the Communist Party and the Socialist Party in France of 27 June 1972 is probably the most comprehensive nationalization programme that has been worked out recently in Europe, although the French Communist Party has made some concessions to the Socialists. It is proposed that five industries be transferred immediately to complete public ownership (raw minerals, armaments, space and aircraft, atomic power and pharmaceuticals), two others are declared ready for part nationalization (computers and chemicals). Companies are listed by name. The following measures are to safeguard against state bureaucracy:

(1) Nationalization must not lead to state-run plants; it must be combined with the 'demands of the masses' and means of realizing workers' control.

(2) The interests of the small investor are to be protected.

(3) Compensation for shareholders is to be on 'equalization principles'.[350]

In many countries there is now a recognizable trend as democratic Socialism develops to give more concrete criteria for nationalization than the old vague formula of the 'key industries'. The 1972 French 'Joint Programme' had three major criteria:

(1) Companies which are of the nature of public services.

(2) Companies which are fed mainly with public money (armaments and infrastructure industries).

(3) Monopolies which prevent competition.

The unions also list:

(4) Companies of growing social importance. This includes the pharmaceutical industry, especially where there is a national health system. However, even in countries with predominantly private health insurance the pharmaceutical industry is largely regarded as being of the nature of a public service. In Great Britain even the construction industry has been named, although it remains stubbornly fragmented and private despite its increasing share of public funds.[351]

(5) The most advanced technological industries (chemistry, EDP, the motor industry).

(6) Companies which are of decisive importance for industry planning or regional policy (even if they do not correspond to the usual size criteria).

(7) Companies which offend against national legislation (on environment questions, for example).

The CGT's nationalization list was even longer. But nationalization policy can only be implemented if there is a broad consensus on the left, and this was not obtainable on union level without concessions. The CFDT has always been only half-hearted about nationalization, accepting it only on condition of the 'self-administration of nationalized companies'. The CGT, however, was sceptical about *autogestion* for organizational reasons, regarding it as feasible only in small units and fearing that in order to be *autogérable* companies would have to split up, and this did not accord well with the Marxist theory of the development of the forces of production. The CFDT countered this with the fear that *gestion démocratique* in nationalized plants would not affect the principle of hierarchic labour relations but only transfer the monopoly to a different owner. In this view the CGT's 'bureaucratic centralism' could produce unholy alliances between the technocrats on the right and the Communists on the left.[352] The unions, whether Social Democrat or Communist in leaning have otherwise in any case rather encouraged than hindered the concentration process as the supporters of genuine competition justly accuse them of doing.[353]

Although in the programmes of Socialist parties and unions nationalization was conceived as a deliberate act of the policy of the furtherance of Socialism, much undergrowth has developed under the prevailing capitalist conditions. The real expansion of the public sector did not always correspond to the intensity of the will to redistribution of the Socialist groups in the system. There has been a strong expansion of the public sector by governments whose policy was not largely influenced by Socialists and who were not aiming to realize Socialism, for reasons of development or regional policy (in Italy and Spain) or fear of external access to foreign assets (Austria with the nationalization of former German property). The public sector has not been greatly enlarged in the Federal Republic, although by the figures Germany is still rather in the lead here over other countries, and there has been even less expansion in Sweden, sometimes already listed among the Socialist countries, although the structure of ownership in that country is further from the fundamental characteristics of a Socialist economy than that of any other country in Europe. The growth in the public sector in Sweden has been from 14% (1950) to 21% (1972), taking the public sector's share of output.[354]

What are the reasons why so many unions put so little emphasis on the programmatic demands for Socialism although none of them have given up the claims?

(1) A popular left-wing theory puts the blame on 'betrayal by Social Democrat revisionists'. A publication from a German publishing house with strong Communist Party leanings says: 'In connection with the adoption of the Godesberg programme by the SPD efforts are increasing to stop the unions' demand for nationalization of key industries'.[355] In Finland we have the converse argument: the Social Democrats, who were actually in favour of nationalization, were forced to the right, to the bourgeois parties, by the Communist offensive, which gave too much emphasis to the problem. That was why the Social Democrats put up no resistance when at the end of 1949 the Government Commission which had been looking into the prerequisites for nationalization for years had its funds stopped by the non-Socialist majority and had to cease its activities.[356] Each of these views takes only the attitude of the union leadership into account. Surveys among workers have shown that even in countries with a militant Socialist union movement only 25% of the workers regard nationalization as an important claim and even in the CGT, which has devoted the most space to this in its

programme, only 59% are in favour. Most of these were supporters of the Communist Party; however, the demand for nationalization was not limited to the Socialist groups but had been taken up by some of the Gaullists in the sample too. In a 1978 survey of workers only 35% favoured the political transformation of society as one of the functions of trade unionism. 51% were against such far-reaching political aims. Only 14% favoured management of enterprises by the state, 9% by trade unions, 26% by all those employed in a plant. 44% were in favour of the status quo.[357] Again, among the socialistically minded workers the concept of *autogestion* had more followers than the Communist concept of state ownership.

(2) Experience with the way the nationalized industries work has lessened the unions' enthusiasm for nationalization. The big state trusts in Italy (IRI) and Spain (INI) have proved all too willing to integrate into the dominant capitalist system and the state has scarcely ever intervened against the interests of private industry.[358] But even in more highly developed countries where Socialist forces have had more influence on state policy, as in Great Britain, the nationalized industries have not proved satisfactory pioneers in investment policy, management transparency, wage policy or participation rights. In countries with alternating governments, where every constitutency plays a part in deciding which party comes to power, there is moreover a great danger that election tactics will affect the profitability of nationalized enterprises. A Labour member who is fighting to save his seat will oppose the closure of unprofitable railway lines if the measure is going to prove unpopular. This is only one of the examples cited from British experience by opponents of nationalization.[359]

In the Latin countries the biggest unions were in favour of nationalization for a long time, while Social Democrat and Christian Democrat unions rather regarded the nationalization campaigns as a distraction of the workers from more important issues. The revolutionary syndicalist wing of the CGT was against nationalization even before the First World War, arguing: 'The revolution must come first'. But the ardour of the supporters of nationalization has also cooled and one group even warned against enforced nationalization under capitalist conditions. Many unionists entertained doubts of the feasibility of administration on the pattern of *gestion démocratique*, which the CGT wanted, as opposed to the autogestion of the CFDT.[360]

One of the reasons for the loss of enthusiasm for forcing governments on to a course of nationalization policy may have been the unions' experience that the nationalized industries brought no essential change with regard to the wage level and certainly did not offer easier negotiating conditions. The working conditions also largely deteriorated. Georges Séguy, Secretary-General of the French CGT, actually argued in 1975 that the deterioration in the public sector had been greater than in the private sector.[361]

Even if the development of wages in the nationalized industries did not prove to be more favourable than in private industry, some of the aims of a rational wage policy should be more easily attainable with a large nationalized sector, especially the establishment of a national scale of performance groups and wage grades which can help prevent a capitalist hedge of special benefits and the resultant splitting of the ranks through a differentiated use of the wages drift. The workers' disappointment over what nationalization has brought them would presumably have been even greater if the ideas of some Communist ministers to prohibit strikes in nationalized industries had been realized.[362] This might have come close to Lenin's idea of a Socialist transition society but with the political culture as we have it in Western Europe it would have had a powerful de-legitimizing effect for a coalition of parties aiming for Socialism. And for that reason the proposals were not put forward again.

(b) Planning and Steered Investment

Where European unions have adopted Socialist aims, planning figures largely in their programmes. Together with socialization, planning could increase the influence of the state and the unions on the still remaining private sector and also serve to orient the collective actions of the union units at plant and local level to a common political end as only a minority of the unions adhere to an anarchic-syndicalist pattern of the complete autonomy of rank and file groups. It was not only the Communist-oriented unions which opposed the beginning of planning in the bourgeois state. Planning was suspect as an instrument of integration and many statements, even from the ILO, which is now by no means purely integrative in orientation, strengthened this suspicion when participation in planning was referred to as 'the doctrine of the social dialogue'.[363] At first participation in planning was no more than an 'instrument of public relations and collective psychological action' used for the symbolic deployment of policy[364] or the demands remained in general terms, as in Belgium: 'Planning must be made more imperative'.[365]

The reformist organizations like the DGB had much less hesitation in demanding planning after the war. However, their 1949 programme drew a clear distinction between central planning and compulsion. There is no mention of planning in the 1963 Düsseldorf programme, its place is taken by steered investment,[366] which caused the Chairman of the White Collar Workers Union, Brandt, to emphasize in 1974 that his organization had a more consistent relation to the market economy than the DGB.[367] But the DGB has been put on the defensive with regard to steered investment as well. At its Federal Congress in May 1975 the demand was only for the establishment of a central office to which investment must be reported.

In other unions, too, there are signs that more importance is being attached to steered investment than to nationalization. That is particularly the case with the CFDT in France, which usually regards nationalization in itself as running counter to the *autogestion* which it is aiming for. In the Federal Republic the opposition to steered investment grew to an unusual strength with the subsidence of the enthusiasm for reform at the beginning of the seventies. Even semi-official SPD publications deny any claim to steered investment, laying this at the door of the Young Socialists, although a positive feature of their writings, in contrast to the conservative press, is that steered investment is not directly equated with a centrally administered economy.[368] A retreat position is being built up in *structural policy* from a steered investment apparently comprising all sectors of the economy, which few in the Federal Republic would support. It is assumed that there will be a continuous deterioration in the economic conditions for the Federal Republic, which were relatively favourable during the 'fine-weather phase' of reconstruction: there will be more out and out competition instead of the differentiation competition there has been up to now, as the market becomes saturated with major industrial goods, and increasing competition from countries on the same technological level but with different production costs.[369]

However, 'structural policy' as a compromise between ideological market economists and supporters of steered investment was branded in a counter-offensive from the employers as late as 1976 as a kind of union Trojan horse, because they regarded it as a concealed form of steered investment.[370]

A second ideological front which has been built up is the argument that there is a contradiction between autonomy in wage bargaining and economic steering. Actually, unionists also admit that the two principles are not unconditionally reconcilable.[371] They would be reconcilable if a united wage policy were pursued with the appropriate effect on stability policy and if there were a stronger transfer of function from simply putting claims to the claim to a formative political role.

3. THE EMPHASIS ON NEW POLICIES IN THE UNIONS' PROGRAMMES

In almost every European country the unions are now more policy-oriented than they used to be. The better possibilities for participation and consultation on the one hand and the diminishing importance of a simple wage policy on the other through the increase in social consumption is forcing them more and more to adopt or press for policies which reach beyond their traditional circles.

The most important of these are social policy, educational policy and consumers' policy. Recently, the unions' research institutes have greatly contributed to developing a labour market policy (especially in Scandinavia) and new models for incomes policy and co-ownership policy (cf. Chapter 4, 3 and 4). Even in legal policy we increasingly find intervention by head organizations from Britain to Italy.[372]

Since 1971 the Swedish LO has repeatedly had even to deal with the question of the form of government. In the new 1974 constitution the power of the monarch was abolished but the LO continued in its congresses to fight for the old aim of a republic in Sweden.[373]

This preoccupation with policies is increasingly transforming many of the unions into pressure groups, and they are giving up the old global conception of 'counterpower for a Socialist society'. Their role as pressure groups has brought many of them into conceptual conflicts. Only in the Northern European countries has the state been the recipient of many claims which have been realized through intervention by the unions. It was only under the impression of the subsidiary principle that some organizations outside the Christian labour movement as well, like the Swiss Union Federation, put more emphasis on 'collective self-help' and produced the slogan 'Self-help as far as possible — state aid as far as necessary'.[374] But even in Switzerland major economic and socio-political programmes could not be realized without state intervention. The social aspect was apparent in the referenda and initiatives which were an expression of political self-help, although the price that had to be paid was that many progressive suggestions did not find a majority among the largely conservative population, as was the case over participation in 1976 (cf. Chapter 4, 5).

Social policy was closest to the interests of trade unions from the outset. But the attitude of the unions towards state intervention in this field differed from country to country. Nevertheless, two main groups can be distinguished:

(1) In countries with a strong state tradition and a centralized labour movement as in the German-speaking area, the claim has been largely for state social policy. A union system of social benefits in the early German union movement was, in contrast to the guild Socialist or cooperative model in the British labour movement, not an end in itself but a means to an end. In Germany the concept of the fighting union was stronger than that of an insurance society. There were conflicts between the SPD and the union even during the Kaiserreich over the form which statutory unemployment insurance should take. The SPD wanted a general Reich unemployment insurance parallel to the existing social insurance. The unions wanted to maintain the existing union arrangements together with the statutory insurance. But as their own system was becoming increasingly expensive they hoped to obtain state subsidies from the Reich, a system which developed in some Scandinavian countries.

By supporting state social policy the unions weakened their own power in a way they could not foresee. The larger the share of social consumption and infrastructure benefits provided gratis or very cheaply by the state the less possible is it nowadays to achieve redistribution policy with the traditional means of wage policy. This development draws the unions even more strongly into state policy, and they have to try to expand their political influence to effect a redistribution of state benefits to the advantage of the workers.

(2) In the Western European countries where there is a strong syndicalist tradition mistrust of the state was so great that the unions opposed state intervention in the social sphere in many instances. Experiments with Socialist sub-cultures and forms of cooperation were widespread among workers who followed Proudhon's ideas or supported guild Socialism. The mistrust was probably greatest in the USA, where Samuel Gompers firmly rejected any form of unemployment benefit for the AFL because it would force the workers to carry labour books and subject themselves to control by civil servants. Even in 1932 John Frey declared at an AFL congress that lions which were fed on boiled meat did not roar.[375] Similar debates took place in Germany but at the Second Congress of the Book Printers Union in 1896 a big majority declared that unemployment benefit would certainly not detract from the character of the organization as fighting in the class war. The US labour movement did not drop its opposition until it saw its political strength growing step by step with social legislation. The unions increasingly became the social basis of reformism, and bitter as the conflicts were in other areas between the CIO and the AFL the two organizations cooperated well over social legislation.[376]

In Great Britain the unions were quicker to see that unemployment benefits would strengthen their position,[377] not only giving them greater influence in the political process but also creating barriers against any increase in the size of the industrial reserve army by lessening the fear of potential unemployment. It was the opposition of the established and well organized workers in the USA to the repeated waves of immigrants which held back the acceptance of this social and humane concept. The TUC Congress of 1907 in Great Britain put forward a comprehensive list of claims, which had eight major points:[378]

(1) an eight-hour day for the mining industries;
(2) old-age pensions;
(3) unemployment benefits;
(4) obligatory state insurance;
(5) nationalization of land;
(6) amendment of the Poor Laws;
(7) legal restrictions on overtime; and

(8) social housing for the workers.

When the unions recognized that the traditional rise in nominal wages was not bringing them a decisive breakthrough for redistribution they gave high priority in their programmes to incomes and social policy in the broader sense. 'Social contracts' with employers sometimes allowed more room than nominal wage claims did for a plant-oriented wage policy: sickness benefits, old-age pensions, and holiday benefits were improved. The Construction Workers Union was the pioneer in negotiating additional benefits as it was in wealth formation policy; it was especially successful in negotiating retirement pensions for construction workers.[379]

The demands of the German unions in the field of general social policy are moderate in comparison with some of the things that have been achieved in other countries. Their general claims include more consideration for the finality principle (not the *cause* but the *fact* of an insurance case is to be the criterion for the benefit). In pensions the aim is 75% of gross earnings. The demand for coordination of the insurance bodies and a levelling of the groups of claimants are also strongly oriented to the status quo: the unions are demanding neither a national health insurance system nor nationalization of the existing social insurance system, as in some capitalist countries.[380] In view of this restraint it is hardly surprising that in their own sphere of wage negotiations they are trying to give increasing weight to socio-political considerations. The ÖTV's demand for a uniform increase of DM 135 for public sector employees was rejected by the minister concerned as an inadmissible mixture of wage and social policy.[381]

However, the argument overlooked the fact that it was the most conservative unions, like the Construction Workers, which had begun the mixture, and that polemics against the illusion that redistribution can be achieved through wages battles has always driven the unions to orient their wage negotiations to include socio-political aspects. The objection that the claim was detrimental to the benefits system and would have a levelling effect is greatly exaggerated, as some thought will show. The unions calculated that a high government official would drop only 1/15 in relation to a messenger. But of course if the levelling continued every year the social consequences would be considerable and it is questionable whether a more open equalization policy should not be pursued with a new and more rational standard for benefits for all industry; otherwise the levelling process would reflect an obsolete status quo ante. However, the German unions' ideas are not at present so radical. What came to be known as 'Kluncker's hotch-potch' (Kluncker is the Secretary-General of the ÖTV) had its tactical side: the aim was to achieve agreement at least on a basic amount on which linear wage rises could be calculated, and this was certainly a moderate equalization claim. But it would only be possible to develop real solidarity in wage policy throughout industry if negotiations were more strongly centralized as they are in Sweden and attempts were really made to bring wages consistently into line right across the occupations (cf. Chapter 4, 3).

The unions' growing engagement in social policy is involving them more and more in state functions although this cannot be compared with the position of the unions in Socialist countries, who are often little more than an extended arm of the state for the administration of the social insurance system. They have only partially been able to realize their claim as spokesmen of the workers, and this has always been contested by other organizations with reference to the large number of insured who are not union members. Even where elections are held, and not, as is the case with unemployment insurance, where the unions and employers' associations (together with the public authorities) propose their representatives, these have often been a matter of form only due to the unity of the DGB and the unions' opponents have tried to use the democracy argument against union claims.

Cultural and education institutions were at one time the third of four pillars of the labour movement, together with the party, the unions and labour-owned enterprises. In contrast to the other three these institutions have largely lost their independence. With the dissolution of the sub-system of the workers' culture, which could envelop its members from the cradle to the grave with services ranging from the union kindergarten to the left-wing crematorium, the cultural and education organizations have more than any others been absorbed into public institutions or non-party cultural and sports facilities or, if they remained in the hands of the unions, are now bureaucratized and used mainly for specialized training for union officials. However, a linear process of decline of the labour movement's education and cultural policy cannot be established, although some of the functions of the unions' former education work, like all the functions resulting from the lack of public elementary education, cannot be resuscitated, even as a counter-culture.

Education and training policy is acquiring growing importance for workers' organizations now that the increasing automation of work processes is contributing to the decline of the demand for the traditional craft qualifications and it is becoming increasingly important to train workers for greater flexibility. The trend to identification of blue and white collar workers in a wider security claim for what used to be the 'proletarian jobs' as well in a kind of uniform 'new salary scale' is also giving education and training policy growing importance. The unions have always had education policy aims in their programmes but these were no more than indications and they were not central to the lists. In union publications education policy usually concentrated mainly on questions of internal organization to further training within the unions.[382]

The polarization of the interests of the unions and employers' associations has been most apparent in the debate on vocational training.[383] The employers have resisted any attempts to change the training of apprentices in private industry, although specialists have argued that the system meets neither the companies' needs for qualified staff nor the needs of the apprentices.[384] In their attempt to prevent further intervention by the state the employers' associations are trying to mobilize interest and promotional groups from outside industry. The unions have less organized potential for a counter-offensive but there has been some cooperation with academic circles which usually came out in support of the DGB.

The third issue area on which the unions from their inception have tried to build up a self-sufficient sub-system of their own is *consumer policy*.

In their relations with the cooperative movement the unions have always tried to organize consumer interests although it has been argued that when the workers' organizations were still fighting for the existential minimum it was easier than it is today to restrict the unions to the production sphere. In the British union system there was comparatively more awareness that union interests need not necessarily be identical with consumer interests, as there were few of the prerequisites for the priority of the productive sphere as compared with the distributive sphere which derives from it, as Marxism conceived of the relation. The Webbs, who were certainly not theorists of a revolutionary syndicalism, used their great influence to warn against what they called co-partnerships in which capitalists and union leaders could form an unscrupulous alliance of producers against consumers.[385]

In Germany the cooperative consumer movement did not play the same role as it did in Great Britain or Sweden. This was due partly to objective factors connected to subjective and ideological factors which were rooted in the intellectual traditions of the German labour movement. Both the Marxist component which was aiming at de-limitation from the corporative association ideas of the Utopian Socialists and anarcho-syndicalists, and the 'strong inclination to an out-moded State Socialism' which Eduard Bernstein saw in the followers of Lassalle (but not only there) created a climate which was hostile to the cooperative idea, although as there was prejudice for the productive cooperatives and against any attempt at cooperative organizations in the distributive sphere the consumer cooperatives were not regarded as valuable.[386]

Today the unions have to make increasing efforts to break out of the ghetto of the productive sphere into which attempts have been made to force them, for several reasons:

(1) Increasing monopolization is forcing the consumers on the market into weaker and weaker positions, and the individual consumer, who has not the time and knowledge to utilize what room is left for competition by comparing the goods on offer properly, is powerless to prevent this.

(2) Shorter working hours and the tendency to use short time to avoid unemployment mean that the workers' leisure time is an increasingly important sphere for the unions. Even if they do not have an ideological fixation on their members' lives as a whole the unions have to try to gain a foothold in the consumer and leisure field if they are to avoid potential functional loss.

(3) With the growing tendency to public control or nationalization of private industry the possible oligopolistic misuse of power by state-owned or state-controlled enterprises as well is becoming more acute. This is a problem which the Socialist states have not avoided either, as with growing partial autonomy in prices the misuse of monopoly had so much the more impact for the consumer the greater the degree of monopoly in the various industries was.

The aim of the unions' consumer policy now is no longer a

cooperative distribution system of their own, which has everywhere except perhaps in Sweden and Great Britain been drawn into the current of capitalist circulation policy and was not able to hold its lead even with the dividend system. The modern means of consumer policy are:[387]

— influence on prices through participation in and outside the plant;
— action against deceptive advertising;
— the encouragement of positive information to consumers;
— model court cases and legal advice.

Longitudinal studies of social welfare sometimes came to the conclusion that the influence of trade unions on re-distribution in the spheres of social security, education and consumption is not very impressive.[388] The mere correlation of indicators may support this hypothesis. But if the organizational power of unions and the conflicts in the political sphere are taken into consideration in Western Europe, at least the activities of the unions are still one of the most important factors which account for the degree of development of the welfare state.[389]

In most countries the unions support a reform policy in many areas. However, it cannot be taken that they can easily be mobilized for any valuable measure of reform. There have been issues where despite their progressive verbal assurances they have been rather a retrogressive factor. This has been especially apparent in policy areas where the status quo of jobs was affected, in environment policy, structural policy (rationalization measures) and labour market policy (for example where there have been attempts to stop overtime, treat foreign workers more generously during recessions, etc.). The recognizable increasing segmentation of the labour market has often been furthered by well organized unions with the result that the well organized workers have shrugged off on to the lesser privileged groups (foreign workers, women, less well organized occupational groups) the costs of crises.

II

The Unions' External Relations in the System of Labour Relations

3

Conflict and Strike Behaviour by the Unions

Unions in the real sense of the word have always been dependent on militancy to achieve their aims to an extent that other interest groups do not need to be. They have had to compensate for their legal and political weakness with unity in conflict. Strike was a recognized means of conflict right through to the Christian unions and the national workers' associations, as long as these were not sworn to 'economic peace' (cf. Chapter 1, 1). According to the extent of ideological fragmentation, the legal or political position of the unions, their relation to parties, the state of economic development of the various countries and the political culture, however, very different conflict patterns developed. So far no uniform theory has been evolved to explain these conflict patterns and it does not seem likely that a theory which will hold good for every country ever can be developed.

1. THEORIES OF STRIKE BEHAVIOUR

Conflict and strike behaviour has so far proved to be the most fruitful area of union studies for theory. It lends itself most readily to the use of formalized and quantitative data. Theories of bilateral monopoly, which economists have most frequently used, have not proved very fruitful, because the artificial cutback in the labour supply through strikes can always be only temporary.[390]

America has produced the largest number of theories on strike behaviour. As political motives have played a smaller role there than in Europe, economically-oriented theories of collective bargaining have predominated. These attempts were not copied in Germany until the work of Külp and others in the sixties, when 'labour economics' began to establish itself as an independent branch of economics. Until then the explanation of strike behaviour had largely been left to Socialist theory, which was mainly political in orientation. Various hypotheses were developed to explain strike behaviour:

(a) Strike as a Means of Class War

The old liberal political economy — Adam Smith, for instance — did not use the word 'strike' and the phenomenon was rejected because wages were conceived over the longer term as the expression of a natural price level (the result of competition). Even unions were largely regarded as dysfunctional. John Stuart Mill was the first to assess unions and strikes positively provided that they affected only a small number of workers and a local labour market. Under pressure from Marxist political economy the older economics was forced to concern itself with the strike behaviour of the 'coalitions'. The Socialists and even those who felt themselves to be Marxists did not, however, develop a uniform explanation of strikes. Many of the early attempts are rather in the form of imperatives than the beginnings of explanations which would lead to a theory. For Marx and Engels strikes would 'remove competition among workers and enable them to enter into general competition with the employers' (MEW — *Collected works of Marx and Engels*, published by the Institut für Marxismus-Leninismus in East Berlin, Vol. 4, p. 180). The workers can only become a 'class for itself' in conflict, but the battle is largely political and not just economic. According to this concept strikes mainly serve two purposes:

(1) The creation of *class consciousness*.

> The workers have to protest as long as they have not lost all human feeling, and if they protest thus and in no other way, that is because they are Englishmen, practical people, who protest with action, unlike the theoretical Germans who go peacefully to bed as soon as their protest has been properly recorded and put in the files, where it can sleep as peacefully as they do themselves (MEW, Vol. 2, p. 436).

(2) A *training school for workers' militancy*: strikes were regarded by Engels as preliminary skirmishes in the social war. 'They decide nothing, but they are the surest proof that the decisive battle between the bourgeoisie and the proletariat is approaching' (MEW, Vol. 2, p. 441). Marx repeatedly warned against letting strikes become an end in themselves, indeed he regarded them as having failed if they were limited to 'petty warfare against the effects of the existing system, instead of attempting to change it' (MEW, Vol. 16, p. 152).

These warnings were necessary because in France especially, there was a trend in Socialism to mystify strikes in the 'social war', it can be found in variants of syndicalism up to Sorel. On the one hand unions were regarded as the 'school for Socialism', on the other it was concluded that they could only be 'the baby talk of the working class''. In the ideological war Marx and Engels took a stand between positions such as that of Lassalle, according to whose 'iron law' strikes were largely meaningless, and that of the Anarchists (especially the Bakuninists), who glorified strikes as a means of direct progression to Socialism. Engels poured biting scorn on the Bakuninist view, because it was insufficiently based on organization theory.

> In the Bakuninist programme the general strike is the lever to bring about the Socialist revolution. One fine day all the workers in a country or even maybe throughout the world will stop work and force the wealthy classes in at most four weeks either to give in or attack the workers, who in turn will have the right to defend themselves and so can overturn the whole of the old society. The proposal is far from being new: French and Belgian Socialists have been riding that horse since 1848, but the horse is of English descent (MEW, Vol. 18, p. 479).

According to Engels the results of this view of political strike were opportunist programme changes, the fragmentation of revolutionary means of conflict and finally a chance for the opposing side to stamp the movement out rapidly.

So Marx and Engels had a sharper eye for the problems of organization than their opponents. Even though the syndicalists did not (as Engels sarcastically supposed) imagine that the workers would wake up one morning and take common action, they did underestimate the passivity and resistance in their own ranks. The great defeats in general strikes were later to prove the Marxists right. During the British general strike of 1926 the Labour Party leaders opposed the strike because they were afraid that it would cost them parliamentary successes on the road to Socialism.[391] Some of the union leaders, who were at first in favour, turned against the strike when it seemed likely to lead to mass stoppages and other unionists refused right from the start to take part, as a theatre revue later remarked:[392]

COOK: I am the miners' king,
The General Strike's the thing.
THOMAS: I am the railway tsar,
The General Strike I bar.

Despite the dominant position of Marx and Engels in the 1st International these delimitations did not solve the problem of strikes for the international labour movement. The mass strikes of 1891-3 in Belgium caused a heated controversy in the 2nd International. The supporters of a political general strike referred to Marx or like Sorel tried to draw a distinction between themselves and Marx in a strategic area, without querying his whole socio-economic analysis.[393] Although the Central European Socialists and unionists who dominated many points in the 2nd International were inclined to reject the idea of a general strike as 'revolutionary gymnastics' (Pannekoek)[394] even they had to make concessions to syndicalist ideas of conflict, for instance at the Mannheim SPD Congress, which wanted to make mass strike action dependent on the agreement of the central party leadership and the unions.[395] In the reasons for his resolution Bebel demanded certain prerequisites for general strikes and sharpened the Jena resolution, which had been called an 'attack on the general franchise': 'Now I am not going to explain that, if an attack is being planned on the general franchise, or if the workers are to lose their right to form coalitions, there can be no question of whether we want to, we have to'.[396] Legien on the other hand saw in this verbal compromise only 'a concession to anarcho-Socialism' which as the SPD knew very well would in the foreseeable future have no real political significance in Germany.[397]

Between the *Attentismus* of the Kautsky wing and the spontaneity of the syndicalist view of the intellectual labour movement intermediary positions developed, like those of Rosa Luxemburg. On the one hand she opposed generalizations from the experience of the Russian general strikes of 1905 and warned against the idea that a mass strike could be a single or unique act, but on the other she opposed a set of rules as to which tactics should be employed on what occasions, for: 'A mass strike is only the external form of a revolutionary struggle...and any shift in the relation of the combattant forces...will immediately affect a thousand invisible hardly controllable means of strike action'. Her language became almost lyrical over the ubiquity of strike action: 'It will flow like a broad wave over the whole of the Reich, spreading in a vast network of smaller rivers; it will burst forth from the ground like a fresh spring and then trickle back into the earth again'.[398]

Bernstein's revisionist position on the other hand developed a strike theory which is still characteristic of most Social Democrat movements today. Strike as a means of Socialist transformation was rejected. Strike was only to be an auxiliary to the greater use of parliamentary procedure and democratization of the system or a means of defence to ward off attacks by the 'reactionary forces' on the general franchise, the basic rights and above all the freedom to coalition. This opened the way for the view that daily conflict should not be derived from a comprehensive theory of class war but would have to be explained by bourgeois negotiation theories, whereby non-Marxist economics only retained a sense of the political components of labour conflicts in exceptional cases, as in that of the 'legal' Marxist, Tugan-Baranovsky.[399] For Bernstein strike was a transition phenomenon. Political strikes seemed to him a means to complete political democracy, but industrial strikes should still play a part in the extension of industrial democracy even after the democratization of the political system.

In the 2nd International the Central European attitude to strikes more or less dominated. Both the radicals among the Russian Social Democrats and the revisionists voted against the syndicalist resolutions from the French and Italian representatives. When the subject of a general strike was being debated at the International Socialist Congress in Paris in 1900 the German reporter Legien could only remark ironically: 'In the commission we did not have long debates as there were a lot of unionists there'. The London resolution on general strikes of 1896 was repeated: 'The Congress regards strikes and boycotts as a necessary means of achieving the aims of the working class but does not see any possibility of an international general strike'.[400] In 1904 at the Amsterdam Congress a resolution which had been accepted by the commission from the Dutch was discussed:

> In consideration that the necessary prerequisite for the success of a mass strike is a strong organization and voluntary discipline by the workers, the Congress regards an absolute general strike in the sense that everyone stops work as not feasible because it would make life impossible, for the proletariat as well.[401]

The attitude of the delegations was in a sense linked with their attitude to parliament and cooperation in bourgeois coalition governments. The Dutchman Vliegen actually argued that 'the idea of a general strike which is apparently new. . .is from the early years of our movement, from twenty years ago, when we were still quarrelling about participating in parliament'. Henriette Roland-Holst, who published the first comprehensive analysis of the attitude of Socialists to strikes in 1905 with an approving foreword by Kautsky, regarded the preference for a general strike as due to 'opposition to parliament on the part of a working class which is already Socialist in its ideas but not consciously Social Democratic', and rightly regarded a general anti-party feeling as leading to the concept of a general strike.[402]

Not only the relation to parliament and party organization but the organizational strength of the union movement itself were regarded as decisive in this debate. While Briand had still argued at the Paris Congress of 1900 that the general strike was a premium for general union organization and would further the integration and centralization of the labour movement,[403] the supporters of the idea of a general strike had now to submit to the reproach of being Utopian precisely because they were so fragmented and weak. 'Does the idea of a general strike come from the strong organizations in Germany, England or Denmark? No, it comes from France and Holland, where the union movement is very weak, and from Russia, where unions are forbidden altogether (quite right!)'.[404] The overwhelming majority supported the doubts that had been expressed over a general strike and apart from most of the French delegates only marginal organizations in Russia (the Russian Social Democrats voted against!), in Japan and in Switzerland voted for it.

Neither the idea of a general strike nor the Marxist explanation of strikes as a subsidiary weapon in the class war were adequate to explain the larger part of the conflict phenomena in labour relations. As the influence of Communist wings increased in the period between the wars the Marxist explanation seemed to gain in importance. But it appeared that the Communist parties and their allies the unions could hardly afford to keep using the strike weapon for political agitation.[405] After the Second World War the Marxist theory had little applicability until the second half of the sixties and it has only been reintroduced more into the discussion since then through new variants of union conflict theory. Many of the enthusiastic conflict prognoses since 1968/9 were, however, again proved to be over-hasty generalizations in the mid-seventies.

(b) Strikes as a Function of the Economic Cycle

When bourgeois economics abandoned its former abstinence with regard to unions and conflict phenomena, it began to examine strike behaviour largely in its dependence on economic indicators. At first neither the economic indicators nor the strike statistics were sufficiently reliable. Pioneering work in this field of research was done by Alvin Hansen, whose hypothesis on strike behaviour was that the number of those on strike will grow with the boom and drop with the recession.[406] This hypothesis still plays a large part in union publications, although it has been questioned or at least made relative to particular periods by Theodor Levitt and Andrew R. Weintraub.[407]

Improvements have also been made to the indicators used. Ross and Hartmann refined the usual material, 'the number of strikes', 'length of strikes' and 'number on strike', in order to be able to test organizational variables such as 'union members as a percentage of those not employed in agriculture' and 'number of those on strike as a percentage of total union membership' and the role of the unions better. Despite this the relative peace during the reconstruction phase in Germany after the war led them to confirm that there was a general reduction in the militancy of unions and to forecast that this was due to the increase in nationalized enterprises and state guidance in the economy, to social policy and state activity in arbitration.[408]

Later studies, which followed Ross and Hartmann in many typologies also established 'secular' trends, but these did not affect the general reduction in strikes. It could simply be shown that in comparison with the rising wave of conflict towards the end of the nineteenth and beginning of the twentieth centuries there had been a relative decline after the Second World War. It could also be shown that strikes were generally shorter while the number on strike was rising.[409] With the growing concentration in industry and increasing organization on the part of the unions as a countermeasure this is hardly surprising.

Since the increase in militant union policy in the second half of the sixties the quietist evolution theories have experienced a renaissance. A team in the Frankfurt Institut für Sozialforschung worked on German material with an adaptation of the Hansen hypothesis. Their study came to the conclusion that wage conflicts on a larger scale occurred mainly in phases of cyclical downswing (1962/63, 1967, 1971). Their studies of the cycle showed that there had been real wage rises in the third and fifth growth phases in the Federal Republic which were above the rise in productivity. 'Over-corrections' instead of adjustment, however, were the result of acute wage lags which were a feature of most of the boom phases in the Federal Republic.[410] The modification of older theses such as Hansen's was that the intensification of the conflict and the resultant wage adjustments usually came only after the peak of the cycle had been passed. It appeared, however, that these over-corrections were not due simply to the intensification of union militancy as older correlation studies generally assumed. The over-correction in the Federal Republic in 1961/62 was rather the result of a shortage of labour (the end of the supply of labour from the GDR and fewer foreign workers, who accounted for only 2.4% in 1961) and in 1969 it was the result of spontaneous strikes, which then forced the unions to abandon the restraint they had practised during the Coalition and the first big recession.

These country studies do not claim to offer a general causality between cyclical movements and the frequency of strikes. That can only come from comparative studies over a longer period of time. Weintraub and others realized that more detailed studies were necessary but recognized the methodological difficulties of these. In 1971 one author was still very pessimistic about the use of the cyclical hypothesis altogether in the Federal Republic because the country had an 'almost unbroken boom and was also a-typical in having very few strikes, so that statements on phase features were extremely problematic'.[411]

(c) Strikes in their Dependence on Subjective Factors in the Life of the Workers

A number of theses were based on subjective factors in the lives of the workers without attempting to explain all strike behaviour in this way. The aim was more limited, concentrating on the average seasonal distribution of strikes throughout the year. The explanations produced on this basis were:

(1) The seasonal influence. However, climatic influences are not the same in the various countries. There is even a difference between the seasonal movements in France and the USA. The main strike activity in France is not so clearly concentrated in the Spring, it begins a little earlier (about March). There are more strikes in the Autumn than in America and sometimes, although not always,

Figure 1
Seasonal pattern of strike activity

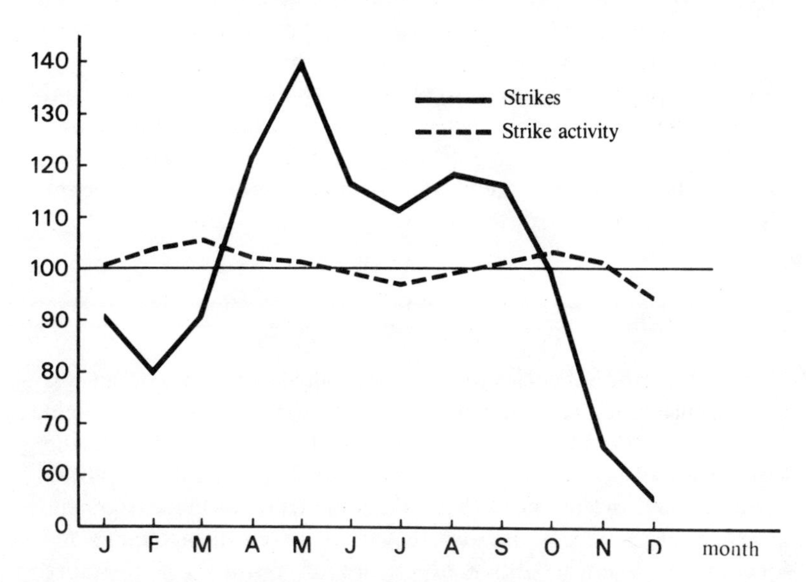

Source: Dale Yoder: 'Seasonality in Strikes', *Quarterly Publication of the American Statistical Association,* 1938, pp. 687-693.

these are more intense than those in the Spring.[412] For the UK it has been shown that March is replacing October as the seasonal peak of strike activities.[413]

(2) One variant of the seasonal hypothesis explains the increase in strikes by the workers' cash position. The evidence for this is not very convincing — it is based on the relative lack of strikes during the holiday period and before Christmas. When social activity by the state is being expanded any hypothesis is bound to become increasingly questionable if it only considers individual consumption by the workers and leaves social consumption out of consideration. However, considerations of social consumption should not tempt to the other extreme, the assumption that is sometimes made that the number of strikes increases with the growth of the social state because there is less risk of loss of income for the individual. If this were so strike activity should correlate with the growth of social expenditure but it does not.[414] Other factors in the lives of the workers do not offer very convincing explanations for strike behaviour.

(3) For the USA it has also been argued that militancy depends on the age of the workers. A lower average age is said to make for greater militancy.[415] This hypothesis has so far not been systematically tested if only because it is easiest to obtain comparative data on the age of members from the least militant unions. However, there is reason to suppose that such unconditional statements are unreliable: when there is greater youth unemployment, as was the case in many countries in Europe with the expansion of the education system after the mid-seventies, the statement is probably simply wrong.

(d) Organization Theories

The organization theories were to overcome the political deficits of the cyclical theories. One of the oldest hypotheses in this field assumes that the age of a union and its membership trend affect the frequency of strikes. American scientists (Kerr, Ira Cross, John Griffin) have often argued that young unions strike more frequently than older unions because they have to create an image for themselves, want to obtain experience in conflict and are more strongly convinced of their ideology. Old unions are more often content with the threat of strikes and unions which are not militant often justify their attitude by pointing to the success of these tactics. So the hypothesis may be right, but it is becoming increasingly less relevant because there are hardly any new unions now in Europe. On the contrary, there is a remarkable process of concentration and shrinkage (cf. Chapter 1, 4). There are still radical groups, Maoists and Trotskyists, for example, who occasionally experiment with unions of their own but these are not successful and the present tactics of these groups is deliberately aimed against the experiment of a 'red union opposition' (cf. Chapter 1, 1). Old unions may be brought down by re-politicization and protest movements in periods of hectic militancy, as was apparent in the case of the CGT and CGIL and a progressive linear debility is not apparent even in the DGB or the Swedish LO. Among the organizational factors the centralization of a union is significant as has often been shown. The higher the degree of centralization and the more participation the head office has been able to achieve in conflicts, the less frequent are strikes.[416]

(e) Strikes and Finances

The financial strength of unions has little influence on the frequency of strikes (cf. Chapter 1, 8). The richest unions, like the LO in Sweden and the DGB, have had the lowest frequency since the war. The LO grants financial aid to affiliated unions involved in open conflicts, provided that the strike was duly authorized. The main financial burden, however, as in most countries, falls on the unions. The LO does not enter until the strike has lasted for some time. The regulations differ. The Metal Workers Union entitles its members to benefits from the union from the seventh day after their entry into the conflict. The LO's expenses for supporting strikers in the seventies varied from only 36,444 kroner (in 1974) to 252,008 kroner in 1972.[417]

In countries where strikes are frequent, like Great Britain, most are so spontaneous and short-term that they would not qualify for support under continental rules. In the TUC, budget expenditure on strikes rarely accounts for more than one-tenth of total expenditure per member. This, however, is still considerably higher than the German proportion, which is between 4.5% and 7% of income from membership fees.[418] In Britain strikers usually cannot claim benefits until they have been out for at least two weeks.[419] Sixty-three unions in the TUC have formal strike rules and strike benefit rules, most of them lay down a set amount of benefit for officially sanctioned stoppages.[420] De facto the unions seem to have considerable discretion to decide how much to pay. They decide whether to sanction spontaneous disputes and vary the rate of payments according to the state of their funds. Since 1968 the unions have paid out between £1.1 million (1968) and £5.5 million (1972). The average appears to be about £3 million per annum. With the increasing duration of strikes the amount of strike benefits is going up. For the individual worker strike benefits usually amount to less than 10% of adult male manual earnings, one of the reasons why state subsidies to strikers' families in 1971 were already 113 times higher than in 1960, whereas the expenditure of the unions in disputes was only eight and a half times higher over the same period.[421]

On a historical comparison expenses for strike benefits in some countries — especially in Central Europe — have decreased. In Germany strike benefits in 1900 amounted to 34% and in 1913 they were still 17.5% of union expenditure.[422] In its report the Austrian Federation says that only 2.8% of its income went into the strike section of the solidarity fund which must be an international record for economy in strike costs.[423]

What is generally referred to as the 'strike fund' in the Federal Republic is actually, from the accounting point of view, only reserves. Insofar as these are not added to the unions' own funds and trust companies but remain as organizational assets they can be used for strike pay but for other purposes as well, like compensation for losses which DGB unions have also incurred during the last few years (cf. Chapter 1, 7). The strike pay in the unions' budgets covers not only support for strikers but other important items such as support for workers penalized by their bosses and travel costs for activists who are organizing the strike above local level. Only in a few countries is the legal right for members to claim strike pay from their organization contained in the statutes. Even the statutes of most of the German unions only state that support 'can' be given. The Metal Workers Union is one exception, stating that support 'will be given'. The statutes of the Luxembourg LAV are exceptionally detailed. In §11 they state that strike support 'will on principle be two months' contributions per strike day after 6 months membership contributions have been paid, but as a minimum 200 francs'. The claim begins after the third day on strike, as in Germany.[424]

As the head associations are not usually responsible for settling this question they can only try to obtain uniform practice by issuing guidelines. Two principles have emerged among the DGB unions:

(1) Voluntary support, which usually excludes a legal claim. The guidelines make support dependent on approval of the strike by the main board of the union; and

(2) Dependence on membership fees. Despite the strong emphasis on solidarity among unions the amount of support depends on the length and amount of the membership fees, which is actually a concession to the 'insurance principle' which the unions do not support in state social policy.

The fact that support is becoming increasingly more regulated in detail has certainly not increased strike frequency. But if there is no correlation between the unions' finances and their militancy one cannot — as left-wing literature occasionally does — draw the opposite conclusion: it is a gross over-simplification to suggest that the German and Swedish unions strike so seldom simply in order not to draw on their accumulated funds.

There is growing opposition to the increase in strike benefits from two wings. Conservative circles in many countries resent the fact that the state is meeting living expenses for strikers' families, even in the United States, where the social system is less state directed than in many European countries. As an alternative to indirect state support to strikers the exploration of possibilities to establish strike insurance programmes with private insurance companies has been proposed.[425] Left-wing circles, on the other hand, even in Britain, Germany and Sweden, are developing a kind of nostalgia for the anarcho-syndicalist tradition of the Latin countries where the development of strikes remains in the hands of strikers themselves and is not manipulable by strike benefits from the unions and/or the state.

(f) Theories of Collective Bargaining

Theories of collective bargaining only developed after recognition by the parties concerned of each other's status, and recognition of both by the state as autonomous factors. This did not happen in Germany until 1919 (Article 157 of the Weimar Constitution). As long as the unions rejected wage agreements there was no basis for such theories. It was not until 1873 that the first wage agreement in Germany was concluded by the Typographers Union.[426]

It was a foreigner who first raised the question in German literature of the non-economic factors determining wages, a Russian, Michael Tugan-Baranovsky.[427] In his view a kind of political equilibrium wage develops between productivity and the existential minimum. However, in his eyes the working class is clearly at a disadvantage in the process of political bullying (strike-lock-out) because technical developments are constantly making labour superfluous and monopolization is giving companies organizational advantages. This imperfect balance entails increasing intervention by the state if the system is to remain stable. Tugan-Baranovsky clearly here had mainly Great Britain in mind. The development he outlined, however, occurred more quickly later in some continental countries. According to his theory the state has to legislate to prevent wages dropping below a certain minimum and as a reformist Socialist he actually approved this. However, it was clear to him that his hopes of increasing political determination of wages would make him enemies of all the theorists of a purely economic wage movement, the Marxists no less than the school of 'marginal benefiters'. In his theory the role of strikes remained relatively unclear. From some of his remarks one can assume that state intervention would lessen the importance of strikes. The hope that strikes might become obsolete as the system matured was expressed in many variations in the English-speaking countries.

John Hicks developed a theory of strikes as operating accidents of collective negotiations. To cut down these 'accidents' he suggests that contact between the bargaining partners should be as formalized as possible in order to prevent unexpected interruptions to the negotiations. However, Hicks already saw that there might be other reasons for strikes, for instance the unions' need to keep in training, or differences over negotiation policy between the leaders and members. He assumed that a large number of strikes occurred against the wishes of the leaders because the members' aims were more far-reaching.[428] The primary explanation of strikes as a weapon used with rational calculation in the battle to maximize incomes had considerable faults. If incomes were the decisive factor the worst-off groups should strike most frequently. However, the opposite is the case.[429]

More recent attempts have regarded the expected length of the strike as decisive for the amount conceded by the employers and thus led to the political explanation through the back door of mainly economic considerations regarding wage development.[430] All the hypotheses which operate with income calculations are in any case questionable because they can never do justice to the complexity of the motives of strikers. A whole number of reasons for strikes can never be explained by the aim to maximize incomes:[431]

(1) Strikes which are risked by the unions to strengthen the loyalty of members. Strikes are used by unions like any other mass campaigns by other associations to prove that the organization is active or, as an American lobbyist once remarked with regard to relatively unsuccessful mass campaigns: '. . . it's mostly to keep the membership happy'.[432]

(2) There can be another secondary motive, again not concerning the opponents but the members and a potential group of members: strikes can be used by the leaders if the possibility of achieving their aim, raising wages, does not seem very good. The strike lets the members see for themselves how large or small the room for negotiation is. Strikes can ultimately serve to re-direct a certain pressure from the left.[433]

(3) In the eyes of militant union leaders strikes also serve to strengthen class consciousness. Among the opponents of the unions this motive is often seen as a ritual confirmation of class differences. It does not play an equally large part in every country. Where the union leaders are not very militant and the political culture as in Switzerland or Sweden has an old tradition of peaceful negotiation, this kind of mobilization would hardly be possible. English and American researchers have shown little understanding for the 'mystical quality' which strikes have in the eyes of the workers in the Latin countries. In strike literature all kinds of emanations of national characteristics are deduced, as in this remark from one recent comparative study: 'In Germany the strike is always the last resort, in Italy it is the first'.[434]

(4) Strikes may also be addressed to the general public, or the state, to demonstrate the fighting strength of the organization and mobilize external allies to influence the employers to put a quick

end to the conflict. In addition to these aims, however, union leaders can be driven by their employers to further militancy. The aims of the employers can be:

(5) To discredit the unions in public by mobilizing prejudices.

(6) To provoke a strike in order to be able to introduce short-time (in a difficult economic situation).

(7) To provoke the strike at a time when it suits them (if they expect a strike once a year anyway as part of the ritual of negotiation).

Most negotiation theories of strikes derive from the American experience. Unions are associations of suppliers of labour on the market who are tough negotiators and pursue no aims other than the optimization of their incomes. Moreover, they incline to a model of élite pluralism. The negotiations of the wage partners at élite level are decisive. The will of members is not even sufficiently considered as a disturbance factor. These theories are often combined with functionalist attempts at social analysis founded on concepts of balance and considerations regarding the maintenance of the system. The continental and especially the German variant of this view is that the struggle will always be moved more from the social to the state sphere. The state as administrator of the common well-being has to ensure that the means used are socially adequate (by forbidding wild-cat strikes etc.). Attempts at systems theory look as far as possible for permanent solutions which exclude conflict.[435]

The recognition of the complexity of the motives for strikes and the influence of many factors has sharpened the perception of economists for the fact that wage conflicts cannot well be treated as part of the game theory, as was occasionally attempted in America. In games it is clearly defined who wins and who loses. It is easier to establish this even in wars than in wage conflicts. Almost all labour disputes end with a settlement above the previous wage level. So one can say that unions 'in this case by definition are among the winners'.[436] That may be so over the short-term, as long as the extent to which the wage increase will be passed on in prices, the development of profits and the general rate of inflation is not yet certain. It is only over the longer period that it is really possible to say who wins.

(g) Differentiated Partial Theories

All these theories will explain conflict behaviour in certain countries at certain times. But none has yet proved adequate to establish a general theory. The more data was used the more union researchers became aware that explanations of the cycles of militancy are dependent on numerous variables and cannot simply be isolated. On the contrary, they must be analyzed configuratively which means that the whole is more than the sum of the parts, sharply as this principle of functionalist explanation has been attacked by some theorists (e.g. by Carl G. Hempel).

Generalizations on an international comparison have proved problematic: either types were established which appeared to cover conflict behaviour in several countries, or national studies were placed side by side, with even their data bases broken down according to differences which may well distort many a cross-national comparison:

(1) Differences between *function groups* in working life. The conflict behaviour of employees (white collar workers) and civil servants may be similar to that of workers (cf. Chapter 1, 3) but the degree to which these groups are mixed in the hierarchy is still highly influential today.

(2) Differences in the distribution of *forms of ownership*. These can be decisive. If there is a large nationalized industry, as in Great Britain or Italy, militancy under overall market economy conditions is rather greater than in the private sector. It remains to be seen how conflict behaviour would develop under Socialist conditions with free constitution of labour relations. There has hardly been a chance to test this. Even Yugoslavia only permits strike law under compulsion.

(3) The *spread of industry* in the various economies usually determines the extent of the conflict. Here there are relatively easily comparable results and generalizations can be made, such as:

— There are usually fewer strikes in shrinking industries than in expanding ones (e.g. mining and textiles).

— The greatest number of strikes are in medium-sized enterprises (and the size of the enterprise proved to be largely a variable which is dependent on the industry). It is more difficult to coordinate and lead a strike both in small companies and big ones. Where most of the companies are small, as in New Zealand, this rather than the legal basis of labour relations and compulsory arbitration (cf. Chapter 4, 1) has kept the number of strikes relatively low in comparison with that in other English-speaking countries with a similarly fragmented union organization.

— Militancy is relatively strong in industries where the workers form a comparatively homogeneous group, are comparatively isolated from society as a whole and so develop greater solidarity among themselves. However, it becomes more difficult to demonstrate their conflict potential if the workers are very isolated or, conversely, if they are fully integrated (the extreme case is the agricultural workers).[437] However, no conclusions can be drawn from the degree of concentration in an economy as to the frequency of strikes. Small countries which export a considerable share of their production develop a relatively high degree of concentration, as we see in Sweden and Switzerland. Both of these countries are at the bottom end of the strike statistics while countries like France or Italy, which are at the top of the list, are at the bottom of the concentration statistics.[438] It has actually been argued that economies with a high degree of specialization and concentration have produced a high degree of centralization in wage negotiation (cf. Chapter 1, 4) and that this is directly responsible for the reduction in the frequency of strikes.[439] That may seem plausible if the comparison is between Great Britain and Scandinavia, but then one must ask why the situation in Canada, which is similar in concentration of industry to that in Sweden, has not had an equally soothing effect on labour relations, and conversely, why Germany has experienced such a high degree of industrial peace, when it is at the lower end of the concentration scale. In any case we do not yet have reliable figures on the degree of specialization in production which could be correlated with data on strikes.

(4) *Regional peculiarities* should also be taken into account in any comparison: militancy is by no means proportional to objective assessments of the extent to which the group may be underprivileged, as can be seen in the industrial concentration areas today, which were once the pace-setters of the class war and have now lost this position in many capitalist countries: 'Although incomes there are low, unionization is high, living conditions are bad and there is a high proportion of workers among the population, all the big unions avoid wage conflicts in the Ruhr, most of all the traditional union in the area, the Mining and Energy Union'.[440] The ex-

planation that is usually offered for this, that the workers there have deeply absorbed the old employers' maxim 'What's good for the Ruhr is good for Germany', is hardly adequate. It can hardly be coincidence that North Baden and North Württemberg, where the expansion industries have moved to, are generally the first to develop militancy in industrial relations. The 'genius loci' is not the whole explanation. Great Britain shows a similar decrease of industrial disputes in the old strongholds of mining.

(5) Since Ross variables of the *political and legal systems*, which are hardly suited to quantification, have increasingly been drawn into the analyses[441] and political scientists are especially interested in relations such as:

— The influence of centralization and decentralization in the structure of the state. The hypothesis that federal states are less able to limit labour disputes may be plausible for Canada, Australia and the USA. But the Federal Republic, Austria and Switzerland show that federal systems can certainly produce quiet labour relations.

— The extent of legalization (cf. Chapter 4, 1) of labour relations.

— The type of cooperation between the unions and the party. This certainly has an influence, although Great Britain disproves the old assumption that close relations between the party and the unions will minimize labour disputes (cf. Chapter 4, 2). Recent empirical comparisons found evidence that left-wing parties and governments relying upon symbolic, electorally expedient appeals to political solidarity, which are not accompanied by tangible rewards to labour have had little success in discouraging working-class militancy. Strike frequency hardly correlated with the growth of labour parties and the frequency they are in power, but rather with the growth of Communist parties which remain important agencies for the mobilization of the workers.[442]

Better results can be achieved from international comparisons if the types of strike behaviour are differentiated, in three important aspects:

(1) types of conflict which are found in particular countries and derive from the description of certain national peculiarities;

(2) a relation between conflict behaviour and wage development — a kind of input-output analysis of conflict;

(3) consideration of the various types of strike especially in terms of the reaction of the legal system. More recent analyses have

shown that the results obtained on the basis of rough and easily accessible variables, such as 'the length of the strike', become increasingly insignificant if the forms of the conflict are not also classified, of which the length of the strike has increasingly become a function.[443]

2. TYPES OF CONFLICT BEHAVIOUR

Certain types of interest realization correspond to the types of national political cultures. However, there are no unchanging national characteristics which will explain this, as sometimes seems to be the assumption in uncritical statements on national unions. The types of interest articulation are acquired, as are those of conflict, and they can be changed under pressure of circumstances.

While the conflict types appeared to be relatively similar up to the Second World War, differences have now appeared. Three types can be distinguished for capitalist systems:

(1) *The West European type*, which is characterized by a large number of strikes which are relatively widespread, but usually relatively short. Great Britain is an exception to this, as the shop steward system and the strong decentralization of negotiation power makes the strikes rather short. But the duration of strikes has increased during recent years in Britain. The shop steward system has often been made responsible for the frequency of strikes, but a study carried out by the Department of Employment in 1976 revealed that 98% of all plants in manufacturing industry are strike-free during any one year.[444]

The frequency of strikes and the special problems of Britain have been debated more vehemently than those of any other country. Against the assumptions of the Donovan Report and of 'In Place of Strife', H. A. Turner showed in international comparisons that Britain is less strike-prone than many other countries.[445] A comparison of figures alone will hardly settle the matter.[446] The fact remains that it is not so much the frequency of strikes but the effectiveness of the bargaining system and its consequences for inflation that is causing one of Britain's major problems and again and again calls are heard for neo-corporatist strategy to achieve some kind of social contract (cf. Chapter 3, 3).[447]

In the Western European type of conflict behaviour political motives play an important part in addition to distribution policy. Strikes in the form of symbolic action or in order to exert pressure on political bodies are usual. However, this type requires further differentiation. It is not only in Great Britain where there are particular patterns. The smaller Western European countries have divergent traits as well and these have not been sufficiently taken into account in the broad typologies which may seem plausible from a wide perspective, particularly in American literature. Special features of the political culture combine with a strong institutionalization of wage policy in some countries, especially Austria and the Netherlands. In systems with a strongly pillared union sub-culture there are often important groups which object strongly to strikes as a means of conflict. This was the case for many years with the Protestant unions in the Netherlands.[448] In any case strikes have a negative image in that country as they have in other consociational democracies with an inclination to *amicabilis compositio* in public opinion.[449]

(2) *The Northern European type*, which is predominant in countries where the Social Democrats are influential and there is a long tradition of direct negotiation with political bodies (Scandinavia, the Federal Republic). The statement by the former President of the LO in Sweden, Gejer, that a strike is not proof of union militancy but of failure in negotiation, is typical of the attitude of union leaders here. In these systems of industrial relations the number of strikes is low but they are widespread. Sweden is a certain exception: in contrast to countries in Central Europe strikes here last a long time. Quantitative correlation analyses have also produced hypotheses on the influence of the length of the strike on wage increases. A recent study on Australia has shown that the frequency of strikes, but not their length, has influenced wage development.[450] But this conclusion cannot be applied to other countries. In Sweden significant wage increases were often achieved only after particularly long and wearisome strikes. So the usual correlation analyses are questionable on an international comparison if they are not seen in relation to the dominant strike pattern in various groups of countries.

It has become a commonplace of left-wing union criticism that the German unions are very moderate in their demands and in the implementation of them. But sometimes hasty conclusions are drawn from the low frequency of strikes in Germany. The execution of a threat is not the only stage in a conflict which should be assessed. The phrase attributed to Theodor Heuss, 'the sword on the wall', has often led to the wrong conclusions and the unions have been misinterpreted as purely 'insurance' institutions against strikes and lock-outs.[451] The pre-negotiations, the estimation of the employers' position and the counter-strategy of the unions should all be included in the analysis. In addition to 'quietism' other factors could play a part in the relative infrequency of strikes:

(a) The relatively high degree of solidarity among the German unions, which are not torn by ideological strife and do not usually develop leadership neuroses against each other during a strike, as is often the case among the unions in France and Italy, where political motives outweigh economic factors and go further to explain the militancy than the less highly developed counter-power of the employers or a basis of healthy strike funds. As the German unions are not so fragmented their actions can be more easily coordinated from the centre and they can break up the employers' front or at least make their calculations more difficult by organizing warning strikes and strikes concentrated on particular spots.

(b) The relative lack of solidarity among the employers, who fear strikes in individual plants and believe that their high dependence on exports makes them particularly vulnerable to strikes. What Bernhard Külp called 'conjectural strike power' must be taken into consideration. The employers' awareness that the German unions could very easily put their threats into practice as they are fairly unified and have the financial strength to withstand a strike has often been enough to get the unions what they wanted.[452] Efforts to encourage the employers to adopt more rational counter-plans, for instance by suggesting that a strike would not be as damaging as they fear have not proved very effective.[453] But the argument that the solidarity of the employers is further jeopardized by the enterprises under union control is certainly an exaggeration. Even in countries where the unions own a quarter of the enterprises private capital has not been jeopardized (cf. Israel).

(c) A simple comparison of strike figures will not yield definitive conclusions, these must be correlated with what the unions actually achieved in each individual case. Wage increases are of course a major indicator, but they are not the only one, and it must be remembered that the aims of the German unions (especially with regard to co-determination and asset formation policy) differ from those of unions in other Western democracies.

(d) The number of actual strikes is an objective indicator of the militancy of groups but the subjective indicator of the *approval of strikes* as a means of achieving the interests of the group must also be considered. As even the Federation of German Employers Associations (BDA) had to admit, there has been a slight, though hardly spectacular, increase in approval of strikes among the general public: in 1963/64 53% approved strikes and 30% disapproved, while in 1973 57% approved and only 26% disapproved.[454] But these long-term trends can be modified by short-term fluctuations. During the 1974/75 recession the militancy of union members dropped noticeably as the unemployment ratio rose, while the employers toughened their negotiating line to such an extent that it was openly speculated that their aim was to force the unions into a long and useless strike, drain their funds and thus permanently weaken their position.[455]

(3) *The North American type* of union militancy has largely been abstracted in contrast to the Western European type: in the USA and Canada, which is included here, strikes are relatively frequent but they are usually only for economic reasons. Political influence is exerted less through politically motivated strikes than organized lobbying (cf. Chapter 4, 2), as in North America there is not that close relation between the unions and social democracy which is a feature of most of the countries of the Western and Northern European types.[456]

Strikes in the USA tend to be large and mostly constitutional and official. As in Sweden and Germany, in America the unions pride themselves on paying substantial subventions to their members, so that they can afford long strikes. Unlike Sweden and Germany, countries which have large national or at least regional agreements, in America strikes usually involve only one plant, so that the unions can call several official strikes on a small scale without bringing out all the workers in the industry, as in Sweden, or all the workers in one or several regions, as in West Germany.

While generalizations on strike success are hardly possible across the front of national political cultures, quantitative research has been more successful in establishing correlations between factors which exist in all countries: for example, the size of the plant and the success of a strike. While it is often not even possible to establish relations between industries and types of strike (official and wild-cat strikes), it has often been possible to show a relation between the size of the plant and the success of a strike. It appears that medium-sized companies everywhere offer better conditions for strike organization than mammoth concerns or small firms.[457]

3. CONFLICT BEHAVIOUR AND SUCCESS IN WAGE POLICY

Social scientists have undertaken all kinds of more or less useful correlation research. Of decisive strategic-tactical importance for the unions, however, were only analyses on relations between conflict behaviour and union successes, which cannot simply be read off from the wage increases achieved. A prerequisite for these analyses were comparisons of strike statistics. Historical analyses have shown that certain types of conflict pattern stubbornly persist even under changing circumstances (corporatistic-proportionalist institutions) but that the indicator 'strike frequency' does not show a continuous trend. If one looks at countries which are now regarded as centres of union militancy, such as Great Britain, France and Italy, and compared them with countries where a cooperative policy is rather the rule, such as the Federal Republic and Sweden, the groups of countries seem to have almost switched roles after the Second World War (cf. Table 17). A Swedish writer, who produced a standard work on the Swedish labour movement in 1945 and so could not reflect the post-war trend, assumed that the Swedish and German unions were primarily constructed for the purpose of strikes, in contrast to the type of organization in Great Britain.[458] The second column in the table shows that not all the countries which are held to be quietist really deserve the epithet according to all the indicators. Germany, the Netherlands and Sweden have strikes which clearly last longer than those in the so-called militant countries. Ultimately a verdict can only be passed on whether union policy is militant or cooperative when successes in wage policy are calculated.

There are now two variants of the thesis of the lack of function of distribution conflict:

(1) The wage ratio is seen as constant with slight fluctuations, and wage increases obtained above the development of prices and

TABLE 17
Changes in strike frequency in European countries

Country	Strike rate 100,000 workers	Man days lost per striker
Germany		
1900-1929	11.1	15.7
1951-1968	—	5.4
France		
1900-1929	7.8	15.1
1946-1968	12.8	2.3
Great Britain		
1900-1929	3.8	
1911-1929		26.7
1945-1968	9.9	3.4
Italy		
1900-1923	12.1	14.2
1950-1968	18.1	3.3
Netherlands		
1901-1929	13.0	32.0
1945-1968	2.5	5.6
Sweden		
1903-1929	18.0	40.8
1945-1968	1.3	13.5

Source: Edward Shorter and Charles Tilly: *Strikes in France, 1830-1968*. Cambridge University Press, 1974, p. 333.

earnings as ultimately only a short-lived and expensive illusion (cf. Chapter 4, 3, a).

(2) In the literature it is often said that strikes are in no causal relation at all to successes in wage development.[459] Prima vista a comparison of data on strike movements with nominal wage increases would appear to confirm this (cf. Table 18). It is pointed out that countries like Italy and Great Britain, which have the highest strike rates in Europe, have the lowest progress in real incomes and the highest inflation rates, so that success in achieving nominal wage rises is quickly wiped out again. But more careful comparisons show that it is not possible to make definitive statements on this point, and not only because the data from the ILO statistics are not available for a sufficient number of comparable cases among what could be described as cooperative and militant unions.[460]

In academic studies so far attempts have been made to show the ineffectiveness of wage disputes partly through a comparison of industries and partly through comparisons over time. So far, however, all analyses which compared wage rises in strike-prone industries with those in quiet industries have proved extremely problematic.[461] Generally they neglected the spill-over effects of the 'wage round locomotives'. An analysis of the time-lags in wage increases in industries where unionization is low might remove some of the faults of industry comparisons up to now.

Studies of periods when unionization was low (1923-1929) with those of strong organization and greater militancy (1947-1955) have produced better results on the influence of union policy on wages: real hourly wages for industrial workers rose twice as fast in the more militant period. Wage negotiation seems to be rather a ritual, although the author is fully aware of the statistical problems of a study over such limited periods of time. It did not prove possible in these studies to show that other variables could have been equally decisive.[462]

The positive verdict on the influence of union militancy on growth generally refers to the structure of collectively negotiated wages. Wage drift is often seen as the reason why one of the unions' main aims, the levelling of the collective wage structure, is constantly being undermined as the apparent success of the unions in achieving greater uniformity is annulled by the real wages the employers pay, in other words by market forces. Nevertheless, many economists are now inclined, despite wage drift, to regard political factors as one of the main determinants of the wage development.[463]

4. DIFFERENT TYPES OF STRIKE AND VERDICTS ON THEM IN LABOUR LAW

Scarcely any other area of industrial relations has produced so many generalizations as strikes, and the most varied phenomena are grouped under one heading. There are many different aims and motives for strikes. Distinctions are usually drawn between:
— wage strikes;
— strikes over working conditions, appointments and dismissals;
— political strikes.

Some generalizations can be made on the predominance of one or the other of these types:
— wage strikes predominate in countries where the collective negotiating system is not highly developed (France is one example).
— strikes over working conditions, appointments and dismissals are frequent in countries where the employers are in a strong position and the reserve army (immigrants or foreign labour) constantly undermines the negotiating power of the unions (in the USA, for instance). In these countries strikes to achieve union rights, which are a marginal type of political strike, are also frequent. Finally, the reasons for strikes also change with the change in the form of ownership. In public enterprises this type of strike seems to be more frequent than wage strikes.
— political strikes are frequent in countries with a fragmented party and union system, where deficits occur in the representation of aggregate interests by the parties and the unions temporarily enter the breach (as in Italy in 1969).

A further classification is of the involvement of the organization. The main distinction is between official strikes and unofficial or wild-cat strikes.

Where the latter is the dominant type, strikes are usually short and small but frequent, as Ross defined the Western European type in his classification, and in countries where official strikes are the dominant type, as in Sweden and the Federal Republic, we have a pattern which Ross did not group into one type as in Sweden strikes

TABLE 18

The development of strike frequency and nominal wage increases in selected countries

(Column 1: Strikes in 1000 lost working days per year = w.d.l.;
Column 2: Hourly wages in industry = currency p.h.)

Country	1963	1964	1965	1966	1967	1968	1969	1970	1971	1972	1973	1974
Militant unions												
Italy												
w.d.l.	11,395	13,089	6,993	14,474	8,568	9,240	37,825	20,887	14,799	19,497	23,419	19,467
Lire p.h.			400	415	439	459	502	617	712	792	974	1,217
Great Britain												
w.d.l.	1,755	2,277	2,925	2,398	2,787	4,690	6,846	10,980	13,551	23,909	7,197	14,750
Pence p.h.		38,0	41,7	44,1	46,3	49,6	53,4	61,4	69,2	79,6	89,7	107,8
France												
w.d.l.			979,9	2,523	4,203	n.d.	2,223	1,742	4,387	3,755	3,914	3,379
Frs. p.h.			3,06	3,24	3,43	3,83	4,24	4,68	5,17	5,80	6,93	8,24
Cooperative unions												
Denmark												
w.d.l.		23,6	242,1	15,4	9,9	33,6	56,2	102,0	20,6	21,8	3 901,0	184,3
Öre p.h.		880	985	1,104	1,206	1,347	1,510	1,670	1,917	2,149	2,486 486	2,967

Switzerland												
w.d.l.	7,0	4,5	0,1	0,06	1,6	1,7	0,2	2,6	7,4	2,0	—	2,7
Sfrs. p.h.	4,27	4,93	5,28	5,53	6,16	6,53	6,86	7,38	8,25	9,16	10,44	11,96
FRG												
w.d.l.			48,5	27,0	389,5	25,2	249,1	93,2	4,483,7	766,0	563,0	1 051,3
DM p.h.			4,26	4,55	4,69	4,88	5,37	6,09	6,82	7,42	8,23	9,13

Source: Yearbook of Labour Statistics 1975. Geneva, 1975, pp. 601ff., 802ff.

tend to be lengthy and it is only the relative infrequency of strikes that the two countries have in common. The indicator 'spontaneous' is especially important in the distinction between these categories. Simply on a comparison of numbers of strikes, the Federal Republic, even in its quiet period from 1948 to 1969, had 55% spontaneous strikes.[464] In many cases it is a matter of definition whether strikes are spontaneous or wild-cat. Where there are strict legal rules many strikes are labelled as wild-cat strikes (in Sweden and Germany). In France, which prides itself on having the least stringent strike laws,[465] most of the strikes, even if they are unofficial, are lawful and constitutional. In Germany the problem is complicated by the works councils, as they, rather than the unions, are responsible for plant issues. In all the other countries which do not have the German type of dualist structure, the growing tendency to make the plants the centre of bargaining (what is known in Germany as *betriebsnahe Lohnpolitik*) tends to blur the former distinction between spontaneous and official strikes.

This 'labelling approach' is used not only by political actors and the courts in some countries with highly institutionalized labour relations, but even by the unions themselves. In countries such as the USA, Sweden and Germany where unions pay considerable amounts of benefits to strikers, the need for a sharp distinction between official and unofficial strikes is greater. Some generalizations in the comparisons between Germany and Britain are no longer valid in the light of developments in the seventies and the three strike patterns elaborated after Ross need to be modified. In Germany the number of spontaneous and short strikes has increased. In Britain, on the other hand, the number of short strikes has begun to drop but the number of national and official confrontations, especially in the public sector, has risen sharply.[466]

In neo-Marxist literature spontaneous strikes are particularly adulated, even by Moscow-oriented Marxists, regardless of the fact that spontaneous strikes are the only type possible in Socialist countries and even they are threatened with severe repression (most recently in the relatively liberal Poland during the crisis over price increases in 1976). The share of spontaneous strikes does not, however, correlate with general militancy, as can be seen in America and even in the case of individual German unions:

Share of spontaneous strikes in five unions in % (1949-1968)

IG Bau (Construction)	IG Bergbau (Mining)	G. Holz (Wood)	IG Metall (Metal)	G. Textil (Textiles)
34.7	64.5	23.1	78.8	52.8

The latent hypotheses of conflict-oriented union theoreticians, that conservatism on the part of the union leaders towards strikes tends to increase the number of spontaneous strikes, is not altogether wrong for certain crisis periods (1969, 1973 in the Federal Republic), but it cannot be proved on a comparison of individual unions. The high number of spontaneous strikes in the mining industry might perhaps support the argument as the leaders here were conservative. On the other hand, the 'wage round locomotive', the Metal Workers Union, which in Germany is the pace-maker of militancy, also has the largest number of spontaneous strikes.[467]

Finally, the classification of legal and illegal strikes is important. The peculiarities of the political system are especially important because they illustrate the success of the authorities in their attempts to reduce strike frequency with legal means. The state and the employers have tried many means of reducing strikes. There have been three major ways of doing this:

(1) Offering bonuses as an inducement to the unions to keep the peace. In Belgium these can amount to as much as 0.6% of gross earnings[468] (cf. Chapter 1, 7).

(2) Ideological discrimination against strikes. It has been possible, after long waves of strikes, for the government to mobilize public opinion against strikes and force the unions to a quieter policy (this happened in France and Great Britain in 1975). But the supporters of a more militant union policy can produce impressive figures to counter the use of the concept that 'everyone is in the same boat' as a weapon against strikes: in 1968 Great Britain lost 4.7 million working days through strikes but 146 million through unemployment and 324 million through accidents. In France it has been shown that the flu costs many more working days every year than strikes and absenteeism — twenty to thirty times more.[469]

(3) The legal restriction of strikes. Repressive means of stopping

strike movements are in most political systems still the most frequent way of channelling conflicts. In many countries the right to strike was only established after long struggles. It only appears as a constitutional right after the Second World War. The preamble to the Constitution of the 4th French Republic of 1946 and Article 40 of the Italian Constitution of 1947 do not, however, ensure the right to strike unconditionally, in almost identical wording they bind its execution to the 'framework of the law'. In the Federal Republic, Article 9 of the Basic Law did not contain the right to strike; this was only introduced in Article 9.3 when the Emergency Laws were passed, and then the condition was included that the Emergency Articles must not be applied to labour disputes. In the Parliamentary Council which worked out the Constitution the right to strike was unopposed. It was not included in the Constitution, however, because agreement could not be reached on political strikes,[470] and there is little agreement on this problem now in legal writings. All those forms of conflict which are not directed to working conditions and economic conditions are regarded as outside the province of Article 9.3 of the Basic Law. But some legal experts argue:

> That does not mean, however, that strikers are automatically doing something illegal, but simply that they have moved from the protection of autonomy in collective bargaining to the 'draughtier region' of other legal norms. This is where the wide and legally still partly unploughed field opens up of all those actions which, like political strikes, are taken only *in* the employment relation but not *because of* it...[471]

In most of the Western democracies with older constitutions there is no explicit acknowledgement of the right to strike, although the unions — in the Netherlands, for instance — have frequently made efforts to have this changed.

But even in countries where the right to strike is guaranteed in the constitution there have been legal conflicts not only over certain forms of strike activity but also over the restrictions 'within the framework of the law'. In Italy a law to regulate the right to strike was, like so many of the other declarations of this progressive Constitution, never passed. The unions always bitterly opposed legal restrictions on strikes and they referred here to the constitution itself, which in Article 3 lays upon the Republic the task of 'removing those obstacles of an economic and social nature to the full development of human personality and effective participation of all workers in the political, economic and social formation of the country'.[472] In other countries attempts to limit the right to strike through the legislature and the judiciary have been more successful than in Italy. The state has attempted to impose legal restrictions on strikes on several levels:

(1) By the use of emergency laws against major strikes.

(2) By declaring certain forms of strike illegal.

(3) By limiting the right to strike for certain groups, mainly in the public sector.

(4) By the use of state arbitration.

(a) The Use of Emergency Laws against Strikes

Even in old democracies with a strong tradition of protection of basic rights the state has always been tempted to use its emergency laws during major strikes. In a liberal country like Great Britain this happened during the general strike of 1926, the dock strikes of 1948, 1949 and 1970, during the railway strike of 1955, the seamen's strike in 1966, the power workers' strike in 1970 and the miners' strike in 1972.[473] The emergency paragraphs in the German Constitution include a regulation that the measures are not to be used in labour disputes which are 'conducted to maintain and improve working and economic conditions by the associations in the meaning of Sentence 1' (the freedom of coalition in Article 9) (Article 9.3). But this was not enough to dispel the concern of opponents of the emergency laws that there might be intervention between the partners in collective negotiations.

(b) Declaring Certain Forms of Strike Illegal

As the labour movement grew and new forms of work and company organization developed the unions, in a growing monopolization of industry, had to be inventive in the evolution of new forms of conflict. In countries where the workers are disciplined and highly organized the classical strike has remained the dominant method; it is as ritualized as a medieval feud and largely follows well channelled legal forms. Particularly in the Scandinavian countries arbitration procedures which were precisely defined by the state had to be gone through before a strike was permissible. In the case of official strikes legal proceedings were often instigated if labour law procedures were infringed. Where the labour courts were largely concerned with the problems of the individual workers and not so much those of the unions, as in the Latin countries, there were always fewer legal restrictions on strikes than in Scandinavia or Germany. A 'non-strike clause' has occasionally been included in the wage agreements in the Latin countries in recent years, but only on a voluntary basis. It was not only the easier legal situation but also the existence of fragmented and comparatively weak unions which in these countries produced greater inventiveness in the development of new energy-saving forms of conflict. Even where there were direct acts of violence, as during the Luddite riots, power was never used quite arbitrarily but always in a carefully dosed combination of measures which had been legally well tested.[474]

The employers tried to prevent an extensive interpretation of the existing legislation and repeatedly used restrictive interpretations of the law against the new forms of conflict. In the early capitalist period aid was often forthcoming from the judiciary and the legislature, where strikes were at best tolerated unwillingly as 'a bit outside the law'. But in highly industrialized capitalist countries, where the right to strike is accepted by all the groups and agencies of the state, the necessity for restrictions on strikes is justified not for legal but economic reasons: as industry becomes more capital-intensive and the production procedures and business activity become more closely integrated strikes become more and more expensive and the costs are increasigly borne by the public at large. The more 'moral suasion', appeals to consideration for the general good, and political integration are used as weapons against the unions, the less necessary it is to use the judiciary or even the legislature as repressive weapons against certain forms of conflict. It did not even prove possible to declare some unorthodox forms of strike illegal.

One can distinguish between the following forms of strike:

(1) Lightning strikes. These are strikes for which no period of notice is given. They are generally not regarded as illegal by courts in the Latin countries provided that the wage agreement did not

contain a period of notice. The unions in these countries usually successfully resisted the inclusion of such clauses in their agreements. But the French legislation of 1963 on strikes in the public sector did declare lightning strikes illegal. This was for two reasons: firstly those unions which have been given the right to announce a strike are privileged, and secondly the measure makes unofficial strikes, which are usually lightning strikes, more difficult.[475]

(2) Unofficial strikes. These are strikes which are not organized by a union. But the borders between these and official strikes are fluid. Unofficial strikes are often tolerated or even secretly encouraged by unions whose hands are tied by peace clauses or lack of funds.[476] The term 'wild-cat strikes', which is often used, is in itself derogatory and in many systems of industrial relations unofficial strikes have a taint of illegality. Nevertheless, there has been an increasing number of these strikes since the end of the reconstruction phase in Europe, and they are often approved both for their tactical efficiency and their normal basis, as they are often the expression of legitimate claims by the workers which the unions cannot adequately represent owing to legal ties.[477] If it used to be difficult for the union leaders to mobilize their members for strikes the trend was reversed at the end of the sixties: after about 1968/69 the union leaders were often drawn unwillingly into strikes which they had not planned, or unofficial strikes were organized without their knowledge, sometimes with a strong anti-union bias.

There are several reasons for this increase in unofficial strikes:

(a) Rising inflation made large sections of the workers dissatisfied as they felt that they had lost out in the wage round.

(b) The composition of the workers changed. The growing number of younger workers made mobilization easier.

(c) The large number of foreign workers were also easier to mobilize for unofficial strikes and they were often less scrupulous than domestic workers, because they did not have a detailed knowledge of the legal system of the country or its practice in disputes. The actions by the North Africans at Renault and the Turks at Ford in Cologne are illustrative of this.

(d) The growing ideological base of conflicts may well be a further reason for the increase in unofficial strikes. The lack of success in redistribution through straightforward wage disputes and the necessity to exercise pressure, not only against the employers but against the system as a whole, are eroding the legitimation base of the rules of labour disputes as they have been practised so far. Even in countries where the labour movement is not on a markedly ideological base, as in the USA, there has been an increase in spontaneous strikes because with the 'revolution of rising expectations' members are more frequently rejecting the results obtained by the unions.[478]

(e) The tendency to centralize negotiations, which is usually encouraged by the employers (cf. Chapter 1, 4), and the centralization of union organizations, is loosening the ties to the rank and file. Small militant groups find it easier to win support for criticism of the centre.

(f) The spread of syndicalist patterns of conflict among groups which have so far been largely middle class in orientation, like the white collar workers and the civil servants, is another reason for the rise in the number of unofficial strikes. The assumption in older strike literature, like that of Ross and Hartmann (1960), that strike frequency would generally decline in capitalist countries as the nationalized sector grew, has not proved correct over time. Certainly it does not reflect the change in strike motives and forms of strike. In France we have seen that there are certainly no fewer strikes in the public sector than in the private sector, on the contrary. But the motives were largely different. It was not wage disputes but working conditions (in 32.5% of all strikes examined in the public sector) and the assignment to wage and salary grades (22%) which predominated, while wage disputes at 14.5% were only in third place. If these figures are correlated with the results of the strikes, then wage disputes drop even further down the scale because the state proved relatively tough over this issue (only 25% of strikes ended with a victory) while the strikers were more successful over union rights (43%) and wage and salary grades (36.5%).[479] However, the public sector has not proved to be an innovation area for conflict forms. In the public sector there were fewer conflicts which would have been illegal under French law than in the private sector. But it is difficult to make definitive judgements on militancy in the public sector because the size of this in the national economy, legal regulations on strikes in the public sector and the behaviour of civil servants vary too much from one country to another.

The more frequently the weapon of the unofficial strike is used in systems with strongly legalized industrial relations, the less effective is the legal weapon and the less effective are sanctions against individual workers or unions for participating in them. That can be seen in Sweden, where industrial relations are very highly legalized in many areas. According to the Swedish legislation of 1928 a union can be taken to court for infringement of a collective agreement and an individual worker for going on unofficial strike. The maximum fine, 200 Kroner, for breach of contract, does not seem very severe today, but that is only because the amount has never been changed. At the time it was a ruinous sum for a worker.[480] The employers in Sweden have rarely used this weapon as there were very few unofficial strikes until 1969. But even in the first spectacular case among the dockers in Gothenburg in 1969 the employers did not use the sanction for the sake of industrial peace. There was a similar trend in reactions from the employers in the Federal Republic during the period of full employment. But that does not mean that they had no means of sanction against activists on unofficial strike.

In countries where the unofficial strike is punishable by law as 'refusal to work', as in the verdict from the German Federal Labour Court, the union leaders with their monopoly on strike have a kind of concealed 'lock-out sub-culture'.[481] Certainly the unions in Germany do usually succeed in having the men reinstated but the sanction remains effective because certain fringe benefits which are bound to the length of time the worker has been in the plant are then lost. As considerable wage rises have been gained through unofficial strikes (after an initial period of refusal to negotiate with the strikers) in Sweden, the Netherlands and the Federal Republic even the unions are coming to the conclusion that occasional unofficial strikes are a necessary safety valve in centralized and bureaucratized collective negotiations to prevent the wage ratio from dropping.

The attempt to illegalize unofficial strikes has repeatedly been justified by reference to the needs of the market economy. This argument was used by the Donovan Report. It was not the number of working days lost which appeared serious (this is relatively low as these strikes are usually short) but the danger that individual entrepreneurs could be pressurized and the competition mechanisms jammed by spontaneous strikes when there are delivery dates.[482] Nevertheless, even in Germany there is less inclination to regard all unofficial strikes as against the law and this is finding expression in wage agreements. The agreement concluded in the metal industry in 1976 provided for 'moderation clauses' in which the employer promised not to take steps against workers who went on unofficial strike. Conservative critics saw this as formal legalization of 'wildcat strikes'. But the strong emphasis some authors put on the individual right to strike is hardly likely to become the prevalent creed. It is clearly coloured by aggression against the 'monopoly of the unions', which is in their view putting 'legal means of conflict' in place of the daily justification to the rank and file.[483] This view is too strongly influenced by the syndicalist radicalism of Southern Europe, where union pluralism prevents a monopoly and individual conflicts are more strongly emphasized than collective ones (also because union membership is lower).

(3) Selective strikes (*grèves bouchons*). These are strikes which affect only some of the workers in a plant and they are frequent in countries where disputes are not often the subject of legal controversy (France and Great Britain). In countries where labour disputes are strongly determined by concepts of 'parity' and 'social adequacy' (Sweden and Germany) this type of strike is more difficult because under current legislation a lock-out is permissible when some of the workers are on strike and it is often practised.[484]

(4) Rota strikes (*grèves tournantes*). These are a form of partial strikes which follow one upon another in different departments and in specific rhythms. In labour movement theory this is justified by the fragmented character of work in modern industry. It is also the most frequent form of strike in highly modernized and highly technical plants. It minimizes wage loss and maximizes the damage to the employer who has to pay most of his wage bill all the time but has his work greatly disrupted. There are two different forms of this strike: the horizontal type, which is exercised by one occupational group, and the vertical type, which halts work in one particular sector of the plant.[485] This type of strike is frequent in private industry in France and Italy but it was prohibited in the public sector by the legislation of 31 July 1963.[486] These strikes have often been regarded as legal even if a wage agreement was still in force in the plant and this had not been terminated nor come to an end. There is only an obligation to keep the peace if this is expressly laid down in the wage agreement and the unions try to avoid this. But the following forms of strike are regarded as illegal in

many countries:

(5) Sympathy strikes. According to the current view strikes may not be for third parties. The solidarity concept of the labour movement is still not accepted in the labour legislation of many countries. In France there have been verdicts which suggest that this form of strike would be regarded as illegal but French experts in labour law have been doubtful that this would be followed in practice.[487] A new form of sympathy strike has evolved through the increasing coordination of conflict against measures by multinational companies. In Scandinavia the unions have therefore regarded solidarity and sympathy strikes as permissible especially as there are often restrictions on strikes in other countries.[488]

(6) Go-slow (*grèves perlées*). As strikes are usually defined as a 'collective stoppage' the go-slow is not regarded as a strike by the judiciary in many countries. In France the Supreme Court of Appeal ruled in 1960 that a go-slow was 'inefficient work' and not a strike.[489] Nevertheless, this form of obstruction is extremely effective in paralyzing the plant and it is often used by groups who are legally not able to strike. In Germany the civil servants have developed the 'work-to-rule' as a form of go-slow. It is very difficult for the judiciary to assemble the facts under the concept of illegal action as the differences in activity by various groups require different definitions of the go-slow. When the employees concerned are highly qualified and their activity cannot be measured on a time basis it is almost impossible to prove that there is a go-slow (cf. the strike by the air traffic control staff).

(7) Occupation of the plant. This was largely developed in revolutionary periods, in 1917 by the Russian workers, in 1920 by the Italian metal workers and in 1936 by almost 2 million strikers in France. Up to the sixties it was a rare form of conflict but it became more frequent, firstly in the mining industry and in ship-building and then mainly when works were to be closed or to prevent lockouts. In France there have been different verdicts in cases of occupation. In several the workers were ordered to clear the plant, sometimes their action was judged to be a serious infringement of their duty, in order to justify the dismissal of the 'ringleaders'. It is registered with satisfaction abroad that even in the conservative Federal Republic plants have been occupied. One case was at Seibel & Söhne in Erwitte.[490] However, too much importance should not be attached to this case. There was no need for militancy on the

part of the unions to show the hair-raising attitude on the part of the management of the cement works in Erwitte. Even the employers' associations and the conservative parties would not support them. The court gave a verdict in favour of the workers who had protested at wrongful dismissal. But however well-meaning the court may have been the weakness of the workers' position is clear: the re-instigations could result in a wage back-log amounting to a huge sum of money but no-one can force an employer to continue in business and a political and legal victory for the workers may well prove a pyrrhic one.[491]

Where the conflict situation is not so open as it was in Erwitte workers have sometimes tried to save a plant by investing in it themselves. In May 1975 the mechanical engineering firm Bammesberger in Leonberg made headlines when 240 of 600 employees without waiting for advice from the Metal Workers Union said they would put up DM 2.1 million to save the company. But this kind of experiment has rather a symbolic significance: it is to encourage the provision of public funds. In this case the Landeskreditbank Baden-Württemberg declined to grant a loan of DM 3 million as there was a deficit of DM 20 million in the company and the Land Government declared that on principle bankrupt companies were not to be rescued with public money, and very certainly not if there was a risk that the workers would lose their savings as well.

In this connection the question was raised whether the unions should invest money in companies like this in order to help save their members' jobs. The Chairman of the German Chemical Industry Workers Union said flatly: 'We can give advice but we can never put money in because we are not allowed to risk our members' fees in chancy investments'.[492] Only rich unions, like those in Sweden and Germany, could in any case ever entertain such an idea. But it would be contrary to the firm principles of the finance policy of these organizations to embark on rescue operations of this kind (cf. Chapter 1, 8) and the unions would fear repercussions. A number of cases like this would over-strain their finances and it would be very difficult to find rational criteria why one company should be supported and another not. Moreover the unions would fear to be used as 'the motors of cold socialization' if the members in any particular region should become more militant. The unions do not suggest that their funds should be used to rescue weak companies but that unhealthy companies should be treated prophylactically and re-training introduced in case there should be a closure. The Swedish unions have been practising this since the fifties as part of their 'labour market policy'.[493]

For successful cases of occupation we must now look outside the Federal Republic. But there has only been partial success with this weapon in other Western democracies too. In Great Britain occupation has seemed to promise more since 1969 than the individual action by employees in other countries because workers in plants threatened with closures and dismissals could attempt to secure the practical and theoretical advice of experienced union groups. In the summer of 1969 the workers in GEC in Liverpool applied to the Institute for Workers' Control (founded in 1968) and the Joint Shop Stewards Committee. Although they tried to win the participation of sympathetic union officials no meaningful plan for the operation was produced and Ken Coates, one of the theoreticians of the left wing of the union movement, retrospectively concluded that a sit-in would have been better than a work-in.[494] Writers who were rather oriented to Moscow Communism came to the opposite conclusion and welcomed the fact that the shop stewards 'despite the attempts to preach the contrary by Trotskyist groups, who come mainly from the university towns' had chosen the work-in because it entailed little physical force but demonstrated particularly well the will to work and the superfluity of capitalists.[495]

In its statements the TUC refrains from such global judgements and simply classifies the new forms of conflict as:[496]

— work-ins, where work is continued;
— sit-ins, on account of important decisions by the management;
— sit-ins to give pressure to collective bargaining;
— tactical sit-ins.

The last two types are used only as ammunition in the battle for traditional union aims, and even the second type is not necessarily directed to a take-over of the plant by the workers.

The most spectacular case of a partially successful action was between 1971 and October 1972 in Upper Clyde Shipbuilders (UCS). While other cases of a work-in were not so successful because they suffered from a lack of fuel and material supplies, this was a success because the workers were controlling real assets which became more valuable with every working day spent on them, the ships which were under construction and which were worth about £90 million. As the Government also wanted to see the ships finished for foreign trade policy reasons the action by the workers forced it to reconsider the financial aid it had at first refused. But on a sit-in the work is not continued. The TUC gives four examples of full or partial sit-ins: Plessey (Alexandria), Fisher-Bendix, Allis Chalmers and the former BLMC Thorneycroft factory in Basingstoke. The TUC takes a very much more positive attitude to these new forms of conflict than the DGB. It does admit: 'Technically they are all illegal' but it confirms that they are useful under 'certain' circumstances (which are not defined), because the process of collective bargaining clearly has weaknesses when the decision is taken far away from the plants.[497]

Most famous is a work-in in France, the occupation of the LIP watch factory in Besançon. LIP became the model for a whole range of new conflict forms, such as

— detention of directors of the company;
— street blockades to inform the general public of the workers' case;
— breaches of company confidentiality;
— the organization and sale of products in the form of about 25,000 watches after the management had secretly removed about the same number. But the value (about F. 5 million) was only enough to cover about two months wages and salaries for the workers.

In this conflict the action suffered firstly from the rivalry between union ideologies. The CGT was in favour of negotiations and a continuance of work, the CFDT under Charles Piaget organized unified workers' committees and set an example of more far-reaching forms of conflict.[498] Success was achieved in preventing partial closures and forcing the management to withdraw charges it had brought. But it did not prove possible to maintain the plant and continue sales beyond the first wave of solidarity purchases by other workers. The hidden 'booty' of the watches had a largely symbolic value. The Left produced different verdicts on the experiment. Some groups saw in it a progressive form of multi-frontal class war which involved wide sections of the population, a symbol for the achievement of the 'open factory' and the mobilization of further sympathisers in the general public. Others saw it rather as a romantic sublimation of an anachronism, one manufacturing plant against the growing international mobility of capital and the technological revolution of late capitalism. There is an element of truth in both interpretations. The big unions never set the experiment up as something which could be generally followed or did anything in particular to create a number of LIPs. Nevertheless, this form of conflict was copied. Between July 1974 and July 1975 the CFDT registered fourteen occupations in which unofficial sales (*ventes sauvages*) had a symbolic and mobilization function.[499] But when LIP again found itself in financial difficulties in 1976 neither the public nor the Government were again ready to save it at any price.[500] But beside these progressive mobilization aspects there were also conservative aspects to the occupations to which many a left-wing enthusiast turned a blind eye. Occupations have been interpreted as the most revolutionary forms of conflict the working class now have, but this is unjustified. Often they are much more the expression of a *reorientation* from the traditional concept of performance to the expectation of adequate participation in the growing social wealth and a claim to job security. Recent occupations were much less frequently part of a mass strike by the revolutionary avant-garde, they were motivated by the very conservative need for security and carried out by highly disciplined workers full of the desire to go on working. The Communist unionists in France are still sceptical about occupations. Séguy, the Secretary-General of the CGT, said that the LIP methods should not be used systematically and he actually rejected certain measures, such as detaining the management, on principle, because they were more likely to produce reactionary counter-mobilization than concessions.[501] So, even by adherents of the Christian social theory, greater rights of co-determination by the workers when plants are to be closed or re-organized are now generally regarded as alternatives to occupations, for even union theories from the Catholic school, which is certainly not militant, while accepting the doctrine of factors, recognize for human considerations that 'decrees cannot be issued over the factor labour in the same way as over the factor capital'.[502]

(8) Finally, political strikes. These are most harshly criticized in the literature on labour legislation. But they are often not easy to define. Even in France in 1968 political and economic factors were closely inter-related and even in minor cases of unrest the aims proclaimed by the unions are not necessarily their main ones or the real source of pressure on the Government. The main feature of a

political strike is the enemy: these strikes are not directed against the employers but against the political leadership. The extent of the strike is not such a clear indicator. Not all *general strikes* have deserved the name. In 1914 a Social Democrat writer concluded: 'No political strike has ever yet grown to the proportions of a general strike. Even the strikes during the Russian revolution only affected a minority of the workers'.[503] Particularly in the Latin countries with their syndicalist tradition the expression 'general strike' is often an exaggeration. The protest in the Basque country at the vicious action by the police in Victoria at the beginning of March 1976 was certainly a political strike but in other countries it would not have been regarded as a 'general strike' because it was largely limited to one region. It was the syndicalist tradition in Spain which kept leaders like Camacho fascinated by the idea of a general strike right up to the seventies, although their inflationary typology made the weapon less effective.[504] Any strike which went beyond a particular region came to be classed as a general strike and the term largely lost its real implications.

In most countries political strikes are illegal.[505] This is especially so in countries where union policy is not particularly militant. That is certainly the case in Germany although the unions have not always been as politically abstinent as they are today — one need only recall the oppositon to the Company Constitution Act of 1952, to re-armament and atomic warfare. Political strikes are also illegal in more militant countries such as Italy; nevertheless they are frequent there.

In countries where union militancy is not sublimated per se political strikes have been condemned not so much for legal as for tactical reasons. The Secretary-General of the Letzeburger Arbechter-Verband (LAV) stated at the 1970 Congress that the union had voluntarily limited the right to strike firstly by recognizing a national arbitration council and secondly by refraining from political strikes:

> This may not suit those workers or unionists who do not see strikes as a means to an end but as an end in themselves, with an ideological or political background. But it is the only right way and the only possible way to maximize results without exposing the workers to unnecessary hardship which would consume anything that might be gained from the action in advance.[506]

Although political strikes were rejected on a cool cost-benefit calculation of income improvement the Luxembourg union did threaten a 'general strike' if further restrictions were imposed on the right to strike without the unions' agreement.

Practice in Western European countries has shown that a schematic distinction cannot be drawn between the attitude of militant and of cooperative unions to a political strike. The cooperative unions, too, especially in Northern Europe, do not exclude the possibility of political strikes altogether. Although there is strong legal discrimination political strikes are regarded as justified under certain conditions in most countries and the political leaders have accepted this and refrained from sanctions.

(a) That is particularly true of political strikes in exercise of the democratic right to offer resistance if constitutional order is jeopardized or basic rights are threatened (e.g. during the Kapp Putsch in Germany in 1920, the prevention of a coup d'etat by the generals in Algeria in 1961). The DGB has always regarded a political strike as justified under such circumstances and these have not been interpreted as illegal by the German judiciary.[507]

(b) Strikes when union rights are being attacked (in 1904 in the Netherlands when legislation was brought in against the right of railway workers to strike, 1920 in Ireland during the hunger strike by Republican political prisoners[508] or in 1941 in Great Britain when unionists who tried to strike despite the war-time restrictions were arrested). The Dutch episode was a fiasco. But the two other actions brought the release of the prisoners and in Britain in 1972 the threat of a general strike was enough to obtain the release of five dockers who had been arrested.[509]

(c) Strike to support a resistance movement which the majority regard as legitimate (in 1944 in France; there were several unsuccessful general strikes of this nature in Spain after the Second World War).

(d) Strikes against an imperialist foreign policy (in 1961 in Belgium over the Congo policy).

(e) Strikes against discredited heads of state or heads of government or to enforce the formation of a desired government (strikes led to the abdication of Leopold III of Belgium, who was suspected of collaboration with the Nazis and there were strikes against the investiture of Scelba in Italy in 1954). A political strike becomes problematic, however much justification there may be for the unions' criticism, if it systematically intervenes in the constitutional mechanisms of the formation of a government. In systems with a large number of parties and instability in the cabinet many attempts at coalition have come to grief partly through union action, especially in Italy and Finland.[510] But in these systems the unions are rarely in a position to put the party or coalition they support into power. This kind of influence is more easily exercised in the two or three party system prevalent in the English-speaking countries.

When a general strike was called at the beginning of July 1976 in Australia 90% of the workers but only 30% of the white collar workers joined in. The occasion was the proposed change in the state sickness benefit scheme to which all Australians automatically belonged without special contracts ('Medibank'), a system of contributions to the amount of 2.5% of income. The radical union wings would have liked to see this as the beginning of a partisan war against the Conservative Government, which they believed had conspired to bring down Whitlam's Labour Government although the majority of the voters confirmed this in the ensuing general election.[511] If Willy Brandt was careful to prevent 'pressure from the street' by a constructive vote of no confidence when it seemed likely that his Government would fall, in some countries there is a growing inclination for unions to exercise pressure in support of Socialist governments or to try to keep them in office. But the political effects of union pressure should not be over-estimated. There is a great risk of a swing round to the conservatives in public opinion and the Australian figures for participation in the general strike show that the white collar workers are certainly not so much in favour of this weapon as the workers are. Among other occupational groups political strikes rather tend to produce counter-mobilization against concerted action by the labour party and the unions. In the English-speaking countries members of Parliament who are supported by the unions (cf. chapter 4, 2) and have strong ideological ties to a Labour philosophy have rarely been inclined to support direct action.[512] Membership of Parliament has generally proved stronger than ideological ties and members have remained loyal to the rules of representative parliamentary democracy even where they have been generally recognized as a union group inside the party spectrum.[513]

Political strikes for other causes have been more controversial:

(f) As a protest against the economic policy of a legal government in order to improve the unions' distribution position (in France against Daladier in 1938, against Laniel in 1953 and against Pompidou in 1963 and 1964; in 1956 in Finland, in 1973 in Denmark and in 1976 in Australia). In Germany a strike which uses social means to enforce sovereign acts of parliament is regarded as illegal because it takes away the sovereign rights of the people and the organizational power of the unions is used to suspend the principle of equality of opportunity for everyone in political life.[514]

(g) Solidarity strikes against multinational concerns. These have been discussed more frequently in the seventies and unions which were otherwise sceptical about political strikes except in exercise of resistance rights have re-assessed their position. The Swedish Labour Law Commission in 1975 after a detailed comparison of Western European rulings voted as a majority against political strikes.[515] But at a congress on multinational corporations of the Scandinavian unions Nordens Fackliga Samorganisation (NFS), a resolution which the LO also supported to admit political strikes at least if they were of short duration was accepted.[516] It seems typical of the self-confidence felt with regard to basic rights in most democracies that political strikes are rarely envisaged; as a case of national resistance as in Germany, it is rather feared that there may be attacks on freedom and basic rights abroad and it was to enable solidarity with these cases that the Swedish workers were to be given the right to political strike.

(h) In most countries strikes to exercise a general political mandate by the unions are illegal. There were heated controversies over this question during the creation of the Federal Republic's Basic Law. It was because agreement could not be reached over the question of political strike that the right to strike was not included in Article 9. In more recent labour legislation, as in 1976 in Greece, attempts have been made to forbid political strikes expressis verbis but a general strike was called against the Karamanlis Government over this issue. In practice the borderline between a labour dispute and a political strike is often hard to find. If unions are striking over certain formative rights which are later recognized by the legislature, and the strike is continued, the Rubicon is quickly crossed and the addressee of the strike changes.

Union theoreticians still justify political strikes with the right to exercise a political mandate for the progressive development of the constitutional system. The Constitution of the Finnish SAK goes furthest here, although it does not refer directly to conflict as a means of realizing its constitutional aims. (cf. Chapter 2, 1). And in the Federal Republic it is by no means only ultra-radical sociologists who justify political action, and political strikes if need be, as a means of countering the constant influence exercised behind the scenes by the employers and prevailing interests.[517] The majority in the middle-class parties, which are now strictly opposed to political strikes, has generally forgotten that the most successful general strikes in history were those in which the workers fought with the support of large sections of the liberal bourgeoisie against the conservatives for a full bourgeois democracy, the extension of the franchise, for instance, as in 1893 in Belgium and 1902 in Sweden. It was clear then that if a political strike is to be successful it needs at least tolerance on the part of large sections of the middle class. Belgium in 1893 is still quoted as an example today but the defeat of 1902 is forgotten, although twice as many workers participated as in 1893 to bring down the plural franchise in Belgium, the last bastion of a privileged electorate. Where working-class organizations are increasingly incorporated directly into the political system (Chapter 4, 2) there have generally been fewer general strikes. The British general strike of 1926 is a certain exception but it is usually seen in historical literature as non-revolutionary, an accident of history, as one might say, the result of a mis-calculation of the union negotiating position.[518] It has even been argued for the Kapp Putsch that the general strike would have progressively broken down if only union members had joined in.[519]

It is not possible to judge political strikes strictly in legal terms and even the most rigid legalists have justified political strikes in support of liberalization movements which were later victorious. The number of conflict patterns and the objects of conflict have multiplied since the world-wide protest movement and patterns of behaviour, which were formerly largely confined to the working class, have appeared in other classes too. Political strikes will have to be assessed by the legitimacy of their cause in the eyes of the majority and the constitutional bases of the consensus. As any misuse of its political mandate by a group representing partial interests is inadmissible the unions cannot claim that they are representing the numerical majority of the population because their potential group is greater than the number of their members. Where general strikes were rashly entered into they have almost always had negative repercussions on the interests of the labour movement over the longer term. (This was the case with the strike on 1 May 1920 in France, in 1909 in Sweden, and in 1926 in Great Britain.) The large responsible organizations of today have therefore been extremely cautious in the use of this weapon.

On the other hand the opponents of political strikes also have to admit that an increasing number of strikes are taking on a political aspect. In countries like Great Britain wage strikes which are directed against the employers are often hard to distinguish from more far-reaching claims which involve action on the part of the legislature.[520] The unions do not have the same political force in every country nor is labour legislation equally tolerant to many forms of conflict. But in all highly capitalized countries there is a recognizable trend for the employer to be only the front line opponent and for major conflicts to involve a confrontation with the government. As the nationalized and public sectors grow and other socialized elements in the economy increase this will also increase. The more Socialist a country is the more does any strike take on a political character.

In many countries the various forms of strike cannot simply be divided into strikes which are legal and those which are not legal. The judiciary generally defends the essential interests of private entrepreneurs and the profitability of companies. Rota strikes and selective strikes have also, if taken too far, been declared illegal. Even in the case of legal strikes certain forms of action are not allowed. The use of picketing against those who are willing to work is illegal in many countries. Picketing is the ultimate form of the use of mass power but it was frequent in the early capitalist period. But where there used to be riots and machine wrecking, sabotage and mass violence, now even occupations, which are the harshest use of force to be regarded as illegal, are comparatively well regulated and channelled, however colourfully radical groups may describe them as the dawning of more intense class conflicts. Even with the generally not gentle use of power in pickets the legal systems of the capitalist countries have often found a modus vivendi with the strikers. But even in the relatively liberal system of labour relations in Great Britain cases of picketing have been brought to court until very recently. The court cited Common Law and the unions were never sure that their struggle for the repeal of the Conspiracy and Protection of Property Act of 1876 would remove the basis for action against pickets. In the Trades Union and Labour Relations Act of 1974 which replaced the Industrial Relations Act of 1971 peaceful picketing was not declared illegal: 'For the purpose only of peacefully obtaining or communicating information, or peacefully persuading any person to work or abstain from working'.[521]

Forms of conflict which have been bitterly contested as illegal have from time to time established themselves, and like unofficial strikes where there are sanction or reprimand clauses, are increasingly being made admissible in voluntary agreements between the negotiating partners, so that there is another shift in the borderline between what is 'legal' and 'illegal'. The over-regulation of strikes has detrimental consequences for labour law itself. Precisely in countries which tend to over-regulate labour relations a kind of double legality develops as soon as non-reprimand clauses and others which bind the partners not to call for court decisions on the basis of the existing law are included in collective agreements. Similar experience of the development of a quasi-legitimization of a number of disputes which started unofficially and illegally in the times of the British Industrial Relations Act must be a warning to legislators and courts not to define legality too narrrowly.[522] An Australian study on political strikes comes to the conclusion that the law will never be in a position to isolate political strikes fully and that the problem can only be solved by not forbidding any kind of strike. There would then be no need for a definition of political strikes.[523]

(c) Restricting the Right to Strike for Certain Groups, Particularly in the Public Sector

We can distinguish between two groups of countries with regard to their restriction on the right to strike for certain groups:

The Western European type (France, Italy, Great Britain), where white collar workers and civil servants largely have the right to strike. In Great Britain the civil servants have usually exercised the right to strike in the Trade Disputes Act of 1906 in the same way as the workers. From 1927 to 1947 civil servants were forbidden to strike with few exceptions. Only a few groups in the public sector are still denied the right to strike, the police (Police Act 1919 and 1964), the merchant navy and post office workers (Post Office Act of 1953). But there have often been infringements of these Acts or they have not been upheld by the courts. In France those who are not allowed to strike include the police (Act of 28 September 1948) and the external prison service (legislation of 6 August 1958) but this did not prevent these employees from striking in 1974.[524] The French courts base their verdicts on the fact that the right to strike in the public sector must not be exercised immoderately or without regulation. A period of notice of five days by the representative unions is prescribed. Lightning strikes are forbidden but the unions evade this by giving notice several times and so leaving their opponents in uncertainty as to when the strike is due to start. Rota strikes (*grèves tournantes*) are forbidden and so are unofficial strikes.[525] In France too the tendency is becoming established to declare strike forms which on principle are permitted to be illegal if excessive use is made of them. The doctrine of the social adequacy of the means is not upheld with the consistency that it is in Germany but there are indications of it. Negative verdicts can be given on 'concerted disorganization' of a plant or a series of short, repeated stoppages, so that in addition to the objective limits to strike action laid down in the law there are subjective limits arising from interpretation by the judiciary.

The Central European type. In few countries is the number of those not allowed to strike as high as in the Federal Republic. According to the current doctrine it is concluded from the 'form of state and the aims of the state as laid down in the Constitution' that independent of the regulations on the civil service which can add a further specific and stricter element, there is a 'political prohibition' on strikes in the public sector. The claims made on the state as a political organization and the claims which this political organization must make on its administrators 'are greater than the claims which can be made within the service'.[526] Opinions which diverge from this interpretation[527] have not succeeded in establishing themselves.

Outside Germany the right to strike in the public sector is becoming increasingly established, partly through the simple fact of the occurrence of a large number of these strikes and partly through formal legislation as in Sweden in 1965 and Finland in 1970, although both these countries long held to the German ideology of the greater need for loyalty on the part of civil servants in their literature on constitutional law. In Sweden certain limits are set through the usual peace-keeping clauses (cf. Chapter 4, 1) and the fact that only official strikes are possible. In Finland legislation was envisaged to limit strikes in the public sector during a state of emergency but it was never passed.

In some countries there is increasing pressure from below for greater right to strike in the public sector. In 1976 there were mass demonstrations in Japan but the Government remained firm. It simply promised to examine the possibility of changing the law on certain points.[528] A threat to remove privileges in exchange for the right to strike has always caused controversy in the ranks of the civil service. In many countries it will not be possible to solve the problem without basic changes to the career patterns and privileges structure.

(d) State Arbitration

With the growing trend to state-steered incomes policy the tendency also grew in capitalist countries to try to channel union strike activity through state arbitration. In many countries there are possibilities for voluntary arbitration; in Sweden there is the *rikslönenämnd* where arbitration is generally on a voluntary basis at the request of the partners. Australia, New Zealand, Denmark and Norway experimented for a long time with institutions of compulsory arbitration. In the thirties the Social Democrats in Norway opposed compulsory arbitration and abolished it when they came to power. After 1945, however, it was re-introduced with the agreement of the LO to help the reconstruction process. But it survived beyond the envisaged temporary phase. The high degree of union fragmentation in Denmark and Norway is one of the reasons why compulsory arbitration was retained longer in these countries than in Sweden (and to a certain extent Finland). In Denmark, as industrial relations worsened at the beginning of the seventies, the tendency grew to reduce the interventionist system.[529]

In addition to voluntary and compulsory arbitration the British system has the possibility of the appointment of a commission of enquiry by the Minister of Labour. Great Britain was one of the first countries to introduce legislation on arbitration, in the Conciliation Act of 1896, the Industrial Courts Act of 1919 and the Industrial Disputes Act of 1951. Most countries have introduced various combinations of the 'mediation', 'conciliation' and 'arbitration' for which the British system provides.

But none of these combinations has been able to prevent strikes altogether. In Australia it has been argued that compulsory arbitration has made no contribution to reducing labour disputes. But more recent studies are more cautious on this point because there is no reliable strike data in Australia for the period before the introduction of compulsory arbitration and its influence in lessening disputes cannot be reliably isolated even where the figures are clear.[530] But even in the public sector arbitration cannot replace the right to strike and experts have argued that it would be better to expand the right to strike in the public sector (except for the police and the fire service) rather than the cumbersome arbitration mechanism.[531]

Restrictive anti-strike legislation has repeatedly been introduced in an attempt to limit the power of the unions, but it has never really been effective. There are several reasons for this:

(1) Strikes are mass actions, which — especially when labour disputes are strongly political — exceed the limits of what can be regulated by private or even criminal law. It is very difficult to enforce obligations to keep industrial peace against a big majority of the workers, as was apparent under the British Industrial Relations Act of 1971. Even the Donovan Report was sceptical that sanctions against unions for failing to keep the peace would be effective in view of the established practice of collective bargaining. Unofficial strikes could easily outmanoeuvre a union bureaucracy which attempted to keep the peace. Swedish regulations have occasionally been cited as an example. But financial weakness would prevent most unions from following the Swedish example. Criminal proceedings against strike leaders have also proved ineffective if the majority of the workers supported the leaders. Since the Taft-Hartley Act of 1947 in the USA and the National Arbitration Order in Great Britain in 1940 restrictive regulations have been effectively used when radical groups were not supported by the majority. This legislation was occasionally used against members of the Left during the McCarthy period without provoking more than a verbal protest from the unions. But even arrests were ineffective when the

majority supported the strike. In Great Britain, even in 1940 when the country was in dire peril and the enemy was at Calais, repressive measures did not stop the Kent miners from striking and until the Arbitration Act was repealed in 1951 there were further examples of the fact that sanctions under criminal law cannot force workers to keep the peace.

(2) Strikes are largely no longer regarded as 'deviant behaviour' as they were when they were the weapon of a sub-culture which was not generally accepted. They are now a weapon used increasingly by middle-class groups. If this sometimes produces strange parallels (when, for example, strikes take the form of boycotting lectures in universities) the fact cannot be overlooked that the syndicalist terminology and attitude are spreading among the middle class.

(3) State social policy is limiting the possibilities for the employers to use a withdrawal of social benefits as a weapon against strikers. In Germany the verdict over payment of short-time pay to those indirectly affected by a strike broke new ground. It reduced the possibility of mobilizing workers who were affected by the strike against the strike. The verdict came from the Federal Social Court in Kassel in 1975 and concluded a labour dispute in the metal industry in North Baden and North Württemberg and it was an attempt to create an equilibrium of power. The court ruled that the Federal Labour Office had been right in paying short-time money in 1971 to 100,000 workers in other parts of the country, when the employers had to lay them off or put them on short time because of lack of supplies from the strike area or reduced sales. The conservatives regarded this as infringing neutrality which as in war time should mean that one of the parties in the dispute should not be supported financially. But the DGB argued that the payments were necessary to maintain parity in the dispute and prevent the employers from putting pressure on strikers by showing the consequences of their action. The Federal Labour Office was an insurance institution for the workers and it could not refuse benefits at the moment when those insured needed them. The verdict was criticized as being 'a blow for the workers' for the following reasons:[532] All those who are directly affected by the strike receive strike pay. Unemployment benefits are only to be stopped if identical claims are made in all the areas covered by the wage agreement. (This is analogous to the principle that chemical workers do

not profit from a metal workers' strike except indirectly as the strike signalizes a wage round.) The workers should refrain from making identical claims if there is no longer an obligation to keep the peace in the areas not on strike, if the ballot has been held and the majority are in favour of strike. The conservatives fear that by skilful timing of the ballot the unions could exploit this arrangement and let the Federal Labour Office pay out while conserving their own funds. However one may opt on this issue, the development was certainly an important instance of the use of social policy measures to safeguard the right to strike in addition to a simple extension of rights which cannot be realized because there are no funds available.

5. LOCK-OUTS

Three types can be distinguished:

(1) Legalized lock-outs in the name of a fictitious parity in conflict (FRG).

(2) Considerable restriction of the right to lock out which is permissible only in reaction to unusual forms of strike (chequer-board strikes, staggered strikes, slow downs — France, Italy).

(3) A watering-down of the effects through continued wage payments by the employer (Netherlands).

(1) In no country is the lock-out so firmly legalized as in the Federal Republic. With its verdict of 28 January 1955 the Greater Senate of the Federal Labour Court recognized the lock-out as 'a socially adequate form of conflict'. The prohibition on lock-outs in Article 29, Subpara. 5 of the Constitution of the Land of Hesse, however, is often regarded as 'unconstitutional', and did not prevent the SPD from proposing prohibiton of a lock-out to dissolve a contract in its framework guidelines for 1975-1985.[533]

In the early days of industrial relations lock-outs were sometimes used to smash union organizations in the plant. As these became more legalized lock-outs went through a functional change in many countries and they came to be used mainly to enable wage negotiations to be carried out over a large area. The quantitative importance of the lock-out is controversial. Statistics on labour disputes in this field are particularly unreliable. About thirty lock-outs have been registered in the Federal Republic since 1949 but it is estimated that there must have been well over a hundred.[534] The most spectacular cases were in 1963 and in 1971 and in 1978 in the German engineering industry and they show that even the employers do not like to use this weapon and that their associations have great difficulty in achieving widespread solidarity. There are three reasons for this:

(a) Lock-outs are unpopular in public opinion. They have a negative effect particularly on the press, which may well start by being very critical to the union standpoint in a major dispute,[535] objecting not so much to the left-wing ideology as to the consequences of a long drawn-out conflict. Although lock-outs are legal the general public appears to regard them as 'socially inadequate'. On the employers' side as well there does not appear to be that unity of opinion which the Left occasionally assumes. The reasons for this scepticism towards lock-outs are:

(b) It is recognized that they may escalate the conflict and that a passive acceptance of the strike may bring about a speedier conclusion.

(c) It is feared that the unions might be strengthened as those who were willing to work would be driven to join them. But with progressive automation it is possible in some sectors, with the help of some of those who are willing to work, to make some plants increasingly immune to strikes.[536] Moreover, the process of concentration, international integration and the resultant production alternatives these offer mean that the negative effects of a strike are decreasing in importance for the employers. The threat to the employers is rather through the effect on third parties and the mobilization of public opinion among consumers with a possibility of intervention by the state. Many employers therefore prefer to develop strategies which will help them to withstand a long strike rather than have recourse to the sanctions which the law permits.

(2) Considerable restriction of the right to lock-out. In contrast to the right to strike, which is expressly guaranteed in more recent constitutions (Article 40 of the Italian constitution), the problem of the lock-out is not mentioned in constitutions or major legislation on labour disputes (in France of 11 February 1950). But there is no right to lock-out in France. On principle it has been established that lock-outs as a reaction to legal strikes are not permissible and that the employer is obliged to pay the wages (Social Senate, 16

December 1963, 8 January 1965, 26 January 1972). In France and Italy at most a defensive lock-out is permitted against illegal and unusual forms of strike (rota strikes and go-slows). It is up to the employer to prove that he is justified by a strike on the part of some of his workers in technically preventing the others from working, and this is scrupulously observed. The judiciary have prevented misuse by rarely accepting the profitability argument as proof.[537]

The constitution of Hesse, which is the only federal Land to forbid lock-outs, is often cited as an example in demands for a general prohibition on lock-outs. But according to the principle that federal law has precedence over Land law (Article 32 of the Constitution) the prohibition, in the generally accepted view, could not in any case be upheld. The 'powerful phalanx' and their auxiliaries, the owners of capital, who base their argument on the basic right to coalition, the general principle of equality or the apparent necessity for neutrality on the part of the state in labour disputes and on the European Social Charter, although this has not had legal implications, have occasionally been contradicted.[538] The Government of the Land of Hessen have been hesitant to use their prohibition and have obtained reports from experts on the subject. In certain cases of lock-out in Hesse the Government has not intervened and the unions have not insisted on ultimate clarification either, after two administration courts declared that they were not competent to order the Government not to intervene to stop a lock-out. The European Social Charter which the Federal Government has signed recognizes the right of workers and employers to take collective measures and thus approves in many interpretations the right to lock out. In Great Britain and Sweden this is expressly, and in the USA and Japan implicitly, recognized by law.

In 1976 and 1978 the German unions renewed their vociferous demands for a general prohibition of lock-outs. But since the increase in the number of unofficial strikes it is hard to avoid the impression that there is a tacit agreement between the unions and the employers that the lock-out can be used with moderation to the advantage of established unions in the case of unofficial strikes, to combat radicals who are outside or even opposed to the union movement. Since the unusually tough use of the lock-out by the employers' associations in the spring of 1978 (24,819 working days were lost through the lock-out which was used against an official strike which only cost 55,773 working days) the German trade unions have tried to get favourable verdicts from the labour courts. In the majority of cases the courts upheld the legality of the lock-outs as a counter-measure against strikes which had negative consequences for production in plants where the workers were not on strike. Pressure on the SPD Government to forbid lock-outs is being stepped up.

In the relevant literature the opinion is increasingly being put forward that in the Federal Republic the legislature is not constitutionally prevented from forbidding an aggressive lock-out. The tendency to differentiate between types of lock-out also means that the defensive lock-out is regarded as dispensable for the employers under the prevailing views on parity in conflict. The real aim of the unions' policy, however, is to outlaw the suspensive and defensive lock-out. Their creativity in evolving new forms of conflict has rather hardened views on parity here. Where it is not individual companies that are the object of the unions' strike activity the danger is recognized that the employer may be put under intolerable pressure and be unable to defend himself even with mass lay-offs and other legal means. It is therefore often assumed that the legislature is not empowered to annul the protection offered by Article 9, Subpara. 3 of the Basic Law and forbid suspensive and defensive lock-outs.[539] It is only to defensive lock-outs which would widen the dispute beyond one wage contract area (sympathy lock-outs) that these parity considerations do not apply. It cannot be expected that the initiatives on prohibition of lock-outs will be very effective over the short term. But even if lock-outs were forbidden in the Federal Republic the employers would still have three means of sanction against the workers which are the functional equivalent of a lock-out:

(1) Mass lay-offs to reduce bonuses above the agreed rates and dismissals in cases of unofficial strikes.

(2) Forms of discrimination through cyclical fluctuations, which can be introduced on a large scale at any time, such as lay-offs, closures or transfers. These can be countered only by a comprehensive structural policy and political action by the state and the unions.

(3) 'Cold lock-outs', when plants cease production on the grounds that they are affected by strikes in other plants.

4

State Measures to Integrate the Unions

Supporters of a militant union policy often welcome any strike, and particularly unofficial strikes, as they entertain exaggerated hopes of this form of conflict. In the enthusiasm for the battle, especially in the Latin countries, the counter-effect of the many levels on which the unions are increasingly being drawn into legal and political participation and responsibility is often overlooked. Most modern capitalist states turn a deaf ear to the arguments of anti-union theorists and aim to give their policies a firm foundation by reaching preliminary consensus with the unions.

Integration is taking place mainly on the following levels:

(1) Legal integration
- (a) an extension of union rights in the plant
- (b) assurance of parity in conflict
- (c) the transfer of sovereign functions to the unions.

(2) The extension of co-determination and participation in the plants.

(3) State incomes policy.

(4) Profit-sharing, part of wages re-invested in the plant, asset formation.

(5) The institutionalization of interest articulation.

1. A LEGAL FRAMEWORK FOR LABOUR RELATIONS

(a) Labour Law or Industrial Relations?

More perhaps than any other branch of the law, labour law is to a particular degree 'political law and geared to a system'. The unions were therefore ambivalent towards the emergence of labour law: on the one hand it filled them with understandable suspicion because it helped to make the labour movement less articulate, on the other it was in many cases recognized as a vehicle of progress to greater freedom of movement. Union theory took different positions between two poles according to the country and political group concerned: the Marxists usually bitterly opposed increasing legalization of labour relations. In a Red Union Opposition publication in 1930 Walter Ulbricht wrote: 'In fact the wage contracts signed by the reformists with the employers' associations are always directed against the interests of the workers, as are the verdicts by state arbitrators'.[541] That does not mean that Marxists are opposed to a legal basis for industrial relations per se, but they have a different view of the law. While bourgeois law saw labour legislation largely as part of a 'work contract', the 'proletarian concept' was of public law, designed to ensure a 'labour constitution'. This still characterizes the attitude to labour law in Socialist countries.[542] Soviet literature accuses capitalist countries of a 'monopoly bourgeoisie' who are not interested in a 'long-term and comprehensive regulation of these questions' but prefer to rely mainly on collective agreements and the norms of compulsory arbitration in addition to the norms created by the legislature. But it has not escaped Soviet labour law experts either that the same tendencies are not apparent in every European country. In the English-speaking countries, for example, greater emphasis is placed on the first category and it is the legislative norms which dominate on the continent.[543] But English writers have also expressed doubts that regulation through collective agreement is a better method than legislation. Sidney and Beatrice Webb in their work *Industrial Democracy* argue that the unions will have to introduce into their legal battle 'common rules' to stabilize their successes. Both the Marxist and the Labour view see political action as of prime importance, in contrast to theorists like Selig Perlman, who believes that the labour movement will go through a maturation process in which political action will increasingly give way to purely economic considerations. This view, with its pragmatic evolutionary approach, is largely conditioned by the American experience, but the two poles of the theory of the role of law in labour relations are also abstractions from experience in various countries which should not really be generalized in this way. Even in countries which have a common tradition of continental Roman law there have been different developments in regulations of this kind.

In the nineteenth century the law did not only play a repressive role in the battle by the labour movement for organization. The right to form unions (conceded in Great Britain in 1825, in France in 1884) was only achieved after a bitter struggle although it might have seemed to derive from certain civil rights. In Great Britain the unions received legal status in 1871 and the Trade Union Act of 1875 fully legalized them and practically freed them from all the former criminal law sanctions in labour disputes. The Conciliation Act of 1896 was occasionally seen as a fall from grace in that it over-legalized industrial relations but it too spoke of intervention by the Government to settle disputes only on a voluntary basis. The Trade Disputes Act of 1906 and the legislation of 1913 and 1945 gave the unions further legal privileges. Great Britain probably best demonstrates the ambivalent function of the law. Since the founding of the TUC in 1868 one can identify five legal offensives by the supporters of the status quo ante: (1) the formation of the Royal Commission on Trade Unions in 1868 and the ensuing legislation of 1871 and 1875; (2) campaigns by the employers in the nineties culminating in the Vale judgement of 1901; (3) the Osborne judgement of 1909 as reaction to the growing strength of the Labour Party and the Trade Union Act of 1913; (4) the Trade Disputes and Trade Unions Act of 1927 in reaction to the failure of the general strike in 1926; and (5) the Industrial Relations Act of 1971. These conservative offensives were countered with an improvement of union organization and greater militancy and since the Second World War the unions have been able to undermine or obtain the repeal of verdicts and legislation which imposed restrictions on them with increasing speed.

There were many setbacks in the process of the expansion of the legal base for labour relations in Great Britain, but the long period in which the American unions existed largely outside the sphere of state legislation did not prove entirely to their advantage. It was not until 1912 and 1932 that they were fully legalized. In various states legislation still existed which placed considerable obstacles in the way of the exercise of the right to coalition and it was only after 1935 that union rights were really given a legal base in the European sense.[544] The effects of this lengthy process are still apparent today. While legislation which effectively limits union rights, like the Taft-Hartley Act of 1947, has still not been changed, the British unions succeeded in shaking off the chains of the Industrial Relations Act of 1971 three years later.

Many left-wing union theoreticians believe that the border from the positive to the negative effects of the law is crossed where the law passes from ensuring the right to coalition and free collective bargaining to the regulation of details and when wage agreements are legally recognized (in France in 1919). In Germany the labour movement is more legalist and after the early conflicts it has since 1919 been less inclined to reject labour legislation. There is a long tradition of interest in legal regulation in the German labour movement. As early as 1848 when the typographers held a national meeting — the first by representatives of a trade — in Mainz, there were demands for legislation on unions.[545] In its framework guidelines for 1975 to 1985 the SPD accords great prominence to labour legislation, placing it next to co-determination 'on the road to the restriction of business power'.[546]

But to many in the Federal Republic this degree of legalism is a thorn in the flesh. It has actually been argued that labour law is a German speciality and can only be explained by the patriarchal traditions of the country.[547] A quick look at the French 1968 Constitution will show that that is not tenable. Article 34 of that constitution in fact treats labour law, the rights of the workers' and employers' associations, as material for parliamentary legislation. At best it could be said that some particular German traits have developed in legislation on labour disputes. It is also true that there are many relations between the genesis of the labour movement and attempts to throttle it on the one hand and the extent of legislation on labour relations on the other. Paradoxically, it could be said that the more repressive labour legislation was at the outset, the more ready the trade unions were to accept integrative legislation as soon as the repression stopped.

The law has been used to persecute the unions to various extents in different countries; on the continent there has been more recourse to criminal law and in Great Britain to civil law. This has given the unions a justifiable mistrust of the bourgeois state, and even regulations such as the draft of a law on unions in the German Reich in 1906, which would have brought some improvement of their legal situation, have met with rejection. As spokesman of the

Social Democrats in the Reichstag Carl Legien rejected the government draft on the grounds that there must first be complete freedom of coalition, association and organization before private legislation could be introduced to regulate the union movement. He was supported by the representatives of the Christian unions in the centre.[548]

In Sweden the conflict was extremely bitter over union rights. A large number of the very high early strike figures are due to the battle for legal recognition. But Sweden is not now one of the countries which have detailed legislation on industrial relations. In the USA the unions had altogether a more difficult time than they did in most of the European countries, as the employers' associations did not as in Europe cooperate in the legalization of institutional relations. A low degree of normative regulation of industrial relations is not therefore necessarily identical with a better starting position on the union side. When Switzerland — the first country to do so — made collective agreements enforceable by law in 1911, this was regarded as a great victory for the unions. The increasing legalization of collective agreements was progress in so far as legally binding contracts ended the isolation of the individual worker and improved the position of the organization. That has been the case in the Scandinavian countries, Germany, Austria and Switzerland.[549] It is not a coincidence that the Swiss Federation still has as a crucial point in its statutes (Article 2, e) the demand for 'the extension of labour law and progress towards a comprehensive labour contract'.[550]

But what the unions have gained in the legal recognition of collective action they have been in danger of losing in freedom of manoeuvre in strikes, and in the Latin countries and Great Britain they have not aimed to make collective agreements legally binding because they reject the obligation to keep the peace while the agreement is in force. This is a reflection of the desire for flexibility in conflict. Where the right to strike was restricted, as it was even in Great Britain for a time in 1940, legal sanctions had to be imposed on collective agreements. But there have been freely agreed peace clauses in British agreements as well.

The greater the trend to centralization (cf. Chapter 1, 5), the greater has also been the pressure to make collective agreements legally binding and to involve the state either loosely as mediator or even as compulsory arbitrator. The use of an incomes policy and the move to a social contract (in the Netherlands in 1972 and Great Britain in 1975) have strengthened the tendency to legalization. There was necessarily bitter opposition to legal regulation wherever the legislature intervened too far in the internal affairs of the unions. It proved a costly mistake when the British Government tried to introduce the secret ballot, which has developed on a voluntary basis in Sweden and Germany, by law and so tie the progressive union leaders more tightly to their conservative rank and file.[551]

Since the 1928 legislation Sweden has been regarded as having the most successful combination of little intervention by the state and some state steering mechanism in legally binding collective agreements. In the present climate of industrial peace in Sweden it is often forgotten that the Swedish unions bitterly opposed the 1928 legislation and called a general protest strike. But when the Social Democrats came to power in 1932 the unions did not attempt to induce them to repeal the law and in 1938 the LO explicitly opposed a parliamentary motion to annul the legislation.[552]

That was not the only occasion on which unions have come to value legislation which they first opposed. That was of course easier where the legislation was brought about by progressive majorities and included the legal recognition of collective agreements (1919 in France and 1918 in Germany) than in the Swedish case, where the legislation had come from a conservative government. Perhaps it was still too early for such legislation in Sweden and the relation between the employers and the state was such as to justify the unions' mistrust. Up to then there had been no legislation in Sweden comparable to the Trade Disputes Acts of 1871, 1875 and 1906 in Britain. One can venture to make the generalization that legislation on industrial relations and collective agreements seemed acceptable to the unions where they were stronger in the political field than in the plants and could play a real part in the formulation of the regulations. During recent years the Luxembourg LAV has most clearly illustrated the ambivalent attitude of the unions to labour legislation: on the one hand it regards this as an 'absolute necessity' to safeguard minimim wages and remove discriminations against the workers in every field from job security to holiday regulations, on the other hand 'legislation on industrial relations is only a supplementary way of legalizing conditions which are largely already realized in contracts generally applicable to all workers and of making them legally binding in future'.[553]

The historical development and strength of the opposition to the unions in society and government has hardly enabled the unions to isolate the beneficial elements in legislation on industrial relations and eliminate those which were repressive or bound them too much. But modern states do not attempt to regulate every detail, they rather aim for a balance between framework guidelines and freedom of negotiation. Today we can distinguish between three groups of systems of industrial relations in Europe with regard to the legal handling of disputes:

(1) Systems in which collective agreements are not legally binding (Great Britain, Ireland).

(2) Systems which differentiate between individual and collective disputes. Collective disputes in this type are generally subject to conciliation or mediation procedures. Individual disputes are brought to court, either civil courts as in Italy or labour courts as in Belgium and France. But the borders between the types of disputes are more fluid in the Latin countries than in Northern Europe. Individual disputes there (unfair dismissal, for instance) are more frequently settled with strikes and not by taking the case to court, although not as frequently as in Britain.

(3) Systems where the obligation to keep the peace is largely legally binding and where legal sanctions are possible if contracts are infringed (Germany, Austria, Luxembourg, Switzerland, Scandinavia). This attitude to industrial relations with its strong patrimonial elements is sometimes contrasted with the free contract system in the English-speaking world. But industrial relations in countries where state intervention was for a long time rejected certainly have their framework regulations, and the process of setting norms in industrial relations is by no means uniform. There are several different types of rules:

— the unions are the only side to induce its members to follow rules;

— the employers' associations prescribe rules to the plants;

— the rules are worked out in negotiations between three parties, the employers, the unions and representatives of the state, as on the British Wage Councils;

— the rules are determined by the state.

Long before experiments such as the Industrial Relations Act of 1971 the fourth type had gained ground in Britain and de facto even in systems which emphasize that rules should be set in voluntary agreements, there are always elements of the other types. That is especially true of Scandinavia, where Denmark and Sweden proved more resistant to state intervention than Finland, where through the civil war, the war and the marginal situation industrial disputes have always been more severe than in the richer neighbouring countries. Although there is a similar development in the establishment of norms now all over Europe, the systems which adhere to the principle of contractual industrial relations still lay greater emphasis on rules of procedure and less on regulations on contents. State intervention to set norms has not only been encouraged by disputes between the partners but also, where there was rivalry between unions, by disputes inside the union movement. That was particularly the case in the USA. The more ruthlessly the craft unions tried to gain privileges for their members over other workers and win for themselves a monopoly position in certain industries, the more concern was there to have relations between unions regulated through legislation as well (Norris-La Guardia Act, National Labor Relations Act).

France is one of the countries where the idea of collective bargaining was established fairly late. The first comprehensive agreement was the Matignon Agrément of 1936 under the Popular Front Government. By 1960, 189 national agreements were in force. After the Grenelle declaration of 1968 collective bargaining became more widespread. There was further legislation in July 1971 to strengthen the contractual basis and expand the areas affected by such agreements.

(b) Legal Institutions to Settle Disputes (Labour Courts, Arbitration)

In Socialist visions of a labour constitution based on self-administration the only permissible type of mediation in disputes is *autonomous settlement* by those who will be affected by the results of the settlement. In fact in Socialist systems, however, *heteronomous settlement* by the courts is increasing. In capitalist systems autonomous settlement means settlement by the parties to the wage agreement. As the number of disputes increased the states increasingly felt the need for settlement not simply to be left to the organized groups and more heteronomous systems developed. But these still differ strongly according to the traditions of the various legal systems and labour relations:

As collective wage agreements became more binding the tendency also grew for legal systems to develop a functionally differentiated *labour jurisidiction*, both in countries with a strong cooperative labour movement, like Sweden and Germany (after 1926) and in countries with a fragmented and very militant union movement (France). The terse statement in the DGB's programme of principles: 'The realization of the state based on social right calls for independent labour, social and administrative jurisdiction'[554] is a generalization untroubled by any comparative awareness of labour relations in other Western democracies and it implies taking the much-criticized legalism of German unions as an ideological base for legal institutions which may have developed by chance in a country. In the same way it is illusory to hope that a jurisdiction overstrained by a growing flood of cases will break down as a major instrument of the realization of interests, thus re-instating the direct form of agreement.[555] There is a similar trend even in Socialist countries.[556] Experience has shown that there is no unilinear development in labour verdicts. These tend to be more repressive in crisis periods than during a boom, when the employers are less interested in enforcing their rights.[557]

The development of legal arbitration is not bound to the development of a particular jurisdiction. Italy is a country which had developed neither a system of labour courts nor a system of private arbitration and labour disputes are handled by the ordinary courts. Great Britain is another example where cases of industrial dispute are very rarely taken to court at all. At the beginning of 1976 Michael Foot refused to give the opposition legal assurances against the consequences of the closed shop which had again been permitted, on the grounds that it would be disastrous to burden the courts with a growing number of industrial cases.

Labour jurisdiction has often been felt as a repressive instrument in Germany as well. Thilo Ramm regretted that labour courts had become part of the social establishment which no-one could now remove.[558] Ireland has a middle solution with its labour court on the basis of the Industrial Relations Act of 1946. The court is a mediation body but not a court of law which can give binding verdicts.

The institutionalization of norms of behaviour for the parties in industrial relations need not necessarily be through differentiated jurisdiction. In Scandinavia, Australia and New Zealand *state arbitration* is used to enable state intervention during a crisis while maintaining the fiction of the free contract. In Denmark state arbitration and, if this was not successful, ad hoc legislation has played an important part in settling disputes between the partners (in 1956, 1963). Norway experimented for a long time with compulsory arbitration. This was reduced in 1949 and abolished in 1952. But emergency procedures for compulsory arbitration reappeared later (1958, legislation of 1964). In Australia and New Zealand state arbitration ceased to be regarded as the fire brigade and became the normal procedure for fixing wages. In New Zealand there were periodic revolts against the arbitration system (especially in 1913 and 1951) with a militancy which occasionally dropped the traditional pragmatism of New Zealand union policy and took on clear political undertones.[559]

It is not possible today to identify an 'Anglo-Saxon type' of free collective bargaining and contrast it with a global continental trend of state intervention with legislation and judicial verdicts. Among the English-speaking countries Australia has progressed furthest in developing a mixture of collective bargaining, compulsory arbitration and a semi-legislative process in which the unions, the employers and some state institutions participate. An arbitration system has developed since 1900 in some Australian states (Western Australia in 1900, New South Wales in 1901, Commonwealth in 1904, Queensland and South Australia in 1912, and in Victoria and Tasmania there is a wages board system which can take authoritative decisons. This highly legalized system with provision for compulsory arbitration added on to the British system of free collective bargaining has often been criticized as throttling but it was not really questioned even by the left wing of the Labour Party or the Communist-influenced unions as long as it clearly favoured the unions' growth and strengthened their political influence. Although there has been considerable anger at some decisions by industrial courts, especially when fines were imposed for unofficial strikes, the unions have recognized that both the arbitration commissions and the courts often emphatically support the workers and union interests.[560] Even where unions do not profit so clearly from a state arbitration system as the Australian ACTU they often regard arbitration procedures as beneficial as long as there are restrictions on the right to strike. That is true in many countries in the public sector (cf. Chapter 3, 3, c). In the USA many states have arbitration in the public sector and as the public financial crisis worsened, especially for the local authorities, the greater grew the pressure to keep down the number of strikes with arbitration. But in America too experts have argued that it would be better to give further groups in the public sector (but not the fire brigade or the police) the right to strike rather than further expand the arbitration mechanisms.[561]

Sweden shows that differentiated labour legislation can certainly be combined with a tradition of free collective bargaining. The partners here formed a labour market committee (*Arbetsmarknadskommitté*) in 1936 of SAF-LO representatives to develop a system of voluntary arbitration. In an agreement of 20 December 1938 a kind of limitation on strikes was imposed: Article 1, Section IV postulated a renunciation of any 'direct action' as long as the possibilities of peaceful settlement according to the 'basic agreement' had not been fully exploited.

In countries like Great Britain and Sweden, where there is a long tradition of free collective bargaining, much less use has been made of legal procedures even when the appropriate legislation had come into force. One may well say that it is not legislation which makes industrial relations less conflict-prone. Conversely, the fact that contracts are legally binding has not been able to guarantee peace even in countries where industrial relations are relatively harmonious, like Sweden, as can be seen with the deterioration after 1970. The tendency to use preventive measures, the emergence of a new 'corporatism' and a political culture which is based on consensus have presumably had a stronger influence.[562] Nevertheless, the Swedish balance between formal legislation and informal practices to reach consensus remains remarkable, although it would be hard to imitate in other political cultures.

Even where there was relatively highly developed legislation on labour relations it has not been so much the force of the legal sanctions as the power of the organizations which were a party to them and could use militant strength to enforce them which has ensured that they were kept.

(c) The Further Development of the Law by the Unions

On a comparative examination one should be cautious in assuming that legal arbitration is always more repressive. The law has played a very ambivalent role for the unions and there have been great changes over time. In the nineteenth century legal regulation of the freedom of coalition and union activities was regarded in almost every continental country as a paternalist relic and the English freedom of contract and free collective bargaining seemed an advantage. In the twentieth century it has appeared that if the unions consistently make the most of labour legislation the workers are better off with regard to dismissals, transfers and other arbitrary acts by the employer under the continental system than the British or North American workers are, and even German jurisdiction is not simply criticized from Great Britian, it is acknowledged that the verdict in the labour courts often goes against the employer. But the legal situation is not an independent variable. It is undergoing a process of constant development; some writers regard the unions as largely responsible for progress, for the following reasons:

(1) When appealing to the legislature the unions are not passive, they develop criticial theories (on co-determination or parity in conflict, etc.).

(2) Constitutional positions are defended and extended. Even when there has been a successful initiative on legislation it is not always possible to enforce the law. This was apparent over the five-day period of notice which was to have been given for a strike in the public sector in France, according to the 1963 legislation, and the obligation of British unions to register under the Industrial Relations Act of 1971 (cf. Chapter 1, 5).

The development in legislation is now taking three main directions:

(1) The Extension of Union Rights in Plants and Further Developments in Company Constitutions

The battle over the recognition of union activity in the plant is still going on. The employers resisted collective bargaining for a long time on the grounds that it was external intervention. When their position became untenable they tried to limit union influence in the plant as far as possible to negotiations which were governed by legal regulations. But they were not always consistent. They often preferred to give the workers time off on full pay to attend union institutions outside the company rather than make any concessions to union activity inside the plant unless they were forced to do so by state legislation.

In the Federal Republic the unions have had to come to terms with the dual system of representation through the works councils and the unions in one plant since the works councils were reinstated as an independent institution during the restoration phase after the Second World War (against the conception of the unions and actually against the original intentions of the British Labour Government for its occupied zone) (Cf. Chapter 1, 5). It is not felt that it would at present be possible to change this dual system but the present limited extent of union rights in the plant even after the amendment to the Company Constitution Act is not acceptable to the unions. It is possible that there may be some improvement of the situation through government concessions although the employers' associations will combat every attempt at politicization or apparent politicization in the plants with reference to the flood of Marxist agitation which is often directed against the unions themselves.

(2) Securing the Legal Position of Union Officials

There is occasional progress in securing the rights of union officials. The Postal Workers Union in Germany worked out with the Post Minister an agreement whereby union officials should receive equal status with the staff representatives. That meant that they and the *Vertrauensleute* could not simply be transferred or moved from their position for longer than three months. That was a privilege for 5% of the union's members. There was criticism of the agreement on the grounds that the Minister (Gscheidle) had formerly been Chairman of the Postal Workers Union. Theodor Eschenburg called the agreement 'A great step on the way to the union state' and the slogan went round: 'From the postal union to the union post', for if equal representation were to be introduced in the administrative council of an independent organization like the Post Office, unionists would be in the majority on both sides.[563] However, the Federal Republic has remained rigidly against attempts at politization. Paragraphs 45 and 74.2 of the Company

Constitution Act forbid party political activities in the plant. But this has been undermined. There are several ways of doing this:
— If the management has close ties with a party. SPD candidates particularly try during an election campaign to use their connections and get into companies, disguising their visits as information-gathering over problems in the constituency. The workers have never protested at these visits and where there are no complaints there will be no judgement.
— The cumulation of offices can bring politics into the plant.[564] This does not happen so frequently in Germany as in countries with strong left-wing parties. But even in the French unions, which are very much more political, there are opponents of over-politicization. In contrast to the Federal Republic the practice in France is 'Political parties in the plant, yes, but no accumulation of party offices with union offices'.[565]
— Politicization of works council elections. In some plants SPD members and sympathizers were given preference when the lists were being drawn up. In 1973 the SPD members grouped into the AFA (Arbeitsgemeinschaft für Arbeitnehmerfragen — Working Group on Workers and Employees Questions), to strengthen party work in plants. The group was largely formed to combat the influence of left-wing groups but it was taken as a challenge by CDU workers, some of whom threatened that the unity of the DGB's lists would be broken by competition from the social committees of the CDU. But there is no serious threat to DGB unity. Reasonable CDU representatives even regarded the re-formation of the Christian unions as a mistake; these did not flourish but they did group important CDU leaders into a splinter group and strengthened the disparity in the DGB (cf. Chapter 1, 1).

If in Germany union rights have grown only very slowly, step by step, in other countries drastic improvements have sometimes been achieved during revolutionary crises, as in France with the Grenelle agreements made on 25 May 1968 in the French Ministry of Social Affairs between the associations and the Government. The Renault workers at first rejected the draft but many of the regulations later found their way into company agreements. On 27 December 1968 legislation was passed which made many of the Grenelle regulations applicable to any company with more than fifty employees:[566]
— the right of any union to form a group in the plant;
— the collection of union fees in the plant (outside working hours

and outside the workshops);
— the right to distribute information and the use of notice boards;
— the use of a meeting room for plants with more than 200 workers or employees;
— the right to hold a meeting once a month in the plant; and
— a maximum of ten hours a month release for union officials in plants with more than 150 employees.
The unions did not achieve the right for their plant groups to negotiate wages but the practice in many companies comes close to this.

Pilot companies, like Renault, where the unions are very militant, take the lead and are followed by others. The recognition of the union plant sections was an important step towards strengthening the unity of the movement (cf. Chapter 1, 1) but at the same time it was an expansion of the union monopoly of negotiation to neutralize traditional anarcho-syndicalist tendencies and unofficial strikes. In countries where union rights are regulated not so much through legislation but rather through collective bargaining, like Great Britain, groups have achieved very far-reaching rights. In 1972 53% of shop stewards questioned in a survey said that their meetings took place during working hours; in the dual system that would at most be possible for the works councils.[567] But there are still very great differences between the facilities accorded to shop stewards in various companies and the TUC is not generally satisfied. It has a list of minimum facilities which should be accorded to shop stewards and it includes some benefits like a separate room, a notice board or photo-copying facilities, which would be a matter of course in countries where company constitution is legalized. The TUC urges managements to regard this as 'investment for good industrial relations' and not costs.[568]

The 'hot autumn' in Italy in 1969 also brought an extension of union rights, although the unofficial and in part anti-union nature of the trouble was reflected in Article 20 of the Labour Statutes (Statuto dei Lavoratori) of 14 May 1970, which does not tie the rights to union activities. Workers and employees were given the right to meet in their companies outside working hours and inside working hours for a total of ten hours a year. This must be on full pay. The workers' meetings can be called with or without the participation of union representatives. If the management is informed, union officials from unions represented in the company can be called in from outside to attend the meetings. The meetings are intended as an organ of the rank and file which is not exposed to the 'class enemy' and can thus exercise some control over the delegates in the factory councils (*consiglio di fabbrica*). There have been attempts to establish rights of recall of these delegates.[569] Radical syndicalists have always feared that the strong emphasis on union rights in the plant would preserve élitist and bureaucratic structures and not cover the workers as a whole. For André Gorz, recognition and autonomy of the labour organization was not the ultimate goal: 'it is rather the indispensable means which gives the workers the power to challenge and to impose their own policy regarding working conditions'.[570] Of course, union rights in the plant cannot be an end in themselves, but they are the prerequisite for any further claims. The contradiction between what has been called the 'concrete element in the proletarian interests' of the individual and the 'necessary abstraction of union policy'[571] is also apparent in the battle for the extension of 'civil rights for the workers on the job'. But experience has shown that after short phases of spontaneity the pendulum usually swings back in favour of control of all the processes by the union organizations (cf. Chapter 4, 5).

(3) The Demand for Parity in Conflict

There seems to be most urgency about reform policy to improve parity in conflict, for instance by legal prohibition of lock-outs. This already exists in many countries. The Metal Workers Union in Germany has for a long time argued that parity in conflict can only be re-established by militant action on the part of the unions without the possibility of lock-outs for the employers, but the employers have refuted this as 'a retrogressive step in conflict rights'. They point to the cautious attempts by the Federal Labour Court to induce respect for the principle of the relativity of means when using the heavy artillery of the lock-out.[572] Since the Federal Labour Court again confirmed the employers' right to lock out (on 21 April 1971), as a critic said, 'Without being asked but in the full sense of its role as ersatz legislator',[573] criticism of the inequality of the weapons has become much fiercer. The 9th DGB Congress took up the demand for a prohibition of lock-outs.[574]

There are three reasons in favour of this:

— experts have also argued for a long time that a lock-out hits the

workers harder than a strike the employers;[575]
— equality of weapons is now no longer regarded as identity of weapons, as strikes and lock-outs are unequal weapons in the hands of unequal partners;
— lock-outs are heavy blow to workers who want to go on working. If political groups organize boycotts of lectures at universities this is held to be impermissible but the same thing in industrial relations is held to be legal.

Discussions on parity in conflict in the Federal Republic are still too characterized by the dualist ideas of American industrial relations research. The unions apparently shared these views for a long time. This is the only way surveys can be explained which showed that unions believed they had generally been more successful than the employers' associations.[576] Representatives of organizations for the under-privileged clearly need more manifestations of success to reduce cognitive dissonance, while the representatives of privileged interests can more easily afford to be seen by their members to 'Complain without suffering' without immediately being accused of being incapable of leading the organization. The impression of greater success in negotiation which Schmölders and his team established is only possible with a reduced perception of the success that could be achieved by the workers in negotiation on the one hand and an exaggerated idea of the long-term resistance of the employers' associations on the other, which still contains something of the old 'Master in the shop' concept. This misconception of what was really achieved in early phases of union policy also leads one to suppose that in subjective terms there is no parity in conflict, although the partners often speak as if there were. Parity is also always assumed in the game theory constructions which have been used in America in industrial relations and are increasingly being adopted by economists with the German associations.[577] But these are not so applicable in the German context as they are in America, apart from the subjective and objective conflict disparity, because the conflict in Germany is not limited to wage rises and working conditions. The range and type of benefits which are the subject of conflict is made much more complex in the Federal Republic through the fringe benefits and side-effects. The concept of a 'system of threats', an analogy from the Cold War, is also less appropriate in Germany on account of the strong integration of the associations on a political level. In addition to income advantages and other material benefits legal privileges and public functions are becoming increasingly important. The tough view that only the egoistic motives of the organizations count may not be actually wrong but there are greater limits to its expression than in the pure market pattern. The more the benefits in question are outside the wage sector, the greater is the dilemma that 'free riders' benefit as well and see no reason to join an organization if they can obtain the results of all its negotiations without doing so.

Only if there is an open market with more or less equal associations can success over claims and participation be shown with the instruments for measuring commercial and advertising success, which association economists are concerned with.[578] The more the associations become integrated in a national process of will formation the less plausible is the measurement of success for one of the protagonists and the lower is the inclination of outsiders to join even where the organization can clearly book a success. But when membership drops to a certain level the negotiating position becomes so weak that two dangers arise: the organization either demands compulsory membership and throws itself into the arms of the state or it aims to take in the militancy of the dissatisfied potential group and draw this into its own ranks. Both these options are now latent in the Federal Republic. Those groups which follow a status policy are rather inclined to the first option while the unions with their tradition of class policy incline to the second.

But as union policy makes progress in legalization the counter-concept is invoked: freedom of movement for the associations is restricted under the motto 'War on the misuse of power by the associations', and one may recall the unfair labour practices legislation in the USA. In Austria the unions mounted bitter opposition to attempts to legalize industrial relations by 'public control' of the unions[579] and in the Federal Republic, too, plans which the conservative party tried to launch have been successfully opposed by the unions and sections of the SPD.[580]

2. THE INTEGRATION OF THE UNIONS IN THE POLITICAL SYSTEM

As the labour movement, as far as it was Socialist in orientation, had a perception of its role which prevented it from integrating into the system as one interest group among many, its concept of power was different from that of other interest groups (cf. Chapter 2, 1). But as the much discussed concepts of counter-power increased the mistrust of the bourgeoisie the less militant unions have usually been cautious about statements on a desire for political influence, although this has not softened the campaign against the threat of a union state. Few unionists have made statements like this one from the Secretary-General of the Luxembourg LAV: 'Let us shock our opponents for once by saying loudly and clearly: the free unions are aiming for power and influence, in the state, in the economy and in society as a whole!'[581] But he also made it clear that the influence was not to be through direct participation in the political process. The Secretary-General was actually rather disdainful of the transitory nature of the political battle: 'Parties depend on the favour of voters and governments come and go. But the unions remain, they exercise a constant influence on economic life as a whole and they are the best, indeed they are often the only guarantee of social political progress and further development'.[582]

These statements cannot disguise the fact that in democratic states the unions have by no means declined to participate in the day-to-day business of politics; their power is well rooted in the political system. The employers in Germany see seven sources of union power:[583]

(1) A monopoly in negotiation on the labour market;
(2) Co-determination in the plants;
(3) Union enterprises;
(4) Union publications;
(5) Strong union representation in parliament;
(6) Strong personal ties with the executive; and
(7) a strong position in vocational training, social administration, labour administration and labour and social jurisdiction.

In Germany, unlike Sweden, the union press is of little importance. Criticism of its relative lack of significance in the media as a whole is usually related to the fact that during strikes the unions undermine freedom of speech by refusing to print the views of the opposing side. There have been examples of this in Portugal in 1974/75 but hardly in the Federal Republic. More important is the influence of the unions through the acceptance of new public functions in administration, or in an advisory or participative capacity.[584] But as the organs concerned have balanced representation even those who believe we are heading for a state dominated by the unions do not believe that this will be the source of future union power. They feel that it will come through extension of co-determination in the plants and outside companies (cf. Chapter 4, 6) and the increase in direct political representation.

Lawyers, too, who are concerned with the question of restrictions on unions' power (over the individual worker and parallel to cartel law on monopolies) say of the unions in Germany: 'No-one can say that there have been flagrant cases of misuse of power on the path the unions have taken so far to extend their influence. . .the unions' current claims cannot simply be dismissed as too far-reaching'.[585] Nevertheless, the argument that the associations have a social obligation (from Kurt Biedenkopf) has become the vehicle for discussion of the question of public control of the unions.

But an international comparison will show that a growth in union power does not necessarily go hand in hand with direct representation in government and parliament, any more than it does for the employers. The integration of the unions into the bourgeois political system of democracy brought only a temporary strengthening of direct participation in the representative bodies and this is not a unilinear trend.

As the unions become more integrated in the existing political system two main forms have developed for the exercise of their influence on the government:

(a) representation by unionists among the political élite, in government and parliament, and

(b) cooperation between unions and political parties.

(a) Union Representatives among the Political Elite, in Government and Parliament

Militant unions originally refused direct representation or leading positions in the bourgeois state. Even the use of the institutionalized channels in the system for the exercise of influence and pressure through lobbying was resisted by most unions outside the English-speaking world. When the first Socialist parties decided to support 'ministerial Socialism' and let some of their representatives join bourgeois coalitions as ministers (the first case was Millerand, who joined the Waldeck-Rousseau Government in 1899 and caused a heated debate in the 2nd International but found many followers in the First World War), the unions also had to re-think their position. Many of their members were Socialist members of parliament and there were actually many union officials in the Reichstag under the Kaiser, although (or perhaps because?) parliament had little influence on the Government.[586]

It has become usual for Social Democrat governments to try to secure the cooperation of high union officials. There were two members of the union General Commission (Bauer and Schmidt) in the first Government of the Weimar Republic, together with the head of the Central Labour Secretariat of the unions, Wissell. A Christian unionist, Giesberts, became Reich Post Minister. After Scheidemann's resignation there were four leading unionists in the eleven-department Government headed by Gustav Bauer. But political office made union work difficult and it was decided that members of the board could only accept political mandates with the approval of the Federal Committee. After the Kapp Putsch in 1920, which was quickly brought to an end with the help of a general strike called by the unions, the union leaders under Carl Legien had a formal veto position over the appointments to Reich government offices, which made the formation of a government extremely difficult.[587] To make approval for unionists to join the Government easier unionists were offered portfolios in which they would have a direct interest, so that they could assure members that participation by unionists could alter policy in certain areas if not as a whole. This was particularly true of the Ministry of Labour. It was not one of the traditonal portfolios and in most countries was not created until the unions were so strong that their cooperation was needed (in France in 1906, the USA 1913, Great Britain 1917, Germany 1918, Austria 1932 and Italy 1947).[588]

But demands for a ministry of labour played a part in the 1848 revolution in many countries. In France it was realized for a time with Louis Blanc as head of the Committee on Labour Questions and member of the Provisional Government. In Germany it remained a claim and was first put by the national meeting of the Book Printers Union in Mainz to the German National Assembly in Frankfurt. The first point on this eight-point programme contained the concept of equal representation: 'The establishment of a German Ministry of Labour, to be elected by workers and employers'.[589]

In Great Britain the first majority Labour Government in 1945 brought many unionists to the levers of power. There were 120 members of the new Parliament who had been supported by the unions in the election campaign. They received twenty-nine of the eighty-one government offices, six with Cabinet rank, and they included George Isaacs, President of the TUC in 1945, as Minister of Labour and Ernest Bevin as Foreign Secretary,[590] but this did not prevent conflicts with the unions from developing. And the increase in the number of unionists in the Government, which the Conservatives had feared, did not take place. When the Attlee Government was formed there were six unionists with and twenty-three without Cabinet rank in it, but in 1951 there were only four with and eighteen without Cabinet rank, and young intellectuals without a union background had become the predominant type of labour minister.[591]

But union representation in parliament is more widespread than union achievement of government office. Again this did not develop uniformly in the Western democracies. We can distinguish four different patterns:

— the unions cooperate closely with the labour party and support labour candidates (Great Britain, Australia, Sweden);

— the unions cooperate with one of the political parties and form wings in delegates conferences (Federal Republic);

— the unions cooperate with one associated party in countries with a pluralist union system (France and Italy), a symbiosis which is only now being reduced to further union unity;

— the unions support parliamentary candidates, but the unions see themselves largely as lobbyists and are not mainly interested in direct parliamentary representation for their officials (USA).

(1) In *Great Britain* the TUC in 1905 produced its own election programme and organized conferences all over the country. Its Parliamentary Committee supported fifty-one labour candidates, fifteen of whom were not even supported by the labour Representation Committee, mainly because they were miners' representatives and relatively remote from the political arena. There is close cooperation between the Labour Party and the unions and this is where the parliamentary influence of the unions is concentrated. The election system and the financing method, which is not state supported to the extent that it is in some continental countries,

notably the Federal Republic, strengthen the trend in Great Britain to direct representation by unionists in Parliament. The unions' influence on the lists appears to have increased during the sixties. In the 1959 election ninety-three of the 258 successful labour candidates were supported by the unions. Altogether the unions supported 129 out of 618 candidates, which shows that their influence was important for success in the constituency. English election studies usually yield exact figures: studies on the choice of candidates showed that in 1964 38% of Labour members had been supported by the unions. In 1970 it was 112 out of 287 candidates, in 1974 155 and a larger number which received individual grants. In 1974 the Labour Party made greater attempts to win support from the unions than in 1970, as relations had cooled noticeably owing to the plans to introduce legislation on industrial relations ('In Place of Strife'). Although the unions had every reason to wish for the return of a Labour Government in 1974, they did not give strong support and about a third of the unionists supported the Conservative Party.[592]

In 1976 fifty-nine out of 113 TUC unions were affiliated to the party. They accounted for 5.8 million of the party's membership of 6.4 million. About 90% of the votes cast at the Labour Party Annual Conference come from the unions.[593]

The number of Labour candidates supported by the unions was highest at the beginning of the thirties. After the war it varied between 31% and 39% and did not rise above 40% until the seventies.

TABLE 19
Labour members supported by the unions
(in % of the total number of Labour MPs)

1929	1931	1935	1945	1950	1951	1955	1959
40	76	51	31	35	37	34	36

1964	1966	1970	1974 (Feb.)	1974 (Oct.)
38	37	40	42	40

Source: Timothy C. May: *Trade Unions and Pressure Group Politics*. Westmead/Lexington, 1975, p. 29.

Finance is as important as personal representation. In 1970 it was established that up to 78% of the general Labour Party fund had come from the unions. But a quantitative assessment of support in either form can easily give an exaggerated picture of the extent of the ties either before or after an election. These will be of varying intensity before the election according to the situation in any particular constituency. We can distinguish three types:[594]

(a) Some unions support any Labour candidate in a Labour constituency or in a Conservative constituency which looks likely to fall to Labour.

(b) Others form formal parliamentary panels, to which members are elected according to their union membership.

(c) In some constituencies candidates are tested to see whether they are well disposed towards the unions. This is certainly closest to the German practice.

After the election, too, the dependence which union support can bring varies considerably. In Parliament the unions usually leave their members free to vote on questions which do not affect industrial matters. But on industrial relations solidarity is expected, whether the government is Labour or Conservative.[595]

A study of the channels of information and influence open to union members of Parliament has also shown that the unions do not provide their members with information and 'commissions' on every question although they have an extensive list of claims, but generally only on questions which affect vital union interests.[596] A chairman of the Parliamentary Labour Party once complained that the relation between the union MPs and the rest of the party is not free from conflict as the union MPs meet in secret sessions.[597] But their cohesion is rather a matter of free will than something which can be enforced with sanctions. The unions have rarely brought in resolutions containing criticism of their MPs at congresses; this is so as not to jeopardize their privileges in access to Parliament. They are clearly aware that the close symbiosis between the party and the unions is rather a fact which has developed over time than a form of cooperation which is genuinely accepted by all their members. The majority of the public has always been in favour of a reduction of the close organizational links between the two, as surveys have shown.[598]

That of course does not mean that sanctions have never been imposed by the unions. If necessary their support can be withdrawn.

(George Brown in 1963 was the most spectacular case.) But union pressure is not always clearly recognizable. Sometimes there is a voluntary retreat in conflicts between the party and the unions (Frank Cousins' resignation in 1966 has sometimes been interpreted in this way). It is not always possible to assess how successful union pressure has been. Sometimes this is directed against members who were not supported by the unions during the election and sometimes the pressure does not succeed. MPs who have been supported by the unions do not reveal a noticeably higher tendency to follow the union if it is in conflict with the Labour Party. In fact the sponsored MPs have often been regarded as bastions of party loyalty in conflict.[599] In any case there are few sanctions available to the unions. Even the withdrawal of support has frequently not adversely affected a political career. Dependence on the unions is rather a matter of general ideological solidarity which can break down on specific issues where the unions and the party diverge.

On this point the Australian Labour Party is very much less liberal. Here the unions dominate the party machine to a much greater extent than in Britain and they leave their members less autonomy in voting.[600] The influence of the unions on the parties in this first type is also clearly reflected in election behaviour. Both in Great Britain and Australia class loyalty in elections is greater than in comparable political cultures such as the USA and Canada where there is no such cooperation.[601] The thesis of the move to the middle class dominated in studies of the fifties on the election behaviour of workers.[602] It was largely discredited after the end of the sixties[603] although the tendencies which disproved it were also too hastily generalized in the hectic period during the turn of the seventies.

Surveys have been conducted to establish the proportion of unionists in the Swedish Parliament. In 1963 of 328 who answered seventy-five said that they were members of the LO and fifty-eight of the TCO, while 102 said they were members of the KF. This means that cooperation in Sweden plays a much greater part than in England. But in view of its position the LO is hardly over-represented with these figures if — as in Germany — parliamentary representation (22.9%) is correlated with the percentage of union members in the population as a whole (20.3%) and among those entitled to vote in Sweden (30.4%).[604]

(2) In *Germany* the unions have always numerically played a big

part but their political influence has often been over-estimated. In the Reichstag in 1912 32.7% of the SPD members were union leaders and in the Weimar National Assembly in 1919 38.2% of SPD members and 13.6% of USPD members were unionists. Their political influence was generally moderate which may be one reason why motions were put forward at the founding congress of the German Communist Party in December 1918 to forbid membership of a union. But Rosa Luxemburg delayed the motions by handing them on to a committee.[605]

A study on the federal elections of 1969 showed that the unions had a monopoly of the representation of economic interests in the constituencies examined. 'But the monopoly was not worth much because economic group interests altogether played a very minor role in SPD nominations and their representation was regarded as illegitimate'.[606] The support of the unions is still important for any prospective SPD candidate but far fewer unionists stand directly as candidates than in Great Britain. The other candidates are such strong union members that union membership is often no longer a differentiating factor. Measured only by formal criteria of representation the 'union state' has long since come into being, for unionists form the majority of the members of the Bundestag (see Table 20).

TABLE 20
Trade union members in the German Bundestag (1977)

Bundestag	I 1949	II 1953	III 1957	IV 1961	V 1965	VI 1969	VII 1972	VIII 1976
Members (including Berlin)	410	509	519	521	518	518	518	518
Members organized in unions (in %)	28	38.1	38.9	42.6	46.7	55.2	61.4	63.1

Source: E. P. Müller: 'Vertreter von Arbeitnehmerorganisationen im 8. Deutschen Bundestag', *Zeitschrift für Parlamentsfragen*, 1977 (184-188), p. 185.

But the growing number of unionists is not giving the unions a corresponding increase in power as the trend for representation by officials is rather declining (twenty-two in the 7th parliament, twenty-five in the 6th and twenty-eight in the 5th). There is also a decline in the number of union board members (only four in the 7th parliament). Insofar the question raised by some lawyers as to whether parallel to the incompatibility regulations relating to mandates in some Land parliaments and certain groups of civil servants there should not be legislation on the incompatibility of a mandate and a top union position does not seem very crucial.[607] It would only be possible to achieve this without discrimination if all the top union officials were excluded which would be detrimental to the work of some of the parliamentary committees. It might be better to settle the matter on the social level, for instance by introducing regulations on incompatibility between parties and unions as in Italy. This would help to sever the connections in an indirect way without making a rigorous principle of the issue.

Membership of a union today says little on actual political behaviour. It is increasingly becoming a ubiquitous sign of progressive politicization. But it is only in some unions that the influx of left-wing intellectuals is having a temporary radical and political effect. Generally it is rather tending to integrate the unions into the system. But the large number of unionists in parliament is not making the unions any less militant. In 1974 the German Public Sector and Transport Union had ninety-seven members in parliament, by far the largest contingent. This did not prevent the union from entering into a head-on confrontation with the Government in its wage round at the beginning of that year. Indeed, the unions' political activity in and outside the state organs is more likely to further intervention by the state than the takeover of more political responsibility by the unions. Georg Benz, executive board member of the IG Metall once said: 'In that sense we wouldn't object to more of the state and less of the unions'.[608]

(3) In the *Latin countries*, where ideology unions cooperate largely with one party, parliamentary representation by the unions does not play a large part. French studies on the recruitment of candidates do not even mention membership of a union as a career vehicle.[609] But union membership is of growing importance for Italian parliamentarians and the number of unionists in parliament rose from 4.9% to 11.6% between the 1st and 3rd legislatures.[610]

The growth in the number of union leaders in the first legislature of the Republic was thus much greater than the growth in party leaders, who had always accounted for between one-fifth and one-quarter of the total number of deputies.[611] In the Communist Party especially the percentage of local union leaders rose from 21.7% (1st legislature) to 31.4% (3rd legislature) of deputies.[612] The 10% union members who represented the CGIL in 1953 were not only Communists as is often assumed. Of fifty CGIL representatives thirty-five belonged to the Communist Party and fifteen to the PSI. It was actually in the Communist Party that the greatest efforts were made to keep the number of unionists down. Long before the unions and the party established incompatibility regulations Togliatti often forced provincial union secretaries to choose between a parliamentary mandate and union office.[613] In 1969 membership of the CGIL and the CISL was declared incompatible. This did not completely prevent political inter-relations but it reduced the incentive for direct parliamentary representation.[614]

In a multi-party system like that in Italy the influence of union activity on the legislature is more difficult to assess than in a two or three-party system. A recent quantitative study of legislative output in Italy shows that most of the initiatives on labour and social legislation came from the Left and assumes that the unions were behind the initiatives from the Communists and Socialists without being able to prove this on individual points.[615]

(4) In the USA the relation between the unions and direct parliamentary representation differs from that in the Western European parliamentary systems. This is mainly because the unions traditionally do not see themselves as playing a political role and put more emphasis on a tough battle for income rises calculated on a capitalist basis than the European unions with their many different functions. The system of institutions and the franchise also contributed to the fact that an independent labour party has never emerged in the United States. In Lipset's view this could have happened with a proportional franchise or majority franchise with two election rounds in America as well.[616] The weakness of third parties and temporary movements made the unions shy away in good time from backing them. In 1895 the AFL added an eighth section to Article III of its constitution declaring that there was no room in AFL conventions for party politics, either Democratic, Republican, Socialist, Populist, Prohibitionist or any other.[617]

Like any other interest group the unions have accepted that there is no better way to exercise political influence than to 'reward one's friends and punish one's enemies'. There has been more inclination to tackle political problems directly since the New Deal but the unions again do not try to do this so much through direct representation among the members of the party they generally favour (the Democrats) as indirectly by lobbying. American unions have proved to be rather oriented to micro-areas of individual pieces of legislation and have shown little interest in macro-areas of global national integration possibilities such as incomes and structural policy. The AFL-CIO works all the time with sympathetic parliamentarians on all levels and even the President is an important target. President Johnson registered forty-nine personal meetings and eighty-two telephone calls with the head of the AFL-CIO and said he knew of no other single group which had done more for progress in the field of labour and wages legislation over the past five years than the AFL-CIO under George Meany.[618] The fragmentation of the party system according to the issue at stake also furthers this type of influence. On socio-political projects in Congress the labour lobbyists have often done more to coordinate the efforts of the Democrats than the party leaders. During the selection of candidates the unions have always tried to win the acceptance of candidates who were sympathetic to them and generally progressive against the conservative office holders and newcomers among the Democrats but their efforts have often been foiled by the conservative party establishment.[619]

The AFL-CIO has never attempted to establish its own labour party. The unions cooperate with both major parties to an extent that would not be possible in Europe. Big organizations have always used their influence especially before elections. With the looser party organization in the USA and the special features of the procedure for choosing candidates through primaries the unions have excellent opportunities to help their candidates by bringing them large parcels of votes. In 1944 the CIO founded the Political Action Committee (PAC) and in 1948 the AFL founded the Labour League for Political Education (LLPE) in order to maintain their political influence while adjusting to the restrictions of the Smith Connolly Act. When the two organizations merged in 1955 the committees were amalgamated to form the Committee on Political Education. AFL-CIO President George Meany is said to have stated, 'We have a political party, and it is known as COPE'. Maybe this was meant to be only a bon mot. In official statements the AFL-CIO emphasizes on the contrary: 'COPE...is not a political party, nor is it wedded to either major party'. In the 1976 campaign, COPE estimated that 120,000 volunteers manned 20,000 telephones and placed more than 10 million calls in the course of registration and voter drives. In most states, the Democratic Party is financed and run by organized labour. Recent studies emphasize also the predominant role of the unions in the early planning and execution of the campaigns. There are speculations that after Meany the New Left might capture control of the Democratic Party and the entire labour movement might move from its centrist position to become part of the New Politics, assuring the Democratic Socialists control of the Democratic Party.[620]

In the recent past, the AFL-CIO has not been formally involved in the presidential primaries, although individual unions and labour leaders have supported favourites. Generally the unions support Democratic candidates. But, at state level, in view of their regional power centres, they cannot afford to be exclusive with their political engagement. In a Report of the AFL-CIO Executive Council in October 1975, it was reported that COPE had a 70% success in election of its endorsed candidates for the US House, US Senate and governorships.[621] In 1972, the AFL-CIO broke with the tradition they had upheld since President Roosevelt, of always supporting the Democratic candidate. McGovern was not supported by the majority. The pretext was that McGovern was not sufficiently anti-Communist. At the heart of Meany's break with McGovern was said to be his passionate belief that the candidate intentionally tried to freeze labour out of the ruling circle within the Democratic Party.

In the 1976 presidential election the AFL—CIO exerted considerable influence over the choice of candidates of both parties. Over 660 labourites were delegates to the 1976 Democratic Convention, 418 from unions, but by this time Carter's nomination was already assured. It was accomplished without the official help or support of the AFL-CIO. The more important was the unionists' contribution to Carter's election. In 1976, 63% of the union voters, against 36% of the non-union voters, supported Carter, second only to the non-whites (85%).

Labour's ability to finance electoral activities at the federal level has been affected significantly by legal developments which have occurred since 1972, such as the Federal Election Campaign Act Amendments in 1974 and 1976. Financial involvement in the federal elections will at least be more in the open than previously. In 1976, AFL-CIO COPE and eleven individual trade unions are reported to have spent 5.4 million dollars.

Generally, one can say that direct parliamentary representation of all four types is declining in importance for the unions' activities because new channels of articulation are opening up, co-determination institutions outside the company, social and economic councils, advisory councils and so on (cf. Chapter 5, 5-6).

Integration of trade union élites today in many countries with tendencies towards a liberal neo-corporatism is achieved less by parliamentary representation of trade unionists than by indirect governmental patronage in the so-called 'Quango' type of organization (Quasi Autonomous Non-Governmental Organization), which play an increasing role in recruiting trade union leaders even in the USA, where direct political activities of the unions are less developed than in the countries in Northern Europe.

(b) Cooperation Between Unions and Parties

During the historical development of the labour movement very different forms of cooperation between parties and unions have emerged despite the early attempts at coordination between the various organizations. The genesis of the unions and the parties is still affecting these relations today in many countries. Three main types have appeared in Europe:

(1) A labour party was formed on union initiatives to achieve parliamentary representation (England, Norway, Sweden).

(2) Ideologically and personally the party played a large part in the establishment of the unions (Germany).

(3) Fragmented union groups maintained a distance from party political and parliamentary struggles. Sometimes they even developed a strong mistrust of centralized union organization and only formed alliances with certain parties very late. In comparison with the SPD or the British Labour Party these had little continuity in the early days of organized parties (the Latin countries, especial-

ly France, Italy and Spain).

Materialist attempts to explain this difference between the various forms of organization have sometimes seen the priority of the unions over the labour party as due to the early days of industrialization and the state of the productive forces, rightly for England, less so for the Scandinavian countries. But ideological and cultural traditions have been equally important. Although Engels recognized that '. . . if there are to be mass movements it will have to start with the trades unions etc. . .' (MEW, Vol. 37, p. 353), both Marx and Engels always emphasized the primacy of the party for all the European countries. Nevertheless, their view was not generally accepted either in England or in the Latin countries but only in countries in Central Europe where the political culture was more strongly influenced by the dialectics of Hegel and Marx. In England the unions first formed a political alliance with the Liberals and they were for a long time characterized by a pragmatism which was far removed from any ideology of fundamental change.

Ireland retained archaic patterns of organization for a long time. The Irish Trades Union Congress and Labour Party existed from 1914 to 1931 and it was not until 1931 that the Labour Party split off as a separate institution within the labour movement.[622] In the Latin countries, too, different forms of organization developed from those envisaged by Marx and Engels. Anarchist and syndicalist ideas penetrated deep into the Socialist unions and parties.

But the state of the political system at the time when the labour movement began to form must be included as a variable together with the economic and ideological factors. Party priority in active class struggles and the consequent ideological support for party primacy are particularly apparent in countries where strong autocratic elements were obstacles to bourgeois democracy, as in Germany and particularly Russia. It can hardly be coincidence that the Bolsheviks put most emphasis on party primacy despite the influence of Anarchist ideas on the Russian labour movement. Conversely unions were most strongly inclined to unrevolutionary pragmatism in the Northern European monarchies where the bourgeois movement for democracy and parliament seemed to offer the greatest legal scope for working-class organizations as well.

(1) In the countries of the first type the links between the labour parties and the unions are still strongest today. Externally it is the

genetic and now not necessarily the political priority of the unions which is reflected in the fact that the majority of the party members are unionists. Union majorities in the fifties were:

British Labour Party	87.2%
Australian Labour Party	62%
Swedish Social Democrats	71%
Norwegian Labour Party	55.3%
Indian Socialist Party	17%

Sources: Raymond Fusilier: *Le parti socialiste suédois*, Paris, 1954, p. 71; Aksel Zachariassen: *Det kollektive medlamskap*, Oslo, Tiden Norsk, 1966, pp. 16ff.

English-speaking writers have attempted to classify this type of party with collective union support as a 'labour party', in contrast to the Socialist or Social Democrat parties.[623] But this creates difficulties because the organization structure of membership is made the only criteria in such a typology. The Swedish Social Democrats, who in their early phase were rather oriented to the German Social Democrats in many points, are then included as a labour party on account of a few superficial analogies in spite of their programmatic declarations. The definition has the further disadvantage that it designates a dying type without being able to make any pronouncements on the regenerative ability of these parties in other areas. In most countries where there are close organizational links between the party and the unions there is a tendency for collective union membership of the party to decline (Great Britain 1956 70%, 1965 64%, 1972 55%; Australia 1954 62%, 1964 56%).[624] Sweden is an exception (1957 71%, 1967 75%; in 1957 38% of LO members were in the party and in 1967 42%). This is due to the merger of local unions into larger organizations which often then decided to join the party.[625]

One reason for the general tendency for collective union party membership to decline is that more middle-class members are joing the party, so that there is a relative drop in the union figure. The increase in state financing for parties means that parties in some countries are now less dependent on financial aid from the unions. A related factor is the growth in syndicalization of white collar workers and non-craftsmen who are usually less willing than workers to join a labour party (cf. Chapter 1, 3). This tendency is particularly marked in Sweden, where the central organization of the white collar workers (TCO) has almost half the membership of the union head organization, LO. In the 1970 election 75% of the LO members voted for the Social Democrats, according to surveys, but only 38% of the TCO members and only 15% of the academics' association SACO did.

A survey of manufacturing workers in 1973 showed that about 22% of the workers sympathized with the 'bourgeois parties' and nearly two-thirds with the Social Democrats. Another study showed this latter proportion to be higher (nearly 97%) and it is much higher the greater the standing of activists among trade union members (up to 98%).[626]

In view of this development the criticism of the symbiosis is now fiercer from the Left than from the Right. The alliance of the two pillars formerly seemed more frightening to the bourgeois groups than it does today and there is less inclination to aim for restrictive legislation.

In England the Conservatives in 1927 after their election victory passed the (short-sighted) Trade Disputes and Trade Unions Act which not only forbad general strikes like that in 1926 but also forced on union members a system which was a speculation on their political apathy. While since the Trade Union Act of 1913 every worker who did not want to be a member of the Labour party as well could give a written declaration to that effect when joining the union (contract out), under the new Act (which was repealed by the Labour Government in 1946) new union members had expressly to declare that they were ready to have part of their membership fee given to the Labour Party (contract in).[627] Neither the unions nor the party are very forthcoming with figures on contracting out. Studies by industrial sociologists such as Goldthorpe and others show that about a quarter of those questioned contracted out, although a large number of them were actually Labour supporters. Even those who did not object to their fees going to the party should not be assumed to have very strong political interests. 50% of the workers questioned by the Goldthorpe team who intended to vote for the Labour Party at the next election willingly paid fees to it and 27% of those questioned knew nothing about the arrangement.[628] This figure is higher than the usual one, which suggests that at most 20% of union members contract out.[629] Perhaps the higher figure is due to the fact that the study focussed on affluent workers. When the parties debated the principle of contracting out in 1946[630] the mood was outwardly cool but the debate concealed a real conflict of interests between the parties. In 1926 the Conservatives had openly admitted that the new Act was intended to channel funds away from the Labour Party.[631] When the Labour Party repealed the Act in 1946 the Conservatives' worst fears seemed realized. The number of unionists giving funds to the party rose from 48.5% (1945) to 90.6% (1947).[632] Support for the party from the unions was at its lowest in 1943 at 41.8%. The figure of 90% is higher than that of admitted Labour voters. In Sweden as well there have repeatedly been cases of Communists or conservatives who have knowingly or carelessly supported the labour party in this way. But surveys show that active support for the labour party and its aims is by no means as great as the conservatives fear, at any rate it is not as great as the finance figures suggest. The unions have not been able to use their close relations with the party to exclude anyone to the Left of them or the many liberals from office. But these minorities still only play a relatively small part in the political lives of the unions. Paradoxically even the Communist Party owes a lot of its growing importance in Britain to the union element. The shop stewards, where they achieved a fundamental opposition to the system, have greatly contributed to the growth of the party with their recognition of the necessity for unity outside the plant, although this can sometimes drive them into a triangular conflict of loyalties with the rank and file who elected them and the unions they belong to.[633]

Sweden has a long and eventful history of the divergence of the two pillars of the labour movement. Between 1895 and 1899 between 95 and 97% of the total membership of the Social Democrat Party were collective members from the local union organizations.[634] Before the LO was established in 1898 the party was the only central organization of the labour movement; very few of the unions were organized on a national level and they were politically weak. When the LO was founded it was decided by 175 votes to eighty-three that the local unions must join the SDAP within three years of joining the LO but this was never fully implemented and the requirement was then dropped (1900). Many members both of the party and the unions were very doubtful about making union members compulsory members of the party. Branting, the party leader, justified it with the 'compulsion to freedom' in a capitalist world in which the workers did not even have the general franchise.[635] As might have been expected, the party then developed strong regional units when the franchise barriers fell, and the two pillars of the labour movement moved further away from each other. The failure of the general strike in 1909 strengthened the party further. But even in the early phase, when the party was still largely a political off-shoot of local unions, the party leaders were not greatly dependent on the unions. It is not coincidence that the first President of the LO, Frederik Sterky, was an active party politician and not a unionist and two members of the five-man secretariat of the LO had to be nominated by the party executive.[636] The relation between the party and the unions was one of mutual dependence. The idea that the unions gradually freed themselves of the party is rather a generalization from German history than a reflection of the reality in Sweden, although the party occasionally acted as censor of good and bad strikes with an eye rather to the agitation effect of the strikes than their economic benefit to union members.[637] The strong ties between the LO and the party came under increasing criticism not only from the Left but also from the Right. The white collar workers' association, TCO, especially opposed the one-party loyalty of the LO for a long time. According to a survey among Swedish trade unionists 18% of members collectively affiliated to the Social Democrats had reservations and favoured either the Communists or the 'bourgeois' parties. Only a tiny minority contracts out — usually they are Communists. Among the trade union members nearly two-thirds are not in favour of collective membership (64%) and even a third of the officials (33%) have mental reservations about this institutional link.[638]

In Denmark some unions passed resolutions in 1974 to give support to parties on the left of the Social Democrats as well. Otherwise here as in all the Scandinavian countries cooperation with the Social Democrats is a programmatic principle for the unions.[639] The Danish union federation, LO, has two representatives on the Executive Committee of the Social Democrat Party and the party has two on the LO Executive.[640]

In Norway the LO Chairman is traditionally a member of the Central Committee of the labour party and generally all the members of the LO Secretariat are party members.[641] In Norway and until 1955 in Sweden there was a liaison committee between the party and the unions. After 1955 in Sweden the party tried to loosen its ties to the unions. What Sweden was trying to undo, Great Britain began to practise to a greater extent in the seventies. After 1972 the Liaison Committee became a more important organ of union influence on the party in many respects than the national Executive Council of the party. The Liaison Committee is comprised of equal numbers of representatives of the National Executive Council of the party and the TUC. The influence of the Liaison Committee has been overrated because of Conservative misgivings about the development of a state dominated by the trade unions. The committee boasts of having contributed in the last five years to the nation's economic recovery and to a 'marked improvement in the climate of industrial relations'. If that is so, it can also be said that the Liaison Committee was sometimes concerned with very premature problems, as can be seen from the blunt statement: 'We look forward to the abolition of the House of Lords'.[642] On the other hand more urgent problems such as agreement on a social contract and the Government's economic policy were not settled by the committee.

It seems that the work of the Liaison Committee was more important when the Labour Party was in opposition. Since 1974 direct access for the unions to the ministries was more regular than before and the committee was generally not used as a forum through which the unions sought to use party pressure in pursuit of their policies.

In Norway early evidence has been found that most trade unionists (60%) prefer their organization to remain politically more neutral, and in the second half of the seventies there has been pressure within the unions to dissolve their ties with the labour party.[643]

In a country like Finland, where two Socialist parties, the Social Democrats and the Communists, have been fighting for years with varying intensity for influence in the union movement, it is not possible for the unions to take a stand clearly on the one side or the other. The SAK Statutes of 1971 only refer to 'cooperation with the labour parties' on all questions of interest to wage earners and the aims of the union movement.[644]

In Denmark and Norway there is a relatively good balance between the two sides. It is difficult to say in these countries which of the two organizations would, if it came to the point, have the final say. But industrial relations specialists have recognized a danger in

Scandinavia too that with the constant growth in the policy areas for which the party feels competent its influence on the unions will grow inexorably the longer it remains in power.[645] Since the reactivation of the Left in the Scandinavian countries at the end of the sixties there has been increasing criticism of the close relations between the unions and the party as these discriminate against left-wing parties. The hegemony of the Social Democrats is further strengthened by union support for its press. Every year millions flow from union funds in Denmark and in Sweden to Social Democrat press organs.

In 1945 the British Communists argued that their party should be aligned with the Labour Party as they were already collective members of the party through their union membership and were giving their funds to it. But this, like other similar motions, was rejected by the Labour Party. It was only in Australia that the dilemma led to divided loyalty for union members because some unions collectively joined the Democratic Labor Party. There was less conflict between the unions and the party in Sweden and more unionists supported the party than in Great Britain where more than 10% availed themselves of the opportunity to contract out. In Sweden it has been estimated that the comparable figure is below 1%.[646]

Close cooperation between a Social Democrat party and the unions as we find it in this first type does not mean that the relations are free of conflict. The unions themselves are too fragmented and there are too many inter-union disputes for there not to be attempts to transfer these to the party or use the party as a battleground. This can be seen in Great Britain and particularly in Australia.[647] In Great Britain the conflicts increased partly because the Labour Party was in power longer after the Second World War than in Australia. Before the war there were only minority Labour governments (in 1924, and 1929 to 1931) and it was then clear that a weak government could not simply be a political arm of the unions. Nor did the unions expect the Government to give way to their demands. It was in opposition that the Labour Party increasingly became 'the General Council's party', as a well-known party historian once put it.[648]

The first Labour Government after the war, and the first ever to have a sufficiently strong majority to be able to pursue a genuinely Socialist policy, the Attlee Government from 1945 to 1951, went through phases of bitter conflict. From 1945 to the autumn of 1947 the unions were friendly and critically detached. From 1947 to 1950 there was close cooperation and after 1950 union opposition to the policy of a wage stop grew. The first major confrontation occurred in 1948 when Stafford Cripps in a White Paper, 'Statement on Personal Incomes, Costs and Prices', advocated a prices and incomes stop.[649] Wages and incomes policy is a cause of conflict between the unions and the party in every country (cf. Chapter 4, 5). In Great Britain the relation between the Labour Government and the unions became increasingly tense from 1964 to 1970 and it was only the attempts of the Heath Government to shackle the unions with the Industrial Relations Act in 1971 which brought the unions and the party closer together again.

Over the question of entry to the European Community the unions in Great Britain, Norway and Denmark were generally more decisively against entry than the leaders of the Social Democrat or Labour parties. The result of the referendum in favour of entry in Great Britain was interpreted by many people as a defeat for the unions. It showed that the left wing of the union movement, analogous perhaps to the conflict between the Industry Secretary Anthony Wedgwood Benn and the conservative majority in his party, had overestimated its influence. Conviction is therefore growing that even well-meant pressure policy from the left wing in the Labour Party will not be successful with support from anti-capitalist forces in the unions and that the reformism in the party cannot be overcome with parliamentary strategies without a readiness to mass mobilization.[650]

(2) Where religious differences did not fragment the union movement, as they did in the Netherlands and Switzerland, the second, Middle European type shows a close relation between the party and the unions; the *Social Democrat-oriented unions* predominate strongly under the influence of the party (Germany, Austria). While the English type was connected with a strong splintering of the union movement, in Germany Social Democrat leadership was undisputed even before there was a general union; the Christian unions (404,682 members in 1918) and the liberal Hirsch-Dunker Gewerkvereine (189,831 members in 1918)[651] only played a marginal role in comparison to the Social Democrat unions. So it is very surprising to see Germany cited as a prime example of a fragmented union movement in an 'anti-revisionist'

pamphlet from Albania, with conclusions drawn from this as to the 'revisionism' of German unions.[652]

The Central European type of cooperation between the party and the unions where there is formal equality between the two but the party factually dominates in political questions was developed in theory by the Central European Socialists at various international congresses after the beginning of the twentieth century. At the Socialist Congress in Stuttgart in 1907 this type of cooperation (still known as the Austrian model) was regarded as ideal. The reporter of a resolution on the relation between the party and the unions, Heinrich Beer (Vienna), recommended this type with these words: 'We see in the exchange of personnel the means of reaching understanding. There are unionists in the party leadership and well-known party members are on the union committees'.[653]

But in fact the aim was difficult to realize. Even where there was a federal central organization to which the majority of the relevant unions belonged, like the British TUC, direct relations did not develop between this and the party. Institutionally the TUC has far fewer formal relations with the Labour Party than the LO in Sweden or Denmark with their Social Democrat parties. In England it is rather the individual unions which have institutional relations to the party. Where there was an ideological split between the unions and the party the Austrian model was not practicable. The Socialist politicians of the 2nd International were well aware of this when they attempted to regulate the relations between the parties and the unions. Karl Kautsky, one of the main ideologists of the 2nd International, declared in 1907 in Stuttgart:

> Now there are comrades, who agree with the standpoint of the Austrian resolution but believe that it would not be practicable where the party is split. They are afraid that a closer relation between the party and the unions would then mean that the union would split as well. That would certainly be a very serious matter, the unity of the union movement is of major importance and if it is threatened by a split in the party this can lead to estrangement between the party and the union.[654]

Kautsky was criticizing the French union movement and indirectly accusing it of not paying enough attention to the party. Legien was more brusque when he pointed out what the Austrian reporter was trying to avoid:

> The French do not have a union organization. As soon as they have there will be no more discussion and propaganda for a general strike, direct action and sabotage. We will not be able to move the bourgeoisie with fine words but only with a unified working class ready for conflict.[655]

The verdict that France did not have a union movement was too hard. But Legien rightly saw that anarcho-syndicalist traditions were partly responsible for the split in the labour movement both on the level of the party and in the unions. These traditions are still active today although France now has far more verbal Marxists on both sides of the labour movement than the Federal Republic.

The theoretical model developed by the international Socialist congresses is still part of the concept of the unions in Germany and Austria. In both countries the development of a general union prevented too great a dominance by the party, for fear that the union would be jeopardized. On the other hand in both countries the unionists often had to accept the fact that the party had to make many compromises against union interests and see unionists who held party offices or parliamentary mandates agree to these compromises because they had no alternative.[656] Despite this relative distance between the party and the unions, the relation of groups outside the Social Democrat party is always sharply criticized. That is especially true of Germany, less so of Austria, where the other political groups can form party groups and thus have retained a certain political influence as minorities (cf. Chapter 1, 1). The threat of the German conservative parties to form an ideology union need not be taken too seriously but although there is a certain exchange of staff between the SPD and the DGB it has helped to loosen the ties between the party and the unions, so that these are not so close as in the English/Scandinavian type.[657] Nevertheless, party surveys have shown that union ties are three times as high in the SPD (38% of members) than in the CDU (12%),[658] so the thesis of the resultant increasing political disorientation of the unions should be reflected in a growth in their membership, but this is not the case. The membership of the SPD is growing while that of many unions is dropping, which rather leads to the conclusion that the parties are becoming more attractive through the range of services they offer than that the unions are becoming a potential ersatz party. The opening of the SPD as a popular party has reduced the number of offices which are exchanged between the unions and the party but even those that remain are rather regarded as the expression of traditional ties than agreement on political aims. This did not, however, prevent the conservative parties from conducting an unusually fierce campaign against the integration between the SPD and the DGB in its 1976 federal election campaign.

In the Middle European type of interaction between the party and the unions the party has always been both ideologically and organizationally superior. Until the anti-Socialist legislation in Germany the unions were regarded as inferior to the political movement and even after the repeal of the legislation this opinion was to be heard in the party although there was a more cooperative attitude in the party towards the unions. The Party Congress addressed a resolution to its members, asking them to join a union. In 1892 there were more conflicts when the first Union congress in Halberstadt expressed scepticism with regard to the SPD's revolutionary vision of the future. At the SPD Mannheim Congress in 1906 a compromise formula was found for a modus vivendi in Bebel's resolution on political mass strike: 'The unions are essential for the improvement of the class position of the workers within bourgeois society. They are no less important than the Social Democrat Party. So the two organizations are dependent on mutual understanding and cooperation in their fight'.[659] But this division of labour on the road to Socialism did not reflect the real balance of strength between the two organizations, and the unions in this second type have never played the independent political role they have in Great Britain or the Latin countries. In the framework guidelines laid down by the SPD for 1975-1985 the traditional superiority of the party is still apparent: 'The unions cannot perform for the party the function of political leadership nor can they activate and mobilize party members, supporters or the population at large. The same is true of the further development of the social state through the legislature and acts of Government'.[660]

(3) In the Latin countries with their fragmented ideology unions the tradition of an independent union strategy for the Socialist transformation of society was strongest. However, the weakness of the rivalling unions had to be compensated by ties with particular parties and the unions only began slowly to free themselves from this embrace in the sixties. In France and Italy union unity was actually jeopardized by too close ties with a party, and relations with a party often had to be bought with a sacrifice of union unity. At the 26th Congress of the CGT in April 1946 the Left (then the

Unitaires) succeeded in obtaining an amendment to the statutes repealing the prohibition on members holding office in the CGT and in a party at the same time. This considerably strengthened the influence of the Communists and the group 'Force ouvrière' split off again under Léon Jouhaux, who had been Secretary-General of the CGT for many years. The group accused the majority of aiming to make the CGT the transmission belt of the Communist Party. The former reformist Confédérés wing largely gathered round the new group, which at first only formed a parliamentary group. The Communists in the CGT tried to mobilize the majority in resolution of the conflict and at the beginning of 1947 won a vote in the Federal Committee with 857 to 101 in favour of a survey in the plants (not only of union members) to counter the accusation that they had won by a majority of votes. Two events completed the breach: the conflict over the Marshall Plan and the controversy over tactics on major strikes. The FO wing was ready to negotiate and declared that a continuance of the strike would be foolhardy. In April 1948 the FO was founded. But the new organization did not succeed in attracting all the reformists. Whole organizations, the book printers for instance, and the majority of the civil servants, remained loyal to the old union. The FO mobilized between 800,000 and a million workers and achieved only a third of the membership of the CGT. Formally, independence of a party was included in the statutes, in fact Jouhaux cooperated closely with the SFIO.

The more political the workers became in certain countries and the greater the number that opted for a left-wing coalition, the easier was it for the union leaders to exercise a political mandate in their members' interests. But in the Latin countries there remained a danger that the leaders and the majority of the members would find themselves in different political camps with occasional friction in will formation. But this rarely appeared in as extreme a form as Eugène Descamps, Secretary-General of the Christian CFTC (predecessor of the CFDT) described: 'Our cadres belong to the PSU, our supporters to the MRP, and our voters vote UNR'.[661] But there was cause to remember the thesis put forward by Alain Touraine on the relative independence between political and union action in France. The dictum of some eminent French scholars, however, that the CGT is less linked with the PCF than the German DGB is with the SPD may become true in the future. For the past it is an exaggeration.[662]

Nowhere in the latin countries has the relation between the parties and unions changed as much as it has in France: firstly the unions changed their ideology, then the Socialist party and the left party spectrum shifted in its internal structure and in its position in the French party system. There was least change in the relations between the CGT and the Communist Party and most between the CFDT and the left-wing parties. The orientation of the Parti Socialiste (the former SFIO) to the left after the resignation of Guy Mollet and the election of Alain Savary in 1969, strengthened by the May unrest in 1968, was also due in part to pressure from union members of the party's Executive Committee. The party Congress was against any further allinace with the bourgeois parties and in favour of negotiations with the Communist Party. The leaders of the former Christian union CFDT were at the beginning of the seventies rather to the left of the Socialist Party and felt many ties to the left-wing Socialist PSU. Under Rocard the PSU moved away from the Leninist concept of the transmission belt and came increasingly into ideological conflict with the Communist Party.

The CFDT issued a political statement in January 1974 which again clarified its relation to the Communist Party: its aim of a union of popular forces meant that the Communist Party would have a major role to play. On the other hand mental reservations are still apparent: 'That does not mean that the CFDT holds the view that the Communist Party has changed to such an extent that all risk of bureaucratic and centralist tendency can be excluded'.[663] The union showed its pluralist attitude to the left by putting forward the argument, in contrast to the Communist Party and the CGT, that the extreme Left organizations could make a contribution to action by progressive forces. But the relations between the PSU and the CFDT were not always free of conflict either. The PSU was increasingly in favour of political militancy in plants while the CFDT regarded it as inopportune and dangerous to build up political groups in the plants.

In times of increased political conflict the relations between the party and the unions have always been troubled with Socialist parties tried to approach the workers by by-passing the unions. The influence of the PSU decreased as time passed after the 1968 unrest when it had become more highly profiled, and the re-strengthening of the Socialist Party under Mitterand brought a re-grouping of the Socialists which Mitterand tried to further by gaining a mass base among the workers through CFDT members. In scarcely any other

European union do the leaders have such a complex history of party political engagements as the CFDT leaders. Gilbert Declercq told an interviewer than he had supported, one after the other, the Popular Front (before the Second World War), the left-wing Catholic MRP (after the war), the SFIO, the PSU and after 1969 the new-formed Socialist party under Mitterand.[664] This would not be worth mentioning if it were not typical of many CFDT leaders. In 1973 62% of CFDT members voted for the Left (PC 21%, PS 30%, PSU 11%, but of CGT members 58% voted for the PC, 29% for the PS, 1% for the PSU).[665] According to surveys by Sofres 73% of CFDT members voted for Mitterand in the presidential elections in 1974. This refutes the accusation which is often made that union leaders have moved too far away from the rank and file with their orientation to the Left. Clearly about three-quarters of the members were in favour of this decision.[666] A Soviet analyst of the French labour movement concluded in 1975 from a comparison of the various surveys published in the *Nouvel Observateur* that there was a growing class consciousness among the workers but she did not pay enough attention to the growth in the number of Socialists under Mitterand and the groups to the left of the Communist Party, which she dismissed as 'left-wing anarchist pseudo-revolutionary phraseology', although as a consequence the new 'class-consciousness' was not to the unsullied delight of the Communist-oriented unions.[667] Even the Force Ouvrière, which was often criticized by left-wing parties and unions for its ideological revisionism and loyalty to the opportunist SFIO policy under Guy Mollet and its international orientation to the German DGB, increasingly voted Left. In 1973 43% of its members voted for the Socialist Party, 20% for the Communist Party, 3% for the extreme Left. However, one third of the FO was still on the Right. 34% of their votes (in contrast with 38% of the CFDT and 12% of the CGT) went to the Centre or the Right. In the presidential elections the FO voters proved to be much more right-wing than the CFDT members. The voting according to the Sofres surveys was as follows:

	Mitterand	**Giscard d'Estaing**
FO	52%	48%
CFDT	73%	27%
CGT	90%	10%

Source: Alain Bergounioux: *Force Ouvrière,* Paris, Seuil, 1975, pp. 159, 161.

The orientation of the CGT and the CFDT to a Socialist programme has been welcomed by Roger Garaudy as of fundamental importance:

> It is the beginning of the end of a murderous dualism, the radical differentiation between unions which strictly limit themselves to economic claims and parties which tackle only political aims and approach only 'from the outside' the problems which arise in labour relations and spread with irresistable continuity to all sections of society.[668]

Although many of Garaudy's suggestions appear to be rather bound to the French syndicalist tradition he, like others who have moved away from Moscow orthodoxy, is contributing with his views on an unmanipulated democracy of the rank and file to overcoming the old dualism between the parties and the unions in theory at least. Surveys among members have shown that about 60% of French workers (in 1970) were in favour of joint programmatic work between the parties and the unions, but only 34% wanted to see this as exclusive cooperation between a union and 'its own' party. The workers were also of the opinion that the three big unions in France could not be 'assigned' to specific parties. Even the CGT was only characterized as 'Communist' by 34%.[669]

There has also been a strong change in the relation between the party and the unions in Italy, where the shift in the coalition spectrum at government level has also played a part. In the sixties the Christian unions were no longer prepared to accept the dominance of the party as they formerly did.[670] But they did not emancipate themselves from this as far as the CFDT in France. Moreover, the parties re-oriented between the two big blocs of the Communists and the Christian Democrats (the Socialists [PSI], the Social Democrats [PSDI], and the Republicans [PRI]) under the motto of an 'opening to the left' and entered a phase of increased cooperation with the unions. The UIL particularly sensed that it could strengthen its own position in the *centrosinistra*. This caused many difficulties for the Communist-dominated CGIL, because it rejected the opening to the left which was approved by many union members who were not Communists.[671]

The idea that the unions are only transmission belts for the parties is increasingly being discredited. The Communists are also verbally moving away from this concept[672] although party dominance is still relatively strongest on the CGIL. The Executive Committee of the French CGT on 31 March 1971 accepted theses on Socialism which speak of a 'fully sovereign role...for the CGT in a Socialist France'.[673] The unions feel stronger towards the parties, and in some cases parties which have a much more Socialist programme than the unions could afford have been criticized:

> Here, too [in the Socialist Party], the outlines have been blurred by a rather pragmatic day-to-day policy and it is difficult to estimate in how far the principles which are in the declaration but are not described in detail in the programmes are still valid, in how far the leaders have already given them up and in how far they are just being covered up because of electioneering tactics.[674]

Precisely in countries with a pluralist union structure and left-wing parties we find the paradox that the unions usually have the less Socialist programme but are more Socialist in their statements than the parties which share government responsibility. It is easier for the unions to take this line since even those unionists who hold government office do not make the union as a whole responsible for any particular policy on the part of the government. In the immobility of a multi-party system, in which only a few groups in the centre have so far been regarded as generally appropriate for a coalition, there is little point in a strict separation between parties and unions. In many cases since the hot autumn the Italian unions have performed functions for the parties without usurping their role in any way over the longer term.[675]

Too close relations between unions and parties has been recognized as a disadvantage by the unions in many countries. In this third type of organization pattern two counter-measures have been tried by the labour movement:

— encouragement of unity to remove fragmentation (cf. Chapter 1, 1);

— a loosening of the ties to the parties by introducing incompatibility regulations on a combination of top posts in the union and the party (cf. Chapter 1, 1).

It remained controversial which side should take the leading role in this loose alliance: neo-syndicalist theories in France and Italy largely supported union primacy, because they held that in a neo-capitalist system the unions are much more of a catalyst than the party and are the centre of the formation of class consciousness.[676]

But radical Marxist-Leninist groups regarded even a demand for stronger independence of the unions from the party as 'bourgeois ideology' because the capitalists were largely independent of their party (in Italy this meant the DC) and hence tried to force the workers into the same position to isolate them and split them off from their political organizations.[677] But these left-wing arguments did not prevent the Communist parties in France and Italy from accepting this separatist trend. In a joint declaration on 18 November 1975 they supported the 'free activities and autonomy of the unions', although this is certainly not in keeping with Leninist organizational principles.[678]

The functional change for the unions as they again became more political after the fine weather phase of the re-construction period in Western Europe has made the former division of labour between the unions and the parties increasingly questionable. In many cases the necessary process of differentiation between their functions has been seen as a revisionist fall from Grace, as it was once in Sweden, where the union function was separated from the Social Democrat party and the LO created (1898).[679]

Different factors determine the unions' militancy towards parties they cooperate with:

(1) Whether a general union encourages or discourages militancy cannot be generalized from the German case. On the one hand the pluralism of party-organized unions is said to be stimulating, on the other fragmentation rather limits the field for action. Often the big Communist unions particularly have only participated in strikes if they were sure that they would be able to take the lead in the action. The relatively quietist development in the German union movement after the war cannot be primarily deduced from the existence of a general union and its interaction with the SPD. Other factors like the strong redistributive capacity after the war, the orientation of the German economy to exports, the development of anti-Communism in the western half of the country which was much stronger than that in any other Western European country and many integrative institutions (ranging from co-determination to Concerted Action) are important causes of the lack of militancy.

(2) On a comparative basis the position of the labour party in the party system is an important determinant. While theoretically party primacy can be a stronger deterrent to de-politicization than purely syndicalist conceptions, the party loses this possibility under certain circumstances, especially if it is not, as in the third type of pluralism of unions and left-wing parties, exposed to competition on the left, like the big Communist cadre parties which follow the Moscow line and have constantly to battle with left-wing Socialist,

Trotskyist and Maoist splinter groups. These may not show a very continuous development in France and Italy but they are a stimulus to a more energetic representation of the workers' interests. From this point of view the 5% clause on the innovative capacity of the system in the Federal Republic and the 4% clause in Sweden are a disadvantage, because they give the party and union leaders a false sense of security.

(3) A functional equivalent of the protection of the party against competiton from the Left in the second type is the preference given to the Social Democrat Party in the first type of cooperation through collective membership. It was firstly the conservative parties which produced propaganda and repressive measures against this organizational strengthening of the labour parties. As long as this was the only line of conflict the labour parties could justify the preference as compensation for the weakness of their financial position as compared with the capitalist side. But recently there has been criticism from the Left of collective membership in Great Britain and Scandinavia, especially in Sweden, because the labour parties were able to expand their hegemony over smaller Socialist and Communist parties. It is hardly possible to make prognoses for the future from the development so far of the relation between the parties and the unions in Western Europe. Future development will depend on success in reactivating other forms of conflict outside the established parties and unions. But attempts to set up councils have so far proved most successful where the unions are only an extended arm of the state, as in Spain under Franco. But here the workers' councils had a different aim, they were to combat the dominance of the obsolete cadres of the exile parties and unions. Whether they will be able to play a creative anti-bureaucratic role now that parties and unions can operate legally again in Spain remains to be seen. The successes of multi-functional 'soviet' structures in times of a latent (Spain) or manifest (Russia from the Spring to the Autumn of 1917) double rulership are not sufficient to show that they will function in a different system. Workers' delegations in Italy have, however, acquired considerable importance regionally and in companies. National conferences for these delegations have been organized by a federation of the CGIL-CISL-UIL. But it would be illusory to wait for this structure to emerge as the third pillar of the labour movement as long as Socialist parties and unions cannot meet on the ground of a Socialist pluralism, with the 'soviet' structure — at best but not necessarily — forming an

organizational framework. Territorial and functional representation could be combined in such a way as not to reproduce the old schematic division between the parties and the unions which is characteristic of most capitalist states today.

3. STATE WAGES AND INCOMES POLICY

(a) Economic Theory and Incomes Policy

State incomes policy has been explained as the result of fiercer competition on world markets, particularly through the advent of some latecomers, and the resultant balance of payments problems.[680]

That may be applicable to Great Britain. But it is not applicable to countries which were experimenting with an incomes policy during the reconstruction phase after the war, like the Netherlands. But certainly an incomes policy in any country is partly a product of the collapse of economic theories which are now inadequate to explain the mechanisms of the distribution of incomes and certainly cannot help regulate them. The bundle of economic aims which is grouped under the concept of the 'magic rectangle' (full employment, monetary stability, balance of payments equilibrium and adequate economic growth) overlooks the political dimensions of economic development. Keynes' theory attempted to remove the weaknesses of the older theories which came to grief over full employment. But it was no longer fully adequate to cope with the mechanisms of a more political distribution battle after the Second World War. The 'magical hexagon' includes free wage formation and free price formation. These were the factors which repeatedly threatened not only full employment but also monetary stability during the period of stagflation, and monetary stability did not always prove compatible with the other five factors. Incomes policy is designed to improve the harmonization of these factors. The state intervenes with restrictive measures in the process of income distribution as it becomes increasingly clear that prices and incomes cannot be influenced only through monetary measures and global steering of demand. In view of the change in economic theory Andrew Shonfield has pointed out that paradoxically the two nations (Great Britain and the USA) where Keynes' theory was first and most eagerly accepted have been least successful of all capitalist countries in guiding their economies.[681] This will only appear not so surprising or paradoxical if Keynes' theory is seen as confirmation of Marx's discoveries, the realization of which is to be prevented by voluntary political intervention in the market mechanisms.[682]

In a positive formulation one can say that the coincidence of strong paternalist relics in the state and among the employers on the one hand and a readiness, inspired by Marxism, in the organized labour movement to accept planning and steering on the other facilitated the acceptance of state dirigism on the continent in comparison to the English-speaking countries. Perhaps the fact that people had become accustomed to dirigism during the occupation all over the continent caused less resistance to state intervention after the war. It is hardly possible to point to a uniform Anglo-Saxon tradition, although it is occasionally mentioned in literature and Shonfield also suggests this. In Australia and New Zealand the institutionalization of arbitration has gone so far that, in contrast to Norway, which experimented with compulsory arbitration for a long time, arbitration became an instrument of national incomes policy while in Norway negotiation has remained the normal route and arbitration was used only as a safety valve.[683]

In view of the weak steering mechanisms of modern capitalism and the lack of relevant economic theory the union movement today has in many countries to combat strong anti-union theories. Some recent economists explain post-war inflation with the wage-push theory. It is suggested that the monopoly power of the unions pushes nominal wages up above the growth in productivity so that the employers try to pass on excessive costs in prices. With this theory Lindblom and others develop a formal thesis of the irreconcilability of trade unions and a market economy and the consequences drawn range from the abolition of the unions[684] to the resigned acceptance that this would be impossible in a Western democracy because there would be too much social resistance and there is no functional equivalent for them.[685]

But many economists simply conclude from this that the power of the unions must be drastically reduced.[686] Three ways of doing this are put forward:

— a reduction of their privileges over unorganized workers;

— a modification of legislation on minimum wages because this favours unskilled workers at the expense of skilled;

— a change in the policy of indirectly supporting strikes by paying benefits to strikers (some American states even pay unemployment benefits if the strike has lasted for eight weeks).[687]

In making these suggestions Haberler assumed that cost-push inflation, or seller's inflation, a new form, was a result of the strong position of the unions. The other alternative for incomes policy regards the effects of the unions' position as limited: incomes policy can at most break through the vicious circle of inflationary spirals in coordination with monetary and fiscal policy.[688] It is objected that there are social prejudices against the unions and that they cannot be treated like any other monopoly.

At the 1974 TUC Congress a British union put forward a motion that the congress, recognizing the evil of inflation, rejected the theory that wage increases were one of the main causes.[689] But the resolution was rejected as too global. The attempt to refute a theory with a majority vote must remain a curiosity although in left-wing groups it is a frequent practice against established theses of bourgeois science.

TABLE 21
Gross earnings and the cost of living (rise in 1976 over the preceding year in percent)

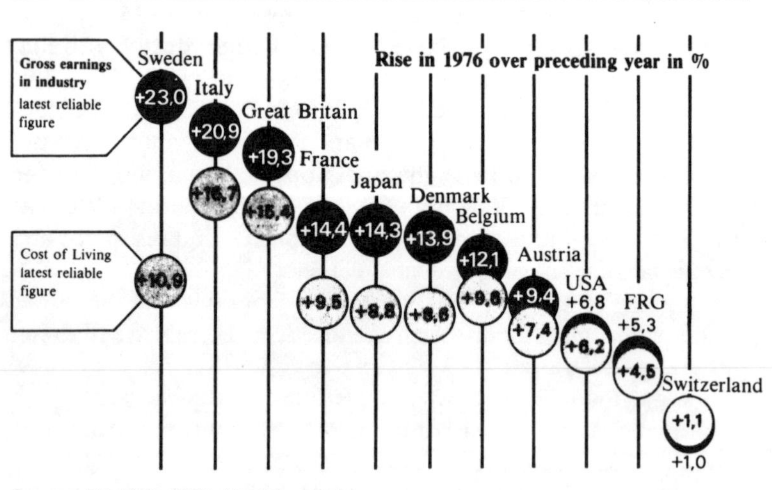

Source: Die Zeit, 1976, No. 31, p. 24.

A recent British study gives a broader answer to the polemical question: do trade unions cause inflation? Almost everybody causes inflation, including the unions, but in what the authors call 'strato-inflationary economies' the unions are not seen in quite such a vicious light as in some American studies. In the views of these authors inflation is hard to cure and certainly agreement with the unions over meaningful measures is necessary. Even Socialist societies are included here. They are supposed to have the same latent inflationary tendencies but with the difference, which no-one wants to eliminate, that the unions there have no free bargaining powers.[690] This brings economics back to its former political premises. The search is no longer for the relation between economic factors, it is recognized that modern inflation needs a political theory of inflation, because it is first and foremost the result of claims by politically organized and articulate groups.[691] The campaign against the inflationary tendencies of union negotiating power has been softened by the recognition that the inflationary trend could not be eliminated without organized labour, as can be seen from the large number of unofficial strikes, which are spontaneous action by workers who feel that the results obtained by the unions are not good enough.[692] The various suggestions to limit union power would therefore have serious repercussions, unofficial strikes to satisfy rising expectations have much more disruptive power than the more moderate policy of the unions, at least in Northern Europe (though Great Britain may be an exception).

At the beginning of the sixties the OECD also increasingly recommended incomes policy to achieve monetary and price stability. In 1973 twenty-one out of twenty-four members of the OECD used wage and price controls, only Japan, Canada and the Federal Republic remained below that level of state intervention and restrained themselves to moral suasion.[693] At first the illusion was internationally entertained that incomes policy could be neutral with regard to distribution. A group of research workers commissioned by the EEC in 1967 established that any incomes policy would have repercussions on distribution and thus could only be protected from dysfunctional effects if consciously used as an incomes and distribution policy.[694] This was taken up by the European Parliament but it has not become general practice.[695]

Different methods of state intervention have emerged in incomes policy, according to the position of the interest groups in the state and the conflict patterns which have developed in the various political cultures:

In the 'input area' we can differentiate between:

(1) a policy of wage guidelines and moral suasion with little or only loose institutionalization (Great Britain, USA, FRG, Sweden in the fifties);

(2) direct state intervention in wage autonomy with stronger institutionalization (Austria, the Netherlands, Australia in 1962, Denmark in 1963 and Finland).

However, the borders between the types are fluid. The USA in 1971 and Great Britain in 1966 both entered the second escalation stage. The main measures are a wage and price freeze; further intervention in wage autonomy has so far been resisted in most democracies. Where that is not the case, in Spain for instance, and many developing countries, the Rubicon to dictatorial regulation of social organizations has generally already been crossed.

In the 'output area' again different policies and measures with varying degrees of severity have been used:

(1) Wage policy in the above sense has often proved insufficient and it is supplemented with

(2) Incomes policy in the wider case.

Where negative parallel measures have been adopted, like restrictions on dividend payments, they are generally regarded as largely ineffective, and some types of income cannot be controlled at all (rent, fees, capital gains, income of managerial staff).

(3) Price policy. This is generally regarded as an emergency measure. Only in a few systems does the state aim to have a consistent influence on prices. These are mainly countries in which relatively little can be achieved with a policy of moral suasion because the unions are organizationally weak but very militant (France and Italy), or countries where there are strong ties between the labour party and the unions (Scandinavia and Great Britain) and the unions can often persuade the government to be more energetic over price controls than wage controls.

In Britain the Council of Prices, Productivity and Incomes recommended in its third report in 1959 that incomes should be adjusted to the growth in productivity rather through price reductions than wage increases.[696] The Luxembourg CGT in its 1974 programme demanded rigorous measures of price control, publicity duties, sanctions and price reductions where prices were excessive. This was to be decided by an independent *office des prix*.[697] In Finland at the beginning of 1976 it was only possible to reach agreement on moderate wage increases from 6.4% to 7% after legislation had been introduced giving power to regulate prices. This was only achieved after intervention and concrete promises by President Kekkonen to the conservative opposition, whose votes were needed for the obligatory majority of five-sixths. But it is questionable whether such a policy is really successful. There was also opposition on the Left and the Finnish Communist Party nearly split over the issue.[698] In Switzerland the second chamber on 5 December 1976 carried out a referendum on the continuance of price controls. The decision was positive although Switzerland then had the lowest inflation rate.[699]

The success of a price policy, which the unions demand to supplement a wage policy together with a generally egalitarian incomes and profits policy, is not regarded as very great in Conservative circles either, and it is felt to be dangerous because it is impossible to prevent 'grey markets' from emerging, while a huge bureaucracy is needed if price controls are to be really effective.[700] Even when there is agreement on principle between the TUC and the Government, this does not necessarily guarantee the success of such a policy in a system where the union movement is so fragmented and the militancy of individual groups of workers and their shop stewards is incalculable, especially where negotiations are highly decentralized. The lack of confidence in the fairness of wage increases can reach catastrophic proportions when anti-inflation policy does not bite and it cannot be restored overnight. Fairness in wage increases is judged on a comparative basis in any case and generalized expectations cannot be changed quickly even by union leaders; at most they can hope to influence these in a long process of enlightenment.[701]

(4) Many measures can be adopted in a structural policy with redistributive effects on income (labour market, consumer, advertising policy measures, etc), but it is difficult to control the success of these in a market economy without a comprehensive systems policy with harmonized long-term aims. The role the unions play is diffuse and contradictory, as outlined in the section on consumer policy (cf. Chapter 3, 3, c).

(b) Incomes Policy Institutions

The unions have a greater influence on incomes policy in the input area than in the output area. Here their ability to exercise a formative influence largely depends on direct representation in the state apparatus. These are two stages of intervention which have different character and institutions in the various systems:

(1) Incomes policy was introduced in a few European countries after the war in a dirigistic phase of transition from the war economy, especially in Austria and the Netherlands. In Sweden a phase of efforts to achieve solidarity in wage policy began in the fifties. Free bargaining was vigorously defended and state intervention rejected; it was only introduced in the seventies in Sweden.[702] Sweden also attempted to maintain solidarity with regard to the emergence of a wages drift. In 1966 the LO achieved a wage drift guarantee, to give compensation to the poorer, less productive regions which could not participate to the same extent in the drift.[703] Solidarity in wage policy was maintained in the seventies to keep state intervention to cases where adjustment of wages between workers was necessary and coordinate various policies such as asset formation, incomes and social policy.[704] But the unions clung to free bargaining and many experts hesitated to recommend far-reaching state intervention because Sweden was stable enough for the uncertain journey into regulation policy not to seem necessary and the country was acutely aware that not everything which appears feasible in economic theory is practicable in a political culture which is geared to autonomous participation.[705]

In the English-speaking countries the first major incomes policy measures were introduced in 1961 and 1962. In Great Britain there was a wage pause, although there had been precedences for this in 1948 under Attlee. In the USA a policy of wage guidelines was introduced after recommendations from the Council of Economic Advisors.[706] But it was never possible to integrate the American unions into a national incomes policy as was the case with some European union movements, although ideologically the American unions are not so opposed to the system as their European counterparts. The reasons for this are the low membership (cf. Chapter 1, 6), the fragmentation which leaves important unions such as the automobile workers, the teamsters and the teachers outside the AFL-CIO, the lack of close contacts with political parties, the relative lack of staff work in the unions and the desire of the employers to prevent the unions from participating in national bodies.[707] Neither a corporatist nor a syndicalist ideology was sufficiently widespread in America to prepare the way for global integration in national economic policy. American unions are held to be more interested in micro-areas of individual items of legislation than macro-areas of national agreements.

The attitude of European unions to incomes policy has been ambivalent. On the one hand the TUC in a report on incomes policy in 1967 admitted the basic necessity for the government to maintain a balance between incomes and productivity. On the other any state intervention was only acceptable to the unions in the context of effective economic and social planning.[708] Moreover, the aim of central regulation proved largely incompatible with the dual system of company constitution in Britain (cf. Chapter 1, 5), where the shop stewards and plant bargaining are a counter trend to incomes policy.[709] The attitude of the TUC also depended on which party was in power and the attitude of the British unions to incomes policy changed as the government changed. Labour governments usually only succeeded in reaching a satisfying compromise with the unions over incomes policy after a long period of Tory rule or if a Conservative come-back seemed likely, as in the wage round from 1 August 1975 to 31 July 1977, when agreement was reached on wage rises limited to 4.5% in return for tax cuts, in the hopes of cutting the inflation rate down to 6%.[710] The Social Contract to the TUC is not a discussion which takes place once a year but a continuous process on a basis of 'mutual trust and understanding' between the TUC and the Government which must be achieved through regular contact between the TUC and the Labour Party Liaison Committee.[711] The main problem for a British social contract is the low degree of influence the TUC can exercise over its affiliated unions to keep the contract. The TUC behaved with unusual harshness to the Seamen's Union in September 1976 and threatened them with expulsion, so that the strike was put off. The unions have in the past formed a successful veto group against Conservative governments. But they were too weak to be able to implement a positive policy of their own. The immobility loosened somewhat under Labour governments but there were often further disappointments. Over greater concessions the TUC was not always in a position to be able to maintain solidarity among its members and many individual unions have gone their own way over wage policy.[712] Only a loose form of institutionalization of wage policy was introduced. There are various organs for cooperation in the formulation of wage guidelines.

(1) Councils of Experts

In the USA a three-member body, the Council of Economic Advisers, was created on the basis of the Employment Act of 1946. It acts within the framework of the President's office and makes recommendations on national economic stability. The results of its enquiries are contained in an economic report which the President by virtue of the same legislation presents to Congress every year. Although the council is a body of experts it sees its role, unlike the German Council of Experts, as to propound a certain economic policy and does not limit itself to purely analytical work.[713]

In the Federal Republic a Council of Experts was formed in 1963. This is not purely an advisory body to the Government, it is to facilitate the formation of opinion in all those responsible for economic policy and in the public at large. Its publications are largely addressed to the general public and in contrast to the American body it is not dependent on the Government. In fact the council is not empowered to make recommendations on specific economic policy measures. The concept is based on a clear mistrust of interest groups and at the same time it presupposes that there is an economic truth which will reveal itself to experts if they can only be sufficiently protected from the influence of the various bodies concerned.[714]

(2) Prices and Incomes Boards

Until 1970 Great Britain moved through increasingly institutionalized advisory bodies. The experiment began in 1957 with an 'economic judiciary', the Council on Prices, Productivity and Incomes under the chairmanship of Lord Cohen, which was to give verdicts on permissible wage increases. The unions generally saw these recommendations, which were disguised as expert opinion, as a veiled politically motivated postulate. In 1962 the National Incomes Commission was created to examine wage agreements for inflationary effects. Three of its five members were full time. The commission was a body of professors without members from the unions or the employers. The TUC refused to have any contact with it mainly because it largely examined wage development but not price and profit trends.[715] The work of the commission did not prove to be a success, although (or because?) it had no special powers. Its five reports appeared with a respectable time-lag after the wage agreements and were usually politically irrelevant for the situation in which they were published. When the Labour Government replaced the Conservatives in 1964 the National Board of Prices and Incomes was set up in April 1965. It was preceded by an agreement between the Government and the TUC. The cooperation of the unions had only been achieved by subjecting all incomes, and not only wages, to the board, which existed until 1970. Its influence on wage policy is disputed. Generally the assessment is lukewarm and there are a number of reasons for this:

— The activity of the board coincided with the beginning of a severe crisis in 1966/67. After that it existed for too short a time for its success to be adequately assessed.

— In 1968 the Department of Economic Affairs was restructured. The Ministry of Labour and later the Department of Employment and Productivity became competent for incomes policy and the standing of the board dropped.

— The board's examinations were too short-term. Fewer studies would also have been more beneficial.

None of these advisory bodies had a great direct influence and in most cases incomes policy was not their only sphere of interest. So a lack of success with incomes policy is not a sufficient reason for a global verdict on them. In turn moral suasion was only indirectly affected by the quality and credibility of the recommendations of such bodies. But governments have repeatedly successfully used these bodies to legitimate a policy of gentle pressure with public opinion on recalcitrant interest groups. The mobilization of prejudices was often more important than the force of rational arguments drawn from the arsenal of expert bodies. Use is made of the fact that in the public at large (in contrast to the workers) the fear of inflation is greater than that of unemployment, which usually only affects the workers. (Figures from an English survey: 71% of those questioned regarded inflation and 52% unemployment as the greatest threat to them personally).[716]

(3) Concerted Action

Another step was taken to institutionalization in the Federal Republic with Concerted Action. The nearest parallel to this in another country is the Harpsund Conferences between the Swedish

Government and the main associations, which like Concerted Action remain a non-binding exchange of views. Concerted Action is the expression of a first attempt at institutionalized conflict settlement between the groups. It is an indirect contribution by the state to changing the patterns of conflict in the Federal Republic. Until 1966 the liberal idea predominated that the economic order did not rest on the acceptance of common aims by the relevant groups but at best on an acceptance of common rules of conflict.[717] Recently, as can be seen from appeals by Schmidt's Government for cohesion on the Government's programme for a 'stable upswing' in December 1974, the concept is gaining ground that certain prescribed basic aims should be jointly followed by groups and the economic protagonists. However, it is too early to see in this 'enlightened market economy' a Socialist note, at any rate in the programme if not in practice,[718] because the concept of group coordination is still far removed from the holistic concept of the identification of aims in Socialist systems.

Attempts to use moral suasion have in several areas not been very successful (especially the maintenance of monetary stability, where it is not expected to be successful in future either), but more severe sanctions which are really essential to a policy of moral suasion have not been applied, although opponents of a state-organized group consensus have been painting in lurid colours the inconsistency with the market economy and the threatening nature of the policy (e.g. in subsidies policy).[719]

Concerted Action emerged from a change in the paradigm in the explanation of the causes of instability. If in boom times inflationary tendencies were explained mainly from the narrow field of fiscal and central bank policy through the change in the money supply, as the distributive power of the state dropped during the crisis the explanation tended to concentrate on the power struggle between the wage partners. Conservative interpreters accused the unions of wage demands in excess of productivity during a period of stagnation. Occasionally extenuating circumstances were seen for the union leaders in pressure from unofficial strikes.

While in Great Britain, the Netherlands and Scandinavia there was some direct intervention in free collective bargaining through wage and price freeze measures, it was no coincidence that the Federal Republic, which was the pioneer of the ideology of the market economy in Europe, tried to evolve means of voluntary coordination which would be, it was hoped, in conformity with that system, especially as direct intervention had not been particularly successful in any of these countries due to the frequent changes of the 'stop-go' policy. The appeal to reason and the idea that there is a 'common interest' for all the groups concerned, however, still held echoes of the old liberal creed that consensus could be reached through recognition of 'proven insights in economic theory'. This became a pluralist variant of the idea of the new *contrat social* in the conceptions of the Council of Experts.[720] The associations were to play a key role in bringing about peace in the distribution battle. It was only after 1970 that a return to a more militant concept became apparent in the view that the government and the associations were not equal discussion partners, the government as guardian of the public interest had a sovereign position over the associations: 'It is the task of economic policy to prevent as far as possible the legitimate particular interests of groups developing against the overall economic interests'.[721]

This was a denigration of Concerted Action from the position of a supreme 'clearing house' to a kind of 'institutionalized hearing'. For a long time the Council of Experts did not have a distribution concept in mind but only some medium-term wage guidelines which were in principle productivity oriented.[722] At best there was 'distribution policy from above' with the limited aim of 'cementing the wage ratio which is the minimum given at the point of departure'. The best that can be said in its economic defence is that it coincided with full employment.[723] This changed in 1972 when the Council of Experts reflected for the first time that its approval of 'behaviour in conformity with stability' by the employers was conservative and valueless for redistributive aims.[724] More detailed figures were now given on income distribution.[725] For the first time the employers were recommended to put forward suggestions and offers as a 'contribution to the reduction of existing social conflict'. When the crisis of 1974 showed that many of the council's recommendations had not been followed the criticism was levied mainly at state economic policy which had not taken the chances offered by the wage lag in the upswing in 1969: 'Instead of bringing the low wage agreements into line with the market by throttling demand and so ensuring stability the boom had been left to take its course'.[726]

This was indirectly also criticism of Concerted Action in particular and moral suasion in general and it was inevitable in view of the doubts the wage partners entertained of such institutions. Nevertheless, a report on the effects of free bargaining in the public sector concluded in 1973: 'The existing institutions of the Council of Experts and Concerted Action would appear to be adequate on principle to influence the contents of wage negotiations in the public sector'.[727]

The two most powerful associations in the Federal Republic gritted their teeth and accepted Concerted Action, though for different motives. The employers' associations saw it as an instrument with which a wage policy could be pursued which ensured economic expansion. Leading members of the conservative parties began to feel it was socially inadequate for unions to refuse to let Concerted Action develop into a means of binding their wage policy and militancy.[728] From the employers' point of view union policy was mainly directed to extending the wage ratio at the expense of the profit ratio to an extent they could not accept. In their view there is so little room for widening the wage ratio without jeopardizing the aims of the 'magic rectangle' that it was suggested that wage policy altogether should be freed from standards of distribution policy. A calculation was presented to the unions according to which, on the basis of the doubtful figure of company profits to the amount of 7-8% of the national income before the 1966/67 recession,[729] all company profits would only yield a single wage increase of just on 10% if distributed to the workers in the form of wage supplements.[730] The employers were therefore implying that the only way out of the dilemma was asset formation, which would bring a double advantage: longer-term wage increases and a higher savings ratio for the workers. Concerted Action was to be a means of reaching a preliminary consensus on this policy.[731]

The unions on the other hand saw Concerted Action as the platform for the articulation of the further development of the economic and social order which they were aiming for.[732] They were therefore quick to criticize the fact that longer-term socio-political aspects were hidden by short-term problems of cyclical policy:[733]

> Hearing the unions within the framework of Concerted Action leaves out the socio-political questions which would have to be decided in medium-term planning. Questions of the public budget, of finance, tax and subsidy policy are excluded as are questions of the distribution of incomes and wealth and investment planning and financing.[734]

Moreover the unions rightly criticized the fact that negotiations in Concerted Action were conducted on the basis of a constellation of overall data which were taken as given, but that only the wage data were fixed and the unions were being forced into the position of the sole guarantor of the parameter which concerned them most while price increase rates and profit growth rates were not be guaranteed by the opposing side in the same way.

The play of forces in the relation between the government, the unions, Concerted Action and the other interests represented in it and the Council of Experts has changed considerably in the course of the development of the German economy. Above all the ideological premises of moral suasion in the Federal Republic have changed. In the sixties a conservative ideology was still apparent in many aspects of the West German discussion. It ignored organizational factors and argued that distribution conflicts were non-functional on a purely economic consideration of a few variables such as wage and price developments. The Council of Experts for a time also put forward the argument that distribution conflict would only cause a loss of benefit to all sides as costs were mutually passed on (increases in wages and prices), leading to higher inflation, a danger to employment and political instability.[735] The associations were told:

> If Concerted Action is to contribute to a lessening of the distribution battle and facilitate greater flexibility on the market, it is more likely to be successful the more clearly the participants recognize that there is very little room under existing conditions, at least over the medium term, for influencing income distribution through a policy aimed at changing nominal incomes.[736]

The concept of a wage policy which was neutral to the cost level, which the council put forward in 1964,[737] met with increasing criticism at the turn from the sixties to the seventies. At the end of the sixties it was still possible for state incomes policy to bind union wage policy to agreements which were in conformity with stability (see Table 22), but after the middle of 1969 the unions changed their policy under the pressure of unofficial strikes. The argument put forward by left-wing union critics, that the unions kept to the orientation data, was only right at the end of the sixties.
Not for nothing was 1968 mainly singled out as the year which proved the docility of the unions.[738] The opposition of the unions grew

TABLE 22
Orientation data and wage increases in the FRG

Year	Orientation data	Increases in agreed wages and salaries (%)
1967	3.5	3.5
1968	4.5	4.3
1969	5.5-6.5	10.3
1970	9.5-10.5	11.6
1971	7-8	9.5

Source: Herman Adam: *Die konzertierte Aktion in der BRD.* Cologne, Bund-Verlag, 1972, 1972, p. 54.

as it became increasingly clear that efforts to keep to the wage orientation data were not being matched by concessions over price orientation data and that the employers were certainly not prepared to concede participation in investment policy to the unions. It is certainly significant that the Federal Minister of Economic Affairs, Friderichs, did not present orientation data for overall economic development at the first Concerted Action session in 1975, in contrast to the last session of 1974. It was to avoid controversy and let the *Council on Cyclical Development* have the first say with its possibly gloomy message. Nevertheless, the conflicts were harder than at almost any time in the past. Loderer, Chairman of the Metal Workers Union, accused the Council of Experts of having finally moved over into the employers' camp.[739]

In contrast to popular left-wing assumptions more detailed studies have shown that the steering capacity of Concerted Action is relatively low. 'Existence outside the constitution' and irresponsible recommendations' are constituent features. Even the name is confusing because the sessions do not usually result in action.[740] Their ability to mitigate conflict and lead to greater integration has been exaggerated, partly because of the strongly harmonized press communiqués which were designed to suggest a consensus. Measured by objective indicators the distribution conflict has intensified since the inception of Concerted Action:[741]

(1) Between 1960 and 1966 356,000 working days a year were lost but this rose to 671,000 between 1967 and 1971.

(2) The disparity between the original claims by the Metal Workers Union and the first offer from the employers' association dropped only slightly during these two periods and fluctuated around 6%.

(3) The length of time taken by wage negotiations was one month until 1966; after that it rose to around two months.

However, it is difficult to draw definite conclusions

— because conflict became altogether fiercer it is hard to say whether it might not have been very much fiercer without Concerted Action;

— it is difficult to isolate the pacifying effect of Concerted Action from other integrationist efforts, i.e. greater cooperation between the SPD and the unions after 1969 and ideological efforts at integration;

— in recessions the ability of institutions such as Concerted Action to achieve consensus is probably generally greater than during an upswing, when the distribution battle usually grows in intensity;

— consensus by the élite was called in question on several occasions by unofficial strikes (in 1969 and 1973).

(4) Strongly Institutionalized Incomes Policy

Few countries have achieved more far-reaching intervention with incomes policy. The second stage of intervention has been easiest in countries with strongly corporatist interest structures. Austria attempted a strongly institutionalized incomes policy with a 'Federal Economic Directorate' (Federal legislation of 4 April 1951). The directorate was to coordinate economic steering measures with unanimous decisions. But the proposal was declared unconstitutional by the Constitutional Court because tying ministers to the decisions of the directorate was regarded as irreconcilable with the principle of ministerial responsibility.[742] Instead, in March 1957 a paritative Price and Wage Commission was set up, to which the Federal Chancellor and the Ministers for Home Affairs, Trade and Industry and Social Administration belonged, together with the two representatives of the Chambers (the Federal Chamber of Trade and Commerce, the Labour Chamber and the Presidents' conference of the Agricultural Chambers) and two representatives of the Austrian Trade Union Federation. In price control the best that has been achieved is a better distribution of price increases but in wage development there may have been a certain delaying effect. The commission was originally created as a temporary measure but as the President of the ÖGB once said, 'Temporary measures have long lives in Austria' and the commission is still working.[743]

It is disputed whether the commission is effective as a steering instrument. However, it is pointed out that Austria has a better price development and better strike statistics than most of the EEC countries.[744] It is difficult to say that the favourable effect is all due to the work of one body, it is rather the result of the many informal contacts which take place before the meetings of the commission during the process of will formation in the associations and in the general system of a 'Chamber State' (*Kammerstaat*) and consociational relations which are similar in Austria to those in the Netherlands.[745] Foreign observers had the impression that the success of Austrian incomes policy and its institutions is not related by the Austrians themselves to quantitative indicators although the usual justification indicators such as 'industrial peace' and 'stability of employment' give favourable results.[746] But judged by these indicators neighbouring countries such as Switzerland and the Federal Republic also have favourable results although they do not have an instrument like the Austrian commission. And so the subjective faith in the desirability of consociational democracy is probably a more important factor in the Austrian success than the objective results of certain institutions. This faith, together with the harmonist ideology which carries it, is, however, increasingly coming under fire in Austria too. There are objections to the depoliticizing effect of the Austrian form of cooperation, the inclination to immobility and the strengthening of the 'non-decision structures', which are let out when social conflict is thematized.[747] But conservative critics are not satisfied with this form of cooperation either, they object that it tends to level out the wage structure, although this is certainly not the case yet. No form of incomes policy has so far made a decisive and systematic attempt at redistribution among wage-earners.

In the Netherlands it is clearer that a highly institutionalized system of incomes policy has not been successful; in 1963 this practically broke down in the face of strikes. An alliance of the Government, the Central Planning Office, the Labour Foundation and the Socio-Economic Council did not succeed in conceiving a continuous incomes policy because the systematic ex-ante coordination of wages and finance policy did not work, cyclical prognoses were relatively unreliable and monetary disturbance variables were neglected for a considerable time.[748] Measured by general indicators the Netherlands system survived fairly well apart from its failures in price policy. Wages rose at times more slowly than in the Federal Republic. But the dysfunctional effects of a moderate wage policy are now too plain for this factor to be evaluated alone. For a time a low wage level brought advantages for the export industry, over the longer term the disadvantages became apparent in a lack of modernization and an emphasis on breadth instead of depth in Dutch investment policy.[749]

The legislation on wage formation of 1970 contained a clause (Article 8) which was to enable the Minister for Social Affairs to declare certain clauses in wage agreements non-binding. At the same time he was to be able to order a wage freeze after hearing the Socio-Economic Council and the Labour Foundation (Article 10). But in October 1970 the Socio-Economic Council recommended to the government, in view of the opposition of the unions, that Article 8 should be suspended and that the powers to intervene in price formation should not be used. This terminated the attempt to use state intervention.[750] The Dutch unions have moved further and further away from the ideology of the 'benevolent democratic state' and turned more towards self-help strategies, especially the NVV.[751] However, the NVV does not reject incomes policy on principle either and in 1975 it announced that it would examine an interim memorandum from the government on incomes policy.[752] In June 1976 negotiations between the wage partners came to grief and the den Uyl Government fixed the rate of wage increases for the second half of the year and began a re-structuring of social insurance contributions. The Christian unions were satisfied, but not the NVV, but its strike threats were not put into practice apart from one action by dockers in Amsterdam and Rotterdam.[753]

Where there is a strongly institutionalized incomes policy there are usually arbitration bodies. In the Netherlands the Labour Foundation has exercised a purely advisory function since 1967. In some countries (Australia, New Zealand) a comprehensive system of compulsory arbitration has developed. In many countries there has only been occasional intervention with wage and price freezes (Australia 1962, Denmark 1963, Great Britain 1966, 1972, Netherlands 1966, 1970, USA 1971).

Generally the more flexible forms of intervention are said to be more successful, although this first type has not always worked well in boom periods (the Federal Republic and Sweden). The higher stage of intervention fails because the wage drift moves over wage restrictions. Regulations on exceptions tend to soften wage norms, a phenomenon which has not escaped a Socialist wage policy either. Other forms of incomes and prices often prove too difficult to control.[754] Most economic studies also overlook the political factors. For the union movement factors such as the organizational form must also be included in an evaluation of the success of wage and incomes policy:

(1) A centralized union movement, as in Sweden or the Federal Republic, is relatively favourable to success. Fragmented union movements can overcome this disadvantage if the pillared structures develop a certain power through formal and informal consultation and interest equalization mechanisms, as in the Netherlands.

(2) But moral suasion does not depend only on the organizational density or degree of centralization, but also on the degree of *ideological penetration*. But in the strongly fragmented ideology unions in the Latin countries this drops with the anarcho-syndicalist behaviour patterns of many unionists even if they make verbal concessions to Marxism.

(3) The success of moral suasion also depends on the degree of industrial unionism. Where the craft unions dominate state moral suasion has little effect. In Denmark, for instance, despite a similar membership density to that in Sweden moral suasion has not developed to the same extent because industrial unionism is not realized.

(4) Where the centre does not have a great deal of power over the basic units in the organization the unions do not have much room for participation in state moral suasion. The internal relations between the party and the unions (even if incompatibility of functions in both organizations is established) weakens the power of persuasion of the union establishment still further. This can be seen from the conflict patterns even in wage policy: where unofficial strikes predominate, as in the Latin countries and Great Britain, it is difficult for the centre to enter into obligations. The defeat of the union leaders after the Grenelle agreements in 1968 in France was a classic case: when the Secretary-General of the CGT, Georges Séguy, appeared before 20,000 workers after the release of the minutes of the meeting in the Renault works at Billancourt, he was confronted with an almost unanimous rejection of the compromise

which had been reached. The leaders retreated into decentralization: the unions called for claims on a regional, industry and company level. Enthusiasts for militancy in union policy often call for unity and centralization but they often overlook that unity does not always bring greater militancy, it can become the vehicle of state integration policy. But faced with the alternative of being militant and weak or cooperative and influential presumably even in the Latin countries more and more unionists will accept a move in the direction of the Northern European pattern. The horizontal integration on EEC level will probably also further this process. It will tend to make not only state intervention policy but also the organizational structures of the interest group more uniform. However, it cannot be denied that within the EEC, with the growing dualism between the two systems of industrial relations which the British Donovan Report established, the informal structures of plant-oriented wage policy are becoming more important because of the national forms of cooperation of the union bureaucracies. Observers of the European scene have felt that it ismore likely that the British system with its informal structures will spread in Europe than that the formal system will come to predominate.[756] Too strong a throttling of social forces through state wage policy can have the opposite effect: it can provoke the outbreak of unofficial strikes as in Finland in 1956 when a general strike brought the collapse of the system of wage controls.

Ultimately the attitude of the unions to incomes policy is bound to be ambivalent: on the one hand a rejection of attempts at a social contract will not serve their power position because it helps to mobilize anti-union prejudice. On the other hand they cannot reconcile their independent role with a smooth and lasting integration into a well-oiled machine of preliminary coordination. Incomes policy always has to be a changing ad hoc agreement during a crisis. A long-term solution with indexing and institutionalization is a dream and not even a very good dream. There is a new tendency in countries with a strong union movement for a voluntary social contract, as the TUC suggested to induce the Wilson Government to drop discipline and an incomes policy in the Industrial Relations Act. The Conservative opposition was highly critical of the social contract which was prepared by the Liaison Committee of TUC and Labour Party members, but found it difficult to achieve discussion on the 'national contract' it proposed with the employers. The vision of a union state was conjured up which would be a condominium between the Labour Party and the unions and in which investors would hardly have a say in policy. Union pressure in such a development would also make a change of government difficult, and the employers' counter measure, a refusal to invest, could be rendered useless by such a coalition with nationalization threats. In the meantime these pessimistic visions have faded as in 1978 Callaghan had to come to terms with the failure of the social contract policy and survive by a retreat to a traditional policy of moral suasion in an admirable mixture of irony and criticism of the unions and with an emphatic appeal to the sense of *bonum commune* in the left wing of his own party.

State incomes policy could be more successful if it were combined with solidarity in wage policy. This has hardly happened so far, even though success with solidarity in wage policy is difficult to estimate as there is insufficient data. Where data is available, as in Denmark, some progress is discernable in the form of higher growth rates among under-privileged groups such as non-skilled workers, women and workers outside the main centres of population (Table 26). But the adjustment has not been spectacular up to now and presumably it could only be so with a comprehensive reorganization of incomes policy.

TABLE 23
Success with solidarity in wage policy in Denmark

Average percentual growth per year from 1963-1974:		
	in Copenhagen	in the provinces
Skilled workers	11.4	11.7
Non-skilled workers (men)	12.1	12.3
Non-skilled workers (women)	13.8	13.9

Source: LO: *Belysning af fagbevaegelsens resultater 1963-1975*. Copenhagen,[2] 1975, p.23.

Solidarity in wage policy seems easier in countries where the civil servants and white collar workers are not for the most part organized in the head associations of the Social Democrat unions, as in Sweden or Denmark. But even among the workers there is much resistance. A Swedish survey of trade union members revealed that the majority of the workers (53%) but only a minority of the civil servants (12%) were not ready to sacrifice possibilities of increasing wages in favour of equalization policy, which is one of the greatest contributions of the Swedish Social Democrats to theory in recent years.[756]

The relative decline in profits and importance of certain industries is reflected in the fear of established unions of losing status. They make immense efforts to stay at the top of the wage scale. This was the case with the miners in the Federal Republic who supported subsidies to ward off competition and protect their position at the top of the scale, although they had bitterly opposed subsidies in agriculture and other areas.[757]

(c) Productivity Rules and Indexing

When the moral suasion bodies in the Federal Republic admitted for the first time that there was a wage lag (the Council of Experts at the end of the sixties) two measures to ease the conflict by recourse to 'objective' economic data came increasingly under discussion:

(1) adjustment to productivity; and

(2) indexing.

(1) *Adjustment to productivity.* During the boom at the turn of the seventies the growth in productivity in comparison to the rise in real wages had been greater than in earlier upswing phases.[758] But with a certain time-lag a considerable long-term adjustment of wages to several factors had gradually been established: the first adjustment was to productivity growth and it was supported by the Council of Experts in their first reports in 1964 and 1965. It was followed by the second *adjustment to inflation rates*, which became known as the *Meinhold formula* in Germany because it was first put forward by Helmut Meinhold in his arbitration proposal in the wage conflict in the metal industry in 1965. Meinhold argued that the workers should also be compensated for the results of failure in economic policy.[759] The third adjustment, which was fought for at the end of the sixties, was to be to the *profits trend*. It was ex-ante the most difficult to achieve. In their 1974/75 report the Council of Experts argued that the workers had improved their position as they remained obdurate in view of expected inflation rates while the employers offered only weak resistance, in the hopes of being able to pass costs on. However, the restrictive monetary policy of

the Central Bank largely prevented this. Unemployment increased. Implicitly the unions were accused of not being prepared to share the costs incurred through the rise in the price of raw materials.[760] Other variations discussed in the circle around the Council of Experts (especially by Giersch) were:
— shortages on the labour market;
— structural employment changes;
— changes in the terms of trade.

Adjustment to the growth in productivity was announced long before the German discussion by the American Council of Economic Advisors (in 1962) and the British Government (also in 1962). In Great Britain polemics against productivity rules are long familiar but the issue is not basically resolved. One study which takes a clear stand against productivity deals even in its title, still after more than 200 pages of polemics recommends steering a course between opportunist adjustment and radicalist isolation and suggests flexibility with regard to the 'capital offensive'. The shop stewards are reminded of a rather cynical basic rule of negotiations: the girl who starts by saying no gets a higher price for her virtue than the girl who starts by talking about money.[761] Even where the unions did not start by rejecting the idea of a productivity deal there was much justified criticism.

But productivity rules have not proved the answer to all ills in any country. Several problems have arisen:

(a) There is no agreement on the best method of measuring productivity growth or the share of the productivity of capital and labour in it. Even if a method is accepted by both sides the period on which this should be based is usually an object of controversy. The picture is distorted by a drop in productivity as workers are hoarded during recessions. So periods have to be chosen which are long enough to cover the usual fluctuations.[762] In Sweden the employers' association SAF put forward a suggestion in 1967 that a group of four experts should present a report on the economic development before wage agreements came to an end, and that this should serve as the basis for the negotiations.[763] The LO rejected the proposal on the grounds that state material was not of even quality, that such reports generally presented the relations between wage and price policy in too generalized a form and that such an automatic way of calculating would force the unions to accept all the underlying irrationalities of a market society. The unions rightly regarded free negotiations as still the most rational way, and the one which did most justice to the political situation.[764]

Economists have also increasingly lost their belief that productivity-oriented wage policy can be derived from some kind of a 'natural order'. It is always a compromise between antagonistic interests and the choice of formula for measurement always has political implications.

(b) Wage increases which are not justified by the productivity rule can be evaded by companies without infringing the agreement by raising the status of the workers instead of giving them higher wages. Generally all the methods of overpaying to avoid the pay guidelines are more difficult to control than underpaying. In view of the generally underprivileged position of wage-earners one can hardly expect the unions to publicize isolated cases of overpaying, even if this makes them tacit accomplices to the breaking of agreements. It is easiest to check individual cases which strengthen the wages drift in countries where the employers' association is strongly centralized. This, as experience has shown, is a reflection of the unity of the labour movement and so it is least developed in countries with a fragmented union movement (cf. Chapter 1, 4).

(c) Productivity growth varies from one industry to another and the arithmetic mean of a general growth rate will hardly prevent unions in prosperous sectors from aiming to participate in the surplus profits through higher wages than agreed as long as there is no solidarity in wage policy to equalize incomes and ensure a relatively stable price level, as there is in Sweden.

(d) All three of the adjustments which have been encouraged in the Federal Republic are oriented to the status quo of equilibrium and they are regarded as concessions which make it easier to refuse more far-reaching claims which may attack the substance of assets. Such claims are often referred to the question of asset formation for the workers without further critical examination. We can quote an example from the 1970 report of the German Council of Experts, which argued from the relative shortage of capital as a production factor:

> The fact that a basic change in income distribution cannot be achieved with a nominal wage policy, in other words that the position of capital in the distribution battle in a market economy is so strong is ultimately due to its shortage (a result of international mobility). It is only possible to participate in the returns on this shortage through asset formation, either voluntary or linked to an agreement.[765]

The attitude of the unions in the Federal Republic to attempts at state incomes policy was ambivalent. At the beginning of the seventies policy alternated between the interests of stability and the interests of wages, with partial success in wage policy (1970) and during periods of stagnation (1973). During the sixties the wage ratio (wages as a percentage of the national income) was about 60-65%, after 1970 it rose from 60.6% (1960) to 71.4% (1974), so that there was talk of a 'necessary wage pause'. Opponents of the unions were eager to point out that wages had quadrupled since 1960 but prices had risen by only two-thirds and that the Federal Republic was at the top of the European table of real incomes and staff costs. This argument is convincing only if one is prepared to accept 1960 as a 'sacred year of the most equal distribution'. Attempts to persuade the unions to renounce more and more of their claims over distribution became increasingly fruitless as the growth rate of the amount to distribute dropped. The process led on the one hand to increased use of class policy. However, on the other hand periods of weaker growth did not automatically bring a more militant union policy because uncertainty over jobs meant that there was not the necessary mass pressure behind the claim for realization of the threefold adjustment of wage development to productivity, prices and profits development.

In crisis periods the argument of the necessary wage pressure, which was used by advocates of militant union policy in the Federal Republic as well, did not fall on such willing ears in the rank and file because the beneficial effects of wage pressure were harder to find. In 1950 Viktor Agartz, for example, had argued that wage pressure would bring:

— incentives to increase performance although experience has shown that these incentives usually only come from wage increases that have been announced but not those long realized;

— an increase in mass purchasing power (an argument he used for his expansive wage policy)[766] coupled with a certain redistribution effect in favour of wage earners, but owing to possibilities of passing on cost increases this did not often happen;

— incentives to rationalization. Attempts at deriving the positive results of wage pressure directly from one indicator — the degree of unionization of an industry, for example — have not been successful, largely because the degree of unionization depends on longer-term trends rather than cyclical fluctuations.[767]

The development of productivity as the main criterion for wage development is not, however, acceptable to the unions:
— firstly, because it is difficult to measure productivity and consideration for differences in productivity in the various sectors can weaken solidarity; moreover, it is assumed that wage pressure will indirectly increase productivity;
— secondly, because other parameters, such as prices and profits ratios, are becoming increasingly important for a fair incomes policy.

The argument in favour of an expansive wage policy which Viktor Agartz used is increasingly being inverted. Agartz refused to consider productivity and prices because the workers could not influence either of these factors. But on the defensive their participation is increasingly being discussed to obtain a more tolerant attitude from the unions — especially with regard to prices, as productivity has always been considered. But the unions have not succeeded any better than the employers in persuading the general public that they are innocent of price rises. In August 1972 27% of those questioned in a survey said they thought the employers were mainly responsible for price rises (after 28% which said the Government was) and the unions came third with 21%.[768] So with regard for their image, the unions have been rather prepared to accept more responsibility for price development than is really their due because the anti-union feelings of a large minority of the population could not easily be dispelled.

Only during the 3rd (1959-1963) and 5th (1968-1972) growth cycles were there over-corrections of the wage lag, wage increases beyond the growth in productivity. But at most during the 5th cycle were these due to more active union policy, during the 3rd cycle at the turn of the sixties full employment and the resultant shortage of labour brought success in wage policy without a militant union policy. The threat of an obstructionist policy was anticipated by economists such as Bombach and the concessions for de facto restrictions on free bargaining (although verbally the unions held to this) moved in two directions:[769]
— asset formation; and
— extension of co-determination rights.

Other writers who doubt the argument put forward by many economists of the lack of function of the distribution battle and the usefulness of thinking in terms of ritual wage increases, try at least not to make the workers the main financiers of reform policy and recommend a redistribution policy by encouraging an equal supply to the public of state and private goods and services.[770]

Infrastructure and social consumption are increasingly moving into the foreground in Socialist countries too, although there they are not regarded as compatible with private asset formation policy as they are by the advocates of a more modern concept of distribution. The unions, however, remain caught in the dilemma of their function as claimants and their participative function, their potential for conflict and their function as a power to maintain order. The very reasonable warnings by economists concerning the possibilities of financing reform policy are abstracted from the need for an organization to be able to produce short-term successes for its members, even if these are the transitory successes of the money illusion. Union spokesmen reject the criticism of union concepts of distribution.[771] It would only be possible for the unions to heed these warnings without risking a greater divergence in wages and profits than during most of the upswing phases of the West German economy if a comprehensive systems policy in many areas could present a united concept of reform within a reasonable space of time (with regard for the fact that reform governments also have to face the electorate), which goes beyond the relatively inexpensive reforms in the field of co-determination and general participation and avoids inflationary distribution effects. But the necessary political constellation is not yet available. Even the Council of Experts has since 1970 recognized the dilemma of weaker organizations which repeatedly take refuge in the money illusion.[772] A new feature of its analysis is the recognition that capital has a stronger position by reason of its international mobility.[773]

Even if the unions try to avoid the money illusion they cannot even maintain the status quo without an active wage policy. Certainly the wage ratio cannot be raised ad lib with a voluntarist policy. But on the other hand a 'fair' wage ratio will not emerge as the result of some kind of economic natural law. With the extension of participation rights and state intervention with the consensus of the union leaders, the full disciplining of the unions in wage policy has certainly not been achieved, as left-wing critics have sometimes suggested. Greater state intervention in the economy in some cases is making an expansive wage policy easier than in the sixties, when the unions still felt strong responsibility for the maintenance of monetary stability and full employment, while now they tend to expect the state to guarantee these aims independent of their behaviour. So there has been no lack of suggestions that the unions should again be made directly responsible for full employment.

(2) Another proposal moved hesitantly in the direction of *indexing*. The Scandinavian countries especially have experimented with this. Giersch suggested that there should be redistribution at the end of the year and the German Council of Experts in its 1973 report suggested that post-negotiation clauses should be included in wage agreements to enable flexibility of nominal and real wages.[774] It was hoped that if a real wage level which had been fixed in agreements proved too high there would be no point in adjusting the price level because wages would follow prices through the sliding scale clause. However, the possibility of a 'quantity effect on workers and employees' remained, in other words the unions would have to pay for excessive claims with some unemployment.

The main objections to this policy come from two sides: the defenders of monetary stability as one of the main aims fear that sliding scale clauses would strengthen the inflationary mentality, no matter which group was mainly responsible for price rises. A minority on the Council of Experts agreed with this.[775] Left-wing critics on the other hand rightly pointed to the internal effect for the interest groups. The powers of the unions would be overstrained if they were to be made responsible for guaranteeing full employment and internal crises would result in the member organizations. But firstly the attractivity of unions can at best be deduced from their achievements as a whole, and secondly it cannot be expected that the members of associations will subjectively release the state from its responsibility towards its citizens and not increasingly hold it responsible for unemployment. But one cannot deduce from the state's benevolent interest in seeing unions which are organizationally strong that no joint responsibility, especially where participation rights are conceded, can be imputed to them.

In the theory and assessment of practice in other countries indexing is controversial.[776] It is said to have advantages such as limiting profits and over-investment or unproductive investment. Some even see in it a means of improving income distribution and restructuring price development in various sectors. But in connection with incomes policy the argument of the anti-inflationary discipline which it is hoped that indexing will bring is decisive. Sliding scale clauses have often been used in Belgium, Denmark and Italy. The Scandinavian countries apart from Denmark on the other hand have worked more with re-negotiation clauses. Since 1952 the legally guaranteed minimum wage in France has been linked to a price index. But it is hard to generalize on these instruments. With a low inflationary trend, as in Brazil, the judgement is largely positive, although it is difficult to separate the anti-inflationary effect of indexing from that of other factors. With moderate inflation rates the unions prefer free bargaining to the fixed arrangements. Adjustment periods which were too short, as in Italy in 1957 (two months) have produced the opposite of the desired effect: the clauses themselves became the main motor of inflation. The degree of employment also plays a part. If the supply of labour is less than the demand indexing loses its attraction in boom periods for the workers as well.

In Germany the scholars and the guardians of stability, the Council of Experts, the Central Bank and the Government were rather sceptical about indexing during the fine weather phase of the economy. The only important indexing of incomes in the Federal Republic is the state pension scheme. Now a certain change is apparent in the attitude of economists.[777] The Central Bank has so far resisted attempts at indexing. Index clauses have only been permitted in exceptional cases, such as:

— rent contracts for at least ten years;
— sales of land and property against a pension for more than ten years or for life.

Paragraph 3 of the Currency Law makes the use of index clauses subject to approval. Index clauses can play a part in bond issues, taxes and wages. The Economic Advisory Council to the Federal Ministry of Economic Affairs suggested cautious experiments with index clauses especially with bond issues. Other experts suggest at most a variable compensation for inflation to be paid subsequently.

The unions have also been rather sceptical about indexing because they fear for their autonomy in wage negotiations and with some justification that once indexing is introduced negotiations may be only over real wages and no longer nominal wages. In Sweden there have been particularly fierce controversies over this question. While the white collar workers' organizations, SACO and TCO, defended their margins after direct tax, the LO insisted that existing discrepancies should be adjusted before tax.[778] In Luxembourg the CGT took up the struggle over indexing less in the wages sphere than over price policy. In its 1974 programme it demanded indexing especially in the building and housing sector and the introduction through legislation of a 'minimum index tranche' for households with a low income is proposed.[779]

After the early experience with index attempts in Austria and Germany even the Christian unions, which were not class conscious, opposed indexing because it perpetuated the status quo of low wages and some which were just on the existential minimum. Oddly enough they supported indexing for civil service salaries on the state-centred grounds that '...the income of civil servants should not be dependent on the fluctuations of the economic cycle, the state should ensure that its employees have the income necessary to maintain their social status'.[780] Only the Hirsch-Duncker unions supported indexing, and the Reich Government opposed it. Braun, the Minister of Labour, objected that it was difficult to find a calculation basis for indexing, that the unions would not receive their adequate share during an upswing and finally — the argument still most frequent today — that 'valuable obstacles to price rises' would be lost.

A number of arguments which are often produced in favour of indexing will not stand up to a comparative analysis. It cannot be proved that countries which experiment with wage-price indexes suffer fewer strikes. Some of the countries which have introduced these indexes (like Finland and Italy) are at the top of the strike table; others, like the Federal Republic, which have largely rejected them, are at the bottom. The effects of indexing on inflation have also varied. Where there was progressive inflation it often acted as a stimulant — it is called the 'in-built inflator', and state prices and incomes policy which was increasingly losing its grip on the situation, tended to manipulate the consumer price index, generally through price policy and subsidies, to be able at least to pretend to some control of the situation.[781] The various forms of 'institutionalized inflation', however, can only stabilize social peace over very short periods, over the longer term they function at the expense of the socially weaker groups and so become the causes of renewed social conflict.[782]

4. CO-OWNERSHIP POLICY

In the mid-twenties a standard work which was certainly not class conscious could limit itself to this brief statement on profit-sharing:

> Profit-sharing has never been of interest to the German union movement and it has really only occasionally stimulated suggestions from socio-political dilettantes. The plans for co-owernship through small shares, etc., which were conceived after the war, never touched the mass at all.[783]

The mass is still hardly affected by these plans but since the sixties union leaders have increasingly had to concern themselves with this subject.

Profit-sharing outside the company is deduced by some economists as a necessity from the changed view of private property: legally, there has for a long time been no formally unlimited ownership but practically no consequences have been drawn from this regarding the legal claim to profits. Those who hold this view are not aiming to abolish private ownership of the means of production for fear of too much administration, but they do not want a 'functionless rentier class like the nobility and the clergy under the ancien régime' either.[784]

Experiments with profit-sharing and asset formation have been stimulated in recent years by two factors:

(1) The criticism had to be acknowledged that in current participation models the weight is distributed so unevenly between participation and profit that participation offers are relatively unattractive to the majority. Especially in countries where there is no strict legal parity arrangements, like Sweden, therefore, participation is increasingly coupled with profit-sharing.

(2) The recognition that a radical redistribution cannot in the capitalist system be achieved through wage policy has repeatedly brought conservative observers particularly to recommend asset formation. The controversies between supporters of types of asset formation which are already being tried out (savings encouragement, asset formation in the company) and types which are still under discussion and whose effects cannot yet be fully estimated has intensified. Several forms of co-ownership policy are being debated:

(a) Savings Encouragement

At present it looks as if consensus is being reached between conservative critics of asset formation measures which have been used so far and unionists that it is better to encourage co-ownership in the company rather than use legislation to encourage asset formation in the population as a whole.

State encouragement of asset formation has proved expensive (about DM 80 billion from 1949 to 1975), and it often proves more to the benefit of higher earners. This was particularly the case with:
— saving with life assurance;
— to a certain extent with saving through building loan plans, and
— saving on a bonus plan which cannot be said to have made any contribution to re-distribution;
— the DM 642 law, under which employees could save up to this amount per year on a bonus plan with tax concessions and a contribution from the employer. This was a mixture between savings encouragement and investment wages and it was only with the amendment of 1970 that it lost the side-effect of benefiting higher income groups, as even the German White Collar Workers Association, which is by no means radical, pointed out.[785]

(b) Voluntary Company Asset Formation Policy

Co-ownership in the company is said to reflect on performance and strengthen the relationship to the company. It also strengthens the company's capital basis and — which makes it rather suspect to the unions — lessens the intensity of wage conflicts.

Big companies in Germany have begun to work voluntarily with staff shares, staff funds and other forms of asset formation related to the company, for various reasons. A study by the Working Group to Spread Share Ownership in Düsseldorf estimates that at the beginning of 1976 about fifty companies had issued shares to their staff and that about 450,000 employees had taken up the offer. This included the 50,000 employees of Preussag, VW and VEBA who acquired shares in these companies when they were being transferred to part private ownership. Siemens is at the top of the list with about 100,000 staff shareholders, followed by Hoechst with 40,000, the Deutsche Bank with 33,000, RWE with 28,000, Bayer with 22,000 and BASF with 18,000. Nevertheless only between 20 and 30% of the employees of these companies are taking advantage of this opportunity. To stimulate the market it is suggested that the period for which the shares must be held and for other tax concessions be lowered from the present five years.[786]

The works council has in some cases rejected profit-sharing, as in 1976 in the Hamburg company Gruner & Jahr, because no cover was given on the share price which could in theory drop below nominal value.[787] Unions have never been interested in holding securities, although it is pointed out that 14.5% of working households in the Federal Republic own securities, as compared with 23.6% of all households and 37.7% of households of the self-employed.[788] Asset formation through wage agreements developed quickly from 1969 to 1971 but the development is now rather stagnating. In addition to the reserved attitude on the part of the unions this is due to the 1973-75 recession and other factors (cf. Table 27).

Among the German unions only the Construction Workers Union has approved and worked out plans for asset formation. This was under the influence of the Catholic social doctrine and in deliberate rejection of Socialist concepts of re-distribution. The influences came directly through the specialist advisers on the Leber Plan for Asset Formation, in which the two Jesuit priests v. Nell-Breuning and Wallraff participated. Indirect influence came from the stimulus to the discussion, which had reached stalemate in the union, after the study group on asset formation in which discussions had been proceeding since 1961 between the DGB and the BDA produced no result after the two major churches had attempted to reactivate it with memoranda. The conflicts intensified between the unions when many observers suspected a latent approach to the BDA standpoint in the Construction Workers Union. The BDA entered somewhat reluctantly into support for asset formation to avoid more far-reaching claims, no doubt in the hope that the concept of partnership, which it was supporting ideologically, could be saved.

But it remained strongly opposed to profit-sharing outside the company. It was also against state intervention and hoped to be able to keep the measures within wage agreements, which was to be the basis of the successes of the Construction Workers Union.[789] Insofar it is not quite right to say that the policy of the 'capital' side was always consistent but that the union strategy was 'highly contradictory', as left-wing critics have done.[790] There was rather a

TABLE 24
Asset formation through wage agreements in the FRG

Year	Employees (in millions)	Participation in asset formation (in billions of DM)
1969	1.0	0.3
1970	8.0	2.0
1971	13.4	3.7
1972	14.4	4.3
1973	15.0	4.5
1974	15.2	4.7
1975	15.2	5.9

Source: From figures issued by the Federal Ministry of Finance in 'Arbeit und Sozialpolitik', 1976, H. 7, p. 241.

contradictory development on both sides the more the clear alternatives between savings encouragement as the only concept on the part of political forces which favoured the employers' side and the socialization concepts of the Left, the SPD and the unions, became blurred at the end of the fifties and the beginning of the sixties. The pacifying effect of the concept was once formulated in the statement that a social system based on private property must be all the more stable, the more 'the opposition of interests between capital and labour. . . becomes rooted in the breast of each individual and is thereby eliminated as a social conflict'.[791]

Although the attempt by the Construction Workers Union to induce the union movement as a whole to share its change of aims was not successful, it did achieve its end in its own sector. For the first time in the history of collective agreements in Germany the contract of 31 July 1965 included asset formation. Although there was strong criticism of the integrative effect from the Left — Rolf Hochhuth spoke of the 'Munich of the German working class' — the BDA opposed the contract because it regarded contracts which provided for asset formation as irreconcilable with a free econony, believed that monetary stability would be jeopardized and feared that future negotiations would be more difficult.[792]

The Leber Plan held asset formation through wage agreements as the best of the alternatives which had been tried out in the system so far:[793]
— asset formation through savings encouragement;
— saving through the company (as under the early version of the DM 624 Law, the DM 312 Law. This was regarded as ineffective); or
— through state legislation.
The main advantage in asset formation through wage contracts was seen in that this gave most influence to the individual workers and the unions.

(c) Collective Profit-Sharing

Co-ownership policy is only acceptable to the majority of the German unions if it touches profits and not wages. The statement by the DGB on profit-sharing of 5 April 1973 emphasizes that participation by the workers in productive wealth 'is not a means of improving incomes'.[794]

This model was first put forward in 1957 by Bruno Gleitze, Director of the union Institute for Economic Research and later supported by the Krelle Report. It has the advantage of only envisaging asset formation where profits have been earned. To prevent differentiation between the wage-earners, however, the certificates were to be distributed free to all the employees, even those in parts of the company which were not making a profit or could not make a profit.

Profit-sharing has the ideological advantage over the other forms of asset formation that it contains a tacit recognition of the doctrine of the value of labour. Participation in capital assumes that only capital has a claim to profits, it is simply spread more widely.[795] Profit-sharing has the disadvantage for the employer of keeping him in the constant fear that he may be pushed into the minority capital position.

Only *collective* profit-sharing is consistent with the unions' standpoint because it can prevent a reconcentration of capital through sales of certificates by individual workers and psychologically does not encourage the use of the assets for private purposes but strengthens the awareness that capital is not for consumption but for investment. The circulation sphere is not touched as it is in the investment wages model and this can have favourable effects on stability policy. For the employers on the other hand it is clear that this comes close to part-socialization, and union theoreticians do not deny this.[796]

Even those who support the idea of co-ownership policy agree that the instrument is a middle way between capitalism and full socialization and would only be meaningful in connection with co-determination, concentration control and a comprehensive social policy.[797] The unions would be bound to reject any plan which touched wages or was a form of investment wage. Firstly, they rightly fear that companies with high labour costs would have a heavier burden to bear than capital intensive companies, which would make solidarity in wage policy even more difficult. The unions agree with the BDA that free collective bargaining must be upheld and are generally opposed to any measure which would presumably entail further state regulation (like the Burgbacher Plan put forward by the CDU). There is a further psychological argument which is decisive in the unions' rejection of plans for wages in the form of investment. The unions generally put their claims forward in a 'package'. Concessions over asset formation could make further concessions over cash wage increases more difficult to achieve and this would create dissatisfaction among members, who naturally prefer the bird in the hand in the form of a cash wage rise. Co-ownership policy in the eyes of unionists always seems a substitute for social policy. But as it is increasingly difficult to create a market to buy and sell individual chances an asset formation policy which puts individual savings before social and collective care becomes an anachronism as more and more spheres of life become politicized and the chances for vertical mobility are collectivized.[798]

For some years asset formation, like co-determination, seemed to be a purely German question. The unions in other Western European countries were generally even more opposed to asset formation plans than they were to co-determination, with the exception of some Christian unions. But here, too, much has changed. At present most unions are reserved over the issue, some are beginning to develop plans of their own (in Austria and the Netherlands) and others after a period of opposition have taken the lead in theory (Scandinavia), putting forward new plans which go beyond the now stagnant German discussion. The unions may be expected to submit to further freezing of class conflict where their influence will increase, as in the Dutch model with 'participation in the growth in company profits', according to which 18% of the growth in taxable company profits is paid into a central fund which is administered by the union with some decision rights for the employers.[799] In Austria, according to the ÖGB President, Benya, 'Consideration is given to any plan for a productive use of wages' and as long as these do not take the form of compulsory saving they are all tested to see if they would be realizable and if they are reconcilable with traditional wage policy.[800]

Many people regard the Swedish model as breaking new ground. At the suggestion of the LO, legislation was passed which enables pension funds to be invested in shares. The unions propose the creation of industry funds to be controlled by employees. This takes the first step towards combining participation and redistribution. So far no other country has been so consistent over this. Scandinavian unions will not accept every form of asset formation either, certainly not in the form of investment wages as proposed by the Swedish employers, they will only accept asset formation in the form of a greater incentive to autonomy for groups in the plants and participation in central steering institutions in the companies. Meidner's plan proposes that all companies — except nationalized and cooperative enterprises for which the ruling is facultative — with more than 500 employees should pay 20% a year of their profits after depreciation into a central equalization fund in the form of shares. This would not be individual profit-sharing for employees. The dividends are to be used to buy new shares, to train union specialists and for enlightenment policy. It is calculated that after twenty years the fund will own one-third of the productive wealth of Sweden. Opponents of the plan have calculated much shorter re-distribution periods and object mainly to the excessive role to be played by the unions on the administrative bodies, on which the local union groups are to have rights of proposal and veto on the appointments to seats on the committee. The head administration of the central fund is to be comprised of representatives of the union industry and occupational groups. The President of the LO, Gunnar Nilsson, said in 1976 that this is firstly a proposal for discussion which needs further work. Palme, the Prime Minister, said the plan was not ripe for discussion during the 1976 election campaign and the unions do not expect it to be realized before the eighties. However, the problem is more urgent in Sweden than in other countries, because solidarity in wage policy without asset formation is threatening to bring wage development as whole behind the development of profits as the most highly-paid groups consistently refrain from extracting wage improvements.[801]

After the victory of the conservative tripartite coalition under Fälldin in the elections in 1976 the plans for collective co-ownership — endorsed by the LO congress in 1976 — were not to be realized.[802]

The Danish LO and the Social Democratic Party have launched wide campaigns in favour of the creation of wage-earner funds and collective co-ownership of the workers. But a bill in parliament introduced by the Social Democrats failed to get a majority.[803]

After the Latin countries Great Britain among the EEC countries has most strongly resisted asset formation plans. The TUC regards all forms of profit-sharing, and enlightened employers have been experimenting with these since the nineteenth century,[804] as discredited. Plans for collective funds are discussed in the Labour Party[805] and the TUC but no concrete projects have yet emerged.[806]

A British student of trade unions commented on Meidner's plans, 'Such a proposal would find no supporters here'.[807] Even the German trade unions, which have partly advocated even non-collective forms of co-ownership and formation of wealth, concluded in some resignation: 'As far as the "great solution" of the problem of co-ownership with the help of collective funds on a nation-wide basis is concerned there seems to be a certain agreement that this postulate cannot be raised with any emphasis in a medium-term perspective'.[808]

5. PARTICIPATION, CO-DETERMINATION, AUTOGESTION OR WORKERS' CONTROL?

Models for participation to realize industrial democracy and link the will formation process in the production sphere with that in the legitimation sphere are as old as Socialist thought. They first flowered after the First World War but authentic participation models did not appear in bourgeois theories of labour until after the Second World War. That was particularly the case in the USA, where Mayo's human relations approach was only increasingly recognized as manipulative in the sixties. Critics began to demand real participation and not simply models to serve the integration of dissent.[809]

(a) Theoretical Participation Models

There are deep differences in the theories of participation held by unions in capitalist countries and three models can be distinguished:

(1) Co-Determination

Co-determination is supported mainly in countries where unions are 'revisionist' in orientation. In other countries it only played a part until the sixties, if at all, in the Christian union movement, especially in Holland and Belgium.[810] This model accepts the dualism of capital and labour. The relation is seen as temporary and at best a concealed *dolus eventualis* (possible deception), which should be transformed into the dominance of labour after a certain development. The formation of a collective counter-power and institutionalized co-determination are seen by theoreticians of a democratic Socialism like Fritz Vilmar not as opposites but as potentially complementary organizational forms of the democratization process.[811] The claim to co-determination is derived from the principle established by a value judgement with its recognition of the dignity of the person and inalienable human rights (Articles 1 and 2).[812] But the concept of co-determination which is generally regarded as 'German' abroad is not uniform by any means in the Federal Republic: there are partnership conceptions ('a mixture of material concessions and partial co-decision rights) in contrast to concepts of workers' control which are based on a fundamental antagonism between capital and labour which might at most temporarily be institutionalized in a class balance in the currently realizable form of co-determination.[813]

Even the very word 'co-determination' is greeted with suspicion abroad, particularly since it became rumoured that the Federal Republic was aiming to export its form of co-determination through the European Community to the rest of Europe. The concept is accepted only with great reluctance by a few foreign unions. We can quote one spokesman of the Dutch NVV:

> There is a lot to suggest that the word 'co-determination' should be avoided. For Socialists it entails the risk that capitalist concepts of ownership are implicitly accepted. On the other hand the concept cannot simply be eliminated from the modern vocabulary. So we will use it, with the proviso that for us it is a collective term for all the ways in which the workers are trying to obtain influence on decisions which are being taken in the economic process and in companies.

So co-determination becomes the term for all the efforts to democratize working conditions.[814]

None of the existing concepts is undisputed. The French term 'participation' seems at first sight to be less restrictive but it is still as suspect to the Left as 'co-determination'. Jokers in the student movement in France distributed posters against the participation campaign by the French Government on which there was a simple but very effective verbal conjugation:[815] 'I participate...' etc. down to 'they profit'. The gap between 'them' and 'us' which this little grammar exercise reveals is in fact still the main problem in any form of participation. The best paritative model only gives at most 50% power and even if it is widened to include some form of asset formation only a tiny percentage of the profit is being distributed and it would be decades before any real effect was felt.

(2) Autogestion

In countries with a syndicalist union tradition, especially France and Italy, the concept is of administration by the workers (*autogestion, autogestione*). This has been most comprehensively developed by the CFDT since it moved from a concept of Christian Socialism to one of a democratic Socialism. The concept of autogestion has a background of varied intellectual traditions, Proudhon to Fourier, for instance.[816] Marxism is not—as in the German SPD after 1959—a 'private matter' but it is only one of the ideological sources.[817] CFDT leaders have even occasionally drawn on Lafargues' *Praise of Idleness* when they were criticizing existing Socialist models for trying to combat capitalism on its own ground, the growth in productivity. Values such as 'non-work' and 'leisure' played a greater part in the CFDT's socio-pedagogic concept of the realization of man than in that of the other French unions.[818]Autogestion is seen as a collective learning process but not as a concrete organizational model which can be achieved with a single revolutionary exercise of power. To fulfil its pedagogic task the union operating under captialist conditions must not allow itself to be fully integrated into the system in the plant. Cumulation of offices in the union leadership and in the company is regarded as harmful. Technical competencies are increasingly to be separated from leadership functions. The means to this, the systematic dialogue, is reminiscent of optimistic theories of the 'ideal discourse situation' and has repeatedly given rise to strong pessimistic criticism.[819] What is new is the concept that a premature institutionalization can be countered by organizing a permanent process of learning.[820] One model which has been influential for autogestion is the Yugoslavian type of worker administration. In its theoretical work the CFDT is trying to learn from the Yugoslav mistakes. In a foreword to an analysis of the Yugoslavian model Michel Rocard drew attention to the danger that the most highly qualified cadres may misuse autogestion and that the system could be increasingly manipulated from above by the party bureaucracy and specialists.[821] But in France there is rightly more optimism that with the greater degree of education the mistakes of a developing country like Yugoslavia can be avoided.[822] Autogestion is often seen as the characteristic system of the Latin countries and certainly it corresponds to the anarcho-syndicalist traditions of large sections of the labour movement there. But syndicalism is not the only, and numerically it is not even the dominant direction. It must be remembered that the Communist-oriented unions CGT and CGIL in France and Italy have never fully accepted autogestion and are still highly critical of the concept today. Apart from the CFDT, it is accepted, by large sections of the PSU, the Anarchists and syndicalists and some of the Trotskyists. Their reference to Trotsky over this, however, is not justified, and they have some difficulties in reconciling Trotsky's policy of the militarization of working life and his hostility to 'the workers' opposition', which was in no way less than Lenin's, with modern Trotskyist views. But the Trotskyists are not unconditional supporters of the ideas of the CFDT. They agree with other Marxist-Leninist groups that the CFDT concept has little sense of power because it neglects the priority of the party's political struggle. Ernest Mandel believes that Socialism would be bound to come to grief over the dualism between business and politics which would arise under the autogestion model. Even if Socialism could be instated through the overthrow of the bourgeois power in the state, he sees a continuance of the dualism of economic leaders and political leaders, which would perpetuate the dualism of parliamentary democracies and further the tendency to bureaucratization which the CFDT is honestly trying to combat.[823]

The main opponents of autogestion are the Maoists, who object that it is confused, and that it is putting the cart before the horse because it announces organization models which there is no realistic chance of putting into practice under present conditions. The model of Yugoslavia makes the concept even more suspect to the Maoists because to them Yugoslavia is a mixture of a neo-bourgeois market economy without the dictatorship of the proletariat but with an encrusted authoritarianism, because the system no longer aims for the permanent mobilization of the masses.[824] But the Maoists are of little importance in the labour movement in the Latin countries and the real opponents for the CFDT are the CGT and the Moscow-oriented Communists who can still mobilize the greatest number of workers in the unions and the party.

The CGT's criticism of autogestion is that it is full of illusions over the possibility of realizing such ideas under capitalist conditions. The CFDT leaders answer that they are not 'idealistic boy-scouts' and that they are aware of the difficulties of realizing the model.[825] The CFDT counters the other criticism that it is blind to political power relations with models to counter the danger of anarcho-syndicalist fragmentation of the will formation processes which can lead back to a petty plant egoism by extending central planning — but not planning which is steered authoritatively from above.[826] It is only in recent contributions that the naivete in organization theory of which the autogestion ideologists were rightly accused has been eliminated and concrete organization models are now being put forward which are showing signs of taking proper account of modern capital relations and even multi-national structures.[827]

The concept which the CGT and the Communists oppose to autogestion is no longer simply the old Leninist concept of workers' control. For tactical reasons the concept *gestion démocratique* has been evolved for medium-term strategic planning. As the CGT and the CFDT are aiming to join forces, the CGT leaders are taking a conciliatory line and avoid the shrill tones of the Maoist critics: 'We told our comrades in the CFDT that if they have a better suggestion to make, one that is concrete and realistic, they should let us see it'.[828] The CFDT emphasizes to the CGT that they agree over the necessity for further democratization but object that the CGT is only aiming to change those in authority in the plant and replace the capitalist boards with the paritative *conseil d'administration démocratique* on which there would be representatives of the workers, the consumers and the state. The CGT is accused of an unbroken relationship to the hierarchy which is oriented to 'behaviour of the classical religious type', while the CFDT claims that it is 'much more iconoclastic'.[829] Great as the differences appear to be between the concepts of the two major French unions the CFDT is quite prepared to make tactical concessions. Its presence in existing participation institutions in France, particularly the *comités d'entreprise* is seen as an act of 'workers' control', which serves to acquire the necessary information for the struggle and retain influence on concrete working conditions in the plants.[830] In this way new means of participation can be won. Like the CGT the CFDT rejects any form of integration through the employers.[831] It remains to be seen in how far the battle over seats on the existing participation bodies will in fact be gradual integration.

(3) Workers' Control

The theoretical model of Marxist-Leninist groups for participation in the production sphere is the concept of workers' control. Theoreticians of this model reject any participation by unionists or elected representatives of the workers in running the plants. The obligation to keep the peace and to respect business secrets is not accepted and any institutionalization of conflict is rejected as there is a danger that militancy will be degraded to an instrument of integration and class reconciliation. The concept of workers' control is not uniform, especially in Great Britain, where ideas ranging from individual approaches to counter-power to complete control of production are all covered by the same term.[832] There were terminological conflicts even just after the First World War, when the concept began to spread. The Brandler-Thalheimer group, which propagated the concept in the twenties in Germany, was severely criticized by Trotsky for having a misconception of control and diluting the term to a purely technical concept of mass mobilization.[833]

The Belgian Socialist union FGTB aimed at a special congress on workers' control in 1970 to bring order into the terminological chaos which had been making the debate increasingly confused after the end of the sixties. 'Participation' was defined negatively for France as an integration offer by the government, for Belgium it was more neutral. *Co-gestion* (co-determination) was bitterly rejected as a German revisionist error and *contrôle ouvrier* (workers' control) was demanded. After a vague acknowledgement of Socialism, however, the terminological excursion concluded with a characteristic dilution: the attitude of the FGTB was described as *participation contestatrice et donc transformatrice* (militant participation to change the system).[834] Two lines above this, however, there is also an acceptance of productivity growth and one must conclude from this that participation cannot be intended to challenge the economic system every day. The narrower definition of workers' control was no more consistent: the union would have to 'have the means (but not be obliged) to exercise its right to militancy'. The union claims for itself the right to choose the moment, the conditions, the length of time and the problems that are opportune to challenge the system.[835] This is certainly different from German co-determination as 'sharing power' but a transformist-Socialist attitude as a permanency must at least be prepared for empirical tests.

The fact that workers' control is largely seen as a process has occasionally caused it to be seen in the capitalist system as the preliminary stage to workers' administration in Socialism, although in the main no organic institutional continuity has been established.[836] There is now agreement that workers' control is an anti-capitalist strategy within capitalism and that it moves through various phases. In the first, individual claims for control (over appointments and dismissals, breaks and working time, tempo and transfers in the plant) are made, firstly to produce greater militancy. It is only in a second phase that capitalist authority in the plant is generally challenged.[837] Unlike the idea of autogestion, concepts of workers' control are more aware of inter-relations with the political sphere, although English models of workers' control do not generally represent Leninist theories of leadership. As the concepts of workers' control in Great Britain too are usually only upheld consistently by left-wing minorities in the relevant specialized institutes and are not a dominant concept even in the shop steward movement, despite its militancy, the relation to the party as to the union was not without conflict. The British union movement especially seems ill-suited to act as catalyst for such aims: its local organizational structure, the fragmentation through the shop steward movement, the insistence on the occupational or craft principle and the reformism of the Labour Party with which it cooperates closely, all these elements make it unlikely that the British union movement will put itself at the head of a strong movement for workers' control.

The British tradition has always been ambivalent over participation. Sidney and Beatrice Webb, who are often criticized as the supreme example of revisionist union theory issued clear warnings after the first forms of participation appeared in the Whitley Councils after 1919. They feared that the solidarity of the working class would be undermined and that there could be agreement on profit-sharing between unscrupulous unionists and entrepreneurs at the expense of consumers.[838] Industrial democracy has been set up as a counter-concept to integrative participation but it has remained ambivalent. In theory it is more than co-determination and less than autogestion. The literature on workers' control in Great Britain often produced verbal compromises although it was radical in tone: workers' control and administration were seen as a continuum which is not schematized into periods: 'The strategic aim of worker control is worker administration...'[839]

Workers' control appears as a historically realistic concept for Marxist-Leninists in contrast to Utopian models like those put forward by some radicals in the labour movement at the end of the sixties, especially in Italy under the motto *tutto e subito* (everything and all at once). Nevertheless, for tactical reasons some Communist parties hold more flexible positions so as not to be pushed to one side in the debate on co-determination. The French CGT and the Communist Party in France generally use weakened variants of the concept such as 'democratic control' or *gestion démocratique* and in its 11th Statement at its 1971 Düsseldorf Congress the German Communist Party actually accepted the word 'co-determination'. Critics of co-determination among sociologists, who prefer the concept of workers' control, have nevertheless occasionally recommended the unions in the Federal Republic to make progressive use of this in order to achieve more far-reaching aims rather than leave it to the 'revisionists' because it is unsuitable as a vehicle for conflict strategy.[840]

Writers close to the Communist Party accuse the left-wing Social

Democrats and non-Leninist Marxists of over-estimating co-determination on the job and not paying enough attention to the problems of coordination and planning. This has its parallels in the criticism from the French Communist Party and the CGT of the anarcho-syndicalism of autogestion. The ties to workers' organizations outside the company, especially the unions, are therefore given special emphasis. Co-determination proposals are not, however, rejected a priori, they are put to the test of several critical questions to find out whether the models encourage initiatives by wage-earners, whether the initiative is really directed against the real centres of the power of monopoly capitalism, whether they broaden the information base of the working class and enable positions of counter-power to be built up.[841] Co-determination as a free gift is rejected, but an active struggle for further rights makes the Moscow-oriented Communists more inclined to accept this.

In every country in which more than manipulative participation is envisaged there have been similar adjustments by the Left (except for the Maoist and Trotskyist groups) to the real development of participation opportunities in the production sphere. This has been most evident in Sweden and the Swedish models sensibly leave enough room for initiative in the plant and in the regions for this tendency to be strengthened in future. In no country does the actual development of participation follow the schemes of the theoretical models sketched here, not even in the Latin countries. Whether this trend will be strengthened in future depends partly on the real concessions which the unions manage to win from the employers and the governments, partly on the structure and traditions of the union movement concerned. In the Latin countries particularly the question is bound to keep arising whether the militant tradition of the unions can be united at all with the *esprit gestionnaire* and participation and whether union autonomy will not have to be drastically reduced in exchange for extended participation. An attempt to reduce union autonomy before granting participation rights would certainly be the worst mistake any government could make if it was aiming to introduce new forms of participation where the unions are very militant. Joint responsibility through participation in any case over the longer term narrows the field for autonomous negotiation, not through outside influence but on the basis of voluntary decisions.

(b) Participation Models in Practice

The real development of participation models in Europe did not neatly follow the lines of the three basic theoretical concepts held by the various union movements. Various institutions of participation have emerged, on very different levels, partly spontaneously through the labour movement and partly with state legislation:
— union representatives in the plant, shop stewards committees;
— ad hoc negotiation committees;
— works councils with some participation in management functions;
— delegate bodies to reform syndicalist organizations;
— political councils.

These various levels are not exclusive. Councils against bureaucratic union structures often grow into the functions of negotiating committees or become political councils. Negotiation committees occasionally have unwillingly taken on management functions, as when the German council movement was reduced to a works council movement after 1919.

Most of these, which are representation by the workers only as the beginning of the formation of a counter-power, are unproblematic for the labour movement. Only those forms of participation which bring joint responsibility and daily direct contact with the representatives of capital are controversial. There is only agreement on 'participation' among Europe's unions in a very general sense, to put it neutrally, because the German word *Mitbestimmung* (co-determination) has an integrative taint even in translation. The approaches to the realization of participation in the various systems in Europe differ as much as the theories of participation itself. The degree of legalization of industrial relations, the degree of politicization of the unions and the form in which the councils have emerged is more decisive for the functions which participation instruments assume than abstract theories put forward by intellectuals. This does not mean that there are no connections between the theoretical models prevailing in different labour movements and the political reality. The two main types, control and co-determination, have not developed incidentally. The more radical and powerful the labour movement was the more has the state tried to pacify these demands. This is one of the reasons why Germany first took the road of co-determination: after a radical tradition in the labour movement and with the employers' associations weakened after the war the state and the entrepreneurs made wide concessions which turned into cooperative practices instead of sticking to the old concept of control. When the integrationist device of German *Mitbestimmung* is criticized it should be kept in mind that the German separation of the workers' representatives in the Betriebsrat (Works Council) shows that complete integration was not the concept of this model from the outset. The trade unions in the Latin countries in a more unitary representation have accepted consultative institutions where they sat together with the representatives of the management.[842]

In Europe roughly four models of participatory institution to increase industrial democracy can be discerned:[843]

(1) on the basis of legislation (Belgium — *conseils d'entreprise*, Finland — production committees, France — *comités d'entreprise*, Netherlands, Austria, the Federal Republic);

(2) on the basis of collective agreements (Denmark, Norway, Sweden);

(3) on the basis of local agreements, which differ strongly from one company to another (Great Britain, Japan, Switzerland);

(4) the co-existence of spontaneous councils as a result of labour disputes, collective agreements and institutions created through legislation (Italy).

(1) *Participation Institutions on a Legal Base*

Until 1971 the Federal Republic was the only country in which the workers were represented on the organs of private companies. Co-determination therefore appeared as a German idea which did not make the concept any more acceptable or reduce the traditional mistrust of it in Europe. The first step to co-determination was taken in the Federal Republic in 1951, and this is still exemplary for plans in all other industries: paritative representation was introduced in the coal, iron and steel industry by the conservative parties and the SPD against opposition from the FDP. In 1952 the Company Constitution Act brought workers the right to provide one-third of the members of the Supervisory Board. However, the shareholders remained responsible for entrepreneurial decisions. For a long time co-determination was only a latent claim and even the SPD in its Godesberg Programme did not go into much detail. The discussion was only reactivated by the SPD draft legislation in the final phase of the Grand Coalition and the report presented by the Special Commission under the chairmanship of Kurt Biedenkopf, which was presented by the Brandt Government at the beginning of 1970. The Co-determination Act was finally passed on 18 March 1976 by a large majority after lengthy battles and it came into force on 1 July 1976. It applies to companies with more than 2,000 employees. For the unions the compromise which was achieved with so much difficulty between the SPD and the FDP had some disadvantages: the addition of one member of the managerial staff to the workers'/employees' contingent, the fragmentation of the workers because three groups are involved, an election procedure which favours radical splinter groups and conservative 'yellow' groups and can lead to phony majorities.[844] Additional conflicts arose when the employers' association BDA — on the basis of an expert opinion from conservative lawyers[845] — tried to prove the unconstitutionality of the Co-determination Act by a 'constitutional complaint' (*Verfassungsbeschwerde*), a step which caused the temporary suspension of the DGB's participation in Concerted Action.[846]

In other countries in Western Europe comparable forms of participation have at most appeared in the public sector. In French and Belgian companies employee representatives take part in board meetings but they cannot vote. In France especially the unions were bitterly opposed to this form of participation with so few rights. Altogether, however, large majorities of unionists have been on the *comités d'entreprise*.[847] Union pluralism has certainly softened the radical opposition to participation, as the FO and the old CFDT were not so doctrinaire in their rejection. This did not prevent the CGT from developing an astonishing degree of cooperation with the management and relatively peaceful relations on the committees on which it held a monopoly, while making highly revolutionary claims.[848] The CFDT, which has become more Socialist in its basic attitude, no longer sees the *comités d'entreprise* as a cause of ideological self-doubt. It rejects integration attempts by the management but its participation in the committees provides the union with more information on the plant, and gives it greater control of working conditions and access to certain funds for social benefits and leisure activities.[849]

Since the beginning of the seventies the German co-determination model has found more supporters abroad, especially in Austria, Luxembourg and Norway. Austria has come closest to the German pattern. Only the size criteria there are different and Austria has no *Arbeitsdirektor* (leading staff member who has the confidence of the unions and is entrusted with recruitment policy). On 1 July 1974 a Labour Constitution Act came into force giving workers one-third representation on the Supervisory Board. But the Austrian model leaves the workers under-privileged in that the Chairman of the Supervisory Board and his first Deputy cannot be appointed against the majority of the votes of the representatives of the shareholders on the board.[850] In Switzerland too the German discussion has had a strong impact. At the beginning of 1976 the three unions under the leadership of the SGB launched an initiative on co-determination.[851] The conservatives argue against the union attempt to have participation settled through legislation that Switzerland already has a measure of co-determination in agreements between the social partners and that there is no reason to aim for a constitutional adoption of the maximal solution containing the most dangerous points from the German model with all the risks it entails.[852] In their dislike of legalized forms of participation the conservatives and the Left are playing into each other's hands. Even a positive declaration from the bishops made no difference. With a relatively good turn-out at the polls of 39.3% the union initiative was approved by only 32.8% of those who voted and none of the twenty-five Swiss cantons produced a majority in favour. The counter proposal from the Federal Assembly was rejected by similar majorities.[853]

The Swiss unions came to grief over their initiative, although they had shown a considerable statemanship in willingness to compromise. It was only in the first phase of the discussion that they bitterly rejected as 'a perfidious and phony solution' the mediation proposal from the Federal Council on the legislative level.[854] But when the conservative Council of States itself took a stand against this 'diluted' version the unions supported the variant proposed by the Federal Council and let it be known that if this proposal were to be accepted by parliament they would consider withdrawing their proposal.[855] But the majority against the union initiative included not only conservative opponents but also a large number of voters from the Left, who felt that the attempt to limit co-determination in the Swiss tradition to plant matters and the staff immediately involved, did not go far enough. The German model played a decisive part in the Swiss debate. But the Dutch model was occasionally discussed as a possible alternative.[856]

The Dutch are proud of the fact that their form of participation is based not so much on labour legislation through a Company Constitution Act as social law, which is why this solution is being discussed in the debate in the European Community over a European limited company as an acceptable alternative to the German model. Since the re-structuring of the limited company in Holland in 1971 the staff as well as the shareholders are participants although with a lower status. The General Shareholders Meeting has the right to propose candidates for election to posts on the board. The works council can exercise a veto right if the persons appear unqualified or if the board does not appear to be appropriately composed. On request by the Supervisory Board the Dutch Social and Economic Council will decide whether the veto is justified. This means that co-determination inside and outside the company are more closely inter-related in this model than in any other system with a comparable national participation organ (e.g. Belgium, France, Italy). The Dutch model is also praised because it avoids the formation of factions. The Supervisory Board is a compact team which works with the confidence of the shareholders and the works council.[857]

But it does not look as if the Dutch unions will be satisfied with only indirect participation, although it would appear at first sight to hold some advantages for unionists who are only willing to accept worker control without participation. To a certain extent this is a more intense version of the FDP solution: the production factor management is not placed on an equal footing with capital and labour, as it is in the Federal Republic, it works above them. So the German system is certainly more militant even if the verdict as to efficiency, if this is questioned, should be in favour of the Dutch solution. The Dutch unions also see it as a disadvantage that the representatives of the workers on the Supervisory Board do not come from the company and do not have to be employees of the unions which negotiate with the company. Many of them regard the system practised in the German coal, iron and steel industry as serving union interests better.[858] In a joint political programme for 1976-66 addressed to the government and to parliament the main emphasis is on strengthening the position of the workers, improving participation outside the company and on the social responsibility of the enterprise. But no concrete proposals were made.[859] The NVV refers to preliminary work by its research department and gives reasons for its objections to the present pattern of the works council and the Supervisory Board.[860]

After the Austrian union federation the Luxembourg CGT drew most on the German model. It demanded paritative co-determination in a *comité mixte d'entreprise*. But in the realization of this it followed the extremely reluctant compromises made by German unions and in its 1974 programme perhaps unwisely made this concession:

> The CGT, as before, demands the introduction of paritative representation in limited companies, as a preliminary stage to the real democratization of the economy, but it might be prepared to accept a minority representation as an interim solution if paritative representation were to be introduced by the latest in 1980 and if there were legislation to that effect.[861]

This kind of compromise may well turn out to be a sign-post. While the German unions have to be content with less than they asked for without any time limit on their compromise, this attempt to attach time conditions to reform policy might well be copied in other countries. An Act of 6 May 1974 created mixed paritative works committees in companies with at least 150 employees. But on all important decisions on structural, financial and investment policy the committee has only the right to be heard (Article 9).[862] So the unions had to make their real concessions where they had not expected to and pay for their victory over parity with loss over the competences on the bodies.

(2) Participation on the Basis of Collective Negotiations

This model has become established in three Scandinavian countries. The Swedish legislation in particular deliberately avoids the German perfectionism. After a commission from the Labour Market Department had carried out preliminary work as from 1971, presenting in January 1975 a 961-page report compiled with typical Swedish thoroughness, the Government presented a draft which would come into force in 1977. It does not provide for the fixed parity over which the various groups and parties spent their energies fighting for many years in the Federal Republic but leaves the details to be settled through negotiation in the company. The workers are granted co-decision rights on jobs, participation in the growth of assets and reorganization or dissolution of company units. Paragraph 26 gives them an influence over the supervision and distribution of work and the appointment and dismissal of staff. Participation in work organization is now in most countries only discussed under the subject of 'The Quality of Working Life'.[863]

The proposals to democratize the plants, put forward by the union movement, were not to be conceived as it were out of a test-tube as 'a co-determination system in a vacuum' because the intention was to build up on what had already been achieved in agreements.[864] It was also emphasized that the LO had not basically changed its views and that it was not taking an uncritical stand over the 'dual loyalty' which would arise for union representatives who were now to participate in running companies.[865] But an initiative was particularly necessary in Sweden because Paragraph 32 of the Statutes of the Employers' Association was still in force, which gave employers the sole right to direct and distribute work. The associations affiliated to the SAF are obliged to make this right a part of any wage agreement, which prevents free negotiation of partial participation in any company.[866] Legislation was needed to break this paternalist reserve, but it was handled with the flexibility which so often characterizes the political process in Sweden.

The Swedish model has undeniable advantages:

(a) It does not create a gulf between small and large companies with all the temptation to manipulation which a system with fixed sizes or legal forms creates.

(b) The claims for democratization are not limited to central bodies but made a matter of concern to self-steering groups. In Norway and since 1969 in Sweden there has been increasing experiment with self-steering groups, not only in marginal plants as in Germany.[867]

(c) It is psychologically an advantage that the workers are not granted participation freely or without a struggle and that unionists who do not want to participate are not forced to do so. Bengtsson, the Minister of Labour explained: 'We are not going to force the workers into participation. If they want to participate they will have to fight for it.'[868]

The Swedish Government was asked by sceptics how long it would take to implement the legislation. Palme told German journalists: 'Admiral Rosa Coutinho and General Carvalho from Portugal recently put the same question to our unionists. . . it will be a few decades yet before the new law is fully effective in all jobs. The Portuguese revolutionaries were astonished and I suppose they were disappointed'.[869] While it is an undisputed advantage if flexible solutions can be found which meet the requirements of each company individually and correspond to the desire for participation of local union units, the German critics especially argue that the Swedish system will lead to an anarchic confusion of institutions and misuse by radical minorities. Central framework regulations are to prevent an anarchic multiplicity of organizational forms. Swedish politicians do not see much danger of misuse by radical groups in view of the dominant position of the Social Democrat LO and its tradition of cooperation, but this does not mean that the Swedish model would prove workable under Italian conditions.

(d) A further advantage of the Swedish model is that it has better flanking measures such as solidarity in wage policy (cf. Chapter 4, 3), asset formation policy (Chapter 4, 4) and social policy, which all union publications emphasize are the prerequisites for co-determination. For other countries the Swedish model would have the advantage that there would not be an inflexible battle over the central parities and that flexible solutions are possible which can be adapted to the requirements of the company and the staff.

In Denmark in 1973 a draft for legislation was presented which had been worked out with the support of the unions, particularly the metal workers. But it had to be postponed due to the mass strikes in April-May 1973. Before the attempts to legislate on industrial democracy there had been numerous attempts at 'cooperation committees' (there were 705 of them in 1971) with joint responsibility for the organization of the factory, social and insurance policy and staff policy.[870] On 1 January 1974 legislation on joint stock companies came into force, according to which all companies employing more than fifty persons must appoint two worker representatives to the board with full rights and duties.[871]

(3) Participation on the Basis of Company Agreements

It is least possible to generalize on countries in which there are only local agreements on participation rights, like Great Britain, Japan and at present Switzerland (since the collapse of the union initiative on co-determination in March 1976). For British theoreticians of worker control co-determination is a vague concept, much more ambivalent than the counter concepts and a typical product of German abstraction in an attempt to combine Socialist ideas with Christian social philsophy.[872] But fewer left-wing specialists on industrial relations in England have also been sceptical about co-determination. The Donovan Commission went to Germany and gathered information. It concluded briefly: 'We found no consensus about the value of these arrangements' and the majority of the members of the commission rather saw in co-determination a danger of further conflict through indiscretion from the central boards, leading to unrest on the shop floor and a conflict of loyalty for the worker representatives.[873]

Many British unionists were only prepared to accept participation if it affected the direct interests of the workers on the job. They saw this as a form of 'job control' on the basis of collective agreements. There was some stronger institutionalization in some companies when 'joint committees' were set up. As the power of the shop stewards grows and they are increasingly accepted by the management as negotiating partners, in some cases over the heads of the local union representatives, 'shop floor' bargaining is developing in many companies. A survey carried out in 1972 showed that about three-quarters of managers questioned could report on 'joint employment-management committees in the workplace', and this appears to have increased since the publication of the Donovan Report.[874]

Not entirely without justification it has been argued that under the continental system participation in board functions has hardly changed the situation for the workers on the job at all and that collective negotiation can produce a wide range of participation in managerial functions without the need for state legislation. The TUC is still reserved towards the German model of co-determination and at most approves the Norwegian system because it is the only one of the continental experiments so far not to leave the shareholders ultimately in control of the company. Naturally they reject the German dual system with its works councils because it brings disadvantages for the unions.

Since its document on nationalization in 1944 the TUC has taken the standpoint that beside free bargaining there can at most be consultative institutions in which unionists participate. This was not revised until the end of the sixties, when there was sufficient evidence to show that labour relations in the nationalized industries, although the management was more favourable to the unions, had not changed so fundamentally as had been hoped. After digesting the results of the Donovan Report the 1970 TUC Congress appealed to the Government for legislation to ensure direct representation by the unions on the management boards of all nationalized enterprises.[875] There were parallel initiatives in the Labour Party. A report by the working party on industrial democracy in 1967 recommended an extension of the system of hard bargaining for private companies while suggesting experiments with union representation on the management board of nationalized companies. Even the ideologists of workers' control supported participation in nationalized enterprises as these were often a bad example to the private sector, particularly where the employment of lower paid workers was concerned.[876]

Much of the original reserve with regard to continental models has changed with Great Britain's orientation to Europe, although the TUC remains on principle opposed to legalized participation. The institutionalist approach of the dominant liberal-pluralist Oxford school of industrial relations theory, which found its politically most effective expression in the Donovan Report, is coming closer to the concept of institutionalized participation on the basis of national regulations.

European integration has become an important vehicle for participation, because it forces national unions to consider the EEC proposals for the uniform European joint stock company. The TUC, which originally rejected the German model of co-determination completely, has modified its attitude a little and now declares that workers' representation on the Supervisory Board is of only limited value as long as the representatives are not elected exclusively by the unions and are members of them. It remains suspicious of any imposition through legislation.

In its 1974 report the TUC suggested a two-tier structure with representation on the top board of the company — concerned with policy-making — to be implemented by the second-tier management board. For a time it was generally assumed that the introduction of workers' representation must entail the importation of the two-tier board system after the German model into British company law.[877] In its supplementary oral evidence the TUC modified this view. It supported the unitary board from fear that the members of one board in a two-tier approach might become remote from the real management decisions. The essence of the TUC's argument was that workers should be represented through the trade union machinery on the supreme policy-making organ of the company and that the workers' representatives at board level should not become involved in the detail of the execution and implementation of the policies. The latter is usually said to be more easily realized in a two-tier system. As a compromise a flexible half-way system was suggested in the Bullock Report. The TUC and the majority of the Bullock Commission found that in practice a kind of two-tier system already operated in Britain with the main boards separate from management operations even though top managers sit on them as shareholders' representatives.[878]

In spite of these compromises few government reports have recieved such a hostile reception as the Bullock Report. Even the TUC had conflicts over whether it should support or oppose the report and remained relatively silent. Only a handful of sincerely committed advocates were left in the Government by the summer of 1977.

The Irish federation, ICTU, in its statements on the European joint stock company, supported a dualist system like the German, as this would enable a distinction to be made between general policy-making in the company, in which the unions would participate, and daily responsibility for routine decisions.[879] The Green Book accepted by the EEC Commission on 12 November 1975 on workers' co-determination also supported the dual system.[880] After the change in direction in the TUC the British union movement is now between the positive attitude of the DGB on the one hand and the critical position of the Latin countries on the other. Like the DGB the TUC in its interim report of January 1973 and a discussion paper on industrial democracy of August of the same year demanded one-half representation instead of one-third as proposed. While the DGB accepted the ruling for companies with more than 500 employees the TUC demanded that this should apply to those employing 200 and more.[881]

(4) The Co-Existence of Spontaneous Participation Arrangements and Legal Institutions

In Italy there is a mixture of participation institutions on a legal basis and institutions the workers have fought for which see themselves rather as control organs of the representative bodies than preliminary organs of participation.

Before the hot autumn the workers' organ of expression was the *commissione interna*. The integration of what was originally a militant office, the departmental commisar (*commissario di reparto*), into the *commissione interna* about 1950 has been represented as taming this militant office. Paradoxically the CISL reproaches the more radical CGIL with having made the *commissioni interne* the centre of its activity and not so much the representation of the trade unions. It claims to re-syndicalize the *commissioni*,[882] a proposal which will probably not meet with resistance from the CGIL.

From 1968 to 1969 the *commissioni interne* were largely rendered inactive by a spontaneous protest movement among the workers. The factory councils (*consigli di fabbrica*) emerged as a co-existent structure, with members usually elected regardless of whether they were members of a particular union or not. Surveys among workers have shown that in most of the Italian factories the factory councils came into being in direct opposition to the bureaucratic unions and the *commissioni interne*.[883]

Italian Socialists have been able to follow Gramsci, who regarded the *consigli* as 'the negation of industrial legality' in 1920, in contrast to the unions whom he regarded as representing an element of legality.[884] However, it became apparent, as for instance during the militant years 1919/20, that this simple distinction was only applicable for short periods at the height of the total confrontation. The *comitati unitari di base* (CUB) were set up after the spring of 1968 particularly in connection with the revolutionary student movement. They proved to be even more short-lived as a counter power to the unions.[885] The management, albeit rather unwillingly, recognized the factory councils in many cases and the union leaders moved to the head of the movement. Their influence on these councils grew, unlike their influence in the company *commissioni*, where they were weak, and where the ideological difference was not even apparent, and communication between the delegates and local union centres intensified.[886] As early as 1969/70 a survey showed that 90% of the delegates were union members and that 80% could be counted as activists.[887] 50% declared that they belonged to the parliamentary Left, 12% to the extra-parliamentary Left, 38% were actually close to the government parties. The criticism of these institutions was in part contradictory. On the one hand they were regarded as too political and accused of neglecting the syndicalist aims of the workers, on the other they were accused by some of being too localized or syndicalized. The situation may have varied from region to region or from one plant to another and there may have been some truth in all of these accusations. But the trend to over-politicization — where it appeared — did not last. Where there was strong political activism the left-wing parties, especially the PCI, were quickly able to extend their influence and activity in the company.

Empirical studies of individual companies have shown that the rank and file democratic councils, which have received excessive praise, had a lot of faults, they were too theoretical, too generally aggressive and too inclined to personal animosities.[888] These faults were exploited, although the relation between the management and the union hierarchy was very strained, to create a new system of labour relations in the company, in which management skilfully channelled the waves of anger through a readiness to impart information.[889] The new system of labour relations proved resistant, because the old institutions were not all abolished or overlaid. In many cases the old *commissioni interne* existed together with the new factory councils and moderate observers welcomed this as fruitful cooperation.[890]

New forms of participation will presumably spread in the Latin countries as well, although they are more resistant to the idea of co-determination than the Northern European countries, and European integration will strengthen this trend, even if the process is bound to be conflict-ridden. Presumably the power of the unions will grow, whether they see their role as militant or not. The less they see their role as militant the more eager they are to proclaim that they are not aiming for dominance of the companies. In contrast to the TUC, which is much more blunt about its desire for power, German politicians and unionists have always bowed to the accusation of a 'union state' and subscribed to this statement from Heinrich Deist: 'The point of co-determination is not control of the companies by the unions...if the unions aimed to take control of the economy they would soon reach the point where they would have to ask whether they were not abandoning and denying their own real task and function'.[891]

Even in countries where a dualist organizational structure in the company is hardly known, like Italy and France, the unions have after a time obtained control of the participation institutions, even if these were originally created in opposition to the unions. In France the unions have always dominated in the *comités d'entreprise* (cf. Table 4). Only for a time did spontaneous movements like that in 1968 tear a breach in union representation. But it has become apparent that the union standpoint cannot be maintained against any form of state participation. Spontaneous movements from the rank and file, which sometimes by-pass the unions and are sometimes actually directed against them, often bring new offers of participation from the political system so that the unions are under double pressure and they sometimes gnash their teeth and accept participation in the system to strengthen their own position towards the rank and file and prevent the integration of the workers from being taken too far against their will. Over participation in the production sphere, as compared with the debate on participation in the political sphere at the beginning of the century, the fronts in Western Europe are reversed. In the 2nd International the German Social Democrats took a hard line against active participation in the political system and had to submit to the question from Western European Socialists as to how far this attitude had got them and accept the criticism that their radicalism was bound up with political illegality in comparison with the Western constitutional states. Today many a unionist in the Latin countries will give a passionate speech on Sunday against the integrative force of German co-determination and on Monday has to submit to the sometimes very much smaller range of participation in his own country. There is little to suggest that the more radical concepts of 'worker control' and autogestion will achieve a decisive breakthrough in the near future. In France at any rate new initiatives by the Barre Government rather seemed to suggest an extension of participation along the lines of *Mitbestimmung*. The situation might perhaps change if there were a victory for the left-wing coalition.

The possibility of mobilizing the workers for participation is limited. Even the legitimation of German co-determination has been shown by surveys to be still very low. One survey at the end of 1975 showed that only 46% of those questioned took a positive attitude to co-determination, 24% were against it and 26% had no views on the subject. More spectacular was the result that about a quarter of the employers supported it.[892] In the hierarchy of union claims co-determination has risen over the last few years but it still occupies a modest position in the middle of members' preferences and there is little militancy to achieve more in this field (cf. Chapter 2, 1). In France a major survey of 1,116 workers has shown that the claim for autogestion gained a lot of ground at the end of the sixties. A claim that was originally put only by activists in the CFDT was supported by 44% in the survey. The results, however, cannot be compared with German surveys on co-determination, because autogestion on the one hand is a much more radical model as far as the rights of the workers are concerned but on the other is much less likely to be realized; so there is less compulsion to a definite attitude by individual members here and now.[893]

The inclination of many Western European countries to leave the battle over concessions to free bargaining rather than attempt to exercise an influence ex ante has proved expensive in many cases in terms of number of working days lost and it is becoming increasingly questionable in view of the growing inter-relations between the unions and the labour parties which are looking for a meaningful reform policy. The further the Western systems move in the direction of Socialism the less justification will there be for only engaging in fresh bargaining ex post facto instead of aiming for a permanent influence on the transformation of company policy ex ante. Socialist planning as a principle is over the longer term hardly reconcilable with the piece-meal technology of a militant and fragmented union policy.

(c) The Institutionalization of Interest Articulation Outside the Company

The institutionalization of interest articulation is being pursued in many Western democracies on two levels:
(1) By institutionalized bodies within the framework of incomes policy (Concerted Action, Advisory Councils), cf. Chapter 4, 3;
(2) By institutionalized bodies which are more oriented to the development of the legal position of the workers altogether and were conceived on initiatives in the socio-political sphere:
There are two salient models:
— Workers' Chambers
— Economic and Social Councils.

(1) Workers' Chambers

Workers' chambers are mainly a feature of the German language area. Best known is the Austrian model, relatively less attention has been focussed on the activity of the chambers in Luxembourg and the two federal German states, Bremen and the Saarland. Mixed chambers comprising members from the employers' side and workers were once a postulate of the Catholic Centre Party and some of the SPD in Germany. Before the First World War the unions were at best prepared to discuss pure workers' chambers.[895]

All workers' chambers have the right of initiative towards parliament and government. In the Saarland state institutions are not obliged to consult the workers' chamber over initiatives but in Austria, Luxembourg and Bremen a statement from the chamber on draft laws and decrees is obligatory.[895] Nevertheless, in its 1974 programme the Luxembourg CGT demanded a revision of the chambers.[896] The Social Committees of the conservative parties in the Federal Republic have several times proposed the creation of workers' chambers in the other Federal Länder. The SPD has been largely indifferent to the question, the DGB and the DAG opposed it.[897] The decision by the German Constitutional Court to reject constitutional complaints against the workers' chambers and confirm the legal existence of the chambers in the Saarland and Bremen did not make the unions' attitude more positive; they complained of undertones of commune orientation and further attempts to integrate the unions into the systems.[898] Since 1971 the DGB has been demanding instead the creation of economic and social councils. There has been no enthusiasm in publications over the idea of more workers' chambers[899] and the Austrian model is regarded in other countries rather as a corporatist relic than a signpost for the future.[900] The main points of criticism are:

— The chambers cannot exercise any meaningful function which is not already being performed by the unions.

— Their compulsory membership limits the freedom to coalition.[901]

— They are likely to lead to the extension of inefficiently coordinated planning by sectoral bodies.

(2) Economic and Social Councils

Economic and social councils derive less from Socialist than from Christian Socialist ideas. The main discussion on them was between the two world wars. But it was in part discredited with Fascist corporatism (Austria, Italy, Spain). The councils were set up after the war mainly where Catholic groups had a strong position in the political process: in France, Italy, Belgium and the Netherlands. The following considerable legal powers have been granted to the councils, not including the Council of Experts (cf. Chapter 4, 3, b):
— they have constitutional status in France and Italy;
— they are institutions under public law in Belgium and the Netherlands;
— the Danish Economic Council has a coordinative function and is part-way between a body of experts and politics.

More important than the constitutional position is the possibility of exercising influence on government and parliament:
— The council has the right to take initiatives over legislation in Italy (and in the DGB 1971 model).
— The French CES has the right to speak in parliament.[902]

The main problems for the unions are the questions of representation. They regard councils as unacceptable where they tend to make the unions one interest group among many and, as was the case with the Reich Economic Council during the Weimar Republic, the interest of the workers is in danger of being lost in a pluralist jungle. This is generally the result of obsolete proportions in the employment structure and contains over-representation of groups pursuing a conservative status policy (like the French farmers).[903] In countries where several union groups are represented on the council particular power relationships also tend to be perpetuated, as on the Dutch Economic and Social Council, on which the Christian unions retained a constant representation although their membership was dropping (NVV 7, NKV 5, CNV 3).[904]

Generally the councils have done valuable service as advisory bodies and produced reports of high standing. This is especially the case in the Netherlands. But they have only occasionally played a part in pacifying industrial relations. A consultative function on wage policy has also been given to other bodies, such as the Labour Foundation in the Netherlands.[905]

At the beginning of the seventies the German unions made it increasingly clear that the looser form of consultation offered by Concerted Action could only be a temporary arrangement for them. After the largely negative experience with the old Reich Economic Council and its slow demise during the period of emergency economic policy under the Reich President the attitude to the formation of an Economic and Social Council has been largely sceptical in the Federal Republic.[906] The negative label 'a supplementary economic democratic constitution', by-passing the Basic Law, has nourished conservative fears for the constitutional status quo.[907] But some CDU members have now drawn up plans for a Federal Economic and Social Council and the DGB has presented its draft on 'Co-Determination throughout the Economy' (3 March 1971).[908] The CDU proposal is only for a parliamentary advisory body but the DGB proposal[909] entails the granting of wide competencies to the council:

— the council is to have constitutional status (as in France and Italy) in contrast to the coordination and advisory function of the Danish council;

— the council is to have the right to the highest form of intervention in the legislative process. In Article 17 right of initiation towards the legislature is proposed.

The DGB model has eliminated the faults of the other councils which largely derive from corporatist ideas and deserves to be realized:

(a) It would eliminate the fragmentation of arbitrary industrial representation which changes rapidly both on the employers' and on the workers' side (Article 3).

(b) It minimizes the danger of blocking through opposing interests because it proposes minority rights (Article 18). A qualified minority (one third) is to have rights of initiation, inquiry and reference which should benefit the innovative function of the body. Critics, however, fear that the council may create further dissent as the minority rights make it hardly worth while to try to reach consensus. Constant blocking of minority initiatives in parliament could therefore intensify conflict if these rights are not exercised responsibly. But doubts have also been expressed in publications that some of the faults of Concerted Action — the information deficit of the organizations as compared with the bureaucracy — might not be eliminated by an Economic and Social council, which would only put the problem off by creating more bodies of experts.

Summary

So complex a subject as trade unions in their various economic and social systems can hardly be summarised. On many points there are no results which are common to all unions in capitalist systems and generalizations are only possible if types are established. But these types in turn should not be too schematized. Types are at most extremes on a continuum and they hardly exist in a pure form. Most unions declare that they are in favour of industrial unionism. But even where, as in West Germany, a break in the continuity gave the union movement the opportunity to re-organize completely there are divergencies from this principle — some organizations break with industrial unionism or are relics of status organizations (DAG, GEW, etc.). It is more difficult to form types according to characteristics in attitude 'Emphasis on class consciousness — strong or weak', 'extent of bureaucratization', 'leaders from the working class or intellectuals', etc.

It is also difficult to make generalizations because the number of cases involved is small. It is no coincidence that the most strongly quantified studies are in fields where a large number of cases are comparable in various regards: the frequency and length of strikes in relation to the size of the plant, the number unemployed and similar easily obtainable data. But a restriction to factors which are easily quantifiable can soon lead to irrelevance and an unpolitical study. The political scientist will gratefully acknowledge the establishment of correlations between the size of the plant and the structure and pattern of strikes but he concentrates more on other and more political influences where full quantification is not possible.

The search for regularity has yielded four conclusions:

(1) Some current assumptions in union literature need correction.

(2) Some of the causal relations established should be qualified and related to certain types of union and industrial relations or certain periods in the development of these types.
(3) Some causal relations can be shown between factors independent of time and space in the majority of cases.
(4) Trend prognoses.

1. SOME MISTAKEN CURRENT ASSUMPTIONS IN UNION LITERATURE

Most of the assumptions that need correcting occur where generalizations have been made for all industrial relations in capitalist countries from one example (usually the USA). We do not need to enumerate all of them. But these are some of the causal relations which occur in literature and are not tenable:
— the lower the union membership the more easily can an incomes policy be pursued;
— the weaker the union the greater the tendency to a closed shop;
— the higher the membership fees the lower the membership;
— the more comprehensive the head federation, the greater is the tendency to industrial unionism;
— the more highly developed social policy is, the less incentive is there to join a union;
— the wealthier a union is the more militant will it be.
And so on. All these hypotheses were plausible for certain cases, but they are variables which are dependent on other factors or which only apply to certain cases of industrial relations.

2. THE NEED FOR A MORE RELATIVE VIEW OF SOME TYPES AND HYPOTHESES ON CAUSAL RELATIONS

Many types of causal relations established in union literature need specification. Many of them are ad hoc hypotheses and critical rationalism has attacked them with the fire and the sword. Eliminating them has been a dream of union research, and not even a very nice dream. For without premature exaggeration many a researcher would not have thought of testing them by comparison. Or we can borrow Paul Feyerabend's irony and say that this

scholarship is much more 'slovenly' and 'irrational' than its methodological mirror image.[910] A large number of assumptions or arguments in union literature need to be relativized historically or limited to groups of countries. Among them are:
— the argument that there are consistent and unchangeable types of militant and integrationist unions; at best these are explained by political cultures acquired over long periods of time, at worst by stereotype national characteristics;
— the assumption that the development of types of industrial relations is exclusive, producing either a tendency to a legalized base or free collective bargaining. 'Social contracts' and symbioses with left-wing parties, as in Great Britain in crisis periods, have taken much of the exclusivity out of the second type particularly;
— the assumption that there is a secular movement towards a cooperative union policy. This is a statement which was only applicable during the fine-weather phase after the war and it worked with not very complex indicators (e.g. the number and length of strikes, without regard for the number on strike or some organizational data on the union movement);
— the correlation between the degree of monopolization and product specialization and strike frequency. This is not tenable, as the widening of the material for comparison is increasingly showing;
— the explanation of the extent of industrial unionism by the degree of concentration of industry;
— the explanation of the degree of union membership among white collar workers by the expansion of the public sector or the postulate that the degree of unionization is conversely proportional to the degree of education and training;
— the explanation of the drop in union membership through cyclical fluctuation, waves of politicization or state wage policy.

Assumptions that white collar workers are less prone to strike than workers and many other hypotheses are only true for certain periods and certain countries. Unchangeable national types and the establishment of certain patterns of behaviour (especially during strikes) also need relativizing. The Westerstahl thesis, that German and Swedish unions are more strongly oriented to strikes than the British, was not entirely wrong up to 1945 (when it was put forward). But later the development of functional equivalents in the British union organization (e.g. decentralized militancy through informal bargaining in the plant and the shop steward system) rather reversed the situation.

3. THE CONFIRMATION OF ASSUMPTIONS ON CAUSAL RELATIONS IN THE SYSTEM OF INDUSTRIAL RELATIONS

Scholarship is not, as some rigorous critical rationalists assume, mainly the correction of established theories and hypotheses. The author in an earlier work followed Lakatos and supported the view that rigorous falsification is sterile and frustrating. Nevertheless, where we are concerned with theories of limited applicability (and that is usually the case in union research) we cannot just accept old hypotheses as valid competitors in the pluralism of academic theories, as Paul Feyerabend recently proposed for the big paradigms on which the theories are based.[911] But a comparative study, while relativizing former hypotheses, should *formulate and classify causal relations*. Only a few monographies make a systematic attempt to relate the results of studies on one country to the general complex of proven hypotheses on the subject, as Shorter and Tilly did in their pioneering work on strikes in France[912] and as the Frankfurt team Projektgruppe Gewerkschaftsforschung (Project Group on Union Research) are aiming to do. A number of hypotheses which are more or less confirmed through comparison of industrial relations are certainly not put forward here for the first time. And there are too many causal relations which have been confirmed for repetition of them, even in summarized form, to be possible here. The diagram on the following pages has therefore been included to show the most important of them. However, the confusing number of lines may mean that the author gained more from drawing the diagram than the reader can from tracing it (pp. 325-327).

A comparison of systems of labour relations shows an astonishing continuity of certain patterns of thought and organization among the unions of various countries. But it is an exaggeration to say that 'unions are the products of the origins of unions'.[913] The development of the political system, the prosperity and relative importance of an economy (the decline of Great Britain as a world leader, for instance, and the revision of the image of Sweden as a poor country), the influences of international integration, monopolization and product specialization in individual economies and whether these are directed mainly to the domestic market or exports (Sweden, Switzerland, the Netherlands) — all these factors have produced far-reaching changes in labour relations and in the ideologies and organizational structures of the unions in the countries concerned.

Certain general trends can be established in all systems of industrial relations. However, they should not be generalized and projected into the future over hastily. This happened at the height of the world-wide protest movement — the first really world-wide revolution in history — when the development of a new class consciousness, the trend to direct action in the company and the growing militancy of workers were given a linear projection into the future. The change in the trend should not bring a denial of everything which cannot be achieved at once. But in the analytical sphere it enables a more objective approach than was possible a few years ago — another reason for refraining from academic analysis of subjects when they are most topical. The closer in time the analysis is, the more quickly is it superseded, and that is true of a large part of the radical literature of 1969 to 1973 even if it tries to avoid rapid obsolescence through a great use of abstractions.

Causal relations in the system of industrial relations

External relations (economic and social system)	**Internal relations**	
	1. Organization	
Secularization of society	General union	Union pluralism
High degree of urbanization	Industrial union	Status groups
Good economic conditions	White collar workers well integrated	White collar workers with their own organization
High unemployment	Centralization	Decentralization
	Small number of unions in head federation	Large number of unions in head federation
Large percentage of foreign workers	Monist company constitution	Dualist company constitution
	Dominance of union officials	Competition from works councils
		Competition from shop stewards

Large tertiary sector	High union membership	Low union membership
	Negative sanctions	
High concentration in industry	Compulsory membership	Closed shop solidarity contribution No right to coalition
Shrinking industry	Wealthy unions	Unions financially weak
	Leadership	
Highly differentiated qualifications	High percentage of union officials Tendency to bureaucratization Leadership by the workers	Low percentage of union officials Strong participation by the rank and file Leadership by intellectuals
	2. Ideology	
	Strong emphasis on class consciousness Socialist Liberal	Little emphasis on class consciousness Christian National

Internal relations		**External relations (political system)**
	3. Conflict	
Frequent strikes	Few strikes	Authoritarian political system
Strikes over wide area	Strikes over small area	Centralized political system
Long strikes	Short strikes	Highly developed systems of social security
Official strikes	Unofficial strikes	Cooperation with left-wing parties
Legal strikes	Illegal strikes	Fragmentation of the international union movement
Strikes over money	Political strikes	Battle against multinationals
Lock-out usual	Lock-out rare or illegal	
	4. Integration	
Strong legal integration	Emphasis on free collective bargaining	
Strong political integration of the union leaders in parliament and government	Weak political integration of union leaders	

Primacy of Labour Party	Equality between unions and party
Strong integration between unions and party	Organizational separation between unions and party
Wage policy oriented to performance and status	Solidarity in wage policy
Inequality in incomes policy	Equality in incomes policy
Unions aiming for asset formation (with collective funds)	Unions reject asset formation
Unions accept co-determination	Unions aim for worker control and informal regulations

4. TREND PROGNOSES

Trend prognoses are often based on ad hoc hypotheses and methodologically they are then of little value. The second source of trend prognoses is the directive interest of the observer and his basic theoretical assumptions. Where *conservative* publications ideologize the status quo (which is often hardly achieved) of symmetrical power relations between the negotiating partners the smallest change is felt as a huge step towards the union state. Where a *progressive* publication on the other hand senses defeat in the current development because its more far-reaching aims are being frustrated, unions in their present form are described as organizations 'of a defensive nature' and their policy is regarded as 'reactive'. The second variant then usually takes refuge in a sublimation of a militant union policy and in praising 'irregular industrial relations' because any further development of fixed regulations and norms appears to be putting new chains on the workers. Even in Great Britain an increasing number of eminent scholars are arguing that only a development in an egalitarian and Socialist direction can create the basis for voluntary cooperation by the workers: one of them has postulated that the disorganized state of relations between company mangement and their staff cannot be regarded as pathological in present social conditions, it must regarded as normal.[914]

Both these views need some modification. The unions which have gone relatively far down the road of cooperation, like those in Sweden and the Federal Republic, can certainly not be described as simply 'reactive sub-systems' of a defensive nature, even if the points in their programmes which are designed to change society are only realized very rarely or in isolated instances. Moreover, the British 'division of labour' could hardly be copied in any other country. Great Britain can afford more decentralized conflict at plant level than other countries because the head organization is an extremely effective instrument of interest representation on the political level. The Latin countries could not achieve this over the foreseeable future and the degree to which negotiation and conflict are centralized in the Northern European countries could not be broken down without jeopardizing the political negotiation power of the general union. It would be dangerous to try to transfer elements from one system of industrial relations to another without careful preparation.

The identification of concepts without regard for their national context — militant = active, cooperative = reactive — will not stand up to comparative analysis. Some of the most radical unions in the Latin countries are at the same time prototypes of purely reactive unions, if more than a purely symbolic output of class-war slogans is taken into account. All efforts to overcome too narrow and restrictive a view of what can be called 'normal' in labour law and collective bargaining are laudable. If industrial disputes are once recognized as 'unrest' in the eyes of a capitalist society it should also be possible to achieve a broad-minded consensus on what constitutes a fruitful unrest. But the consensus will be jeopardized if 'irregularity and disorder' are sublimated in the industrial relations of particular countries. This happens if the values of unchannelled participation are set up against the employers' standpoint which usually recognizes only the efficiency of the economy as a value. However, a comparison of the political development in various countries will show that the satisfaction which comes from irregular participation does not compensate for the losses of the majority of citizens in other fields. Over the longer term it will be hard to satisfy British or Italian workers with the relatively larger degree of unrest in their industrial relations when cooperative union movements abroad (and workers are increasingly looking beyond their own systems when assessing benefits) are producing advantages in the domestic economy and in foreign trade which are reflected in higher growth rates in incomes.

However, there is even less justification for the complaint from the conservative side that irregularity in industrial relations causes a deterioration in the position of the employers, firstly because the workers' organizations tend to put higher claims and secondly because state organs intervene on behalf of the workers. However, the complaint that the traditionally powerful employers' associations (such as the BDI, the Confederation of German Industry, in Germany) are meeting with less and less consideration from the government (in contrast to the situation in the USA and Japan)[915] is not simply a perfidious masking of a continuous growth in power. In some countries the investors are losing ground. Labour governments have sometimes profited in crisis periods from being able to direct criticism of the government on to the employers. But as the area of state intervention grows or as the market economies develop further into democratic Socialist systems this useful buffer zone will gradually disappear. In some Socialist countries, like Poland (in 1970 and 1976) it is already clear that the government is increasingly being made accountable for economic developments with repercussions far beyond those of the four-year elections here. But justified as this view is in many points from the perspective of 'mutual relations between capital and labour' with regard to a harmonizing ideology of the social partners, it would be false if the third party in these mutual relations, the state, were seen simply as the extended arm of the capital side.[916] Disputes between unions and parties during the legislative and regulative process in the fight for progress in industrial relations deserve as much study as the conflicts between capital and labour. The differentiated symbioses in the stage of new 'corporatist' tendencies between reform forces may indeed be those which will prove decisive in achieving union claims in many instances.

The extension of union power is not straightforward nor is it continuous. The group pluralist theory which entered German literature from American research often assumed that all relevant interests were organized or at least latent. But Olson already refuted this with his 'side-product theory': only the big interest groups which exercise other functions beside that of lobbying retain power over the longer term, the unions, the agricultural associations and the organizations of the self-employed. They have been strongest when they were able to use indirect pressure to recruit members: from the closed shop practised by the unions to the control exercised by the farmers through the agricultural cooperatives. The forgotten groups — forgotten because they are large, fragmented and amorphous, like the taxpayers or the consumers — have occasionally made themselves felt, as under Poujadism and Glistrupism. This development has steadily reduced the area which is not dominated by groups. Some large organizations are extending their competencies or smaller groups are merging and this is increasing the relative power of individual groups. Areas not dominated by groups only exist now in the political vestibules of the parties, which irregular groups, extra-parliamentary protest movements and citizens' action groups, try to fill from time to time; the political organizations or clubs of citizens are relatively less developed in the Federal Republic in comparison with other Western democracies with older traditions and in comparison with the general union membership in Germany. The main shift in power is now taking place between the social partners. Usually the side which fears that it will lose out tends to insist on 'social symmetry' and 'parity'. The extension of state intervention is altering the balance of power between the organized groups as the state takes over an increasing number of functions. As it wishes to regulate these but cannot administer them alone it gives some competencies and participation rights back to the associations. The mass organizations which can mobilize the greatest mass loyalty, like the unions, are bound to register a growth in political power over the longer term, whether there is a Labour government or not. The employers' associations are furthering this development by demanding a state guarantee for prices and profits developments and by attempting to control wage development as well, which can only be done with the help of the state through the unions.

The employers have gone on to the offensive during the last few years. The shift in power is now not only demanded with regard to the negotiation partner, with whom a temporary truce can be obtained in a 'historical compromise' over 'parity' but also with regard to the secondary opponent. The DGB's proposal for an Economic and Social Council at federal level with dualist representation of employers and workers is rejected by middle-class groups as an unacceptable levelling (cf. Chapter 4, 5, c). The DGB proposes that the various industries should not be represented according to a strict key but, together with the representatives of scholarship and the professions, according to whether they are employers or employees. If on the one hand it appears unavoidable over the longer term that there will be a further shift of power in favour of the unions, the process is on the other hand so slow that the complaints in conservative publications that we are moving into a 'union state' have found little response from the general public. The Allensbach Institute in Germany established that on the question of people's greatest fears with regard to a distribution of power, fear of too great an influence on the part of the unions was fourth from last (31% of those interviewed) in a list of eighteen items. But fear of excessive influence on the part of the employers was also near the bottom of the list (38% of those questioned). This is different in Great Britain. 'Market and Opinion Research International' found in 1975 that almost two-thirds of trade unionists interviewed agreed with the statement that 'unions have too much power in Britain today' and nearly one-third of the entire sample believed that unions were 'the main cause of Britain's economic problems'.[917]

The thesis of the union state appears in different variants whenever syndicalist forms of conflict spread. It is sometimes suggested that the DGB has left no doubt that it intends to realize the union claim to power and by-pass parliament if necessary, although in numerous official statements the DGB has made it abundantly clear that it always accepts the priority of parliament in decisions. Union ideologists are at best said to have 'a naive and benevolent totalitarianism' in mind[918] although there are conservatives as well who do not see the unions as ready to take over power.[919] Of course the unions are trying to extend their influence but the employers have certainly not been pushed into the position of a marginal group as has sometimes been maintained. But after a time the associations generally rise to the challenge and what once seemed to be an intolerable union claim to power becomes, in a reduced form, part of the programme. This is most striking over the concept of asset formation (cf. Chapter 4, 4). But the reference to foreign models has intensified the conflict because the disruptive element in co-determination and asset formation plans is now being grossly exaggerated in the Federal Republic, particularly by the big employers' associations.[920] These polemics become self-contradictory when co-determination is on the one hand described as concealed Socialism and the unions are warned on the other that they will lose their role as representatives of the workers because a growing number of intellectuals and middle-class members will try to obtain the highly-paid posts.[921]

The second argument rather suggests that the extension of co-determination would have effects counter to Socialism. The undeniable growth in the importance and the functions of unions in a modern capitalist industrial state is not always bound up with a growth in power, as the thesis of the 'union state' supposes. The relative importance of the unions is growing through developments such as:

(1) The tendency to *overcome ideological fragmentation* and integrate those who are not skilled or manual workers (cf. Chapter 1, 1, 3).

(2) The formation of larger units in the organization and the gradual establishment of industrial unionism over wider areas. But this trend also shows the ambivalence of all developments in the shift of power in society. The victory of industrial unionism is threatening to become a Pyrrhic victory: the integration of a growing number of white collar workers and civil servants into the union movement through the extension of the tertiary sector is making conflicts which were once external now internal conflicts for the unions and it is making solidarity in wage policy very much more difficult to achieve (cf. Chapter 1, 2).

(3) *The extension of dualism in company constitution* through the extension of participation is leading to rivalry between works councils and union organizations in the plant and between union organizations and delegates from the rank and file. In both forms of conflict the big organized unions have gained considerable ground despite some losses during waves of unofficial strikes as in 1968/69 in the Latin countries (cf Chapter 1, 5, LV, 5). They are also obtaining a better legalized position, and the old distinction between legalized industrial relations and free bargaining is becoming blurred (cf. Chapter 4, 1). The praise of 'irregular' and unregulated militancy in labour relations which has been a target of criticism in Great Britain since the Donovan Report, may be respectable under the normative premises of a Socialist concept of development. But there is little empirical evidence to support it. Paradoxically one could actually say that over-emphasis on irregular industrial relations over a few years would certainly further

the reversal which has been caused from Britain to Italy since the mid-seventies with the battle over the social contract. It seems more realistic to attempt to find a meaningful combination of the two apparently exclusive processes — the extension of the legalized base for industrial relations but (as in Scandinavia) with a limitation in framework regulations which leaves enough room for collective agreements in the company, can lead to creative experiments and does not reduce progress to the lowest common denominator in the parallelogram of reform and conservative forces.

(4) Important changes are taking place through the restructuring of the relation between the labour parties and the unions. Institutional ties are loosening everywhere but many channels of union influence are becoming more intensive, less through direct political representation, which is being reduced in almost every parliament (though not in governments) than through forms of co-determination outside the company, and more complex forms of consultation and participation (cf. Chapter 4, 2). In some cases when the party system was immobilized the unions have actually taken on for a time interest aggregation functions which are usually ascribed to the parties (e.g. during the hot autumn in Italy). The extension of the list of claims, the more scientific and specialized nature of current programmes and the adoption of direct responsibility for certain areas (especially in social policy, and in some countries in vocational training and other areas of education) is giving the unions more political weight even in countries where the parties still dominate interest aggregation. As the public functions of the associations increase, the unions particularly, however, as the wage partners acquire special privileges, find themselves in the embarrassing position of having to emphasize either their freedom (autonomy in wage negotiation) or their semi-public function (as 'watchdogs' of state intervention), whichever suits the circumstances best. The functional change which the associations are going through is rendering useless the old evolutionist schemes of the development of associations and unions. The simple alternative between 'interest groups' and 'social movement' no longer applies to the unions. Nor is the political or economic standpoint now the decisive criterion which differentiates the unions from other interest groups. As their functions widen the unions become more political simply through the increase in their power, but in contrast to the 'labourist' model the greater division of labour between the

parties and the unions still ensures a certain distance. Even with a purely Social Democrat government the same forms of cooperation could not be developed under the system in the Federal Republic because of the organizational distance between the party and the unions and the need to maintain the general union.

(5) The further development of the 'real' constitution will not be oriented to the narrow view of the old liberal distinction between state and society, as it was once expressed in association research: 'Associations become enemies of freedom when they move beyond their legitimate field of interest. . . '.[922] Certainly, complete integration of the state and the associations in a paternalist-clientalist relationship, as has developed with the growing bureaucratization in Italy would not be desirable, but the move beyond the legitimate field does as little justice to the functional change as the necessity for the state to keep delegating new tasks. The *public functions* of many associations, especially the unions, have always been firmly established in many areas from administration to jurisdiction although a strictly 'legitimate' field of competence could not have been defined at any stage in their development. German union leaders keep emphasizing: 'Neither an "ersatz" party nor a substitute for the party'.[923] This is not only in anticipation of conservative propaganda against the 'union state' but also some renunciation of the traditional leadership of the party which has appeared in the German labour movement with the system of division of labour. Even if it cannot be fully realized in view of the integration of personnel and parallelism of interests this model of division of labour may be regarded as an advantage where an independent union movement is politically active. That is also true on a comparison with Great Britain. What may appear as a disadvantage with regard to the short-term achievement of union ideas in comparison with the labour model in Britain is rather an advantage in an alternating parliamentary system with two and a half parties. The German construction brings less friction between the unions and a government of the conservative parties than occurred between the unions and the British Conservative Party.

(6) In some countries, especially in Northern Europe, after the Second World War a trend towards a *new corporatism* can be established. Neo-corporatism is a theoretical model opposed to the old clear-cut separation of the state and society, governmental agencies and interest groups which prevailed in a competitive socie-

ty. From various definitions the following definition of a corporatist system has been suggested: 'Corporatism is a politico-economic system in which the state directs the activities of predominantly privately-owned industries in partnership with the representatives of a limited number of singular, compulsory, non-competitive, hierarchically ordered and functionally differentiated interest groups'.[924] At first this new model was used to describe Scandinavian systems.[925] Philippe Schmitter, who popularized this notion in the seventies, tended to use it for a whole society.[926] In the light of industrial relations studies one should be cautious about generalizing the corporatist model. It is restricted geographically to Austria and some Northern countries. There are a few traces of it in the Latin countries and the USA. Even in Britain it does not occur in the same way as in Scandinavia. Corporate integration and political bargaining as opposite principles are at least both still relevant. 'Bargained corporatism' seems to be the British shade of corporatism, if it exists.[927] The dependence of the Labour Party on the unions which support it and the failure of the Social Contract and incomes policy shows that corporatism does not yet prevail in Britain. One characteristic feature of neo-corporatism is the tendency to decrease the residual power of liberal-individualist representational institutions. In spite of the importance of consultation and co-determination for German interest groups it cannot be said that the primacy of parties and parliament is already severely challenged. Where clientelist politics prevailed as in the Latin countries and power was transferred to extra-representational bodies (boards, *enti pubblici* and others)[928] this was sometimes only a means of preserving power by the dominant party (Italy) or in a semi-presidential system it weakened both the interest groups and the parties (France). Even in those countries where the strongest corporatist tendencies are to be found this model does not explain the reality of all stages of decision-making.

Usually it does not explain what goes on at the initial stage of policy-making, and it does not explain the process of interest mediation in all the policy areas. Neo-corporatist structures dominate in incomes policy (but with limited success, cf. Chapter 4, 4). They have even failed so far in the field of co-ownership, which can be explained by the fact that corporatism is based on the preservation of a capitalist society, though in a liberalized Socialist system not bourgeois democracy but a kind of liberalized corporatism of the state in cooperation with the 'social organizations' could develop. Corporatist politics have had some impact on economic policy. They have failed so far in environment policy, in social and education policy, in short in all those issue areas which have been termed 'post-materialist politics' or 'new politics'. In many countries from Britain to Italy 'corporatism' in trade union literature has a polemic connotation directed against any integrationist strategy.[929] But there is no doubt that it is precisely the double strategy of many trade unions, to participate in corporatist politics and refuse this, to bargain and fight for a better position, which has increased the power of the trade unions in the last few years.

The relative growth in the importance of the unions is not one-sided, it has disadvantages as well:

(1) Conservative mobilization against the extension of the list of union claims is fairly strong. The 'Trojan horses' of the conservative forces are now deeply integrated in the union movement and they will be the more deeply integrated the wider the circle of union members and the more socially diffuse the groups towards which the unions' work is directed are. Unions have sometimes successfully prevented the realization of aims by conservative governments, especially in Great Britain and Australia, but so far they have not proved strong enough to realize a positive policy of their own on a larger scale.

(2) The search for new ways of determining wage development is widening, despite early failures with the first experiments in incomes policy (cf. Chapter 4, 3). The demand for a social contract is becoming more audible, especially in countries with troubled industrial relations. The closer the relations between the parties and the unions become when there is a new impetus to realize a democratic Socialism, the greater are the concesssions which are demanded from the unions. This trend is apparent in Great Britain too now that the Labour Party has at least in part been won over to a Socialist policy again and since the advance of the Communists in the mid-seventies it is not coincidence that interest in a kind of social contract has been growing in Italy too.

(3) As state intervention increases labour relations move *closer to those in Socialist countries,* although the mistakes of Socialist labour relations (abolition of the right to strike, the degradation of the unions to a transmission belt, a suffocating administration of

the social security system) have been avoided. Planned incomes policy and an active labour market policy, solidarity in wage policy and co-determination outside the company will be less and less likely to leave the process of determining wages to the results of the battle over the interests of one group (the workers, however they may be defined) (cf. Chapter 4, 3).

(4) The *extension of participation* is broadening the horizon of the unions and union power is no longer identical with the increase in value for one group, it is embedded in a process of will formation which enforces consideration for other groups.

(5) As syndicalist patterns of conflict spread, the unions in many modern industrial societies are *losing their monopoly position* in the use of a sophisticated system of pressure instruments. Both conservative fears and radical excesses have occasionally given the impression in the discussion in the Federal Republic that the conflict patterns would take a unilear development in a clearly recognizable direction. That is not the case, and not only in the time perspective of boom and crisis, reform enthusiasm and political stagnation. In the spatial dimension of the overall system of organized groups different patterns of conflict develop simultaneously and in the USA in the sixties the expressions 'status policy' and 'class policy' were used to describe the two different phenomena. But both are related to economic and political crisis cycles: *class policy* is most prominent in times of economic depression when the associations are largely oriented to economic interests, while *status policy* appears to be a symptom of upswing phases. As the pace of growth accelerates some groups lose out in the distribution process and find that they are profiting less than others. There may be a growth in absolute figures but in relative figures (compared with other groups) they are not doing so well and status anxieties and greater radicalism are the result. In the Federal Republic we have seen how some groups have come to take a different position as their long-term economic outlook and the relative growth in benefits which they have calculated change.

However, these two concepts cannot be applied schematically to the system of interest groups in Europe. Functional change means that groups which develop status fear, and at present these are mainly the middle-class, self-employed and farmers' associations, are increasingly adopting the weapons of those which have so far restricted themselves to class policy. We see that patterns of union militancy are spreading among groups which formerly emphasized their difference from the workers, doctors, teachers and even civil servants. Conversely some organizations which traditionally laid claim to a political mandate beyond their economic interests, like the unions, are increasingly working with means which were once regarded as the prerogative of state-prone organizations or the organizations of state officials. The promotional groups have always been ambivalent in their attitude; as they were most strongly based on a coherent ideology their means always appeared to be largely functionalized by their aims. Some promotional groups (the Churches, prohibition movements, and so on) were therefore quicker to learn new strategies than more traditional organizations of professional groups. Finally, the transfer of conflict patterns from one type of organization to another is also furthered by groups outside the system — extra-parliamentary opposition, citizens' action groups and irregular protest movements.

Certainly there are tendencies to a gradual dissolution of the parity between capital and labour, although this is embedded in legislation in some countries, and there is a relative overweight of the organized workers as opposed to the investors. There need be no objections to this shift in power as long as the growth in function does not lead to a growth in bureaucracy and etatization of the unions. Generally there is less reason to accuse the unions than other large aggregates (with the exception of some corruption in the USA) of misuse of power. As a result of their old traditions, their democratic potential is still considerable, even if the internal democracy of many unions leaves a lot to be desired. A temporary increase in union power could actually be an advantage in connection with a growth in power of progressive groups aiming for a democratic Socialism. But the balance between the two independent pillars of the labour movement must not be overstrained by this development. In fact nowhere is it leading to further organizational ties between the party and the unions (cf. Chapter 4, 2). Indeed, too open a support from the unions for their parties, as in Australia (in 1976) and Great Britain, is dangerous because it can lead to unnecessary counter mobilization among the electorate who traditionally dislike too close a symbiosis between the party and the unions. Even Communist parties, like that in France, which despite the strong anarcho-syndicalist traditions of the country at first retained a strong mistrust of the idea of strikes, have in Western

Europe largely resisted the temptation to gain power through mass strikes.[930] The more respect they announce for decisions by the electorate the more reversals they will have to fear if they overstrain the possibilities for action by the party and the unions (as in the elections after the May strikes in 1968).

Many of these trends only develop very slowly and in many countries there is certainly a temporary increase in union power during the process. The development is already implied in the change in the paradigm of the theory of industrial relations. The old concept of industrial relations was liberal-pluralist in a very mechanical sense, in that it assumed that pluralism would mean that all the parties to the conflict would feel obliged to adhere to the 'philosophy of mutual survival'.[931] But these assumptions were revised even by early representatives of the pluralist school in Oxford, Alan Fox, for instance.[932] Even relatively cooperative union leaders are now less willing to give a guarantee for the status quo of the capital side, as there are many reasons beyond union self-interest which speak for increasing socialization (the fight against multinational companies, improved state steering mechanisms, greater facility in the establishment of participation models, environment questions and so on), even if the union leaders now no longer see this process towards Socialism as a revolutionary act of power to achieve 'dictatorship by the proletariat'. The idea that militant or cooperative strategies can be 'bought like hot or cold sausages at the counter of history' (R. Luxemburg) is not realistic. Militant and cooperative elements are mutual determinants at any moment. No union can now embark on a cooperative course unless it maintains its militancy at the same time. This duality of role, when the unions are at once a regulative factor and a counter power, is a condition for the maintenance and achievement of social liberties and it is certainly not a fault, as one neo-Marxist writer has argued.[933] Even in a Socialist system, as long as it remains free and democratic, the unions will not be able to act only as a regulative factor, if only because when the basic opposition between capital and labour is eliminated the importance of the subsidiary conflicts in societies where the means of production are largely nationalized is necessarily reduced. In any transformation to Socialism conflicts between the state power and the unions will be unavoidable if freedom is maintained.

All Socialist movements so far have worked with a good deal of authoritarianism. In many a well-intentioned bourgeois radical view of Socialism this is often overlooked. The authoritarian element with regard to the opposing force, capital, has been held to be essential by Socialists of all directions. Recent experiments with Socialism, in Cuba, Chile or Portugal, have shown that at the beginning of a sweeping process of socialization the aggressive element in unionism is not tamed but fully released. Then, as all these cases have shown, if the experiment is not to fail, fairly authoritarian social contracts have to be drawn up to hold back the unions. In future, we are likely to see a combination of Socialist-egalitarian and authoritarian developments as well. The labour movement will have to try to prevent the authoritarian direction of industrial relations from making the old mistakes of Socialist movements and replacing the private capitalist 'boss' with a bureaucratic state power and forcing the unions into a transmission belt function which leaves them less room for manoeuvre than they had under the capitalist system.

Participation and cooperation always entail the acceptance of some responsibility by the unions. A meaningful strategic concept must aim to find the right combination of militancy and co-responsibility and this will not be the same in every country. There is no point in trying to import models of militant union policy from Great Britain or the Latin countries to Switzerland, the Federal Republic or Scandinavia. But one must recognize that all over Europe the cooperative forces are pretty powerful and that through the European Community they are gaining ground in countries where the unions still have a certain tradition of verbal radicalism. From this point of view the Belgian unions, which have not received much attention so far, would be a valuable study object in dual stance for the competent powers in Brussels.

The increasing involvement of the unions in political responsibility should not lead to a loss in militancy. The inevitable widening of the legalized base, the political integration and the greater involvement of the unions in the system through participation (in Northern Europe mainly through new models of re-distribution and asset formation) and their involvement in incomes policy must now be allowed to undermine their freedom to negotiate and their freedom to strike. Tendencies in the direction of Socialist co-responsibility must take the form of models of democratic socialism while maintaining all the collective rights which are ensured by a constitutional state and they must not be allowed to lead to a throttling of the right to coalition and strike. There is a real possibility of this. Even Communist groups are increasingly coming to abandon the idea that the unions should be a transmission belt for a party which holds ideological primacy (cf. Chapter 1, 1). If on the one hand the unions can resist the temptations of radical ideologies to make themselves the political pace-makers of nationalization (and thus jeopardize the unity and economic efficiency of their organizations) they will on the other hand cautiously have to further this process. Precisely those who fear too great a negotiation power in the hands of the unions will have to approve the development to a democratic Socialism, because it is only when the major means of production are no longer privately owned that the wage discipline and co-responsibility of the unions can be achieved over the longer term without bitter conflict. However, there is one comfort for the critics of a 'union state': the temporary increase in union power is probably not a trend which will continue in unilinear development. The contribution which the unions make to the realization of a democratic and pluralist Socialism should at the same time prove a contribution to the voluntary limitation of their own power.

Notes

I

1. Jean-Daniel Reynaud in: Guy Spitaels (ed.): *La crise des relations industrielles en Europe*. Bruges, De Tempel, 1972, p. 210.

2. Stephen Hill and Keith Thurley: 'Sociology and Industrial Relations', *British Journal of Industrial Relations*, 1974, No. 2, pp. 147-170.

3. For Britain this has been put less bluntly: 'Universities no longer consider it politically disreputable to examine labour problems; but it is not yet academically reputable to do so'. V. L. Allen: *The Sociology of Industrial Relations. Studies in Method*. London, Longman, 1971, p. 17.

4. Allan Flanders: *Collective Bargaining*. Harmondsworth, Penguin, 1969.

5. Hansjörg Weitbrecht: *Effektivität und Legitimität der Tarifautonomie*. Berlin, Duncker & Humblot, 1969; Projektgruppe Gewerkschaftsforschung: *Die Austauschbeziehungen zwischen Kapital und Arbeit im Kontext der sozioökonomischen Entwicklung. Zwischenbericht* (mimeo). Frankfurt, 1976, p. 1.

6. John T. Dunlop: *Industrial Relations Systems*. New York. Holt, 1958, pp. 7, 382.

7. Richard Hyman and Ian Brough: *Social Values and Industrial Relations. A Study of Fairness and Inequality*. Oxford, Blackwell, 1975, p. 247; Richard Hyman: *Industrial Relations. A Marxist Introduction*. London, Macmillan, 1975, p.x., pp. 4ff.

8. Cf. Allen, op. cit. (note 3), p. 5.

9. Cf. for lower level theories: George Sayers Bain and H. A. Clegg: 'A Strategy for Industrial Relations Research in Great Britain', *British Journal of Industrial Relations*, 1974 (91-113), p. 105.

10. Werner Goldschmidt: *Gesellschaftliche Krise und die Perspektive der Arbeiterbewegung in Frankreich*. Marburg PhD, Dissertation, 1973, p. 73.

11. Heinrich Streithofen: *Wertmaßstäbe der Gewerkschaftspolitik*. Hiedelberg, F. H. Kerle, 1967, p. 167.

12. Wolfgang Hirsch-Weber: *Gewerkschaften in der Politik*. Cologne, Westdeutscher Verlag, 1959, p. 51.

13. Jürgen Klein: *Vereint sind sie alles? Untersuchungen zur Entstehung von Einheitsgewerkschaften in Deutschland*. Hamburg, Stiftung Europa-Kolleg, 1972, p. 394.

14. Jacob M. Landau: *The Arabs and the Histadrut*. Tel Aviv, Ranot Printing Press, 1976.

15. *Labor and Society in Israel: A Selection of Studies*. Tel Aviv, Department of Higher Education, Histadrut, 1973, p. 219.

16. EG, Gewerkschaftsinformationen: *Die Gewerkschaftsbewegung in der EG*. Brussels, 1975, Part 1, pp. 2ff; Andrew Boyd: *The Rise of the Irish Trade Unions. 1729-1970*. Tralee, Anvil, 1972.

17. Walter Galenson: *Rival Unionism in the United States*. New York, Russell & Russell, 1966, pp. 32, 34.

18. Jean-Daniel Reynaud: *Les syndicats en France*. Paris, Seuil, 1975, Vol. 1, p. 100.

19. Wolfram Elsner: *Die EWG. Herausforderung und Antwort der Gewerkschaften*. Cologne, Pahl-Rugenstein, 1974, pp. 14ff.

20. Guy Spitaels: *Le mouvement syndical en Belgique*. Brussels, Editions de l'université de Bruxelles, 1974, 3rd edition, pp. 73, 65f.

21. Gerhard Baier: 'Einheitsgewerkschaft. Zur Geschichte eines organisatorischen Prinzips der deutschen Arbeiterbewegung'; *Archiv für Sozialgeschichte*, 1973 (207-242), p. 210.

22. Projektgruppe, op. cit. (note 5), p. 120.

23. AFL-CIO: *Constitution*. Washington DC, 1961, p. 5.

24. Theo Pirker: *Die blinde Macht. Die Gewerkschaftsbewegung in Westdeutschland*. Munich, Mercator, 1960, Vol. 2, pp. 83ff.

25. *Proletariat in der BRD*. Berlin (East), Dietz, 1974, p. 439.

26. *Die Revolutionärre Gewerkschaftsopposition (RGO)*. Berlin, Verlag Rote Fahne, 1972, Vol. 1, p. 88.

27. KBW: *Für klassenbewußte, kampfstarke Einheitsgewerkschaften*. Manheim, Kühl KG, 1975, p. 17.

28. H. Bilstein et al.: *Organisierter Kommunismus in der BRD*. Opladen, Leske, 1975, p. 78.

29. *Hamburger Lehrerzeitung*, 1975, No. 10, p. 437.

30. Erich Frister: 'Von der Grenze der Toleranz', *Erziehung und Wissenschaft*, 1974, No. 4, p. 3.

31. Wolfram Elsner: 'Erich Frister, die DKP und die Einheitsgewerkschaften', *Marxistische Blätter*, 1974, No. 4 (92-99), p. 97.

32. Antonio Gramsci: 'Sindacalismo e Consigli'. Reprinted in: *Scritti politici*. Rome, Editori Riuniti, 1971, 3rd edition (260-263), p. 260f.

33. Antonio Donini: 'Gli extraparlamentari e il sindacato'. *Rassegna sindacale, Quaderni*, 1972, No. 33/34 (105-121), pp. 114, 116.

34. Jean Meynaud: *Rapporto sulla classe dirigente italiana*. Milan, Giuffrè, 1966, p. 109.

35. Joseph La Palombara: *The Italian Labor Movement*. Ithaca, Cornell, 1957, p. 57; Sergio Turone: *Storia del sindacato in Italia. 1943-1969*. Bari, Laterza, 1975, 3rd edition, pp. 191f, 208.

36. Sandro Fontana: *I cattolici e l'unità sindacale 1943-1947*. Bologna, Il Mulino, 1978, p. 21.

37. Centro Studi Nazionale della Cisl: *Strumenti di cultura sindacale*. Bologna, Il Mulino, 1977, p. 21.

38. Cf. Antoine Prost: *la CGT à l'époque du Front Populaire*. Paris, Colin, 1964; Pierre Monatte: *Trois scissions syndicales*. Paris, Editions ouvrières, 1966.

39. Spitaels, op. cit. (note 20), p. 24.

40. Carl Erik Knoellinger: *Labor in Finland*. Cambridge, Mass., Harvard UP, 1960, p. 108.

41. Jaakko Nousiainen: *The Finnish Political System*. Cambridge, Mass., 1971 p. 114.

42. Spitaels, op. cit. (note 20), p. 52.

43. John P. Windmuller: *Labor Relations in the Netherlands*. Ithaca, Cornell, 1969, p. 137.

44. CNV: 'Visieprogram', in: *CNV Informatie*. Utrecht, 1975, p. 4.

45. CNV: *Christian Trade Unionism in the Netherlands*. Utrecht, 1976, p. 10; *Trade Unions Affiliated to the FNV-Partners*. Amsterdam, 1978.

46. *Federatie Nederlandse Vakbeweging FNV*. Amsterdam-Slotermeer, 1976, pp. 3, 5.

47. *Beleidsprogram '76-'77, NVV, NKV, CNV*. 1976.

48. Letzeburger Arbechter-Verband (LAV): *Die freien Gewerkschaften in der modernen Gesellschaft*. Esch-sur-Alzette 1970, p. 14.

49. Franz Mehring: *Die Geschichte der deutschen Sozialdemokratie*. Stuttgart, Dietz, 1898, Vol. 2, p. 326.

50. Klaus Mattheier: *Die Gelben: Nationale Arbeiter zwischen Wirtschaftsfrieden und Streik*. Düsseldorf, Schwann, 1973, pp. 309, 54.

51. Friedrich Zunkel: *Industrie und Staatsozialismus*. Düsseldorf, Schwann, 1974, p. 192f.

52. Tribuna obrera: *Comissiones obreras y Eurocomunismo*. Madrid, Tribuna obrera, 1978, p. 7.

53. CGIL-CISL-UIL: *Esperienze, problemi e sviluppo della prospettiva sindacale unitaria*. Rome, Stasind, 1971; Gino Giugni: *Il sindacato fra contratti e riforme. 1969-1973*. Bari, De Donato, 1973, p. 70f.

54. Edmond Marie and Jacques Julliard: *La CFDT d'aujourd'hui*. Paris, Seuil, 1975, p. 130.

55. Henri Krasucki: 'L'expérience des pays socialistes', in: Krasucki: *Syndicats et socialisme*. Paris, Editions sociales, 1972, pp. 71ff.

56. Federazione CGIL-CISL-UIL: *Per il dibattito sull' unità sindacale*. Rome, Edizioni Seusi, 1974, p. 73; Luciano Lama, *Dieci anni di processo sindacale unitario*. Rome, Editrice Sindacale Italiana, 1976, 4th edition.

57. Santiago Carrillo: *Eurocomunismo y Estado*. Barcelona, Editorial Crítica, 1977, p. 141. Tribuna obrera: *Comisiones obreras y Eurocomunismo*. Madrid, 1978, p. 118.

58. 'Les rapport CFDT-CGT', *CFDT aujourd'hui*, 1976, No. 17, p. 35f.

59. *Lettres ouvertes à Georges Séguy. Réponses à 65 questions*. Paris, 1975, p. 64.

60. Alain Bergounioux: *Force ouvrière*. Paris, Seuil, 1975, p. 179.

61. Franco Gheza: *Cattolici e sindacacto. Un'esperienza di base*. Rome, Coines Edizioni, 1975, pp. 232ff.

62. Spitaels, op. cit. (note 20), p. 58.

63. Edmond Maire: *CFDT. Pour un socialisme démocratique*. Paris, Epi, 1971, pp. 14ff. Krasucki, op. cit. (note 55), pp. 47ff.

64. 'Fühzeitiger Stellungsbezug. Zwei Monate vor dem Entscheid über die Mitbestimmung', *NZZ*, 18/19 January 1976, p. 17.

65. Benjamin Aaron and K. W. Wedderburn (eds.): *Industrial Conflict. A Comparative Legal Survey*. London, Longman, 1972, p. 57. *Strumenti*, op. cit. (note 37), p. 144.

66. Maire and Julliard, op. cit. (note 54), p. 38.

67. L. I. Dvinina: *Problemy mezhdunarodnogo khristianskogo sindikalizma*. Moscow, Nauka, 1974, p. 194f.

68. *CGT Information*, 13 December 1973, p. 7.

69. *Le Monde*, 19 April 1978, p. 37. *Le Monde*, 18 April 1978, pp. 1 and 36.

70. CISL: *Silvano Levrero: Strategia sindacale e società multinazionali*. Rome, Editrice Sindacale Italiana, 1977, p. 21. The Swedish LO favoured international sympathy strikes which it formerly considered with some reserve: LO: *The Trade Union Movement and the Multinationals*. Stockholm, 1977, p. 17. For the documents of the international trade unions see: Angela Sarcina (ed.): *Sindacati e multinazionali*. Rome, Collana documentazione CGIL, 1977. Cf. for a comprehensive study: Ernst Piehl: *Multinationale Konzerne und internationale Gewerkschaftsbewegung*. Frankfurt, EVA, 1974.

71. Anton Benya: *Gewerkschaften in der Gesellschaft von heute*. Vienna, Verlag des ÖGB, 1975, p. 11; Peter Ulrich Lehner: 'Die österreichische Gewerkschaftsbewegung', *GMH*, 1974, No. 8 (486-497), p. 488.

72. 'CC.OO. y U.G.T. controlan el movimiento obrero Español', *Informaciones*, 23 March, 1978, p. 6; 'U.G.T. y CC.OO. denunciadas ante la organización mundial del trabajo', *ABC*, 2 June, 1978, p. 14.

73. *El sindicalismo de clase en Espana (1939-1977)*. Barcelona, Ediciones Península, 1978, pp. 269ff on the unficiation process. Tribuna obrera: *Comisiones obreras y Eurocomunismo*. Madrid, 1978.

74. Maire and Julliard, op. cit. (note 54), p. 122.

75. 'L'unità sindacale', *Rassegna sindacale, Quaderni*, 1971, No. 29, p. 138.

76. L. Lama and B. Manghi: *Il sindacato di classe ieri e oggi*. Rome, Editrice Sindacale Italiana, 1977, 3rd edition, pp. 28, 32.

77. Theodor Cassau: *Die Gewerkschaftsbewegung. Ihre Soziologie und ihr Kampf*. Habberstadt, H. Meyer, 1925, p. 298.

78. Karl Kautsky: *Das Erfurter Programm in seinem grundsätzlichen Theil*. Stuttgart, Dietz, 1910, 10th edition, p. 212.

79. *Internationaler Sozialistenkongress zu Stuttgart, 18.-24.8.1907*. Berlin, Vorwärts, 1907, pp. 50f, 54, 57.

80. For the revisionist position see: Fritz Tarnow: *Das Organisationsproblem im ADGB*. Berlin, 1925. The views of the centre: Robert Dissmann: *Berufsorganisationen oder Industrieverbände?* Stuttgart, 1925.

81. Jong Oh Ra: *Labor at the Polls*. Amherst, University of Massachussetts Press, 1978, pp. 24ff.

82. Peter Lösche: 'Amerikanische Gewerkschaften', *Neue Politische Literatur*, 1974 (40-47), p. 49.

83. John Hutchinson: *The Imperfect Union. A History of Corruption in American Trade Unions*. New York, Dutton, 1972, p. 372.

84. *TUC Report 1975*. London, 1976, p. 37.

85. *Royal Commission on Trade Unions and Employers' Associations 1965-1968* (*Donovan Report*). London, HMSO, June 1968. Reprint, 1975, p. 7, lin 28.

86. *TUC Report 1977*, p. 612.

87. LO: *Kampens gang*. Copenhagen, 1973, p. 518.

88. *Trade Unions Affiliated to the FNV-Partners*. Amsterdam, 1978.

89. LO: *The Danish Trade Union Movement*. Copenhagen, 1977.

90. Hildegard Waschke: *Gewerkschaften in Westeuropa*. Cologne, Deutscher Institutsverlag, 1975, p. 48.

91. Cf. H. A. Turner: 'British Trade Union Structure. A New Approach?', *British Journal of Industrial Relations*, 1964 (165-181), pp. 179ff. TUC: *Trades Union Congress: Structure and Development*, September 1970, p. 4f; *TUC Report 1977*, pp. 3ff.

92. H. A Clegg: *The System of Industrial Relations in Great Britain*. Oxford, Blackwell, 1976, 3rd edition, p. 73.

93. David Coates: *The Labour Party and the Struggle for Socialism*. Cambridge UP, 1975, p. 134.

94. Jörgen Westerstahl: *Svensk fackföreningsrörelse*. Stockholm, Tiden, 1945, p. 46.

95. Bo Carlson: *LO och fackförbunden*. Stockholm, Tiden, 1969, pp. 85-89.

96. *Labour Relations in Norway:* The Norwegian Joint Committee on International Social Policy/The Royal Ministry of Foreign Affairs. Oslo, 1975, p. 49.

97. Knoellinger, op. cit. (note 40), p. 130.

98. Margaret Stewart: *Trade Unions in Europe*. Epping/Essex, Gower Press, 1974, p. 118.

99. LAV, op. cit. (note 48), p. 11f.

100. Yu. P. Chaplygin: *Proletariat v stranach kapitala: pravda i vymysly*. Moscow, Profizdat, 1975, p. 23.

101. Cf. R. M. Blackburn and K. Prandy: 'White-Collar Unionization: A Conceptual Framework', *The British Journal of Sociology*, 1965 (111-122), p. 112.

102. 'Les enfants de Lip', *CFDT aujourd'hui*, September/October 1975, No. 15 (18-26), p. 26.

103. Marcello Lelli: *Tecnici e lotta di classe*. Bari, De Donato, 1973, pp. 147ff; Chiara Sebastiani: *Pubblico impiego e ceti medi*. Rome, Editrice Sindacale Italiana, 1975, p. 3. Against the *operaismo*: Giovanni Battista Chiesa: *Pubblico impiego, sindacato e riforma*. Rome, Editrice Sindacale Italiana, 1977, p. 27; Albert Calderó: *Sindicalismo de los funcionarios publicos*. Barcelona, Editorial Avance, 1977.

104. Roger Lumley: *White-Collar Unionism in Britain. A Survey of the Present Situation*. London, Methuen, 1973, p. 122.

105. Robert H. Connery and William V. Farr (eds.): *Unionization of Municipal Employees*. New York, Columbia University, The Academy of Political Science, 1970, p. 136.

106. William J. Taylor et al. (eds.): *Military Unions. U.S. Trends and Issues*. Beverly Hills/London, Sage, 1977, p. 11; CGIL della Lombardi: *Unità di classe e alleanze nella strategia sindacale*. Rome, Editrice Sindacale Italiana, 1977, p. 50; L. Lama: *Relazione e conclusioni al IX Congresso CGIL*. Rome, Editrice Sindacale Italiana, 1977, p. 6.

107. *Studienkommission für die Reform des öffentlichen Dienstrechts. Bericht der Kommission*. Baden-Baden, Nomos, 1973, pp. 120ff, p. 142. Robert Steiert: 'Gewerkschaft der Polizei verstärkt Einheitsgewerkschaften', *GMH*, 1978, pp. 289-296. On the ÖTV and its fight for a levelling down of the status groups in the civil service: Gerhard Weiss: *Die ÖTV*. Marburg, Verlag Arbeiterbewegung und Gesellschaftswissenschaft, 1978, pp. 306ff.

108. Clegg, op. cit. (note 92), p. 500.

109. Dieter Schneider (ed.): *Zur Theorie und Praxis des Streiks*. Frankfurt, Suhrkamp, 1971.

110. Otto Nordenskiöld: *Förhallendet LO-TCO.* Stockholm, Tiden, 1972, pp. 22, 47ff. Leennart Forsebäck: *Sozialpartner und Arbeitsmarkt in Schweden.* Stockholm, Schwedisches Institut, 1977, p. 19.

111. George Sayers Bain: *The Growth of White Collar-Unionism.* Oxford, Clarendon, 1970, p. 181; B. V. Humphreys: *Clerical Unions in the Civil Service.* Oxford, Blackwell, 1958.

112. Roy J. Adams: 'White-Collar Unions' Growth. The Case of Sweden', *Industrial Relations.* Berkeley, 1972, No. 2 (164-176), p. 174f.

113. Joseph A. Alutto and James A. Belasco: 'Determinants of Attitudinal Militancy among Nurses and Teachers', *Industrial and Labour Review*, 1974, No. 2 (216-227), p. 226.

114. R. D. Coates: *Teachers' Unions and Interest Group Politics.* Cambridge UP, 1972, p. 127.

115. *TUC Report 1974.* London, 1975, p. 65; TUC: *Non-Manual workers. 36th Conference Report*, December 1972, p. 2.

116. *TUC Report 1975*, p. 87.

117. Linda Dickens: 'Staff Associations and the Industrial Relations Act. The Effect of Union Growth', *Industrial Relations Journal*, Nottingham, 1975, No. 3, pp. 29-41.

118. Timothy C. May: *Trade Unions and Pressure Group Politics.* Westmead, Saxon House/Lexington, Lexington Books, 1975, p. 49.

119. J. David Edelstein and Malcolm Warner: *Comparative Union Democracy. Organisation and Opposition in British and American Unions.* London, Allen & Unwin, 1975, p. 8.

120. Gewerkschaften: 'Aufs Trittbrett springen', *Der Spiegel*, 1975, No. 36, p. 43.

121. Siegfried Braun and Jochen Fuhrmann: *Angestelltenmentalität.* Neuwied, Luchterhand, 1970, pp. 417ff.

122. Heinz Seidel: *Das Verhältnis der Angestellten zur Mitbestimmung.* Frankfurt, EVA, 1972, p. 99.

123. Ibidem, pp. 102ff.

124. Walter Nickel: *Zum Verhältnis von Arbeiterschaft und Gewerkschaft.* Cologne, Bund-Verlag, 1974, 2nd edition, pp. 40ff.

125. Michael Jungblut: 'Vernünftiger als ihre Funktionäre', *Die Zeit*, 1974, No. 47, pp. 33, 37.

126. Wolfgang Däubler: *Der Streik im öffentlichen Dienst.* Tübingen, Mohr, 1970, pp. 105.

127. *FAZ*, 18 September 1975.

128. 'Auf dem Weg in die Beamten-Republik', *Der Spiegel*, 1974, No. 51 (28-41), p. 32, col. 1.

129. Bernd Rüthers: 'Interessenverfilzung zu Lasten der Bürger. Die Zerstörung der Tarifautonomie im öffentlichen Dienst', *FAZ*, 14 December, p. 13.

130. Deutscher Beamtenbund: *Ursprung, Weg, Ziel.* Bad Godesberg, Beamtenverlags GmbH, Part III, p. 82.

131. Ibidem, p. 77.

132. 'Der DGB kündigt Widerstand gegen die Sparpläne für den öffentlichen Dienst an', *FAZ*, 5 September, p. 3.

133. Stewart, op. cit. (note 98), p. 174.

134. Braun and Fuhrmann, op. cit. (note 121), p. 134.

135. Arthur M. Ross and Paul T. Hartman: *Patterns of Industrial Conflicts*. New York, Wiley, 1960, p. 50.

136. Pierre Dubois: *Mort de l'état-patron*. Paris, Editions ouvrières, 1974, p. 246.

137. Arnold J. Heidenheimer: 'Professional Unions, Public Sector Growth and the Swedish Equality Policy', *Comparative Politics*, 1976 (49-73), p. 69. Cf. also: Everett M. Kassalow: 'Professional Unionism in Sweden', *Industrial Relations*, 1969 (119-134), pp. 130ff.

138. D. W. Rawson: 'The Frontiers of Trade Unionism', *Australian Journal of Politics and History*, May 1956 (196-209), p. 199. R. M. Blackburn: *Union Character and Social Class. A Study of White-Collar Unionism*. London, Batsford, 1967, pp. 265, 256.

139. B. C. Roberts et al.: *Reluctant Militants: A Study of Industrial Technicians*. London, Heinemann, 1972, p. 326.

140. George Syers et al.: *Social Stratification and Trade Unionism*. London, Heinemann, 1973, p. 148.

141. Gérard Adam et al.: *L'ouvrier francais en 1970*. Paris, Colin, 1970, p. 57.

142. 'Die ÖTV—Politik ist nicht sozial. Gespräch mit Heinz Groteguth über die Differenzen in der Lohnpolitik', *Die Zeit*, No. 14, 1976, p. 19.

143. *FAZ*, 15 June, 1976, p. 1.

144. 'Gegen den Alleinvertretungsanspruch der OTV', *FAZ*, 31 July 1976, p. 11.

145. Cf. 'Disputes in the TUC', *TUC Report 1977*, p. 3ff.

146. *Industrial Democracy*. London, TUC, 1976 (reprint), p. 27.

147. Burkhart Lutz: 'Überlegungen zu einigen Zukunftsproblemen der deutschen Gewerkschaften', *GMH*, 1975, No. 5 (274-277), p. 276.

148. DAG: *Forderungen für leitende und wissenschaftliche Angestellte*. Hamburg, 1970.

149. Günter Witt: *Leitende Angestellte und Einheitsgewerkschaft*. Frankfurt, EVA, 1975, p. 54.

150. Cf. Jacques Doublet and Olivier Passeclercq: *Les cadres*. Paris, PUF, 1972.

151. Maire and Julliard, op. cit. (note 54), p. 53.

152. Georges Séguy: *Lutter*. Paris, Stock, 1975, p. 206.

153. Witt, op. cit (note 149), p. 60.

154. A. Andrieux and J. Lignon: 'Die französischen Gewerkschaften vor dem Problem der Organisierung von Führungskräften', *GMH*, 1970 (234-239), p. 237.

155. ' "Sie werden noch weinen'. Der Testfall "Leitende Angestellte der Lufthansa Service GmbH" vor dem Arbeitsgericht', *FAZ*, 17 March 1976, p. 12.

156. Everett Carl Ladd Jr. and Seymour M. Lipset: *Professors, Unions and American Higher Education*. Berkeley, Carnegie Commission on Higher Education, 1973, p. 97.

157. Dieter Zimmer: 'Autoren als Radikale im öffentlichen Dienst', *Die Zeit*, 1974, No. 48, p. 19.

158. Seymour M. Lipset and Stein Rokkan (eds.): *Party Systems and Voter Alignments: Cross-National Perspectives*. New York, Free Press/London, Collier-Macmillan, 1967, p. 50.

159. Hugh Clegg: *Trade Unionism under Collective Bargaining. A Theory based on comparisons of Six Countries*. Oxford, Blackwell, 1976, p. 39.

160. 'Statuts de la caisse nationale d'action syndicale', in: Reynaud, op. cit. (note 18), Vol. 2, p. 103; *CFDT aujourd'hui*, 1976, No. 17, p. 54.

161. Robert Goetz-Girey: *Le mouvement des grèves en France. 1919-1962*. Páris, Sirey, 1965, p. 35.

162. Richard A. Lester: *As Unions Mature*. Princeton UP, 1966, 3rd edition, p. 151.

163. Edelstein and Warner, op. cit. (note 119), p. 20.

164. Frederick R. Livingston: 'Changing Relations between Union and Management', in: Joel Seidman (ed.): *Trade Union Government and Collective Bargaining*. New York, Praeger, 1970 (285-301), p. 299.

165. *Principprogram för Finlands Fackförbunds Centralorganisation*. Helsinki, 1971, p. 7.

166. Séguy, op. cit. (note 152), p. 203; Knoellinger, op. cit. (note 40), pp. 106ff, 136.

167. Stewart. op. cit. (note 98), p. 58f.

168. F. O. Gundelach: 'Mitbestimmung in Europa'. *Das Mitbestimmungsgespräch*, 1976, No. 2 (23-29), p. 24, col. 2.

169. Johan De Jong: *En aantal recente ontwikkelingen in het Nederlandse systeeem van arbeidsverhoudingen*. Rotterdam, Universitaire Pers, 1974, p. 91f; Bram Peper (ed.): *De Nederlands arbeidsverhoudingen*. Rotterdam, Universitaire Pers, 1973, p. 78.

170. *Chemicals Manpower in Europe*. London, National Economic Development Office, HMSO, 1973, p. 36.

171. N. Robertson and K. I. Sams (eds.): *British Trade Unionism. Select Documents*. Oxford, Blackwell, 1972, Vol. 2, pp. 393ff.

172. *TUC Report 1974*, p. 34.

173. TUC: *Structure and Development*, September 1970, pp. 19ff.

174. Baier, op. cit. (note 21), p. 209.

175. Karl Albin: 'Die verkümmerte Diskussion', *GHM*, 1968, No. 4, pp. 245ff.

176. Rudolf Meidner and Berndt Öhman: *Solidarisk lönepolitik*. Stockholm, Tiden, 1972, pp. 21ff.

177. Sven Jerstedt (ed.): *LO:s linje — strid eller samarbete*? Stockholm, Askild & Kärnekull, 1971, p. 24.

178. *TUC Report 1977*, p. 637.

179. Kurt Hirche: *Die Finanzen der Gewerkschaften*. Düsseldorf, Econ, 1972, p. 219, figures, p. 336.

180. *Labour and Society in Israel*, op. cit. (note 15), p. 257.

181. J. David Greenstone: *Labor in American Politics*. New York, Knopf, 1969, pp. 6ff.

182. Herbert Dorfman: *Labour Relations in Norway*. Oslo, The Norwegian Joint Committee on International Social Policy, 1957, p. 57; *Labour Relations in Norway*. Oslo, Norwegian ILO Committee, 1975. p. 50.

183. Arnold Sölvén: *Landsorganisationens Nya Stadgar*. Stockholm, 1957, 4th edition, p. 47.

184. Gerhard Leminsky: 'Gerwerkschaftsorganisation und Gewerkschaftsstaat', *GMH*, 1974, No. 10 (654-661), p. 661.

185. G. Latta and R. Lewis: 'Trade Union Legal Services', *British Journal of Industrial Relations*, 1974, No. 1, pp. 56-70.

186. B. C. Roberts: *Trade Union Government and Administration in Britain*. London, Bell, 1956, p. 461.

187. W. E. J. McCarthy and S. R. Parker: *Shop Stewards and Workshop Relations*. London, HMSO, 1968; *Donovan Report*, op. cit. (note 85), p. 26, lin. 99. Günther R. Degen: *Shop Stewards. Ihre zentrale Bedeutung für die Gewerkschaftsbewegung in Großbritannien*. Cologne, EVA, 1976.

188. TUC: *Training Full-Time Officers*. London, January 1972, p. 6; Stanley Parker: *Workplace Industrial Relations. 1972*. London, HMSO, 1974, pp. 11.

189. J. D. M. Bell: 'The Development of Industrial Relations in Nationalized Industries in Postwar Britain', *British Journal of Industrial Relations*, 1975, No. 1 (1-22), pp. 18, 22.

190. Department of Employment: *The Reform of Collective Bargaining at Plant and Company Level*. London, HMSO, 1971, p. 84; Ian Boraston et al.: *Workplace and Union*. London, Heinemann, 1975, pp. 153ff.

191. Mike Pedler: 'The Training Implications of the Shop Steward's Leadership Role', *Industrial Relations Journal*, University of Nottingham, 1974, No. 1 (57-69), p. 57.

192. Stan Poppe: 'Mitbestimmung in den Niederlanden', *Amsterdam, NVV*, January 1975, p. 5.

193. Fabrizio D'Agostini: *La condizione operaia e i consigli di fabbrica*. Rome, Editori Riuniti, 1974, pp. xi, 171, 174, 183 et passim.

194. Ibidem, p. 20, 26f.

195. Centro Studi Nazionale della CISL: *Strumenti di cultura sindacale*. Bologna, Il Mulino, 1977, p. 24.

196. Reynaud, op. cit. (note 18), Vol. 1, p. 134.

197. *Der Spiegel*, 1976, No. 29, p. 83.

198. Edvard Bull: 'Die Entwicklung der Arbeiterbewegung in den drei skandinavischen Ländern', *Archiv für die Geschichte der Arbeiterbewegung*, 1922, pp. 329-361. W. M. Lafferty: 'Industrialization and Labor Radicalism in Norway', *Scandinavian Political Studies*, 1972 (157-175), p. 174; Claudio Calvaruso: *Emigrazione e sindacati*. Rome, Coines, 1975.

199. John H. Goldthorpe et al.: *The Affluent Worker*. London, Cambridge UP, 1968.

200. Dieter Otten: *Kapitalentwicklung und Qualifikationsentwicklung*. Berlin, Rossa Verlagskoperativa, 1973, pp. 116ff.

201. Robert Taylor: *The Fifth Estate. Britain's Unions in the Seventies*. London, Routledge & Kegan Paul, 1978, p. 14.

202. Quoted in: Adolf Wagner: *Der Kampf zwischen Kapital und Arbeit*. Tübingen, Mohr, 1921, 4th edition, p. 177f.

203. Cf. for this hypothesis: Gerhard Kessler: *Die deutschen Arbeitgeberverbände*. Leipzig, Duncker & Humblot, 1907, p. 37.

204. *TUC Report 1975*, p. 49.

205. LO: *Verksamhetsberättelse 1973*. Stockholm 1974, p. 4f.

206. CGT: *Les militants de la CGT en formation syndicale*. Paris, n.d., p. 113.

207. 'Il finanziamento del sindacato'. *Rassegna sindacale, Quaderni*, No. 50, 1974, p. 48.

208. Neil McInnes: *The Communist Parties of Western Europe*. London, Oxford UP, 1975, p. 28.

209. Hartmut Schellhoss: *Apathie und Legitimität. Das Problem der neuen Gewerkschaften*. Munich, Piper, 1967, p. 12.

210. Clegg: *Trade Unionism*, op. cit. (note 159), p. 27.

211. Nickel, op. cit. (note 124), 256. *Gewerkschaftschaftsbarometer*, 1974/75, mimeo, p. 2f.

212. Ibidem, p. 2.

213. Goetz Briefs: *Gewerkschaftsprobleme in unserer Zeit*. Stuttgart, Kohlhammer, 1968, pp. 137ff.

214. UdSSR 1973: 97,6% cf.: E. A. Ivanov: *Provosjuzy v politicheskoy sisteme sotsializma*. Moscow, Profizdat, 1974, p. 40.

215. G. D. H. Cole: *The World of Labour*. London, Bell & Sons, 1913, p. 55.

216. V. L. Allen: *Power in Trade Unions*. London, Longmans Green, 1954, p. 56.

217. W. E. McCarthy: *The Closed Shop in Britain*. Oxford, Blackwell, 1964, p. 7.

218. Beatrice and Sidney Webb: *Industrial Democracy*. London, Longmans Green, 1897, p. 207.

219. Cyril Grunfeld: *Modern Trade Union Law*. London, Sweet & Maxwell, 1966, p. 24f, McCarthy, op. cit. (note 217), p. 260.

220. P. R. Jones: 'The British Medical Association and the Closed Shop', *Industrial Relations Journal*, Nottingham, 1974, No. 4 (36-45), p. 37; Ross M. Martin: *Trade Unions in Australia*. Harmondsworth, Penguin/University of Queensland Press, 1975, p. 51.

221. Ronald L. Miller: 'Right To-Work Laws and Compulsory Union Membership in the United States', *British Journal of Industrial Relations*, 1976, No. 2, pp. 186-193.

222. John M. Howells et al. (eds.): *Labour and Industrial Relations in New Zealand*. Carlton/Vic, Pitman House, 1974, pp. 12, 15, 90f, 169.

223. *Donovan Report*, op. cit (note 85), pp. 162ff.

224. Campbell Balfour: *Unions and the Law*. Westmead, Saxon House/Lexington, Lexington Books, D. C. Heath, 1974, 2nd edition, p. 42.

225. *Trade Union and Labour Relations Act 1974*, London, HMSO, 1975 (reprint); Taylor, op. cit. (note 201), p. 18.

226. Rupert Scholz: *Das Grundrecht der Koalitionsfreiheit anhand ausgewählter Entscheidungen zur Rechtsstellung von Gewerkschaften und Arbeitgeberverbänden*. Stuttgart, Boorberg, 1972, p. 28.

227. T. L. Johnston: *Collective Bargaining in Sweden. A Study of the Labour Market and its Institutions*. London, Allen & Unwin, 1962, p. 47f.

228. LAV, op. cit. (note 348), p. 27.

229. Theodor Eschenburg: 'Ein "Gewerkschaftsgroschen"?' *Die Zeit*, No. 5, 1961, reprinted in: idem: *Zur politischen Praxis der Bundesrepublik*. Munich, Piper, 1967, 2nd edition, pp. 238-242.

230. Helmut Ridder: *Gestattet das Grundgesetz für die BRD die Erhebung sogenannter Solidaritätsbeiträge?* Frankfurt, 1961 (mimeo).

231. Alfred Hueck: 'Die Frage der tarifrechtlichen Zulässigkeit von Solidaritätsbeiträgen nach geltendem deutschen Recht', *Recht der Arbeit*, 1961, No. 4, pp. 141ff.

232. *Proletariat in der BRD*. Berlin (East), Dietz, 1974, p. 451.

233. Franz Gamillscheg: *Die Differenzierung nach Gewerkschaftszugehörigkeit*. Berlin, Duncker & Humblot, 1966, pp. 24ff, 103ff.

234. Rolf Seitenzahl et al.: *Vorteilsregelungen für Gewerkschaftsmitglieder*. Cologne. Bund Verlag, 1976.

235. Robert A. Senser: 'Special Bonuses for Belgian Unionists', *Monthly Labor Review*, 1964, p. 928.

236. LAV, op. cit. (note 47), p. 26.

237. Cassau, op. cit. (note 77), p. 86.

238. LO: *Schwedischer Gewerkschaftsbund*. Stockholm, 1970, p. 34.

239. LO: *Verksamhetsberättelse 1973*, p. 142. *Verksamhetsberättelse 1977*, p. 198.

240. LO. *Statistik 1977*. Stockholm, 1978, pp. 23, 46.

241. *TUC Report 1974*, p. 579; *TUC Report 1975*, p. 49. Cf. Taylor, op. cit. (note 201), p. 31.

242. Chester A. Morgan: *Labor Economics*. Georgetown/Ontario, Irwin/Dorsey, 1970, 3rd edition, p. 391.

243. Gerhard Vater: 'Gewerkschaften müssen auch finanziell stark sein', *Die Quelle*, 1978, p. 410f; Peter Müller: 'Die "Wirtschaftsmacht" der Gewerkschaften in der öffentlichen Meinung', *Die Quelle*, 1978, p. 203, col. 2.

244. LO: *Verksamhetsberättelse 1973*. Cf. for Denmark: LO: *Kampens gang*. Copenhagen, 1973, p. 518.

245. Hirche, op. cit. (note 179), p. 377f.

246. Taylor, op. cit. (note 201), p. 30.

247. 'Hier, aujourd'hui, demain: La CGT'. Paris, Supplément *Le peuple*, No. 965, 1 May 1975, p. 73; Reynaud, op. cit. (note 18), Vol. 1, p. 137.

248. ÖGB: *Kurzbericht 1971-74*. Vienna, 1975, p. 14.

249. Windmuller, op. cit. (note 43), p. 15.

250. Johnston, op. cit. (note 227), p. 28; Knoellinger, op. cit. (note 40), p. 142.

251. *LO Statistik 1977*. Stockholm, 1978, p. 26.

252. Knoellinger, op. cit., 130; Martin, op. cit. (note 220), p. 53.

253. TUC: *Structure and Development*. September 1970, p. 4.

254. Hirche, op. cit. (note 179), p. 90.

255. 'Il finanziamento', op. cit. (note 207), p. 63.

256. Lloyd Ulman and Robert J. Flanagan: *Wage Restraint. A Study of Incomes Policies in Western Europe*. Berkeley, California UP, 1971, p. 236.

257. NVV: 'Die Ansichten des Industriebond NVV im Bezug auf Betriebsräte und Aufsichtsräte der Arbeitnehmerseite', Amsterdam, November 1975, p. 12.

258. Hirche, op. cit. (note 179), p. 144.

259. Roberts, op. cit. (note 186), p. 288; *Donovan Report*, op. cit. (note 85), p. 188, lin. 701.

260. Hirche, op. cit. (note 179), p. 179f.

261. Joseph LaPalombara: *Interest Groups in Italian Politics*. Princeton UP, 1964, p. 158f.

262. Sabine Erbès-Seguin: *Démocratie dans les syndicats*. Paris/The Hague, Mouton, 1971, p. 143.

263. Brian Weekes et al.: *Industrial Relations and the Limits of Law. The Industrial Effects of the Industrial Relations Act 1971*. Oxford, Blackwell, 1976, pp. 221ff.

264. Clegg, op. cit. (note 92), p. 92.

265. NVV, op. cit. (note 257).

266. Egil Fivelsdal and John Higley: 'The Labor Union Elite in Norway', *Scandinavian Political Studies*, 1970 (165-207), p. 179; Claus W. Witjes: *Gewerkschaftliche Führungsgruppen*. Berlin, Duncker & Humblot, 1976, p. 92.

267. Leif Lewin: *Hur styrs facket? Om demokratin inom fackföreningsrörelsen*. Stockholm, Rabén & Sjögren, 1977, p. 156.

268. Guy Tyler: *The Political Imperative. The Corporate Character of Unions*. New York, Macmillan 1968, p. 258.

269. Bromley H. Kniveton: 'Industrial Negotiating. Some Training Implications', *Industrial Relations Journal*, 1974, No. 3, pp. 27-37.

270. Lewin: *Hur*, op. cit. (note 267), p. 146.

271. Ludwig Rosenberg: *Entscheidungen für morgen — Gewerkschaftspolitik heute*. Düsseldorf, Econ, 1969, p. 94.

272. Allen, op. cit. (note 216), p. 190.

273. Friedrich Fürstenberg: 'Gewerkschaften in der Industriegesellschaft', in: Rupert Gmoser (ed.): *Die Gewerkschaft auf dem Weg zum Jahre 2000*. Vienna, Verlag des ÖGB, 1971 (29-46), p. 41.

274. H. L. Wilensky: *Intellectuals in Labour Unions*. Glencoe/Ill., Free Press, 1956, p. 35.

275. Morgan, op. cit. (note 242), p. 393.

276. TUC: *Training Full-time officers*. London, January 1972, p. 9.

277. Jack Barbash: *Trade Unions and National Economic Policy*. Baltimore, Johns Hopkins, 1972, p. 196.

278. Cf. Clark Kerr: *Unions and Union Leaders of Their Own Choosing*. Berkeley, California UP, Institute of Industrial Relations, 1958.

279. Alfred Weber: 'Staat und gewerkschaftliche Aktion', *GMH*, 1952, pp. 478ff.

280. Pirker, op. cit. (note 24), Vol. 1, p. 314.

281. Robert Michels: *Zur Sociologie des Parteiwesens in der modernen Demokratie*. Stuttgart, Kröner, 1925, 2nd edition, p. 330.

282. Leonard R. Sayles and George Strauss: 'Are Unions Democratic?' in: Jon M. Shephard (ed.): *Organizational Issues in Industrial Society*. Englewood Cliffs, Prentice Hall, 1972 (207-219), p. 219.

283. Alice H. Cook: *Union Democracy. Practice and Ideal. An Analysis of Four Large Local Unions*. Ithaca/Cornell, 1963, pp. 226ff.

284. Richard J. Willey: *Democracy in West German Trade Unions. A Reappraisal of the 'Iron Law'*. Beverly Hills/London, Sage, 1971, p. 49. Claus W. Witjes: *Gewerkschaftliche Führungsgruppen*. Berlin, Duncker & Humblot, 1976, pp. 126ff, 366ff.'

285. Lewin: *Hur*, op. cit. (note 267), p. 155, pp. 236ff.

286. Seymour M. Lipset et al.: *Union Democracy*. New York, Free Press, 1968, 2nd edition, pp. 414ff. Frieder Naschold: *Organisation und Demokratie*. Stuttgart, Kohlhammer, 1969, pp. 38ff.

287. Cook, op. cit. (note 283); Edelstein and Warner, op. cit. (note 119), pp. 87ff.

288. Eric Wigham: *Trade Unions*. London, Oxford UP, 1969, 2nd edition, p. 54.

289. Frans Leijnse: 'Democratisering van de vakbeweging', *Mens en Maatschappij*, 1973 (62-82), p. 76.

290. LAV, op. cit. (note 48), p. 19.

291. William M. Leiserson: *American Trade Union Democracy*. New York, Columbia UP, 1959, p. 69f.

292. Walter Galenson: *Trade Union Democracy in Western Europe*. Berkeley, University of California Press, 1962, pp. 88ff.

293. S. M. Lipset: 'Der politische Prozeß in den Gewerkschaften', in: B. Külp and W. Schreiber (eds.): *Arbeitsökonomik*. Cologne, Kiepenheuer & Witsch, 1972 (141-180), p. 142.

294. Jacques Jurquet: *Arracher la classe ouvrière du revisionisme*. Paris, Editions du centenaire, 1976.

II

295. Adolf Sturmthal: *Workers' Councils*. Cambridge, Mass., Harvard UP, 1964, p. 180.

296. Quoted in: Vivian Vale: *Labour in American Politics*. London, Routledge & Kegan Paul, 1971, p. 28.

297. *Statuten des ÖGB*. Vienna, 1971, p. 4; SGB: *Tätigkeitsbericht 1972, 1973, 1974*, Berne, n.d., pp. 180-183; LO: *Verksamhetsberättelse för ar 1977*. Stockholm, 1978, pp. 32ff; *Principprogram,* op. cit. (note 165), p. 4.

298. *The AFL-CIO Platform Proposals. Presented to the Democratic and Republican National Conventions 1976*. Washington DC, p. 56, col. 1.

299. *TUC Report 1975*, p. 100.

300. Cf. Joseph A. Banks: *Trade Unionism*. London, Macmillan-Collier, 1974, pp. 58ff.

301. H. A. Turner: *Trade Union Growth, Structure and Policy. A Comparative Study of the Cotton Unions*. London, Allen & Unwin, 1962, p. 364.

302. Rosenberg, op. cit. (note 271), p. 111f.

303. Reinhard Hoffmann: 'Parlamentarismus, soziale Interessen und Gewerkschaften', *Hamburger Jahrbuch für Wirtschafts- und Gesellschaftspolitik*. Tübingen, Mohr, 1971 (250-268), p. 261.

304. Carl Legien: 'Die Stellung der Gewerkschaften zur sozial politischen Gesetzgebung', *Sozialist. Monatshefte*, 1903, I, p. 323f.

305. Henri Krasucki: *Syndicats et lutte de classes*. Paris, Editions sociales, 1969, p. 52.

306. Karl-Otto Hondrich: *Die Ideologien von Interessenverbänden*. Berlin, Duncker & Humblot, 1963, p. 177.

307. Joachim Bergmann et al.: *Gewerkschaften in der Bundesrepublik*. Frankfurt, EVA, 1975, p. 150.

308. Krasucki, op. cit. (note 55), p. 117.

309. 'Sindacati e riforme'. *Rassegna sindacale, Quaderni*, 1972, No. 36, p. 16.

310. Antonio Donini: 'Gli extraparlamentari e il sindacato', *Rassegna sindacale, Quaderni*, 1972, No. 33/34, pp. 105-121.

311. *Principprogram*, op. cit. (note 165), p. 10.

312. V. L. Allen: *Militant Trade Unionism*. London, Merlin, 1972, 3rd edition, p. 18.

313. Edmond Maire: *CFDT. Pour un socialisme démocratique*. Paris, Seuil, 1971, p. 81f.

314. Gilbert Declercq: *Syndicaliste en liberté*. Paris, Seuil, 1974, p. 20.

315. Ibidem, p. 54.

316. Wilfried Höhnen: 'Gedanken zum Konzept eines Langzeitprogramms', *GMH*, 1972 (753-763), p. 763. Gerd Elvers: 'Brauchen wir ein neues Grundsatzprogramm?', *GMH*, 1972, pp. 342-348.

317. Nickel, op. cit. (note 124), p. 106. Elisabeth Noelle-Neumann: 'Werden wir alle Proletarier?', *Die Zeit*, 1975, No. 25, p. 7, col. 3.

318. M.-L. Antoni: 'Les syndicats sont-ils représentatifs?' *Le nouvel économiste*, 1978, No. 155 (44-53), pp. 45, 51, 53.

319. Ursula Jaerisch: *Sind Arbeiter autoritär? Zur Methodenkritik politischer Psychologie*. Frankfurt, EVA, 1975, p. 138.

320. David Butler and Donald Stokes: *Political Change in Britain*. London, Macmillan, 1970, p. 167.

321. Bo Gustafson: *Marxismus und Revisionismus*. Frankfurt, EVA, 1972, Vol. 1, p. 29.

322. Samuel H. Beer: *Modern British Politics*. London, Faber & Faber, 1969, 2nd edition, p. 145.

323. CNV: *Statuten*. Utrecht, n.d., p. 3.

324. LAV, op. cit. (note 48), p. 35f.

325. AFL-CIO: *Constitution*. Washington DC, 1961, p. 5; *The AFL-CIO Platform Proposals*. Washington DC, 1976, p. 59, col. 1.

326. Edelstein and Warner, op. cit. (note 119), p. 191. On the influence of Communists on the American unions: Bert Cochran: *Labor and Communism. The Conflict that Shaped American Unions*. Princeton UP, 1977.

327. *Constitution of the Irish Congress of Trade Unions*. Dublin, n.d. (Separatum), p. 643.

328. CGT: *Programm, angenommen durch den a.o.Kongress vom 6. April 1974*. Luxembourg, 1974, p. 31.

329. Federazione CGIL-CISL-UIL, op. cit. (note 56), p. 70f.

330. Lama/Manghi, op. cit. (note 76), p. 32.

331. Krasucki, op. cit. (note 55), pp. 101ff.

332. FGTB: *Congrès contrôle ouvrier*. Brussels, October 1970, p. 9.

333. *Flash sur la FGTB*. Brussels, n.d. (*Ca.* 1973), p. 17.

334. *Principprogram*, op. cit. (note 165), p. 10.

335. Adam, op. cit. (note 141), p. 50.

336. Maire, op. cit. (note 313), p. 89.

337. Roger Cornu: 'L'influence de l'action syndicale sur la socialisation de la production', *Mens en maatschappij*, Rotterdam, 1973 (126-136), p. 135.

338. *TUC Report 1974*, p. 572.

339. *Labour Party Annual Conference. Main Speeches. Blackpool, November 28/29. 1959*. p. 6.

340. TUC: *Post-War Reconstruction. Interim Report*. London, 1945, p. 9.

341. V. L. Allen: *Trade Unions and Government*. London, Longmans, 1960, p. 271.

342. *Principprogram*, op. cit. (note 165), p. 5f.

343. Nils Elvander: 'Democracy and Large Organizations', in: M. Hancock and Gideon Sjoberg (eds.): *Politics in the Post-Welfare State*. New York, Columbia UP, 1972 (302-324), p. 323.

344. T. L. Johnston (ed.): *Economic Expansion and Structural Change. A Trade Union Manifesto. Report submitted to the 16th Congress of Landsorganisationen i Sverige*. London, Allen & Unwin, 1963, p. 140.

345. Carl Reinhold Tersmeden: 'Sweden. Unofficial Strikes', in: Spitaels, op. cit. (note 1) (194-206), p. 197.

346. *Forcer l'avenir. Plan FGTB 1976-1986*. Brussels, n.d., p. 5.

347. Gerhard Leminsky and Bernd Otto (eds.): *Politik und Programmatik des Deutschen Gewerkschaftsbundes*. Cologne, Bund-Verlag, 1974, p. 51.

348. Gerhard Himmelmann: *Gemeinwirtschaft und Sozialismus*. Frankfurt, EVA, 1975.

349. H. A. Clegg: *Industrial Democracy and Nationalization. A Study prepared for the Fabian Society*. Oxford, Blackwell, 1955, pp. 88ff.

350. *Programme Commun*. Paris, 1972, pp. 42ff.

351. Bill Sampson: *Labour, the Unions and the Party*. London, Allen & Unwin, 1973, p. 73.

352. Dubois, op. cit. (note 136), p. 172; Jacques Gallus and Philippe Brachet: *Les Nationalisations. Quand la droite se sert de la gauche*. Paris, Editions du cerf, 1973, pp. 73, 60ff.

353. Kurt Biedenkopf in: 'Bergedorfer Gesprächskreis zu Fragen der industriellen Gesellschaft', *Protokoll*, 1975, No. 52, p. 35.

354. E. Westerlin and R. Beckman: *Sveriges Ekonomi*. Lund, Gleerup, 1974, p. 87.

355. *Gewerkschaften und Nationalisierung in der BRD*. Frankfurt, Verlag Marxistische Blatter, 1973, p. 10.

356. Knoellinger, op. cit. (note 40), p. 114.

357. Adam, op. cit. (note 141), p. 53; Antoni, op. cit. (note 318), p. 46.

358. Salvatore Luciano and Robert Magri: *Die Gemeinwirtschaft in Italien*. Frankfurt, EVA, 1974, p. 50; Ramón Tamames: *Estructura económica de Espana*. Madrid, 1969, 4th edition, p. 239.

359. Jochen Rudolph: 'Wohin die Sozialisierung führt', *FAZ*, 22 July 1976, p. 15.

360. André Barjonet: *La CGT*. Paris, Seuil, 1968, p. 94f.

361. Séguy, op. cit. (note 152), p. 201.

362. Goetz-Girey, op. cit. (note 161), p. 36.

363. *La participation des organisations d'employeurs et de travailleurs à la planification économique et sociale*. Geneva, ILO, 1973, p. 239.

364. S. Wickham: 'Participation in the National Development Plan and the Concept of Economic Decisions', in: Arthur M. Ross (ed.): *Industrial Relations and Economic Development*. London, Macmillan, 1966 (296-319), p. 318.

365. *Forcer l'avenir*, op. cit. (note 346), p. 4.

366. Leminsky and Otto, op. cit. (note 34), p. 51, col. 1.

367. Hermann Brandt: 'Das Selbstverständnis der Gewerkschaften', in: Helmuth C. F. Liesegang (ed.): *Gewerkschaften in der Bundesrepublik*. Berlin, De Gruyter, 1975 (66-72), p. 71.

368. Hubert Voigtländer: *Investitionslenkung oder Marktsteuerung. Ein Beitrag zur politischen Ökonomie des Godesberger Programms*. Bonn, Verlag Neue Gesellschaft, 1975, pp. 41ff.

369. Volker Hauff and Fritz W. Scharpf: *Modernisierung der Volkswirtschaft*. Frankfurt, EVA, 1975, pp. 22ff.

370. Jürgen Husmann: 'Augenwischerei', *Der Arbeitgeber*, 1976, No. 5, p. 170.

371. Ulrich Steger: 'Gewerkschaften und Wirtschaftsplanung', *GMH*, 1975, No. 4 (230-240), p. 235.

372. *TUC Report 1977*, p. 156 on 'vandalism and antisocial behavior'; Lama, *Relazione*, op. cit. (note 106), p. 77.

373. *LO Kongress 1976. Motioner*. Stockholm, Tiden-Barnängen, 1976, p. 495.

374. *Arbeitsprogramm des Schweizerischen Gewerkschaftsbundes*. Berne, n.d., p. 4.

375. Roy Lubove: *The Struggle for Social Security. 1900-1935*. Cambridge, Mass., Harvard UP, 1968, p. 15f. Everett M. Kassalow; *Trade Unions and Industrial Relations. An International Comparison*. New York, Random House, 1969, p. 68.

376. Daniel S. Sanders: *The Impact of Reform Movements on Social Policy Change: The Case of Social Insurance*. Fair Lawn, NJ, Burdick, 1973, p. 132.

377. John R. Hicks: *The Theory of Wages*. London, Macmillan, 1932, p. 12.

378. TUC: *Annual Report 1907* quoted in R. C. Roberts: *The Trades Union Congress 1868-1921*. London, Allen & Unwin, 1958, p. 206.

379. Gerhard Himmelmann: *Lohnbildung durch Kollektivverhandlungen*. Berlin, Duncker & Humblot, 1971, pp. 97ff.

380. Gerd Muhr: 'Sozialpolitik — Motor für innere Reformen', in: Leminsky and Otto, op. cit. (note 347), pp. 202-207.

381. 'Gewerkschaft bleibt bei ihrer Forderung', *FAZ*, 18 February 1976, p. 4.

382. Gerhard Wuthe: *Gewerkschaften und politische Bildung*. Hanover, Verlag für Literatur und Zeitgeschehen, 1962, pp. 35ff.

383. Martin Baethge: *Ausbildung und Herrschaft. Unternehmerinteressen in der Bildungspolitik*. Frankfurt, EVA, 1970.

384. Wolfgang Lempert: *Berufliche Bildung als Beitrag zur gesellschaftlichen Demokratisierung*. Frankfurt, Suhrkamp, 1974, pp. 134ff.

385. Sidney and Beatrice Webb: *The History of Trade Unionism*. London, Longmans Green, 1956 (reprint), p. 718.

386. Eduard Bernstein: *Die Voraussetzungen des Sozialismus und die Aufgaben der Sozialdemokratie*. Stuttgart, Dietz, 1899, p. 96.

387. Christa von Braunschweig: *Der Konsument und seine Vertretung*. PhD Dissertation. Mainz, 1964, pp. 165ff.

388. Robert W. Jackman: *Politics and Social Equality*. New York, Wiley, 1975, p. 151.

389. Klaus von Beyme: *Sozialismus oder Wohlfahrtsstaat?* Munich, Piper, 1977, p. 124.

III

390. Jan Pen: *Harmony and Conflict in Modern Society*. London, 1966, p. 60f.

391. Ralph Miliband: *Parliamentary Socialism*. London, Allen & Unwin, p. 135f.

392. Quoted in: T. L. Jarman: *Socialism in Britain*. London, Gollancz, 1972, p. 142.

393. Georges Sorel: *Réflexions sur la violence*. Paris, Rivière, 1950, p. 266f.

394. Karl Kautsky: *Der politische Massenstreik*. Berlin, 1914, p. 20.

395. *Protokoll über die Verhandlungen des Parteitages der Sozialdemokratischen Partei Deutschlands. Abgehalten zu Mannheim vom 23. bis 29. September 1906*. Berlin, Vorwärts, 1906, p. 132.

396. Ibidem, p. 233, italics in the text.

397. Ibidem, p. 245.

398. Rosa Luxemburg: *Politische Schriften*, Frankfurt, EVA, 1966, Vol. 1, pp. 173, 172.

399. Eduard Bernstein: *Der Streik*. Frankfurt, Rütten & Loening, 1906, p. 118f.

400. *Internationaler Sozialisten-Kongress zu Paris 1900*. Berlin, Vorwärts, 1900, p. 32.

401. *Internationaler Sozialisten-Kongress zu Amsterdam*. Berlin, Vorwärts, 1904, p. 24.

402. Henriette Roland-Holst: *Generalstreik und Sozialdemokratie*. Dresden, Kaden, 1906, 2nd edition, p. 15f.

403. *Kongress Paris*, op. cit. (note 400), p. 32.

404. *Kongress Amsterdam*, op. cit. (note 401), p. 28.

405. Arthur Ross: *Changing Patterns of Industrial Conflict*. Berkeley, Institute of Industrial Relations, 1960, p. 16.

406. Alvin Hansen; 'Cycles of Strikes', *American Economic Review*, December 1961, pp. 616-621.

407. Theodore Levitt: 'Prosperity versus Strikes', *Industrial and Labor Relations Review*, January 1953, pp. 220-226. Andrew Weintraub: 'Prosperity versus Strikes. An Empirical Approach'. *Industrial and Labour Relations Review*, 1965, pp. 231-238.

408. Ross and Hartman, op. cit. (note 135), p. 50.

409. Edward Shorter and Charles Tilly: *Strikes in France 1830-1968*. London, Cambridge UP, 1974, p. 307.

410. J. Bergmann et al.: *Gewerkschaften in der Bundesrepublik*. Frankfurt, EVA, 1975, pp. 109ff.

411. Klaus Wiedemann: *Streik und Streikdrohung*. Herford, Bonn, Maximilian Verlag, 1971, p. 57, note 116.

412. Tables in: Goetz-Girey, op. cit. (note 161), p. 93.

413. P. Galambos and E. W. Evans: 'Work Stoppages in the UK', in: E. W. Evans and S. W. Creigh (eds.): *Industrial Conflict in Britain*. London, Frank Cass, 1977 (31-57), p. 48f.

414. J. W. Durcan and W. E. J. McCarthy: 'The State Subsidy Theory of Strikes. An Examination of Statistical Data for the Period 1956-1970', *British Journal of Industrial Relations*, 1974, No. 1, pp. 26-47.

415. Daniel Guérin: *Die amerikanische Arbeiterbewegung. 1867-1967*. Frankfurt, Suhrkamp, 1970, p. 157.

416. Myron Roomkin: 'Union Structure, Internal Control, and Strike Activity', *Industrial and Labor Relations Review*, 1976 (198-217), pp. 201, 213.

417. LO: *Statistik 1977.* Stockholm, 1978, p. 33.

418. Hirche, op. cit. (note 179), p. 225.

419. John Gennard: *Financing Strikers.* London, Macmillan, 1977, pp. 25ff.

420. Taylor, op. cit. (note 201), p. 34; Clegg, op. cit. (note 159), p. 79.

421. Taylor, ibidem.

422. O. Eckert: *Die Finanzwirtschaft der Gewerkschaften in Deutschland.* Berlin, 1922, p. 43.

423. ÖGB: *Kurzbericht 1971-1974.* Vienna, 1975, p. 21.

424. LAV: *Verbandsstatut.* Esch-sur-Alzette, 1972, p. 7.

425. A. J. Thieblot and R. M. Cowin: *Welfare and Strikes: The Use of Public Funds to Support Strikers.* University of Pennsylvania, 1972, p. 226.

426. Gerhard Beier: *Schwarze Kunst und Klassenkampf.* Frankfurt, EVA, n.d., p. 437.

427. Michael Tugan-Baranovsky: *Soziale Theorie der Verteilung.* Berlin, Julius Springer, 1913, p. 82.

428. Hicks, op. cit. (note 377), p. 146f.

429. René Wack: *Kollektivverhandlungen in den USA.* Zurich, 1959, p. 32; Arthur Rolls: 'Changing Patterns of Industrial Conflict, *Monthly Labor Review*, 1960, p. 232.

430. Bernhard Külp: *Lohnbildung im Wechselspiel zwischen politischen und wirtschaftlichen Kräften.* Berlin, Duncker & Humblot, 1965, p. 138.

431. Bernhard Külp: *Streik und Streikdrohung.* Berlin, Duncker & Humblot, 1965, pp. 40ff.

432. Quoted in: D. R. Matthews: *US Senators and their World.* New York, 1960, p. 192.

433. O. Ashenfelter and G. Johnson: 'Bargaining Theory. Trade Unions and Industrial Strike Activity', *The American Economic Review*, 1969, pp. 35-49.

434. Stewart, op. cit. (note 98), p. 11.

435. Weitbrecht, op. cit. (note 5).

436. Külp: *Lohnbildung*, op. cit. (note 430), p. 158.

437. Clark Kerr and Abraham Siegel: *Labour and Management in Industrial Society.* New York, 1964, pp. 105ff; Evans and Creigh, op. cit. (note 413), p. 245.

438. Frederic L. Pryor: 'An International Comparison of Concentration Ratios', *Review of Economics and Statistics*, 1970, pp. 130-140.

439. Geoffrey K. Ingham: *Strikes and Industrial Conflict. Britain and Scandinavia.* London, Macmillan, 1974, p. 43f.

440. Rainer Kalbitz: 'Die Entwicklung von Streiks und Aussperrungen in der BRD', in: O. Jacobi et al. (eds.): *Gewerkschaften und Klassenkampf. Kritisches Jahrbuch '73.* Frankfurt, Fischer, 1973 (163-176), p. 170.

441. Ross, op. cit. (note 405), p. 19.

442. Douglas A. Hibbs: 'Industrial Conflict in Advanced Industrial Societies', *APSR*, 1976 (1033-1058), p. 1058.

443. N. Aboud et al.: 'Les grèves', *Sociologie du travail*, 1973, No. 4, p. 363.

444. Taylor, op. cit. (note 201), p. 129.

445. H. A. Turner: 'Is Britain Really Strike Prone?' Cambridge UP, Occasional Paper 20, 1969.

446. For a criticism of his argument: W. E. J. McCarthy: 'The Nature of Britain's Strike Problem', in: Evans and Creigh, op. cit. (note 413), pp. 267-281.

447. Cf. Chapter 3, 3.

448. Convent der Christelijk-Sociale Organisaties: *Rapport inzake arbitrage in arbeidsgeschillen*. The Hague, 1964.

449. J. H. Derksen: *Nationale Loonpolitiek*. 'sHertogenbosch, Zuid-Nederlands Drukkerij, 1963, p. 290.

450. Barry Gordon: 'A Ninety Sector Analysis of Industrial Disputes in Australia 1968-1973', *The Journal of Industrial Relations*, 1975, No. 3 (240-254), p. 248.

451. Alfred Horne (ed.): *Zwischen Stillstand und Bewegung*. Frankfurt, EVA, 1965, p. 16.

452. Bernhard Külp: *Theorie der Drohung*. Stuttgart, Kohlhammer, 1965, p. 48.

453. E. Bardey: *Streikfibel für Unternehmer*. Bremen, 1958, pp. 11ff.

454. Klaus Schneider: 'Gewerkschaftsbarometer. Wer ist der mächtigste im ganzen Land?', *Der Arbeitgeber*, 1974, No. 10, pp. 382ff.

455. *Der Spiegel*, 'Tiefer Graben', 1975, No. 6 (52-64), p. 63.

456. Shorter and Tilly, op. cit. (note 409), pp. 318ff.

457. C. F. Eisele: 'Organization, Size, Technology and Frequency of Strikes', *Industrial Labor Relations Review*, 1974, No. 4 (560-571), p. 569.

458. Westerstahl, op. cit. (note 94), p. 137.

459. Karl Jetter; 'Der Streik — kein Motor des Fortschritts. Eine Erfolgsbilanz europäischer Arbeitskämpfe 1969-1974', *FAZ*, 15 November 1975, p. 11.

460. Fluctuations of nominal wages and strike frequency have been measured on the basis of data from the ILO (Table 21) for Italy, Britain, Denmark and Switzerland in the period of 1962-72.

A correlation analysis (Pearsons' r) was tried with the help of Jörg Ueltzhöffer. In order to get a more specified view of the correlations, the countries have been classified by the predominant character of their industrial relations (conflict-oriented vs cooperation-oriented). In order to get better compatibility of the scales of nominal wages, a Z-transformation was necessary. The analysis for conflict-oriented systems showed a linear correlation of $r = 0.54$ for the cooperation-oriented systems $r = -0.19$. With due caution it can be concluded that in a conflict-oriented system there is some correlation between strike frequency and the development of wages (more so in Britain than in Italy). In cooperative systems, however, this connection is very weak.

461. John E. Maher: 'Union, Nonunion Wage Differentials', *American Economic Review*, June 1956, p. 352.

462. Robert Ozanne: 'DerEinfluß der Gewerkschaften auf das Lohnniveau und die Einkommensverteilung', in: Külp and Schreiber, op. cit. (note 293), p. 324-346.

463. Külp: *Lohnbildung*, op. cit. (note 430), p. 337.

464. Kalbitz, op. cit. (note 440), p. 169.

465. Gérard Adam and Jean-Daniel Reynaud: *Conflits du travail et changement social*. Paris, PUF, 1978, p. 43.

466. Taylor, op. cit. (note 201), p. 17.

467. Kalbitz, op. cit. (note 440), p. 173.

468. Stewart, op. cit. (note 98), p. 59.

469. Tony Cliff: *The Employers' Offensive. Productivity Deals and How to Fight Them*. London, Pluto Press, 1970, p. 199; Reynaud, op. cit. (note 18), Vol. 1, p. 162.

470. *Verhandlungen des Hauptausschusses. 117. Sitzung 3 December 1948, Bonn*, pp. 210ff.

471. Karl Hernekamp (ed.): *Arbeitskampf. Aktuelle Dokumente*. Berlin, De Gruyter, 1975, p. 16.

472. Federazione lavoratori metalmeccanici (FIM-FIOM-UILM): *Poteresindacale e ordinamento giuridico*. Bari, De Donato, 1973, p. 263.

473. D. F. MacDonald: *The State and the Unions*. London, Macmillan, 1960, pp. 101ff.

474. April Carter: *Direct Action and Liberal Democracy*. London, Routledge & Kegan Paul, 1973, p. 37.

475. Jean-Clause Javillier: *Les conflits du travail*. Paris, PUF, 1976, p. 38.

476. Gouldner called this form of strike 'Pseudo wildcat strike'. A. W. Gouldner: *Wildcat Strike*. London, Routledge & Kegan Paul, 1955, p. 95.

477. J. E. T. Eldridge: 'Unofficial Strikes', in: *Industrial Disputes*. London, Routledge & Kegan Paul 1968 (68-90), 90.

478. Jack Barbash: 'The Causes of Rank-and-File Unrest', in: Joel Seidman (ed.): *Trade Union Government and Bargaining*. New York, Praeger, 1970 (39-58), p. 45.

479. Dubois, op. cit. (note 136), pp. 246, 248.

480. Tersmeden, op. cit. (note 345), p. 195.

481. Rainer Erd and Rainer Kalbitz: 'Gerwerkschaften und Arbeitsrecht. Ansatzpunkte einer Neubestimmung gewerkschaftlicher Rechtspolitik — am Beispiel der Aussperrungsdiskussion', *GMH*, 1976, No. 3 (143-154), p. 147.

482. *Donovan Report*, op. cit. (note 85), p. 112, lin. 413f.

483. Spiros Simitis: 'Entwicklungstendenzen im Tarifvertrags und Streikrecht', in: *Krise und Reform in der Industriegesellschaft*. IG-Metall-Tagung, Cologne, 1976, pp. 57-72.

484. Carlson, op. cit. (note 95), p. 176.

485. M. Borysewicz: *Les grèves tournantes*. Paris, Dalloz, 1961, p. 53.

486. Helène Sinay: *La grève*. Paris, Dalloz, 1966, p. 36, pp. 388ff.

487. Gérard Lyon-Caen: 'Streik und Aussperrung in Frankreich', in: Michael Kittner (ed.): *Streik und Aussperrung. Protokoll der wissenschaftlichen Veranstaltung der Industriegewerkschaft Metall vom 13. bis 15. September 1973 in München*. Frankfurt, EVA, 1975 (333-347), p. 337.

488. *LO om § 32. LO's remissvar*. Stockholm, July 1975, p. 33.

489. Javillier, op. cit. (note 475), p. 37.

490. 'Les enfants de Lip', op. cit. (note 102), p. 20.

491. *Die Zeit*, 1976, No. 19, p. 25.

492. Frank Otte: 'Partner in der Pleite. Warum die Sanierung konkursreifer Betriebe durch die Belegschaft selten gelingt', *Die Zeit*, 1975, No. 43, p. 29.

493. Rudolf Meidner: *Svensk arbetsmarknad vid full sysselsättning*. Stockholm, Konjunkturinstitutet, 1954.

494. Ken Coates: 'Fabrikbesetzungen in Großbritannien', in: Jacobi, op. cit. (note 440) (223-241), p. 226. Ernie Johnston: *Industrial Action*. Tiptree, Essex, Anchor Press, 1975, pp. 33ff.

495. Klaus Pickshaus and Dieter Raulf: *Klassenkämpfe in Großbritannien heute*. Frankfurt, Verlag Marxistische Blätter, 1973, p. 88f.

496. *Industrial Democracy*, op. cit. (note 146), p. 10.

497. Ibidem, pp. 11, 31.
498. Edmond Maire and Charles Piaget: *Lip 73*. Paris, Seuil, 1973.
499. 'Les enfants de Lip', op. cit. (note 102), pp. 21-23.
500. 'Requiem für Lip', *NZZ*, 18/19 April 1976, p. 9.
501. Séguy, op. cit. (note 152).
502. Streithofen, op. cit. (note 11), p. 214.
503. Heinrich Laufenberg: *Der politische Streik*. Stuttgart, Dietz, 1914; Reprint, Bonn 1976, p. 247.
504. Marcelino Camacho: *Charlas en la prision*. Paris, Colección Ebro, 1974, p. 91.
505. Joseph H. Kaiser: *Der politische Streik*. Berlin, Duncker & Humblot, 1959.
506. LAV, op. cit. (note 48), p. 22.
507. Otto Brenner: *Gewerkschaftliche Dynamik in unserer Zeit*. Frankfurt, EVA, 1966, p. 12; Hans Brox and Bernd Rüthers: *Arbeitskampfrecht*. Stuttgart, Kohlhammer, 1965, p. 62.
508. Boyd, op. cit. (note 16), p. 102.
509. Ulrich Mückenberger: *Arbeitsrecht und Klassenkampf. Der große englische Dockarbeiterstreik 1972*. Frankfurt, EVA, 1974, p. 7.
510. Klaus von Beyme: *Die parlamentarischen Regierungssysteme in Europa*. Munich, Piper, 1973, 2nd edition, p. 818.
511. 'Erstmals Generalstreik in Australien', *FAZ*, 13 July 1976, p. 5.
512. Robert Benewick and Trevor Smith (eds.): *Direct Action and Democratic Politics*. London, Allen & Unwin, 1972, p. 268.
513. Cf. Giovanni Sartori (ed.): *Correnti, frazioni e fazioni nei partiti politici italiani*. Bologna, Il Mulino, 1973, p. 79.
514. Brox and Rüthers, op. cit. (note 507), p. 58.
515. SOU: 1975: 1: *Demokrati pa arbetsplatsen*. Stockholm, 1975, pp. 373ff.
516. *LO om § 32*. Stockholm, July 1975, p. 33.
517. Reinhard Hoffmann: *Parlamentarismus*, op. cit. (note 303), p. 267, Idem: *Rechtsfortschritt durch gewerkschaftliche Gegenmacht*. Frankfurt, EVA, 1968, p. 110.
518. E. H. Phelps Brown: *The Growth of British Industrial Relations. A Study from the standpoint of 1906-1914*. London, Macmillan, 1965, p. 348.
519. Hirsch-Weber, op. cit. (note 12), p. 133.
520. Eric Wigham: *Strikes and the Government. 1893-1974*. London, Macmillan, 1976, p. 194.
521. *TUC Report 1974*, p. 81; *TUC Report 1975*, p. 105; *Trade Union and Labour Relations Act 1974*, p. 14.
522. Clegg: *Trade Unionism*, op. cit. (note 159), p. 78. For Germany cf. Rainer Erd: *Verrechtlichung industrieller Konflikte*. Frankfurt, Campus, 1978, p. 205.
523. C. J. Arup: 'Political Strikes. A Fresh Look at Spicer's Case', *The Journal of Industrial Relations* (Sidney), 1975, No. 2 (201-206), p. 206.
524. *Le Monde*, 8 August 1974.
525. Javillier, op. cit. (note 475), pp. 37ff.
526. Josef Iseesee: *Beamtenstreik*. Bonn, Godesberger Taschenbuchverlag, 1971, p. 134.
527. Däubler, op. cit. (note 126).
528. 'Japan: Staatsbedienstete stecken auf', *FAZ*, 4 December 1975, p. 11.

529. Nils Elvander: 'The Role of the State in the Settlement of Labor Disputes in the Nordic Countries: A Comparative Analysis', *European Journal of Political Research*, 1974 (363-383), pp. 376ff.

530. E. P. Kelsall: 'Industrial Conflict in Australia', *Economic Record*, August 1959, pp. 255-262; D. W. Oxnam: 'International Comparisons of Industrial Conflict. An Appraisal', *Journal of Industrial Relations*, 1965, No. 2, pp. 149-163; Kenneth P. Walker: *Australian Industrial Relations System*. Cambridge, Mass., Harvard UP, 1970, p. 437.

531. Raymond D. Horton: 'Arbitration, Arbitrators and the Public Interest', *Industrial and Labor Relations Review*, 1975, No. 4 (497-507), p. 505f.

532. Fernando Wasser: 'Neutralität mit Schlagseite. Das Arbeitsamt zwischen den Streikfronten', *FAZ*, 12 September 1975, p. 11.

533. *Ökonomisch-politischer Orientierungsrahmen für die Jahre 1975-1985*. Bonn, SPD, 1975, p. 59, col. 2.

534. Erd and Kalbitz, op. cit. (note 481), p. 145.

535. Peter Märthesheimer: *Publizistik und gewerkschaftliche Aktion. Das Bild der IG Metall in westdeutschen Zeitungen*. Dortmund, Institut für Zeitungsforschung, 1964, pp. 81ff.

536. G. Herzog: 'Der unbestreikbare Betrieb', *Der Arbeitgeber*, 1962, No. 21, pp. 616ff.

537. Lyon-Caen, op. cit. (note 487), p. 340; Giugni, ibidem, p. 278; Sinay, op. cit. (note 486), p. 342ff; Javillier, op. cit. (note 475), pp. 75ff.

538. Peter Lerche: *Verfassungsrechtliche Zentralfragen des Arbeitskampfes*. Bad Homburg v.d.H., Gehlen, 1968, p. 10.

539. Thomas Raiser: *Die Ausperrungen nach dem Grundgesetz*. Berlin, Duncker & Humblot, 1975, p. 92.

IV

540. Bernd Rüthers: *Arbeitsrecht und politisches System*. Frankfurt, Athenäum Fischer, 1973, p. 16.

541. Walter Ulbricht: *Revolutionäre Streikführung*. Berlin, Betrieb und Gewerkschaft, n.d. (about 1930), reprinted in: *Die Revolutionäre Gewerkschaftsopposition (RGO)*, op. cit. (note 26), Vol. 2 (139-185), p. 148.

542. Karl Korsch: *Arbeitsrecht für Betriebsräte (1922)*. Frankfurt (reprint), 1968, p. 26.

543. *Sowjetisches Arbeitrecht*. Berlin (East), Staatsverlag der DDR, 1974, p. 406.

544. C. Northcote Parkinson (ed.): *Industrial Disruption*. London, Leviathan House, 1973, p. 173.

545. Beier, op. cit. (note 426), p. 249.

546. *Orientierungsrahmen*, op. cit. (note 533), p. 32, col. 1.

547. Lutz Unterseher: *Arbeitsrecht — eine deutsche Spezialität. Gewerkschaften und Klassenkampf. Kritisches Jahrbuch '72*. Frankfurt, Fischer, 1972, pp. 190-201.

548. Heinz Josef Varain: *Freie Gewerkschaften. Sozialdemokratie und Staat*. Düsseldorf, Droste, 1956, p. 46.

549. Cf. Johannes Schregle: 'Die Arbeitnehmer-Arbeitgeber-Beziehungen in Westeuropa', *GMH*, 1974, No. 8 (457-472), p. 459.

550. *Statuten des Schweizerischen Gewerkschaftsbundes*. Berne, 1969, Amendments von 1972, p. 1.
551. Weekes, op. cit. (note 263), pp. 221ff.
552. Westerstahl, op. cit. (note 94), pp. 371ff.
553. LAV, op. cit. (note 48), p. 29f.
554. Leminsky and Otto, op. cit. (note 347), p. 57 (Art. XII).
555. Projektgruppe, op. cit. (note 5), p. 134.
556. Klaus von Beyme: *Ökonomie und Politik im Sozialismus*. Munich, Piper, 1977, 2nd edition, p. 252.
557. Ulrich Mückenberger and Marianne Welteke: 'Krisenzyklen, Einkommenspolitik und Arbeitsrechtsentwicklung in der BRD', *Kritische Justiz*, 1975 (1-23), p. 20.
558. Thilo Ramm in: Benjamin Aaron (ed.): *Labor Courts and Grievance Settlement in Western Europe*. Berkeley, University of California Press, 1971, p. 83.
559. Sir Arthur Tyndall: 'The New Zealand System of Industrial Conciliation and Arbitration', *International Labor Review*, 1960, No. 2, pp. 138-162; Howells, op. cit. (note 222), p. 20.
560. Walker, op. cit. (note 530), p. 451; Martin, op. cit. (note 220), pp. 17, 110.
561. Horton, op. cit. (note 531), p. 498.
562. Olof Ruin: 'Participatory Democracy and Corporativism: The Case of Sweden', *Scandinavian Political Studies*, Oslo, 1974, pp. 171-184.
563. 'Umstrittene Privilegien für Funktionsträger der Postgewerkschaft', *FAZ*. 24 May 1975, p. 2; Theodor Eschenburg: 'Gewerkschaftsstaat der Post?', *Die Zeit*, 1975, No. 24, p. 6.
564. 'Wahlkampf in die Betrieben', *FAZ*, 9 April 1974, p. 4.
565. Maire, op. cit. (note 413), p. 82.
566. Law of 27 December 1968, in: *Dossier Notre Temps*, No. 339, January 1969, pp. 339-340.
567. Stanley Parker: *Workplace Relations 1972*. London, HMSO, 1974, p. 10.
568. TUC: *Facilities for Shop Stewards*. London, 1971, 1975, 4th edition, p. 10f.
569. Enrico Taliani: 'Modelle betrieblicher Demokratie in Italien', in: Fritz Vilmar (ed.): *Industrielle Demokratie in Westeuropa*. Reinbek, Rowohoflt, 1975 (194-230), p. 210.
570. André Gorz: *Strategy for Labor. A Radical Proposal*. Boston, Beacon Press, 1967, p. 46.
571. Frank Deppe: *Das Bewußtsein der Arbeiter*. Cologne, Pahl-Rugenstein, 1971, p. 244.
572. Reinhard Richardi: 'Tarifautonomie. Grundpfeiler freiheitsrechtlicher Arbeitsverfassung', *Der Arbeitgeber*, 1974, No. 19 (739-741), p. 741.
573. Michael Kittner: 'Parität im Arbeitskampf. Überlegungen zur Forderung nach dem Verbot der Aussperrung. *GMH*, 1973, No. 2 (91-104), p. 91.
574. DGB: *9. ord Bundeskongress Berlin vom 25.6-1.7.1972, Tagungsprotokoll*, pp. 19ff.
575. Claus Noé: *Gebändigter Klassenkampf. Tarifautonomie in der BRD*. Berlin, Duncker & Humblot, 1970, p. 223.
576. Günter Schmölders (ed.): *Das Selbstbild der Verbände*. Berlin, :Duncker & Humblot, 1965, p. 127.

577. Philipp Herder-Dorneich (ed.): *Zur Verbandsökonomik*. Berlin, Duncker & Humblot, 1975, pp. 195ff.
578. Helmut Reichvilser: *Erfolgskontrolle der Verbandsarbeit*. Berlin, Duncker & Humblot, 1973, pp. 240ff.
579. Benya, op. cit. (note 71), p. 28.
580. On this German discussion: K.-H. Giessen: *Die Gewerkschaften im Prozess der Volks- und Staatswillens-Bildung*. Berlin, Duncker & Humblot, 1976; M. Gerhardt: *Das Koalitionsgesetz*. Berlin, Duncker & Humblot, 1977. G. Teubner: *Organisationsdemokratie und Verbandsverfassung*. Tübingen, Mohr, 1978.
581. LAV, op. cit. (note 48), p. 32.
582. Ibidem, p. 32f.
583. *Unternehmerbrief des Instituts der deutschen Wirtschaft*, 12 September, 1974.
584. Joachim Hirsch: *Die öffentlichen Funktionen der Gewerkschaften*. Stuttgart, Klett, 1966, pp. 155ff.
585. Liesegang, op. cit. (note 367), p. 122.
586. Klaus von Beyme: *Die politische Elite in der BRD*. Munich, Piper, 1974, 2nd edition, p. 46.
587. Varain, op. cit. (note 548), pp. 140, 179.
588. *Donovan Report*, op. cit. (note 85), p. 19, compiled from B. Spuler (ed.): *Regenten und Regierungen der Welt*. Bielefeld, Ploetz, 1953, Part 2.
589. Beier, op. cit. (note 426), p. 248.
590. Leo Panitch: *Social Democracy and Industrial Militancy. The Labour Party, the Trade Unions, and Incomes Policy. 1945-1974*. London, Cambridge UP, 1975, p. 10.
591. Joseph A. Banks: *Trade Unionism*. London, Collier-Macmillan, 1974, p. 66.
592. Austin Ranney: *Pathways to Parliament. Candidate Selection in Britain*. London, Macmillan, 1965, p. 221; Richard Rose: *Politics in England Today*. London, Faber & Faber, 1974, p. 243; David Butler and Dennis Kavanagh: *The British General Election of February 1974*. London, Macmillan, 1974, p. 228.
593. Taylor, op. cit. (note 201), p. 63.
594. Michael Rush: *The Selection of Parliamentary Candidates*. London, Nelson, 1969, p. 179.
595. Lewis Minkin: 'The Party Connection: Divergence and Convergence in the British Labour Movement', *Government and Opposition*, 1978, pp. 458-483.
596. Anthony Barker and Michael Rush: *The Member of Parliament and His Information*. London, Allen & Unwin, 1970, pp. 264ff.
597. Douglas Houghton: 'Trade Union MPs in the British House of Commons', *The Parliamentarian*, October 1968 (215-221), p. 217.
598. David Butler and Donald Stokes: *Political Change in Britain. Forces Shaping Electoral Choice*. London, Macmillan, 1970, 2nd edition, p. 168.
599. William D. Muller: 'Union-MP Conflict: An Overview', *Parliamentary Affairs*, 1973 (336-355), p. 353.
600. James Jupp: *Australian Labour and the World*. London, Fabian Research Series, 246, 1965, p. 30f.
601. Robert R. Alford: *Party and Society. The Anglo-American Democracies*. Chicago, Rand McNally, 1963, p. 94.

602. Arthur Kornhauser et al.: *When Labor votes. A Study of Auto Workers.* New York, University Books, 1956, pp. 273ff.
603. Barry Hindess: *The Decline of Working Class Politics*. London, Paladin, 1971, pp. 20ff; Tom Forester: *The Labour Party and the Working Class*. London, Heinemann, 1976, pp. 124ff.
604. Nils Elvander: *Intresseorganisationerna i dagens Sverige*. Lund, Gleerup, 1972, 2nd edition, pp. 208, 210.
605. Varain, op. cit. (note 548), pp. 45, 161.
606. Bodo Zeuner: *Kandidatenaufstellung zur Bundestagswahl 1965*. The Hague, Nijhoff, 1970, p. 78.
607. Lowisch in: Liesegang, op. cit. (note 367), p. 132.
608. Zeitforum: 'Marsch in den Gewerkschaftsstaat?'*2 Die Zeit*, 1974, No. 49 (9-13), p. 13, col. 4.
609. Roland Cayrol et al.: *Le deputé francais*. Paris, Colin, 1973.
610. Jean Meynaud: *Rapporto sulla classe dirigente italiana*. Milan, Giuffrè, 1966, p. 17.
611. Alberto Spreafico and Joseph LaPalombara (eds.): *Elezioni e comportamento politico in Italia*. Milan, Comunità, 1963, p. 543.
612. Giovanni Sartori (ed.): *Il Parlamento Italiano 1946-1963*. Naples, Edizioni scientifiche italiane, 1963, Table xx, p. 133.
613. LaPalombara, op. cit. (note 261), p. 227f.
614. *La Stampa*, 17 January 1970.
615. Franca Cantelli el al.: *Come lavora il Parlamento*. Milan, Giuffrè, 1974, p. 293.
616. Seymour M. Lipset: *The First New Nation*. Garden City, Doubleday, 1967, p. 343.
617. Vale, op. cit. (note 296), p. 34.
618. *AFL-CIO News*, 18 January 1969, p. 7.
619. J. David Greenstone: *Labor in American Politics*. New York, Knopf, 1969, pp. 322, 330.
620. Douglas Caddy: *The Hundred Million Dollar Payoff*. New Rochelle, Arlington House, 1974, pp. 50f, 83, 98, 107, 114; Charles M. Rehmus et al. (eds.): *Labor and American Politics*. Ann Arbor, University of Michigan Press, 1978, pp. 350ff, 422ff. *This is the AFL-CIO*. Washington DC, 1978, p. 9, col. 2.
621. *Report of the AFL-CIO Executive Council*, 2 October 1975. Reprinted in Rehmus, op. cit. (note 620), p. 203. For the following: Jong Oh Ra: *Labor at the Polls*. Amherst, University of Massachussetts Press, 1978, pp. 118ff. *Statement by the AFL-CIO Executive Council on Financing Federal Election Campaigns*. Bal Harbour/Fla, February 1979.
622. ICTU: *Structure and Function of Congress*. Dublin, 1975, p. 5.
623. D. W. Rawson: 'The Life-Span of Labour Parties', *Political Studies*, 1969 (313-333), p. 313.
624. May, op. cit. (note 118), p. 332.
625. Nils Elvander: 'In Search of New Relationships: Parties, Unions and Salaried Employees' Associations in Sweden', *Industrial and Labor Relations Review*, October 1974 (60-74), p. 62.
626. *Sveriges officella Statistik*: Allmänna valen, 1970, Part 3, p. 100, Lewin: *Hur styrs facket*, op. cit. (note 267), pp. 91, 155.

627. Documents in: G. H. L. LeMay: *British Government 1914-1963. Select Documents*. London, 1964, 2nd edition, p. 37f, 102.

628. Goldthorpe, op. cit. (note 199), p. 110.

629. Martin Harrison: *Trade Unions and the Labour Party since 1945*. London, Allen & Unwin, 1960, p. 33.

630. 419 HC Deb. 5s col. 266.

631. Duff Cooper: *Old Men Forget*. London, Hart-Davis, 1953, p. 143.

632. *Report to the Chief Registrar of Friendly Societies, 1947*, Part IV.

633. Detlev Albers et al.: *Klassenkämpfe in Westeuropa*. Reinbek, Rowohlt, 1971, p. 282.

634. Tage Lindbom: *Den svenska fackföreningsrörelsens uppkomst och tidigare historia*. Stockholm, 1938, p. 216f.

635. Hjalmar Branting: 'Tvang til frihet', in: Idem: *Tal och skrifter*. Stockholm, 1927, Vol. 1, pp. 247-250.

636. Westerstahl, op. cit. (note 94), pp. 217ff.

637. Cf. Donald J. Blake: 'Swedish Trade Unions and the Social Democratic Party: the Formative Years', *The Scandinavian Economic History Review*, 1960, No. 1 (19-44), p. 43.

638. Otto Nordenskiöld: *Förhallendet LO-TCO. En överskikt*. Stockholm, Tiden, 1972, p. 22; Lewin: *Hur*, op. cit. (note 267), p. 144f.

639. Walter Galenson: *The Danish System of Labor Relations*. Cambridge/Mass., Harvard UP, 1952, pp. 40-47; Josef A. Raffaele: *Labor Leadership in Italy and Denmark*. Madison, University of Wisconsin Press, 1962, pp. 181ff.

640. Kenneth E. Miller: *Government and Politics in Denmark*. Boston, Houghton & Mifflin, 1968, p. 117f.

641. Penny Gill Martin: 'Strategic Opportunities and Limitations: The Norwegian Labor Party and the Trade Unions', *Industrial and Labor Relations Review*, October 1974 (75-88), p. 76.

642. TUC-Labour Party Liaison Committee: *Into the Eighties: An Agreement*, July 1978, pp. 3, 16. For the following cf.: Lewis Minkin: 'The Party Connection: Divergence and Convergence in the British Labour Movement ', *Government and Opposition*, 1978 (458-483), p. 474.

643. Henry Valen and Daniel Katz: *Political Parties in Norway*. Oslo, Universitetsforlaget, 1964, p. 325; Robert B. Kvavik: *Interest Groups in Norwegian Politics*. Oslo, Universitetsforlaget, 1976, p. 113.

644. *Principprogram*, op. cit. (note 165), p. 11.

645. Galenson, op. cit. (note 639), p. 45f.

646. Figures for Denmark: Wilfried Lauritzen and Hans-Erik Rasmussen: *Derfor svigter LO*. Copenhagen, Sorte Fane, 1970, p. 31. For Australia cf. Martin, op. cit. (note 220), p. 46.

647. D. J. Murphy (ed.): *Labor in Politics. The State Labor Parties in Australia 1880-1920*. St Lucia, University of Queensland Press, 1975, p. 9.

648. Henry Pelling: *A Short History of the Labour Party*. London, Macmillan, 1961, Chapter 5.

649. Sampson, op. cit. (note 351), p. 101; Robertson and Sams, op. cit. (note 171), Vol. 2, p. 513 (text of the agreement).

650. David Coates: *The Labour Party and the Struggle for Socialism*. Cambridge UP, 1975, pp. 218ff.

651. Varain, op. cit. (note 548), p. 153.

652. Filip Kota: *Deux lignes opposées dans le mouvement syndical mondial.* Paris, nbe, 1974, pp. 20ff.

653. *Kongress Stuttgart*, op. cit. (note 79), p. 106.

654. Ibidem, p. 108.

655. Ibidem, p. 108.

656. Dieter Piel: 'Die zwei Seelen der "Urbaniaks". SPD-Abgeordnete müssen im Bundestag oft gegen ihre gewerkschaftliche Überzeugung stimmen', *Die Zeit*, No. 13, 1976, p. 17.

657. On the local level: B. Vogel and P. Haungs: *Wahlkampf und Wählertradition*. Cologne, Westdeutscher Verlag, 1964, p. 343.

658. Cf. Klaus von Beyme: *Das politische System der Bundesrepublik Deutschland.* Munich, Piper, 1979, pp. 68ff and the quoted literature.

659. *Parteitag Mannheim*, op. cit. (note 395), p. 132.

660. *Orientierungsrahmen*, op. cit. (note 533), p. 59, col. 1.

661. Quoted in: Serge Mallet: *Die neue Arbeiterklasse*. Neuwied, Luchterhand, 1972, p. 311.

662. Adam and Reynaud, op. cit. (note 465), p. 27.

663. 'La CFDT et l'union des forces populaires. Jan. 1974', in CFDT: *Textes de base*. Paris, 1975, p. 109. For the following cf.: Jacques Capdevielle and Roland Cayrol: 'Les groupes d'entreprise du PSU', *Revue francaise de science politique*, 1972 (89-109), p. 106.

664. Declercq, op. cit. (note 314), pp. 29ff.

665. *Nouvel Oberservateur*, 28 March 1973.

666. Ibidem, 10 June 1974.

667. M. V. Kargalova: Frantsiya: *Profsoyuzy i nauchno-technicheskaya revolyutsia*. Moscow, Nauka, 1975, pp. 49, 53.

668. Roger Garaudy: *Die Alternative*. Vienna, Molden, 1973, p. 196.

669. Adam, op. cit. (note 141), pp. 46, 50.

670. Gheza, op. cit. (note 61), p. 234.

671. Giovanni Bechelloni: 'Sindacati ed elezioni politiche', in: Mattei Dogan and Orazio M. Petracca (eds.): *Partiti politici e strutture sociali in Italia*. Milan, Communità, 1968 (205-248), pp. 225, 234.

672. *VIII Congresso del PCI*. Rome, Editori Riuniti, 1956, quoted in: 'Sindacato e partiti', *Rassegna sindacale, Quaderni*, 1971/72, No. 33/34, p. 99.

673. Krasucki, op. cit. (note 55), p. 114.

674. LAV, op. cit. (note 48), p. 40.

675. Alessandro Pizzorno: 'Les syndicats et l'action politique', *Sociologie du travail*, 1971 (115-141), p. 136.

676. Gorz, op. cit. (note 570), p. 15f.

677. 'Quaderni Rossi', Reprinted in: *Spätkapitalismus und Klassenkampf*. Frankfurt, 1972, p. 115.

678. 'Dichiarazione commune di PCI e PCF', *Unità*, 18 November 1975, pp. 1, 13.

679. Victor Pfaff and Mona Wikhäll (eds.): *Das schwedische Modell der Ausbeutung*. Cologne, Kiepenheuer, 1971, p. 19.

680. Cliff, op. cit. (note 469), p. 17.

681. A. Shonfield: *Modern Capitalism,* Oxford UD, 1965, Chapter 4.

682. Paul Mattick: *Marx und Keynes*. Frankfurt, EVA, 1969, p. 142.

683. Tyndall, op. cit. (note 559), pp. 138ff; H. A. Turner and H. Zoeteweij: *Prices, Wages and Incomes Policies in Industrialized Market Economies*. Geneva, ILO, 1966, p. 108.

684. Peter Wiles: 'Are Trade Unions Necessary?', *Encounter*, September 1956, p. 11.

685. Robert M. Dahl and Charles E. Lindblom: *Politics, Economics and Welfare*. New York, Harper & Row (1953), 1963, p. 484.

686. Gottfried Haberler: *Incomes Policy and Inflation*. Washington, Institute of Economic Affairs, 1972, p. 140; J. E. Meade: *Wages and Prices in a Mixed Economy*. London, 1971.

687. Gottfried Haberler: 'Incomes Policies and Inflation', in: idem et al.: *Wages and Prices in a Mixed Economy*. London, The Institute of Economic Affairs, 1972 (1-72), p. 6.

688. Ibidem, p. 32.

689. *TUC Report 1974*, p. 572.

690. Dudley Jackson et al.: *Do Trade Unions Cause Inflation?* Cambridge UP, 1975, 2nd edition, p. 113f.

691. Gottfried Bombach: *Inflation als wirtschafts- und gesellschaftspolitisches Problem*. Bâle, Kyklos, 1973, p. 9.

692. A. Jones: *The New Inflation*. Harmondsworth, Penguin, 1973, p. 25.

693. OECD: *Inflation. The Present Problem*. Paris, 1970, pp. 36ff.

694. Gottfried Bombach et al.: *Grundkriterien für die Festsetzung der Löhne und damit zusammenhängenden Probleme einer Lohn- und Einkommenspolitik*. Brussels, EEC, 1967, p. 83f.

695. Hans-Adam Pfromm: *Einkommenspolitik und Verteilungskonflikt*. Cologne, Bund-Verlag, 1975, p. 59.

696. UK Council on Prices, Productivity and Incomes: *Third Report*. London, 1959, p. 26.

697. *CGT-Programm*. Luxembourg, 1974, p. 42.

698. 'Spaltung der Finnischen Kommunisten?', *FAZ*, 2 February 1976, p. 4.

699. 'Entscheid für Weiterführung der Preisüberwachung', *NZZ*, 10 September 1976, p. 17.

700. Michael Parkin and Michael T. Sumner (eds.): *Incomes Policy and Inflation*. Manchester, University Press, 1972, pp. 11ff.

701. Kevin Hawkins: 'The Miners and Incomes Policy 1972-1975', *Industrial Relations Journal*, 1975, No. 2 (4-22), p. 21.

702. Eric Schiff: *Incomes Policies Abroad*. Washington DC, American Enterprise Institute, 1971, p. 2.

703. Casten von Otter: 'Entwicklungstendenzen bei den Gewerkschaften in Schweden', *GMH*, 1974, No. 8 (472-485), p. 478.

704. Rudolf Meidner and Berndt Öhman: *Solidarisk lönepolitik*. Stockholm, Tiden, 1972, pp. 54ff.

705. Erik Lundberg: 'Incomes Policy in Sweden', in: *On Incomes Policy. Papers and Proceedings from a Conference in Honour of Erik Lundberg*. Stockholm, Ersette (11-20), p. 20.

706. *Economic Report of the President 1964*. Washington, GPO, 1964, p. 185.

707. Jack Barbash: *Trade Unions and National Economic Policy*. Baltimore, Johns Hopkins, 1972, p. 194.

708. *Incomes Policy. Report of a Conference of Executive Committees of Affiliated Organisations of the TUC. Central Hall, London, March 2*, 1967, p. 5.

709. Hugh Clegg: *How to run an Incomes Policy and Why we Made Such a Mess of the Last One*. London, Heinemann, 1971, p. 82; Frank Blackaby: *An Incomes Policy for Britain*. London, Heinemann, 1972.

710. Panitch, op. cit. (note 590), pp. 41ff.

711. TUC: *The Social Contract 1976-77. Report to a Special Trade Union Congress*. June 1976, p. 10.

712. Gerald A. Dorfman: *Wages Politics in Britain 1945-1967*. Ames, Iowa, The Iowa State UP, 1973, pp. 146ff.

713. James W. Davis, Jr.: *The National Executive Branch*. New York, Free Press, 1970, p. 25.

714. Regina Molitor (ed.): *Zehn Jahre Sachverstandigenrat*. Frankfurt, Athenäum, 1973, p. 4.

715. Allan Fels: *The British Prices and Incomes Board*. Cambridge UP, 1972, p. 16.

716. Haberler, op. cit. (note 687), p. xi.

717. Erich Hoppmann: 'Neue Wettbewerbspolitik', *Jahrbücher für Nationalökonomie und Statistik*, 1970, No. 4, pp. 397ff.

718. Watrin in: Erich Hoppmann (ed.): *Konzertierte Aktion*. Frankfurt, Athenäum, 1971 (201-228), p. 215.

719. Tuchtfeld in Hoppmann, op. cit. (note 718), p. 62.

720. Sachverständigenrat: *Jahresgutachten* (quoted as JG) 1965, 8c.

721. JG 1970, p. 69, § 214.

722. JG 1966, p. 216, Appendix VI.

723. Molitor, op. cit. (note 714), p. 158.

724. JG 1972, p. 160, § 493.

725. Ibidem, pp. 141ff.

726. JG 1975, p. 42, § 65.

727. H. Weitbrecht: *Wirkung und Verfahren der Tarifautonomie*. Baden-Baden, Nomos, 1973, p. 28.

728. Kurt H. Biedenkopf: 'Rechtsfragen der Konzertierten Aktion', *Der Betriebsberater*, 10 September 1968, No. 25, p. 1008.

729. Wilfried Schreiber: *Die gesellschaftlichen Funktionen des Unternehmergewinns*. Cologne, Bund Kath. Unternehmer, 1958, p. 4.

730. Walter Eberle: *Grenzen der Umverteilung*. Cologne, Deutsche Industrieverlags GmbH, 1969, No. 4, p. 11.

731. W. Eichler in: Helmut Arndt (ed.): *Lohnpolitik und Einkommensverteilung*. Berlin, Duncker & Humblot, 1969, pp. 744, 748.

732. 'Absage an die Konzertierte Aktion', *FAZ*, 3 June 1972.

733. H. Adam: *Die Konzertierte Aktion in der Bundesrepublik*. Cologne, Bund-Verlag, 1972, p. 31.

734. Leminsky and Otto, op. cit. (note 347), p. 270.

735. JG 1967, p. 155, § 373; JG 1970, pp. 71ff.

736. JG 1970, p. 72, § 232.

737. JG 1964, § 248.

738. E. Hennig: *Zur Kritik der Konzertierten Aktion. Blätter für deutsche und internationale Politik*, 1970, pp. 580ff.

739. *FAZ*, 16 January 1975, 14 February 1975, p. 11.

740. Rolf Seitenzahl: *Einkommenspolitik durch Konzertierte Aktion und Orientierungsdaten*. Dissertation, Cologne, 1973, pp. 72ff, 102.

741. Heinz-Dieter Hardes: *Einkommenspolitik in der BRD*. Frankfurt, Herder & Herder, 1974, pp. 119ff.

742. Karl-Heinz Nassmacher: *Das österreichische Regierungssystem*. Cologne, Westdeutscher Verlag, 1969, p. 104; Werner Lang: *Kooperative Gewerkschaften und Einkommenspolitik. Das Beispiel Österreichs*. Berne, Lang, 1978.

743. Benya, op. cit. (note 71), p. 30.

744. Alfred Klose: *Ein Weg zur Sozialpartnerschaft. Das österreichische Modell*. Munich, Oldenbourg, 1970, pp. 46ff.

745. H. P. Secher: 'Representative Democracy or "Chamber State"?', *The Western Political Quarterly*, 1960, pp. 890-909.

746. H. Suppanz and D. Robinson: *Prices and Incomes Policy. The Austrian Experience*. Paris, OECD, 1972, p. 54f.

747. G. Chaloupek and H. Swoboda: 'Sozialpartnerschaft und Wirtschaftsentwicklung in den fünfziger und sechziger Jahren', *Österreichische Zeitschrift für Politikwiss*, 1975, No. 3 (333-343), p. 342.

748. Hermann Albeck: *Stabilisierungspolitik mit Entscheidungsmodellen. Das Beispiel der niederländischen Lohn- und Finanzpolitik*. Tübingen, Mohr, 1969, pp. 239ff.

749. Stanislaw Wellisz: 'Economic Planning in the Netherland, France and Italy', *Journal of Political Economy*, 1960, No. 3 (252-283), p. 256.

750. *Das Königreich der Niederlande*. The Hague. Ministerium für auswärtige Angelegenheiten, n.d. (*ca.* 1974), p. 18.

751. Jan Pen: 'Trade Union Attitudes Toward Central Wage Policy', in: Adolf Sturmthal and James G. Scoville (eds.): *The International Labor Movement in Transition*. Urbana, Ill., University of Illinois Press, 1973 (259-282), p. 282.

752. *Information bulletin of the Netherlands Federation of Trade Unions*, No. 107, August 1975, p. 12.

753. 'Lohndiktat der holländischen Regierung', *NZZ*, 17 July 1976, p. 13.

754. Pfromm, op. cit. (note 695), p. 92.

755. *Donovan Report*, op. cit. (note 85), p. 36f; Campbell Balfour: *Industrial Relations in the Common Market*. London, Routledge & Kegan Paul, 1972, p. 13.

756. Lewin, op. cit. (note 268), p. 131.

757. H. Gutermuth: *Referat auf dem 8. ord. Gewerkschaftstag der IG Bergbau und Energie. Wiesbaden, 13-18 September 1964*, p. 9.

758. JG 1969, p. 22, § 65.

759. Helmut Meinhold: 'Das Dilemma unserer Lohnpolitik', *Die Zeit*, 17 December 1965, p. 36.

760. JG 1974, p. 63, § 131.

761. Cliff, op. cit. (note 469), p. 217.

762. E. Streissler et al.: *Möglichkeiten und Grenzen einer produktivitätsorientierten Lohnpolitik*. Vienna. Österreichisches Institut für Wirtschaftsforschung, 1960, pp. 15ff.

763. *On Incomes Policy*, op. cit. (note 705), p. 227.

764. Ibidem, p. 236f.

765. JG 1970, p. 72, § 234.

766. Viktor Agartz: 'Die Lohnpolitik der deutschen Gewerkschaften', *GMH*, 1950, pp. 441-447.

767. Rainer Skiba: *Die gewerkschaftliche Lohnpolitik und die Entwicklung der Reallöhne*. Dissertation, Cologne, 1965, p. 126.

768. Elisabeth Noelle and Erich Peter Neumann (eds.): *Jahrbuch der öffentlichen Meinung 1968-1973*. Allensbach, Verlag für Demoskopie, 1974, p. 363.

769. Gottfried Bombach: 'Möglichkeiten und Grenzen einer Verteilungspolitik', in: Helmut Arndt (ed.): *Lohnpolitik und Einkommensverteilung*. Berlin, Duncker & Humblot, 1969 (809-837), p. 825.

770. Bernhard Gahlen: 'Verteilungskampf und Reformpolitik', *GMH*, 1973, No. 9 (524-534), p. 529.

771. Rudolf Henschel: 'Kritik der gewerkschaftlichen Verteilungsvorstellungen', *GMH*, 1973, No. 9, pp. 535-542.

772. JG 1970, p. 71, § 231.

773. JG 1970, p. 72, § 234.

774. JG 1973, p. 124, § 340.

775. JG 1973, p. 137, § 381.

776. Jean-Pierre Gern: *L'indexation des salaires*. Neuchâtel, Thèse, Imprimerie Moser & Fils, 1961, pp. 44ff.

777. *Die Zeit*, 1975, No. 43, p. 19.

778. Lundberg, op. cit. (note 705), p. 19.

779. *CGT Programm*. Luxembourg, 1974, p. 43.

780. Deutscher Gewerkschaftsbund: *Kritische Betrachtungen zur gleitenden Lohnskala*. Berlin-Wilmersdorf, Christlicher Gewerkschaftsverlag, 1922, p. 4.

781. Oscar-Erich Kunze: *Preiskontrollen, Lohnkontrollen und Lohn-Preis-Indexbindung in den europäischen Ländern*. Berlin, Duncker & Humblot, 1973, p. 195f.

782. Bruno Molitor: *Verteilungspolitik in Perspektive*. Hamburg, Verlag Weltarchiv, 1975, p. 39.

783. Cassau, op. cit. (note 77), p. 222.

784. Wilhelm Krelle et al.: *Überbetriebliche Ertragsbeteiligung der Arbeitnehmer*. Tübingen, Mohr, 1968, Vol. 2, p. 481.

785. DAG: *Forderungen zur Beteiligung der Arbeitnehmer am Produktivvermögen*. Hamburg, 1970, pp. 13ff.

786. '450,000 Arbeitnehmer sind Belegschaftsaktionäre', *FAZ*, 29 January 1976, p. 12.

787. *Die Zeit*, 1976, No. 8, p. 23.

788. *FAZ*, 3 March, 1976, p. 12.

789. Ulrich Steger: 'Warum ist die BDA für Vermögensbildung?', *GMH*, 1972, No. 4 (234-241), pp. 235ff.

790. *Gewerkschaften zur Vermögensbildung*. Frankfurt, Verlag Marxistische Blätter, 1974, p. 33.

791. *Protokoll des Wirtschaftstages der CDU/CSU*. Bonn 1969, p. 169.

792. *Jahresbericht der BDA, 1 December 1964-30 November 1965*. Bergisch-Gladbach, n.d., pp. 50ff.

793. Georg Leber: *Vermögensbildung in Arbeitnehmerhand. Ein Programm und sein Echo*. Frankfurt, EVA, 1974, p. 19.

794. Leminsky and Otto, op. cit. (note 347), p. 172, col. 2.

795. Michael Jungblut: *Nicht vom Lohn allein. Elf Modelle für Mitbestimmung und Gewinnbeteiligung*. Hamburg, Hoffmann & Campe, 1973, p. 183f.

796. Hermann Adam: *Macht und Vermögen in der Wirtschaft*. Cologne, Bund-Verlag, 1974, p. 70.

797. Herbert Ehrenberg: *Vermögenspolitik für die siebziger Jahre*. Stuttgart, Kohlhammer, 1971, p. 89; Adam, op. cit. (note 796), p. 83.

798. Karl Neumann: *Vermögensbildung und Vermögenspolitik*. Cologne, EVA, 1976, pp. 99ff.

799. 'Holländische Pläne für betriebliche Vermögenszuwachsverteilung', *NZZ*, 22 May 1975, p. 15. Kommission der EG: *Mitbestimmung der Arbeitnehmer und Struktur der Gesellschaften in der EG*. Luxembourg, 1975, p. 157.

800. Benya, op. cit. (note 71), p. 55.

801. *Löntagarfonder och kapitalbildning. Förslag fran LO-SAPs arbeitsgrupp*. Stockholm, 1978, pp. 36ff. 'Meidners socialism', *Dagens Nyheter*, 1975, August 31, p. 2.

802. *Motioner. LO Kongress 1976*. Stockholm, p. 299.

803. LO: *The Danish Trade Union Movement*. Copenhagen, 1977, p. 9.

804. Less negative is the evaluation of some British models on the basis of the Common Ownership Act in: John Elliott: *Conflict or Cooperation? The Growth of Industrial Democracy*, London, Kogan Page, 1978, pp. 192ff.

805. *Capital and Equality*. London, 1973.

806. In a TUC Paper on 'Distribution on Income and Wealth', London, n.d., the Swedish solution was not even mentioned.

807. Taylor, op. cit. (note 201), p. 36.

808. Hans-Dieter Küller: 'Vor einer Tendenzwende in der Vermögenspolitik', *Die Quelle*, 1978 (17-19), p. 18.

809. Paul Blumberg: *Industrial Democracy. The Sociology of Participation*. New York, Schocken, 1969, p. 129.

810. William Garcin: *Cogestion et participation dans les entreprises des pays du marché commun*. Paris, Editions Jupiter, 1968, p. 293.

811. Vilmar, op. cit. (note 569).

812. Wolfgang Daübler: *Das Grundrecht auf Mitbestimmung*. Frankfurt, EVA, 1973, pp. 129ff.

813. Udo Mayer: *Paritätische Mitbestimmung und Arbeitsverhältnis*. Cologne, 1976, p. 54.

814. Stan Poppe: 'Mitbestimmung in den Niederlanden', *Amsterdam, NVV*, January 1975, p. 3.

815. Ken Coates and Tony Topham: *The New Unionism. The Case for Workers' Control*. Harmondsworth, Penguin, 1974, p. 56.

816. Jean Bancal: *Proudhon, pluralisme et autogestion*. Paris, Aubier-Montaigne, 1970.

817. Yvon Bourdet: *Pour l'autogestion*. Paris, Anthropos, 1974, pp. 10ff.

818. Declercq, op. cit. (note 314), p. 56.

819. Daniel Chauvey: *Autogestion*. Paris, Seuil, 1970, pp. 244ff.

820. Maurice Montculard: 'Autogestion et dialectique', *Autogestion et socialisme*, October 1974/January 1975, Nos. 28/29, pp. 27-60; G. Lapassade: *L'autogestion pédagogique*. Paris, Gauthiers-Villars, 1971.

821. M. Drulovic: *L'autogestion à l'épreuve*. Paris, Fayard, 1973, p. xvf.

822. Olivier Corpet: 'Le socialisme yougoslave entre la bureaucratie et l'autogestion', *Autogestion et socialisme*, March/June 1975, Nos. 30/31, pp. 5-12.

823. Ernest Mandel (ed.): *Arbeiterkontrolle, Arbeiterräte, Arbeiterselbstverwaltung*. Frankfurt, EVA, 1971, p. 32f.

824. 'La gauche, l'extrême-gauche et l'autogestion', *Autogestion et socialisme*, January/March 1973, pp. 165.ff.

825. Krasucki, op. cit. (note 55), p. 25; Maire, op. cit. (note 313), p. 87.

826. Jean-Pierre Oppenheim: *La CFDT et la Planification*. Paris, Tema action, 1973, Christian Pierre and Lucien Praire: *Plan et autogestion*. Paris, Flammarion, 1976.

827. Jacques Brault: *Droits des salariés et autogestion. Des propositions concrètes*. Paris, Tema action, 1975, p. 114.

828. Krasucki, op. cit. (note 55), p. 45.

829. A. Detraz et al.: *La CFDT et l'autogestion*. Paris, Editions du Cerf, 1975, p. 7; Declercq, op. cit. (note 314), p. 26f.

830. CFDT: *Le comité d'entreprise*. Paris, 1975, p. 4.

831. *Autogestion et révolution socialiste*. Paris, Editions Syros, 1973, p. 51.

832. Ken Coates and Tony Topham: *Industrial Democracy in Great Britain*. London, 1968; Ernie Roberts: *Workers' Control*. London, Allen & Unwin, 1973, pp. 29ff.

833. Leo Trotzki: *Was nun?* Berlin, 1932, p. 101.

834. FGTB, op. cit. (note 332).

835. Ibidem, p. 10.

836. Coates and Topham, op. cit. (note 832), p. 361f.

837. Rudolf Kuda: *Arbeiterkontrolle in Großbritannien*. Frankfurt, Suhrkamp, 1970, p. 76f.

838. Webb, op. cit. (note 385).

839. Coates, op. cit. (note 494), p. 232.

840. Frank Deppe et al.: *Kritik der Mitbestimmung*. Frankfurt, Suhrkamp, 1972, 3rd edition, pp. 254ff.

841. Autorenkollektiv des IMSF: *Mitbestimmung als Kampfaufgabe*. Cologne, Pahl-Rugenstein, 1972, 2nd edition, pp. 62, 279, 267.

842. Karlheinz Nagels and Arndt Sorge: *Industrielle Demokratie in Europa*. Frankfurt, Campus, 1977, pp. 122ff.

843. *Demokrati pa arbetsplatsen*, op. cit. (note 515), p. 132.

844. G. Leminsky: 'Der Mitbestimmungsvorschlag der Koalition', *GMH*, 1976, No. 3 (129-134), p. 133.

845. P. Badura et al.: *Mitbestimmungsgesetz 1976 und Grundgesetz*. Munich, 1977.

846. 'Der aktuelle Stand in den verfassungsrechtlichen Auseinandersetzungen um das Mitbestimmungsgesetz 1976', *GMH*, 1978, pp. 297-300.

847. Adam, op. cit. (note 141), p. 49.

848. Maurice Montuclard: *La dynamique des comités d'entreprise*. Paris, CNRS, 1963, p. 498.

849. CFDT: *Le comité d'entreprise*. Paris, 1975, p. 4.
850. *Bundesgesetzblatt für die Republik Österreich*. 15 Jänner 1974, pp. 393-424.
851. *Mitbestimmungsprogramm des SGB*. Separatum, n.d. (*ca*. 1973). SGB: *Mitbestimmung, Mitbestimmungsinitiative. Gegenvorschlag*. Referentenführer des SGB, Berne, September 1975.
852. 'Was steht mit welcher Art Mitbestimmung auf dem Spiel', *NZZ*, 27 January 1976, p. 11.
853. 'Absage an die gewerkschaftliche Mitbestimmungsideologie', *NZZ*, 23 March 1976, p. 9.
854. *Ein Mensch ist mehr als ein Rädchen im Betrieb*. Berne, SGB, n.d., p. 6.
855. SGB: *Tätigkeitsbericht 1972, 1973, 1974*. Berne, 1975, p. 91.
856. Peter Isler: 'Das nie derländische Mitbestimmungsmodell', *NZZ*, 4 November 1975, p. 27; SGB: *Tätigkeitsbericht 1975, 1976, 1977*. Berne, n.d., p. 92.
857. *Das Königreich der Niederlande*, op. cit. (note 750), p. 11f; E. H. van Gorcum: *Industrial Democracy in the Netherlands*. Mappel, Boon en Zoon, 1969.
858. Stewart, op. cit. (note 98), p. 63.
859. *Beleidsprogram '76-'77*. NVV, NKV, CNV, 1976, p. 3, col. 3.
860. 'Die Ansichten des Industrieverbond NVV im Bezug auf Betriebsräte und Aufsichtsräte der Arbeitnehmerseite', *Amsterdam, NVV*, November 1975, p. 20.
861. *CGT-Programm*. Luxembourg, 1974, p. 35.
862. *Gesetz vom 6. Mai 1974 über die Einführung gemischter Betriebsausschüsse in den Betrieben der Privatwirtschaft und über die Vertretung der Arbeitnehmer in den Verwaltungsräten der anonymen Gesellschaft*. Luxembourg, Conseil National des Syndicats, 1974.
863. Fritz Vilmar (ed): *Menschwenwürde im Betrieb*. Reinbek, Rowohlt, 1973.
864. *Betriebsdemokratie. Programm des schwedischen Gewerkschaftsbundes*. Stockholm, Tiden, 1971, p. 12.
865. *Demokrati i företagen. Rapport till LO-Kongressen 1971*. Stockholm, Prisma, 1971, p. 11; Sten Edlund and Per Eklund: *Rätt och arbetsgivarmakt*. Stockholm, Prisma, 1974, p. 74.
866. Ibid.
867. Aake Anker-Ording: *Betriebsdemokratie*. Frankfurt, EVA, 1969, pp. 110ff.
868. *Der Spiegel*, 1975, No. 42, p. 165.
869. 'Mitbestimmung. Modell aus Schweden. Schwedens Premier Olof Palme über seine Mitbestimmungspläne', *Der Spiegel*, 1975, No. 46 (32-38), p. 32.
870. Kampens gang, op. cit. (note 87), pp. 455ff.
871. LO: *Belysning af fagbevaegelsens resultater 1963-1975*. Copenhagen, 1975, p. 44.
872. Coates and Topham, op. cit. (note 815), p. 218.
873. *Donovan Report*, op. cit. (note 85), p. 257f.
874. Bell, op. cit. (note 189), p. 21.
875. TUC: *Industrial Democracy*. London (reprint), 1976, p. 22.
876. Coates and Topham, op. cit. (note 815), p. 150.
877. Eric Batstone and P. L. Davies: *Industrial Democracy. European Experience*. London, HMSO, 1976, p. 53.
878. TUC: *Industrial Democracy*, including supplementary evidence to the Bullock Committee. London, 1977, new edition, p. 47. *Report of the Committee of Inquiry on Industrial Democracy* (*Chairman Lord Bullock*), London, HSMO,

January 1977, pp. 37ff. Elliott, op. cit. (note 804), pp. 241ff.

879. ICTU: *Submission to Minister for Labour on Statute for the European Company proposed by the European Commission*. Dublin, June 1973, p. 3; ICTU: *Statement by Executive Council on the Election of Employees to the Boards of State Enterprises*. Dublin, January 1976, p. 3.

880. Commission of the European Communities: 'Statute for European companies', *Bulletin of the European Communities*, Supplement 4, 1975.

881. Leminsky and Otto, op. cit. (note 347), p. 156f.

882. *Strumenti*, op. cit. (note 37), pp. 21, 35.

883. D'Agostini, op. cit. (note 193), pp. 171, 183.

884. Antonio Gramsci: 'Sindacati e Consigli' (1920), in: idem: *Scritti politici* (note 32) (338-342), p. 339.

885. Aldo Forbice and Emilio Chiaberge: *Il sindacato dei consigli*. Verona, Bertani, 1974, pp. 91ff, 97.

886. Laura Luppi and Emilio Reyneri: *Lotte operaie e sindacato in Italia: 1968-1972. Vol. 1: Autobianchi e Innocenti*. Bologna, Il Mulino, 1974, pp. 36, 87.

887. R. Agleita et al.: *I delegati operai*. Rome, Coines, 1970, p. 87f; Romano Alquati: *Sindacato e Partito*. Turin, Stampatori, 1975, pp. 69ff.

888. Ida Regalia and Marino Regini: *Lotte operaie e sindacato in Italia: 1968-1972. Vol. 4 SIT-Siemens e GTE*. Bologna, Il Mulino, 1975, p. 114f.

889. Giuseppe Abbatecola et al: *Lotte operaie e sindacato in Italia: 1968-1972. Vol. 5. Dalmine, Falck, Redaelli*. Bologna, Il Mulino, 1975, p. 86f.

890. Taliani, op. cit. (note 569), p. 215.

891. SPD: *Protokoll des Gosberger Parteitages*. 1959, p. 212.

892. 'Jeder vierte Unternehmer für Mitbestimmung', *FAZ*, 7 January 1976, p. 9.

893. Adam, op. cit. (note 141), p. 54.

894. *Protokoll der Verhandlungen des 8. Kongresses der Gewerkschaften Deutschlands, abgehalten zu Dresden am 26 Juni und 4 Juli 1911*. Berlin, Verlag der Generalkommission der Gewerkschaften Deutschlands, 1911, p. 54.

895. Jürgen Peters: *Arbeitnehmerkammern in der BRD*. Munich, Olzog, 1973, p. 47.

896. *CGT-Programm*. Luxembourg, 1974, p. 31.

897. *FAZ*, 31 March, 1970.

898. *GMH*, 1973, No. 3, pp. 154-162.

899. Hans Bayer (ed.): *Stellung der Arbeitnehmer in der modernen Wirtschaftspolitik*. Berlin, Duncker & Humblot, 1959, pp. 71-75.

900. Uncritical: Klose, op. cit. (note 744).

901. Dieter Mronz: *Körperschaften und Zwangsmitgliedschaft*. Berlin, Duncker & Humblot, 1973.

902. Brun-Otto Bryde: *Zentrale wirtschaftspolitische Beratungsgremien in der parlamentarischen Verfassungsordnung*. Frankfurt, Metzner, 1972, pp. 146, 148.

903. Jean Meynaud: *Les groupes de pression en France*. Paris, Colin, 1958, p. 218.

904. CNV: *Christian Trade Unionism in the Netherlands*. Utrecht, n.d. (1975), p. 11.

905. Bram Peper (ed.): *De Nederlands arbeidsverhoudingen*. Rotterdam, Universitaire Pers, 1973, p. 38.

906. R. Geberth: *Bundeswirtschaftsrat und Conseil économique*. Dissertation, Mainz, 1966.

907. Günter Triesch: 'Keine wirtschaftsdemokratische Sekundärverfassung', *GMH*, 1967, p. 539.

908. Leminsky and Otto, op. cit. (note 347), pp. 150ff.

909. Seitenzahl, op. cit. (note 740), p. 182.

910. Paul Feyerabend: *Against Method*. Frankfurt, Suhrkamp, 1976, p. 249.

911. Ibidem, pp. 252ff.

912. Shorter and Tilly, op. cit. (note 409), pp. 306-334.

913. Turner, op. cit. (note 301), p. 232.

914. J. H. Goldthorpe: 'Die britische Arbeitskampfverfassung', *Leviathan*, 1974, No. 2 (479-500), p. 500.

915. 'Arbeitnehmer haben die stärkeren Bataillone', *Der Spiegel*, 1973, pp. 42-48.

916. Frankfurter Projektgruppe, op. cit. (note 5), p. 118.

917. Noelle-Neumann (ed.), op. cit. (note 768), p. 350; Taylor, op. cit. (note 201), p. xi.

918. *Der Arbeitgeber*, 1974, No. 6, p. 187.

919. Günter Triesch: *Gewerkschaftsstaat oder sozialer Rechtsstaat?* Stuttgart, Seewald, 1974, pp. 12ff.

920. Hanns Martin Schleyer: 'Gesetzesvorhaben von ordnungssprengender Dimension', *Der Arbeitgeber*, 1974, No. 7, p. 224.

921. Mitbestimmung: 'Doppelvorteil, Halbsozialisierung', *Der Arbeitgeber*, 1974, No. 17, p. 638.

922. Wolf Donner: *Die sozial- und staatspolitische Tätigkeit der Kriegsopferverbände*. Berlin, Duncker & Humblot, 1960, p. 187.

923. Karl Hauenschild: 'Weder Ersatzpartei noch Parteiersatz; *GMH*, 1976, No. 8, pp. 498-503.

924. Alan Cawson: 'Pluralism, Corporatism and the Role of the State', *Government and Opposition*, 1978 (187-199), p. 187.

925. Ruin, op. cit. (note 562); Kvavik, op. cit. (note 643), pp. 124f. Nils Elvander: 'Vad är korporatism', in: idem (ed.): *Demokrati och socialism*. Stockholm, 1975, pp. 181ff. Agne Gustafsson (ed.): *Företagsdemokratin och den offentliga sektorn*. Lund, Studentilitteratur, 1978, p. 14.

926. Philippe Schmitter: 'Modes of Interest Intermediation and Models for Societal Change in Western Europe', *Comparative Political Studies*, 1977, No. 1, pp. 7-38.

927. Colin Crouch: *Class Conflict and the Industrial Relations Crisis. Compromise and Corporatism in the Policies of the British State*. London, Heinemann, 1977, p. 262.

928. Giuseppe Di Palma: *Surviving without Governing. The Italian Parties in Parliament*. University of California Press, 1977, p. 265.

929. Lama and Manghi, op. cit. (note 76), p. 33.

930. Bertrand Badie: *Strategie de la grève*. Paris, Presses de la Fondation Nationale des sciences politiques, 1976, p. 15, pp. 158ff.

931. C. Kerr: *Industrial Relations and the Liberal Pluralist. Proceedings of the 7th Annual Winter Meeting of the Industrial Relations Research Associations*. 28-30 December 1954. Madison, 1954, p. 12.

932. Alan Fox: *Beyond Contract: Worker, Power and Trust Relations*. London, Faber & Faber, 1974, pp. 255ff.

933. Rainer Zoll: *Der Doppelcharakter der Gewerkschaften*. Frankfurt, Suhrkamp, 1976, p. 7.

Bibliography

I. Sources on the organization and programmes of trade unions and governmental sources on labour relations.

Austria

Achter Bundeskongreß des ÖGB. Wien, 15.-19. September 1975. Vienna, ÖGB, 1975.

Arbeitsverfassungsgesetz. Bundesgesetz für die Republik Österreich. 15. Januar 1974. Vienna.

BENYA, Anton: *Gewerkschaften in der Gesellschaft von heute.* Vienna, Verlag des ÖGB, 1975.

Kurzbericht. Information über die Arbeit des ÖGB. 1971-1974. Vienna, ÖGB, n.d.

Der Österreichische Gewerkschaftsbund. Vienna, ÖGB, 1974.

ÖGB-Rednerdienste. Vienna, ÖGB, 1975, Folge 1-8, 1976.

Statuten des Österreichischen Gewerkschaftsbundes (Fassung gemäß Beschluß durch den 7. Bundeskongreß des ÖGB vom 20. bis 24.9.1971). Vienna, ÖGB.

Vernunft in Arbeitswelt und Wirtschaft. Die Wirtschafts und Sozialpartnerschaft in Österreich. Vienna, Staatsdruckerei, n.d.

Belgium

ABVV: *Interne organisatie.* Brussels, May 1978.

ABVV: *Statutair Kongres. Aktivitetsverslag.* Brussels, 1975.

ABVV: *voor het voetlicht.* Brussels, n.d.

COATES, Ken (ed.): *A Trade Union Strategy in the Common Market. The Programme of the Belgian Trade Unions. A Translation of the Report of the FGTB on Workers' Control with Explanatory Documents.* Nottingham, Spokesman Books, 1971.

Connaître la CSC. Brussels, September 1977.

CSC: *Conférence de presse.* Brussels, September 1978.

CSC: *Statuts de la CSC.* Brussels, n.d.

DEBUNNE, G.: *Naar en socialistische maatschappij. Nota aan ABVV.* Limburg, 1977.

Democratisation de l'entreprise. Brussels, Editions CSC, 1971.

FGTB: *Congrès contrôle ouvrier.* Brussels, October 1970.

Flash sur la fgtb. Brussels, n.d. (1974), 1977.

Plan fgtb 1976-1980. Brussels, n.d. (1976).

Denmark

HANSEN, J. F.: *Okonomisk demokrati*. Separatum. Copenhagen, 1978.
KOCH-OLSEN, Ib (Red.): *Kampens Gang. LO gennem 75 ar 1898-1973*. Copenhagen, Landsorganisationen i Danmark, 1973.
LAURITZEN, Wilfried and Hans-Erik RASMUSSEN: *Derfor svigter LO*. Copenhagen, Sorte Fane, 1970.
LO: *Belysning af fagbevaegelsens resultater 1963-1975*. Copenhagen, 1975.
LO: *Beretning 1975*.
LO: *Beretning 1976*.
LO: *The Danish Trade Union Movement*. n.d.

Finland

The Central Organization of Finnish Trade Unions (*SAK*). Helsinki, n.d. (mimeo).
Finlands Fackförbunds Centralorganisation: *Principprogram*. Helsinki, 1974.
Proposal of the Executive Committee of the Central Organization of Finnish Trade Unions (SAK) in the 10th General Congress.
SAK: *Affiliated Unions*. Helsinki, 1975 (mimeo).

France

ADRIEUX, Andrée and Jean LIGNON: *Le militant syndicaliste d'aujourd'hui*. Paris, Denoël Gonthier, 1973.
'Autogestion et révolution socialiste'. Rencontre nationale organisée par les revues: *Autogestion et socialisme, Critique socialiste, Objectif Socialiste, Politique Aujourd'hui*. Paris, January 1973.
Autogestion et socialisme, 1973, No. 22/23: 'La gauche, L'extrême gauche et l'autogestion'.
CAPDEVIELLE, Jacques and René MOURIAUX: *Les syndicats ouvriers en France*. Paris, Colin,[2] 1973 (Collection of documents).
CFDT: *aujourd'hui, Revue d'action et de reflexion*, 1976, January/February Dossier spécial: 'Les rapports CFDT-CGT'.
CFDT: *Pratique syndicale: Le comité d'entreprise*. Paris, 1975.
CFDT *s'addresse aux cadres*. Paris, 1977.
CFDT: *Textes de Base*. Paris, 1975.
CFDT: *Textes de Base (2)*. Paris, June 1977.
CGT: *Congrès 37e. Rapports*. Paris, 1969.
CGT: *Congrès 38e. Les documents*. Paris, 1972.
CGT: *Congrès nationale 38e, Nîmes 1972. Rapports, discussions, documents, 18-21 avril 1972*. Paris, 1972.
CGT et l'armée. Paris, n.d. (*ca*. 1976).
CGT: *Le bilan social de l'année 1975*. Paris, 1977.
CGT: *Les militants de la CGT en formation syndicale*. Paris, n.d.
CGT: *La nationalisation industrialisée. Les raisons, la nécessité de sa realisation*. Paris, 1920.

CGT: Paris, January 1978.

CGT: *Statuts. Articles modifiés, adoptés par le 38e congrès Nîmes, 18-22 avril 1972.*

CGT: *Statuts.* Paris, März, 1970.

Contribution à une politique culturelle de la CGT. Paris, n.d. (*ca.* 1977).

DECLERQ, Gilbert: *Syndicaliste en liberté.* Paris, Seuil, 1974.

Di CRESCENZO, Bernard and Jean GIARD: *Les cadres aussi...* Paris, Editions Sociales, 1977.

Elargir les libertés dans l'entreprise. Paris, CFDT, 1977.

Guide pratique et juridique du délégué du personnel. Paris, October 1975.

Hier, aujourd'hui, demain. La CGT. Paris, 1975.

La hiérarchie. Paris, CFDT, June 1977.

KRASUCKI, Henri: *Syndicats et socialisme.* Paris, Editions Sociales, 1972.

'Lettres ouvertes à Georges Séguy. Réponses à 65 questions'. Supplément au *Peuple*, No. 960, 15 February 1975.

MAGNIADAS, Jean et al.: *Les militants de la CGT en formation syndicale.* Paris, CGT, n.d.

MAIRE, Edmond: *Pour un socialisme democratique. Contribution de la CFDT.* Paris, Epi, 1971.

MAIRE, Edmond and Jacques JUILLIARD: *La CFDT d'aujourd'hui.* Paris, Seuil, 1975.

MAIRE, Edmond, Alfred KRUMNOW and Albert DETRAZ: *La CFDT et l'autogestion.* Paris, Editions du Cerf, 1975.

'Memento juridique des agents de la fonction publique et des agents des collectivités locales'. Paris, *Le droit ouvrier, Revue juridique de la CGT*, Supplement 1972.

Perspectives et problèmes de l'énergie. Paris, November 1977, 2nd edition.

Plate-forme CFDT. Plan & nationalisations. Paris, 1978.

Positions et orientations de la CFDT. Paris, 1978.

SÉGUY, Georges: *Lutter.* Paris, Stock, 1975.

Le syndicat. Paris, CFDT, 1978.

'Les syndicats sont-ils représentatifs?' *Le Nouvel Économiste.* No. 155/44-78, 1978, pp. 44-53 (Interviews with Séguy, Maire and Bergeron).

Germany

ADAM, Hermann: *Macht und Vermögen in der Wirtschaft.* Cologne, Bund-Verlag, 1974.

BRENNER, Otto: *Gewerkschaftliche Dynamik in unserer Zeit.* Frankfurt, EVA, 1966. *Aus Reden und Aufsätzen.* Frankfurt, EVA, 1972.

DAG: *Forderungen zur Novellierung des Betriebsverfassungsgesetzes und Entschließung zum Bericht der Mitbestimmungskommission (Biedenkopf-Kommission).* Hamburg, 1970.

DAG: *Forderungen für leitende und wissenschaftliche Angestellte.* Hamburg, 1970.

DAG: *Forderungen zur Beteiligung der Arbeitnehmer am Produktivivermögen.* Hamburg, 1970.

DAG: *9. Bundeskongreß (ff.), Tagungsbericht.* Hamburg, 1967 (ff.).

DBB: *Ursprung, Weg, Ziel. Zur 50. Wiederkehr des Gründungstages am 4. Dezember 1918.* Bad Godesberg, Beamten-Verlags-GmbH, 1968.

DBB: *Zehn Jahre Deutscher Beamtenbund 1949-1959*. Cologne, 1959.

DGB: *Geschäftsbericht 1962-1965* (ff.). Düsseldorf, 1965 (ff.).

DGB: *Protokoll des Bundeskongresses* (starting with: a.o. Bundeskongreß Düsseldorf 1963). Düsseldorf, 1963ff.

Gewerkschaften zur Vermögensbildung. Dokumente und Materialien. Frankfurt, Institut für Marxistische Studien und Forschungen, 1974.

BORSDORF, U. et al (eds.) *Gewerkschaftliche Politik: Reform aus Solidarität. Zum 60. Geburtstag von Heinz O. Vetter*. Cologne, Bund-Verlag, 1977.

Gewerkschaftsbarometer 1974/75 (mimeo).

'Gewerkschaftstheorie heute. Referate und Diskussionsbeiträge einer öffentlichen Tagung der DGB-Bundesschule Bad Kreuznach'. Sonderdruck aus *GMH*, June-July, 1970.

HERNEKAMP, Karl (ed.): *Arbeitskampf. Aktuelle Dokumente*. Berlin, De Gruyter, 1975.

HIRCHE, Kurt: *Die Finanzen der Gewerkschaften*. Düsseldorf, Econ, 1972.

HOCHGÜRTEL, Gerhard and Barbara STEIGLER: *Die Aufgaben des DGB an der Basis. Zum Berufsbild des DGB-Sekretärs*. Bonn, Verlag Neue Gesellschaft, 1978.

KITTNER, Michael: *Arbeits- und Sozialordnung. Ausgewählte und eingeleitete Gesetzestexte*. Cologne, Bund-Verlag, 1977.

KITTNER, Michael (ed.): *Streik und Aussperrung. Protokoll der wissenschaftlichen Veranstaltung der IG Metall vom 13 bis 15 September 1973 in München*. Frankfurt/Cologne, EVA, 1974.

Krise und Reform in der Industriegesellschaft. Protokoll der IG Metall-Tagung (Red. H.-A. PFROMM). Frankfurt, IG Metall, 1976, 2 vols.

LEMINSKY, Gerhard and Bernd OTTO: *Politik und Programmatik des Deutschen Gewerkschaftsbundes*. Cologne, Bund-Verlag, 1974.

LIESEGANG, Helmut C. F. (ed.): *Gewerkschaften in der Bundesrepublik Deutschland. Dokumente zur Stellung und Aufgabe der Gewerkschaften in Staat und Gesellschaft*. Berlin, De Gruyter, 1975.

Die Mitbestimmung der Arbeitnehmer. Der Bundesminister für Arbeit und Sozialordnung, Bonn, 1974.

NICKEL, Walter: *Zum Verhältnis von Arbeiterschaft und Gewerkschaft*. Cologne, Bund-Verlag, 1974.

PITZ, Karl H. (ed.): *Das Nein zur Vermögenspolitik. Gewerkschaftliche Argumente und Alternativen zur Vermögensbildung*. Reinbek, Rowohlt, 1974.

Protokoll: 3 Außerordentlicher Bundeskongreß Düsseldorf 14 bis 15 Mai 1971.

PULTE, Peter: *Vermögensbildung, Vermögensverteilung*. Berlin, De Gruyter, 1973.

ROSENBERG, Ludwig: *Entscheidungen für morgen. Gewerkschaftspolitik heute*. Düsseldorf, Econ, 1969.

SCHOLZ, Rupert: *Das Grundrecht der Koalitionsfreiheit anhand ausgewählter Entscheidungen zur Rechtsstellung von Gewerkschaften und Arbeitgeberverbänden*. Stuttgart, Boorberg, 1972.

SCHWERDTFEGER, Günther (ed.): *Mitbestimmung in privaten Unternehmen*. Berlin, De Gruyter, 1973.

SEITENZAHL, Rolf: *Gewerkschaften zwischen Kooperation und Konflikt. Von einer quantitativen Tariflohnpolitik zur umfassenden Verteilungspolitik*. Cologne, EVA, 1976.

SEITENZAHL, Rolf et al.: *Vorteilsregelungen für Gewerkschaftsmitglieder*. Cologne, Bund-Verlag, 1976.

VETTER, Heinz O. *Christian Götz befragt und portraitiert den Vorsitzenden des Deutschen Gewerkschaftsbundes*. Cologne, EVA, 1978, 3rd edition.

Great Britain

British Industry Today. Organisation and Production. London, HMSO, 1975.

COATES, Ken and Tony TOPHAM: *The New Unionism. The Case for Workers' Control*. Harmondsworth, Penguin, 1974.

Department of Employment: *The Reform of Collective Bargaining at Plant and Company Level*. London, HMSO, 1971.

Department of Trade (ed.): *Report of the Committee of Inquiry on Industrial Democracy. Chairman Lord Bullock*. London, HMSO, January 1977.

The Distribution of Income and Wealth. London, TUC, 1976.

Employment Protection Act 1975. London, HMSO, 1978 (reprint).

Incomes Policy. Report of a Conference of Executive Committees of Affiliated Organisations of the Trade Unions Congress. Central Hall, London, 2 March, 1967.

Industrial Democracy. A Statement of Policy by the Trade Unions Congress. 1974, 1976 (reprint).

Industrial Democracy. Presented to Parliament by the Prime Minister... London, HMSO, 1978.

Industrial Democracy including supplementary evidence to the Bullock Committee. London, TUC, 1977.

Industrial Relations Bill. Notes and Diagrams. Trade Unions Congress Education Service. London, n.d. (*ca*. 1972).

Industrial Relations. Code of Practice. London, HMSO, 1972.

In Place of Strife. A Policy for Industrial Relations, presented to Parliament by the First Secretary of State and Secretary for Employment and Productivity. London, HMSO, 1969.

Job Security. A Guide for Negotiators. London, TUC, December 1973.

Manpower and Employment in Britain. Trade Unions. London, HMSO, 1978.

McCARTHY, W. E. J.: *Trade Unions. Select Readings*. Harmondsworth, Penguin, 1976.

——— *The Role of the Shop Stewards in British Industrial Relations*. Research Papers 1, Royal Commission of Trade Union and Employers' Associations, HMSO, 1967.

McCARTHY, W. E. J. and S. R. PARKER: *Shop Stewards and Workshop Relations*. Research Papers 10, Royal Commission on Trade Unions and Employers' Associations. London, HMSO, 1968.

Model Rules for the Guidance of Trades Councils. London, TUC, n.d.

Occupations and Conditions of Work. London, HMSO, 1976.

Office of Manpower Economics: Equal Pay. *First Report on the Implementation of the Equal Pay Act 1970*. London, HMSO, 1972.

Paid Release for Union Training. A TUC Guide. London, n.d. (1977).

PARKER, Stanley: *Workplace Industrial Relations 1972. An enquiry carried out on behalf of the Department of Employment*. London, HSMO, 1974.

Reason. The Case against the Government's Proposals on Industrial Relations. TUC, London, n.d.

ROBERTSON, N. and K. I. SAMS (eds.): *British Trade Unionism. Select Documents*. Oxford, Blackwell, 1972, 2 vols.

Royal Commission on Trade Unions and Employers' Associations 1965-1968. London, HMSO, 1968. Reprinted 1975 (frequently mentioned as: Donovan Report).

SINGLETON, Norman: *Industrial Relations Procedures*. Department of Employment, Manpower Paper No. 14. London, HMSO, 1975.

The Social Contract 1976-77. London, TUC, 1976.

Time Off for Union Activities. London, TUC, 1978.

Trade Unions and Labour Relations Act. London, HMSO, 1974.

Trade Union Recognition, CIR Experience. London, HMSO, 1974.

The Trade Union Role in Industrial Policy. Report of a Conference of Affiliated Unions to Discuss the Trade Union Role in Industrial Policy. London, Congress House, October 31, 1977.

TUC: *ABC of the TUC*. London, 1964, revised edition, April 1975.

TUC: *Action on Donovan*. London, 1968.

TUC: *Disputes Principles and Procedures*. London, n.d.

TUC: *Economic Policy and Collective Bargaining in 1973. Report of a Special TUC. London, March 1973.*

TUC: *Economic Review 1978*. London, 1978 (and earlier issues).

TUC: *Facilities for Shop Stewards. A Statement of Policy*. London, 1971, 1975.

TUC: *Labour Party Liaison Committee: Into the Eighties: An Agreement*. London, July 1978.

TUC: *Non-Manual Workers. 36th Conference Report*. London, December 1972.

TUC: *Report 1974*, London, 1975; *Report 1975*, London, 1976, *1977*, London, 1978.

TUC: *Report of Proceedings, Annual Trades Union Congress*. London 1969ff.

TUC: *Statistical Statement and List of Delegates appointed to Attend the One Hundred and Ninth Annual Congress 1977.*

TUC: *The Industrial Relations Bill. Report of the Special Trades Union Congress*, London, June 1976.

TUC: *Trade Unions and Contracting-Out*. London, 1975.

TUC: *Training Full-Time Officers*. London, 1972. *Wage Drift Review of Literature and Research*. London, HMSO (Office of Manpower Economics), 1973.

Ireland

Constitution of the Irish Congress of Trade Unions, Separatum, Dublin, n.d.

ICTU: *List of Affiliated Organizations. 17th Annual Conference, Cork, Juli 1975.*

ICTU: *Operating the All-out Strike*. Dublin, 1974.

ICTU: *Statement by Executive Council on the Election of Employees in the Boards of State Enterprise*. Dublin, January 1976 (mimeo).

ICTU: *Structure and Function of Congress*, Dublin, 1975.

ICTU: *Submission to Minister for Labour on Statute for the European Company proposed by the European Commission*. Dublin, June 1973 (mimeo).

Italy

D'AGOSTINI, Fabrizio: *La condizione operaia e i consigli di fabbrica*. Rome, Editori Riuniti, 1974.
ALQUATI, Romando: *Sindacato e Partito. Antologia di interventi di sindaalisti sul rapporto fra sindacato e sistema politico in Italia*. Turin, Stampatori, 1974.
BAGLIONI, Guido: *Il sindacato dell'autonomia. L'evoluzione della Cisl nella pratica e nella cultura*. Bari, De Donato, 1977.
CELATA, G. and M. MAGNO: *Sindacato, programmazione e democrazia industriale*. Rome, Editrice Sindacale Italiana, 1977.
Centro Studi CISL: *Sindacato e sistema democratico*. Bologna, Il Mulino, 1975.
Centro Studi federlibro, FIM, SISM-CISL di Verona: *Piccola azienda, grande sfruttamento*. Verona, Bertani, 1974.
Centro Studi Nazionale della CISL (ed.): *Strumenti di cultura sindacale*. Bologna, Il Mulino, 1977.
CGIL-CISL-UIL: *Attività, atti, documentazione della Federazione Sindacale unitaria*. Rome, Società Editrice Unitaria Sindacale, n.d. (1974?).
La CGIL dall 8' al 9' congresso. Atti e documenti. Rome, Editrice Sindacale Italiana, 1977, 2 vols.
CGIL-CISL-UIL: *Esperienze, problemi e sviluppo della prospettiva sindacale unitaria*. Rome, Stasind, 1971.
CGIL: *Lotte unitarie e unità sindacale. Atti. Consiglio generale della CGIL*. Rome, Edizione Sindacale Italiana, 1970.
CHIAROMONTE, Ferdinando: *Sindacato Restrutturazione Organizzazione del lavoro*. Rome, Editrice Sindacale Italiana, 1978.
CHIESA, Giovanni Battista: *Pubblico impiego sindacato e riforma*. Rome, Editrice Sindacale Italiana, 1977.
CISL: *Domenti della CISL*. Rome, Edizione di Conquiste di Lavoro, 1971.
CISL: *Lo statuto dei diritti dei lavoratori*. Rome, 1970.
CISL: *Una CISL forte e unita per l'unità e per lo sviluppo della società italiana. Atti*. Rome, 1974.
I congressi della CGIL. Vol 8: 7° congresso della CGIL, Livorno 16-21 giugno 1969, vol. 9: 8° congresso della CGIL, Bari 2-7 luglio 1973, vol. 10: 9° congresso della CGIL, Rimini 6-11 giugno 1977. 2 vols. Rome, Editrice Sindacale Italiana.
Federazione CGIL-CISL-UIL per il dibattito sull'unità sindacale. Rome, Società Editrice Unitaria Sindacale, n.d. (1974).
Federazione lavoratori metalmeccanici (FIM-FIOM-UILM): *Potere sindacale e ordinamento giuridico. Diritto di sciopero, consigli di fabbrica, forme della contrattazione*. Bari, De Donato, 1972.
Fondazione Giacomo Brodolini (ed.): *Sindacati e contrattazione collettiva in Italia nel 1972-74*. Milan, Franco Angeli, 1978 (with documents on collective agreements).
FORBICE, Aldo and Ricardo CHIABERGE: *Il sindacato dei consigli*. Verona, Bertani, 1974.

Guida pratica per l'attivista di patronato. Rome, Tipografia Lugli, 1976.
I 30 anni della CGIL. Rome, Editrice Sindacale Italiana, 1975.
I giornali sindacali. Catalogo dei periodici CGIL 1944-1976. Rome, Editrice Sindacale Italiana, 1977.
'Il finanziamento del sindacato'. *Quaderni di Rassegna sindacale*, No. 50, Rome, 1974.
LAMA, Luciano: *Dieci anni di processo sindacale unitario*. Rome, Editrice Sindacale Italiana (Proposte No. 1), 1976.
LAMA, Luciano: *Il potere del sindacato*. Rome, Editori Riuniti, 1978.
LAMA, Luciano and B. MANGHI: *Il sindacato di classe ieri e oggi*. Rome, Editrice Sindacale Italiana (Proposte No. 10), 1977.
LAMA, Luciano: *Intervista sul sindacato*. Bari, Laterza, 1976.
LAMA, Luciano: *Relazione e conclusioni al IX Congresso CGIL*. Rome, Editrice Sindacale Italiana, 1977.
LEVRERO, Silvano: *Strategia sindacale e società multinazionali*. Rome, Editrice Sindacale Italiana (Proposte No. 57), 1977.
LIBERTINI, Lucio and Bruno TRENTIN: *L'industria italiana alla svolta. Sindacato, partiti e grande capitale di fronte alla crisi*. Bari, De Donato, 1975.
'L'Unità sindacale'. *Quaderni di Rassegna sindacale*, No. 29, Rome, 1971.
PEPE, A. and G. GUERRA: *Riformismo e riforme nell'esperienza sindacale italiana*. Rome, Editrice Sindacale Italian (Proposte No. 9), 1974.
PERNA, Corrado: *Breve Storia del sindacato*. Bari, De Donato, 1978.
SEBASTIANI, Chiara: *Pubblico impiego e ceti medi*. Rome, Editrice Sindacale Italiana (Proposte No. 29/30), 1975.
Sindacati e multinazionali. I documenti ufficiali della CES, della CISL internazionale, della CMT, della FSM e dell'OIL. Rome, Collana documentazione CGIL, 1977.
'Sindacato e partiti'. *Quaderni di Rassegna sindacale*, No. 33/34, 1972.
TRESPIDI, Aldo: *Lotte operaie e autonomie sindacale*. Rome, Editrice Sindacale Italiana, 1975.
Unità di classe e alleanze nella strategia sindacale. A cura della CGIL della Lombardia. Rome, Editrice Sindacale Italiana, 1977.

Luxembourg

CGT Programm angenommen durch den außerordentlichen Kongreß vom 6. April 1974. Esch-sur-Alzette, Imprimerie Coopérative Luxemburgeoise, 1974.
Conseil National des syndicats: *Gesetz vom 6. Mai 1974 über die Einführung gemischter Betriebsausschüsse in den Betrieben der Privatwirtschaft und über die Vertretung der Arbeitnehmer in den Verwaltungsräten der anonymen Gesellschaften*. Esch-sur-Alzette, 1974.
LAV: *Aktionsprogramm des LAV und Erklärung über die Ziele und Aufgaben der Freien Gewerkschaften*. Esch-sur-Alzette, 1964.
LAV Generalsekretariat: *Dreierkonferenz. Schlussfolgerungen*. Esch-sur-Alzette, 1977.
Letzeburger Arbechter-Verband (LAV): *Die freien Gewerkschaften in der modernen Gesellschaft*. Esch-sur-Alzette, 1970.

Letzeburger Arbechter-Verband. 1916-1966. Esch-sur-Alzette, 1966.
Programme d'action à moyen terme du LAV. Esch-sur-Alzette, 1968.
Verbandsstatut LAV. Esch-sur-Alzette, 1972. Revised edition, 1976.

Netherlands

Aktionsprogramm 1971-1975 von NVV, NKV, CNV. n.d. (mimeo).
Beleidsprogram '76-'77, NVV, NKV, CNV. n.d. (1975).
CNV: *Christian Trade Unionism in the Netherlands.* Utrecht, n.d. (1976).
CNV: *Informatie.* Utrecht, 1975.
CNV: *Statuten van het Christelijk Nationaal Vakverbond in Nederland.* Utrecht, n.d.
Federatie Nederlandse Vakbeweging. Bund Niederländischer Gewerkschaftsbewegung. Amsterdam-Slotemeer, 1976.
FVN: *Trade Union Movement.* Amsterdam-Slotermeer, February 1976.
Informatie Nederlands Verbond van Vakverenigingen. Amsterdam, n.d. (*ca.* 1975).
Nota van het CNV inzake het te voeren beleid met betrecking tot de medezeggenschap in de onderneming in het algemeen en de positie van de C.R. in het bijzonder. Utrecht, n.d.
NVV Informatie. Amsterdam, January 1976.
NVV Jahresbericht, 1972, 1973, 1974.
NVV Mitbestimmung in den Niederlanden. Amsterdam 1975. Die Ansichten des Industriebond NVV in Bezug auf Betriebsräte und Aufsichtsräte der Arbeitnehmerseite. Amsterdam, 1975.
NVV Statuten en huishoudelijk reglement. Amsterdam, n.d.
Statuten en huishoudelijk reglement van de Federatie Nederlandse Vakbeweging. Amsterdam, 1976.
Trade Unions affiliated to the FNV-Partners. Amsterdam, 1978.
Urgency Programme 1975 of NVV, NKV and CNV. o.O. 1975.
Vakbeweging & Maatschappij: *Ontwerp Maatschappij-visie.* NVV, Amsterdam, January 1977.
Vakbeweging & Maatschappij: *Resolutie.* Amsterdam, NVV, February 1978.
Visie NKV. Amsterdam, January 1978.

Norway

Arbeidsdirektoratet: *Labour Market Problems and Programs in Norway.* Oslo, 1974.
Basic Agreement of 1978. Oslo, LO, 1978.
LO: *Norwegischer Gewerkschaftsbund.* Oslo, 1977.
LO i Norge: *Vedtekter (med endringer vedtatt på kongressen i 1977.* Oslo, 1977.
Norwegischer Gewerkschaftsbund: *Betriebsdemokratie.* Oslo, October 1975.
The Norwegian Joint Committee on International Social Policy: *Labour Relations in Norway.* Oslo, 1975.

Spain

ALMDENDROS MORCILLO, F. et al: *El sindicalismo de clase en Espana (1939-1977)*. Barcelona, Ediciones Peninsula, 1978.

ARTES, Marco: *Sindicato y Partido*. Paris, Editions de la Tour Mauresque, 1976.

CALDERÓ, Albert: *El sindicalismo de los funcionarios publicos*. Barcelona, Editorial Avance, 1977.

CAMACHO, Marcelino: *Charlas en la prisión. El movimiento obrero sindical*. Paris, Colección Ebro, 1974.

FRANZ, Hans-Werner and Santiago TOVAR (eds.): *Gewerkschaftsbewegung in Spanien — Auf dem Weg zur Einheit?* Berlin, VSA, 1976 (Collection of documents).

Tribuna obrera: *Comisiones obreras y Eurocomunismo*. Madrid, Tribuna Obrera, 1978.

UGT: *Conoce tus derechos*. Madrid, Solidaridad Ediciones, 1977.

Sweden

Arbetsmarktnadsdepartementet (ed.): *Towards Democracy at the Workplace. New Legislation on the Joint Regulation of Working Life*. Stockholm, 1977.

Basic Agreement between the Swedish Employers Confederation and the Confederation of Swedish Trade Unions (as amended in 1947). Stockholm, Adrén & Holmes, 1956.

CARLSON, Bo: *L och fackförbunden*. Stockholm, Tiden, 1969.

Demokrati i företagen. Rapport till LO-kongressen 1971. Stockholm, Prisma (&LO), 1971.

Demokrati och Arbetsmiljö på den statliga sektorn. Program för TCO. Stockholm, 1973.

EDLUNG, Sten and Per EKLUND: *Rätt och arbetsgivarmarkt*. Stockholm, Prisma, 1974.

Förslag till lag om demokrati på arbetsplatsen. Stockholm, Liber Tryck, 1975.

FORSEBÄCK, Lennart: *Sozialpartner und Arbeitsmarkt in Schweden*. Stockholm, Schwedisches Institut, 1977.

KORPI, Walter: *Varför strejkar arbetarna?* Stockholm, Tidens Förlag, 1974.

Lagen om styrelse representation — en handledning. Stockholm, Tiden, 1974.

LEWIN, Leif: *Hur styrs facket? Om demokratin inom fackföreningsrörelsen*. Stockholm, Rabén & Sjögren, 1977 (This book is an important source because of its extremely useful survey data on the internal life of LO).

LO: *En presentation av Landsorganisation i Sverige*. Stockholm, Tiden, 1975.

LO: *Lönepolitik. Rapport till LO-Kongressen*. Stockholm, Prisma/LO, 1971.

LO om § 32. LO's remissvar. Stockholm, July 1975.

LOs Program för arbetsmarknadspolitiken. Stockholm, n.d. (1976).

LOs Program för Socialpolitiken. Stockholm, n.d. (1976).

LO: *Stadgar 1977*. Stockholm, 1977.

LO: *Statistik. 77*. Stockholm, 1978.

LO: *The Trade Union Movement and the Multinationals*. Stockholm, 1977.

LO: *Verksamhetsberättelse. 1977*. Stockholm, 1978 (and earlier issues).

Löntagarfonder och kapitalbildning. Förslag fran LO-SAPs arbetsgrupp. Stockholm, 1978.

MEIDNER, Rudolf: *Samordning och solidarisk lönepolitik.* Stockholm, Prisma/LO, 1973.

MEIDNER, Rudolf, Anna HEDBORG and Gunnar FOND: *Löntagarfonder.* Stockholm, Tiden, 1975.

MEIDNER, Ruldolf and Berndt ÖHMAN: *Solidarisk lönepolitik. Erfarenheter, problem, framtidsutsikter.* Stockholm, Tiden, 1972.

Motioner. LOs 19: e ordinarie Kongress 12-19 Juni 1976. Stockholm, Tiden, 1976.

NORDENSKIÖLD, Otto: *Förhållendet LO-TCO. En oversikt.* Stockholm, Tiden, 1972.

Normal Stadgar 1977 för till Landsorganisationen i Sverige anslutna förbund. Stockholm, 1977.

Reservation. Gemensamma reservationer och yttranden i arbetsrättskommiteen av Lars Westerberg och Sten Edlund, LO, samt Stig Gustafsson, TCO. Stockholm, Tiden, 1975.

SCHILLER, Bernt: *LO, paragraf 32 och företagsdemokratin.* Stockholm, Prisma/LO, 1974.

SCHMIDT, Folke and Anders VICTORIN (eds.): *Arbetslagstiftning.* Stockholm, Liber Förlag, 1978, 7th edition.

SMITH, Göran: *Parterna på arbetsmarknaden.* Stockholm, Prisma, 1978.

Solidarskt medbestämmande. Rapport till LO-Kongressen 1976. Stockholm, Prisma, 1976.

Towards Democracy at Workplace. Ministry of Labour. Stockholm, 1977.

Utlatande över motioner. LOs 19: e ordinarie kongress 12-19 Juni 1976. Stockholm, Tiden, 1976.

Switzerland

Arbeitsprogramm des Schweizerischen Gewerkschaftsbundes. Berne, n.d. (gebilligt auf dem 36. Gewerkschaftskongreß in Basel 1960).

Kurzreferat zur Mitbestimmung. Berne, December 1975 (mimeo).

Mitbestimmung, Mitbestimmungsinitiative, Gegenvorschlag. Referentenführer des SGB, Berne, September 1975.

'Mitbestimmungsprogramm des SGB'. Separatdruck aus *Gewerkschaftliche Rundschau* (*ca.* 1972).

SGB: *Tätigkeitsbericht 1972, 1973, 1974.* Berne, n.d.

SGB: *Tätigkeitsbericht 1975, 1976, 1977.* Berne, n.d.

Statuten des Schweizerischen Gewerkschaftsbundes. Berne, 1969 (with Amendments of 1972).

USA

AFL-CIO: *Constitution.* Washington DC, 1961.

AFL-CIO: *The Intimidation of Job Tests.* January 1979.

Labor Relations Yearbook. Washington DC, 1978 (and earlier issues).

Statement and Reports adopted by the AFL-CIO Executive Council on the National Economy. Bal Harbour, Fla., February 1979.

Statement by the AFL-CIO Executive Council on Financing Federal Election Campaigns. Bal Harbour, Fla., February 1979.

The AFL-CIO Platform Proposals presented to the Democratic and Republican National Conventions 1976. Washington DC, 1976.

This is AFL-CIO. Washington DC, Revised Edition, March 1978.

II. Comparative literature on labour relations and trade unions (Only comparative titles are mentioned. Studies on trade unions in the different countries are quoted in the footnotes.)

AARON, Benjamin (ed): *Labour Courts and Grievance Settlement in Western Europe*. Berkeley/Los Angeles, University of California Press, 1971.

AARON, Benjamin and K. W. WEDDERBURN (eds.): *Industrial Conflict. A Comparative Legal Survey*. London, Longman, 1972.

ADAM, G. and J. D. REYNAUD: *Conflicts du travail et changement social*. Paris, PUF, 1978.

ADLERCREUTZ, Axel: *Kollektivavtalet. Studier över dess tillkommsthistoria*. Lund, Gleerup, 1954.

ALBERS, Detlev, Werner GOLDSCHMIDT and Paul OEHLKE: *Klassenkämpfe in Westeuropa. England, Frankreich, Italien*. Reinbek, Rowohlt, 1971.

BAIN, George Sayers, David COATES and Valerie ELLIS: *Social Stratification and Trade Unionism. A Critique*. London, Heinemann, 1973.

BAIN, Joe S.: *International Differences in the Industrial Structures. Eight Nations in the 1950s*. New Haven, Yale UP, 1966.

BALFOUR, Campbell: *Industrial Relations in the Common Market*. London, Routledge & Kegan Paul, 1972.

——— *Unions and the Law*. Westmead/Lexington/Mass. Saxon House D.C. Heath/Lexington Books D.C. Heath, 1973.

BANKS, J. A.: *Trade Unionism*. London, Collier-Macmillan, 1974 (mainly on Britain and the USA).

BARKIN, S. (ed.): *Workers' Militancy and its Consequences*. New York, Praeger, 1975.

Basic Agreements and Joint Statement on Labour-Management Relations. Geneva, ILO, 1971.

BATSTONE, Eric and P. L. DAVIES: *Industrial Democracy. European Experience*. London, HMSO, 1977.

BELLASI, Pietro, Michele LA ROSA and Giovanni PELLICCIARI (eds.): *Fabbrica e società. Autogestione e participazione operaia in Europa*. Milan, Franco Angeli, 1972.

von BEYME, Klaus: *Interessengruppen in der Demokratie*. Munich, Piper, 1974, 4th edition.

BLACKMER, Donald L. M. and Sidney TARROW (eds.): *Communism in Italy and France*. Princeton UP, 1975.

BLUMBERG, Paul: *Industrial Democracy. The Sociology of Participation*. New York, Schocken, 1969.

BONVARD, Marguerite: *Labor Movements in the Common Market Countries. The Growth of a European Pressure Group*. New York, Praeger, 1973.

BUTLER, Arthur D.: 'Labor Costs in the Common Market'. *Industrial Relations*, 1967, pp. 166-183.

CAIRE, Guy: *Les syndicats ouvriers*. Paris, PUF, 1971.

CAREW, Anthony: *Democracy and Government in European Trade Unions*. London, Allen & Unwin, 1976.

CHAPLYGIN, Ju. P.: *Proletariat v stranach kapitala: Pravda i vymysly*. Moscow, Profizdat, 1975.

CLEGG, H. A.: *Trade Unionism under Collective Bargaining. A Theory Based on Comparisons of Six Countries*. Oxford, Blackwell, 1976.

COATES, Ken (ed.): *A Trade Union Strategy in the Common Market*. London, Spokesman Books, 1971.

La confederazione europea dei sindacati attraverso i suoi documenti. Rome, CGIL, 1974.

La crise des relations industrielles en Europe: Diversité et unité, les responses possibles. Bruges, Collège d'Europe (De Tempel), 1972.

CROUCH, Colin and Alesandro PIZZORNO (eds.): *The Resurgence of Class Conflict in Western Europe since 1968*. London, Macmillan, 1978, 2 vols.

Demokrati på arbetsplatsen. Förslag till ny lagstiftning om förhandlingsrätt och kollektivavtal. Stockholm, SOU, 1975: 1 (with many comparisons).

DUNLOP, John T.: *Industrial Relations Systems*. New York, Holt, 1958.

DVININA, L. I.: *Problemy mezhdunarodnogo khristianskogo sindikalizma*. Moscow, Nauka, 1974.

EDELMAN, Murray and R. FLEMING: *The Politics of Wage Price Decisions*. Urbana, University of Illinois Press, 1965.

EDELSTEIN, J. David and Malcolm WARNER: *Comparative Union Democracy. Organisation and Opposition in British and American Unions*. London, Allen & Unwin, 1975.

EICKHOF, Norber: *Eine Theorie der Gewerkschaftsentwicklung*. Tübingen Mohr, 1973.

ELVANDER, Nils: 'Collective Bargaining and Incomes Policy in the Nordic Countries: A Comparative Analysis'. *British Journal of Industrial Relations*, 1974, pp. 417-437.

——— 'The Role of the State in Settlement of Labor Disputes in the Nordic Countries: A Comparative Analysis'. *European Journal of Political Research*, 1974, pp. 363-383.

Der Europäische Gewerkschaftsbund und der Ausbau der Zusammenarbeit der Gewerkschaften. Brüssel, Europäische Dokumentation 1973.

EVANS, E. W. and S. W. CREIGH (eds.): *Industrial Conflict in Britain*. London, Frank Cass, 1977 (in spite of the limitation of the title this book contains important contributions on comparisons of the causes of industrial disputes).

FOX, Alan: *Beyond Contract: Work, Power and Trust Relations*. London, Faber & Faber, 1974.

FROMMEL, S. N. and J. H. THOMPSON (eds.): *Company Law in Europe*. Deventer, Kluwer Law Publishing Division, 1976.

GALENSON, Walter: *Trade Union Democracy in Western Europe*. Berkeley, University of California Press, 1962.

——— (ed.): *Comparative Labor Movements*. New York, Prentice Hall, 1952.

GALENSON, Walter and Seymour M. LIPSET: *Labor and Trade Unionism. An Interdisplinary Reader*. New York, 1960.

GARCIN, William: *Cogestion et participation dans les entreprises des pays du Marché Commun*. Paris, Jupiter, 1968.

GAULT, Francois: *Les nouveaux syndicalistes. Suède — Japon — Italie*. Paris, Editions France- Empire, 1978.

GERN, Jean-Pierre: *L'indexation des salaires*. Neuchâtel, Thèse, Imprimerie E. Moser & Fils, 1961.

Gewerkschaften im Klassenkampf. Entwicklung der Gewerkschaftsbewegung in Westeuropa. Argument-Sonderband 2, Berlin, Argument-Verlag, 1974.

GUINEA, José Luis: *Los sindicatos en la Europa de hoy*. Madrid, Iberico Europea de Ediciones, 1977.

HIBBS, Douglas A: 'Industrial Conflict in Advanced Industrial Societies', *APSR*, 1976, pp. 1033-1058.

HILL, Stephen and Keith THURLEY: 'Sociology and Industrial Relations'. *British Journal of Industrial Relations*, 1974, No. 2, pp. 147-170.

HONDRICH, Karl Otto: *Mitbestimmung in Europa. Ein Diskussionsbeitrag*. Cologne, Europa Union-Verlag, 1970.

HORTON, Raymond D.: 'Arbitration, Arbitrators and the Public Interest'. *Industrial and Labor Relations Review*, July 1975, Vol. 28, No. 4, pp. 497-507.

INGHAM, Geoffrey K.: *Strikes and Industrial Conflict. Britian and Scandinavia*. London/New York, Macmillan, 1974.

International Conference on Trends in Industrial and Labor Relations. Jerusalem, 1974.

JAVILLIER, Jean-Claude: *Les conflicts du travail*. Paris, PUF, 1976.

KASSALOW, Everett M.: 'White-Collar Unionism in Western Europe'. *Monthly Labor Review*, July 1963, pp. 765-71, August 1963, pp. 889-896.

——— *Trade Unions and Industrial Relations. An International Comparison*. New York, Random House, 1969.

——— (ed.): *National Labor Movements in the Postwar World*. Evanston/Ill., North-Western University Press, 1963.

KELLER, Berndt: *Theorien der Kollektivverhandlungen. Ein Beitrag zur Problematik der Arbeitsökonomik*. Berlin, Duncker & Humblot, 1974.

KENDALL, Walter: *The Labour Movement in Europe*. London, Allen Lane, 1975.

KITTNER, Michael (ed.): *Streik und Aussperrung. Protokoll der wissenschaftlichen Veranstaltung der IG Metall vom 13-15 September 1973 in München*. Frankfurt, EVA, 1974.

KUNTZE, Oscar-Erich: *Preiskontrollen, Lohnkontrollen und Lohn-Preis-Indexbindung in den europäischen Ländern*. Berlin, Duncker & Humblot, 1973.

LAFFERTY, W. M.: *Economic Development and the Response of Labor in Scandinavia. A Multi-Level Analysis*. Oslo, Universitetsforlaget, 1971.

LEFRANC, Georges: *Les expériences syndicales internationales des origines à nos jours*. Paris, Aubier, 1952.

——— *Grèves d'hier et d'aujourd'hui*. Paris, Aubier-Montaigne, 1970.

——— *Le syndicalisme dans le monde*. Paris, PUF, 1975.

LESTER, Richard A.: 'Reflections on Collective Bargaining in Britain and Sweden'. *Industrial and Labor Relations Review*, 1956/57,m pp. 375-401.

——— *As Unions Mature*, Princeton UP, 1958, 1966.

LEVINSON, Charles: *Industry's Democratic Revolution*. London, Allen & Unwin, 1974 (Views of trade union leaders).

LORWIN, Val. R.: 'Working-Class Politics and Economic Development in Western Europe'. *American Historical Review*, 1958, pp. 338-351.

MANN, Michael (ed.): *Social Stratification and Industrial Relations. Proceedings of a Social Science Research Council Conference, Cambridge 1968*. London, The Council, 1969.

MARX, Eli and Walter DENDALL: *Unions in Europe*. University of Sussex, 1971.

McPHERSON, William H.: *Grievance Settlement Procedures in Western Europe*. Urbana/Ill., Institute of Labor and Industrial Relations, 1963.

MUKHERJEE, Santosh: *Making Labour Markets Work. A Comparison of the UK and Swedish Systems*. London, PEP, 1972.

NAGELS, Karlheinz and Arndt SORGE: *Industrielle Demokratie in Europa. Mitbestimmung und Kontrolle in der Europäischen Aktiengesellschaft*. Frankfurt/New York, Campus, 1977.

NAGELS, Karlheinz: *Überbetriebliche Partizipation von Arbeitnehmern in Europa*. Frankfurt/New York, Campus, 1978.

Objectifs et instruments des politiques industrielles. Paris, OECD, 1975.

OXNAM, D. W.: 'International Comparisons of Industrial Conflict. An Appraisal'. *Journal of Industrial Relations*, 1965, No. 2, pp. 149-163.

PARKINSON, C. Northcote (ed.): *Industrial Disruption*. London/New York, Leviathan House, 1973.

La participation des employeurs et des travailleurs à la planification. Geneva, Bureau international du travail, 1973.

PERLMAN, Selig: *A Theory of the Labour Movement*. New York, A. M. Kelley, 1928, 1949.

Prospects for Labour-Management Cooperation in the Enterprise. Paris, OECD, 1972.

RAWSON, D. W.: 'The Life-Span of Labour Parties'. *Political Studies*, 1969, pp. 313-333.

ROSS, Arthur M.: *Changing Patterns of Industrial Conflict*. Berkeley, Institute of Industrial Relations, 1960.

——— (ed.): *Industrial Relations and Economic Development*. London, Macmillan, 1966.

ROSS, Arthur M. and Paul T. HARTMANN: *Changing Patterns of Industrial Conflict*. New York, Wiley, 1960.

ROSS, Arthur M. and Donald IRWIN: 'Strike Experience in Five Countries, 1927-1947'. *Industrial and Labor Relations Review*, 1951, No. 4, pp. 323-342.

RUBTSOV, V.: *Sila — v edinstve. Mezhdunarodnye monopoly i bor'ba profesoyuzov s nimi*. Moscow. Profizdat, 1974.

SARCINA, Angela: *Sindacato e partecipazione dei lavoratori nella Comunità europea*. Rome, Editrice Sindacale Italiana, 1974.

SCHIFF, Eric: *Incomes Policies Abroad*. Washington DC, American Enterprise Institute, 1971.

SCHREGLE, Johannes: 'Die Arbeitnehmer — Arbeitgeberbeziehungen in Westeuropa'. *GMH,* 1974, No. 8, pp. 457-472.

SHORTER, Edward and Charles TILLY: *Strikes in France 1830-1969.* London/ New York, Cambridge, UP, 1974, Chapter 12: 'French Strikes in International Perspective', pp. 306-334.

SILVESTRE, Paul and Paul WAGRET: *Le syndicalisme contemporain.* Paris, Colin, 1970.

SINAY, Hélène: *La grève.* Paris, Dalloz, 1966.

SPITAELS, Guy: *Notes de sociologie du travail.* Brüssels, Editions de l'université de Bruxelles, 1969.

STEWART, Margaret: *Trade Unions in Europe.* Epping/Essex, Gower Press Limited (Employment Conditions Abroad Ltd/Gower Economic Publications), 1974.

STURMTHAL, Adolf: *Workers Councils. A Study of Workplace Organization on both sides of the Iron Curtain.* Cambridge, Mass., Harvard UP, 1964.

——— (ed.): *Contemporary Collective Bargaining in Seven Countries.* New York, Cornell University, The Institute of International Industrial and Labor Relations, 1957.

——— (ed.): *White-Collar Trade Unions.* Urbana, University of Illinois Press, 1966.

TAYLOR, William J. et al. (eds.): *Military Unions. U.S. Trends and Issues.* Beverley Hills/London, Sage, 1977.

'Trade Unions and Political Parties', *Government and Opposition,* 1978, No. 4.

TURNER, H. A. and H. ZOETEWEIJ: *Prices, Wages and Incomes Policies in Industrialized Market Economies.* Gene a, ILO, 1966.

ULMAN, Lloyd and Robert J. FLANAGAN: *Wage Restraint. A Study of Incomes Policies in Western-Europe.* Berkeley, University of California Press, 1971.

VAN DE VALL, Mark: *Die Gewerkschaften im Wohlfahrtsstaat.* Cologne/ Opladen, Westdeutscher Verlag, 1966.

VILLINGER, Andreas: *Aufbau und Verfassung der britischen und amerikanischen Gewerkschaften.* Berlin, Duncker & Humblot, 1966.

VILMAR, Firtz (ed.): *Industrielle Demokratie in Westeuropa.* Reinbek, Rowohlt, 1975.

WASCHKE, Hildegard: *Gewerkschaften in Westeuropa.* Cologne, Deutscher Instituts-Verlag, 1975.

WINDMULLER, John P. (ed.): 'European Labor and Politics. A Symposium'. *Industrial and Labor Relations Review,* October 1974, January 1975.

Worker Participation and Collective Bargaining in Europe. Commission on Industrial Relations (CIR) Study 4, London HMSO, 1974.

Index

The most frequent abbreviations are explained in the index.

Klaus von Beyme

is Professor of Political Science at the University of Heidelberg. His books include *Interessengruppen in der Demokratie* (1969), *Die Parlamentarischen Regierungssysteme in Europa* (1970), *Die Politischen Theorien der Gegenwart* (1972), *Ökonomie und Politik im Sozialismus* (1975), *German Political Studies* (SAGE, 1975), *German Political Systems: Theory and Practice in the Two Germanies* (SAGE, 1976), *Elections and Parties* (Edited with Max Kaase, SAGE, 1978), and *Das politische System der Bundesrepublik Deutschland* (1979).

Eileen Martin

is a freelance translator and interpreter. From 1959-68 she held a teaching post in the English Department of the University of Frankfurt am Main, from where she became Head Translator with Deutsche Bank AG. From 1974-77 she was an Executive Assistant with the Anglo-German Foundation for the Study of Industrial Society, London.